THE
MIGHT
OF THE
MULTINATIONALS

THE
MIGHT
OF THE
MULTINATIONALS
THE RISE AND FALL
OF THE
CORPORATE LEGEND

ALEX RUBNER

PRAEGER

New York
Westport, Connecticut
London

Library of Congress Cataloging-in-Publication Data

Rubner, Alex.
    The might of the multinationals : the rise and fall of the
corporate legend / Alex Rubner.
        p.   cm.
    Includes bibliographical references (p.
    ISBN 0–275–93531–0 (alk. paper)
    1. International business enterprises.   I. Title.
HD2755.5.R82   1990
338.8'8—dc20   89–26526

Library of Congress Catalog Card Number: 89–26526
ISBN: 0–275–93531–0

First published in 1990

Praeger Publishers, One Madison Avenue, New York, NY 10010
An imprint of Greenwood Publishing Group, Inc.

Printed in the United States of America

∞

The paper used in this book complies with the
Permanent Paper Standard issued by the National
Information Standards Organization (Z39.48–1984).

10 9 8 7 6 5 4 3 2 1

To my grandchildren

CONTENTS

Abbreviations   ix

Introduction   xi

Part I   Theories, Fantasies, Denigrations

1   Four World Conspiracies   3
2   Definitions Do Matter   11
3   The Image of the Beast   19
4   Their Combined Might   31
5   Howard's Perfect Multis   39
6   One Hundred Percent   45
7   Executives Sans Patrie   55
8   Charles Levinson   69
9   Business International Corporation   79
10   The Multi Brotherhood   91

Part II   The Harsh Reality

11   The Birth of Multis   101
12   An Internecine Fraternity   121

13   The Clay Feet of the Corporate Dinosaurs   131
14   Workers Have a Motherland   153
15   No More Gunboats   171
16   The Inhospitable Host Countries   187
17   Multis Are Hypersensitive   199

Part III   Living with the Future

18   The Tide Is Receding   225
19   The Multis of the Twenty-First Century   245
20   Not Bigger But Smaller   259

Bibliography of Cited Sources   277
Index   285

ABBREVIATIONS

AGM	Annual general meeting
BoP	Balance of payments
CEO	Chief executive officer
COMECON	Soviet Trading Club (the USSR, allied European states, Cuba, Mongolia, and Vietnam)
EC	European Community
GDP	Gross domestic product
GNP	Gross national product
IMD	International Management Development
IMEDE	Institut pour l'Etude des Methodes de Direction de l'Enterprise
IMI	International Management Institute
LDC	Less developed country
MITI	Ministry of International Trade and Industry, Tokyo
MNC	Multinational corporation
OECD	Organization for Economic Cooperation and Development
TNC	Transnational corporation
WCC	World Council of Churches

Companies

AMOCO	Standard Oil (Indiana)
BASF	Badische Anilin Soda Fabrik
BAT	British-American Tobacco
BINCO	Business International
BL	British Leyland
BOC	British Oxygen
BP	British Petroleum
BSN	Boussois-Souchon-Neuvesel
ESSO	Standard Oil (New Jersey)-EXXON
GM	General Motors
HLR	Hoffmann-La Roche
IBM	International Business Machines
ICI	Imperial Chemical Industries
ICL	International Computers
ITT	International Telephone & Telegraph
OXY	Occidental Petroleum
P&O	Peninsular & Oriental Steam Navigation
RTZ	Rio Tinto-Zinc
SKF	Svenska Kullagerfabriken
3M	Minnesota Mining and Manufacturing
UFCO	United Fruit
USM	United Shoe Machinery

Union Organizations

AFL-CIO	American Federation of Labor-Congress of Industrial Organizations (U.S.)
CGT	Confederation Generale du Travail (France)
DGB	Deutscher Gewerkschaftsbund (Germany)
ICF	International Federation of Chemical and General Workers' Unions (Switzerland)
IMF	International Metalworkers Federation (Switzerland)
ITS	International Trade Secretariat
IUF	International Union of Food and Allied Workers Associations (Switzerland)
LO	Landsorganisationen i Sverige (Sweden)
TUC	Trades Union Congress (UK)
UAW	United Automobile Workers (U.S.)

INTRODUCTION

The first multinational corporations (MNCs or TNCs) were reared in the nineteenth century, and no doubt some of the species will still be with us in the twenty-first century. However, the pervasive populist perceptions of the powers of MNCs are of recent vintage. They became politically significant only in the 1960s and were in full flower by the beginning of the 1980s. The fabulous legendary tales on the influence of the present-day MNCs are now losing credence. I surmise that by the year 2000 few disgruntled businessmen, ambitious trade union bosses, charlatan politicians, and secular-oriented religious leaders will find it expedient to dwell on multinational conspiracies.

The following two stories are meant to break the ice, to illustrate the constraints under which multinational corporations perform. In the first half of the 1960s, the foreign investments of U.S. MNCs aroused worldwide indignation. Governments were urged to halt the rapacious American invaders in their tracks and, in particular, to prohibit the acquisition of indigenous companies. Quite unconnected with this agitation, the U.S. administration initiated in 1965 several measures to halt the outflow of capital in order to improve its balance of payments (BoP). President Johnson actually ordered U.S. MNCs to curtail heavily their direct investments overseas. J. Behrman has researched the global reactions to this injunction, which was out of character with U.S. free enterprise (95). Alas, foreign governments did not applaud but instead used this opportunity to denounce the United States. Politicians in France, Spain, and Japan were among the first to castigate Washington for halting the exploitation of foreign nations by U.S. capitalists. Australia and Canada, previously among the more virulent opponents of the activities of U.S. MNCs on their terrorities, now bellowed that President Johnson was about to damage their economies. In a letter to the president, Australia's prime minister uttered veiled threats about what he would instigate if the inflow of U.S. capital into Australia were reduced. Ottawa was outraged at Washington's instructions to U.S. MNCs (with Canadian subsidiaries), which would effectively prevent them from expanding in Canada by injecting additional resources. The restrictions were described perversely as "interfering in our internal affairs."

Chrysler's British subsidiary was frequently mentioned in the press of North America because of the antics of its bloody-minded union representatives. Slogans such as "Yankees, go home" adorned the factory walls. In 1975 the chief shop steward publicly threw down the gauntlet to John Ricardo, Chrysler's CEO, who was told to "pay up or get out." The world media were informed that UK workers would rather become unemployed than be the poor relations of Chrysler: "We are not going to be the puppets of a multinational corporation." A few months later the parent in Detroit announced its complete withdrawal from manufacturing in Britain. Once again the shop stewards manifested their revolutionary fervor on the television screens; this time they scorned the Yankee MNC for the impertinent declaration that it was going home.

Four men, all from North America, stood at the cradle of the MNC legend. The leftist Stephen Hymer, of MIT and Yale, traced the evolution of capitalist businesses from one-product workshops to multidivisional international corporations. He shared the view of Howard Perlmutter, MIT and Wharton School, that the centralized head offices of MNCs demand subservience from their subsidiaries. Hymer opined that private sector MNCs were bad for mankind (especially for the host countries), while Perlmutter thought they would be a blessing all round. These two theoreticians were joined by two "practical" individuals: Charles Levinson and Eldridge Haynes. Levinson, a devout socialist, accepted that MNCs are here to stay. Their evil impact could be warded off when trade unions were organized to bargain globally. According to Haynes's credo, MNCs were marvellous creatures. By supporting them, one advanced the cause of world government. Haynes aimed at organizing TNCs of different countries into a global association.

With hindsight it is now known that the four founding fathers had exaggerated the influence of the international companies. Thus Haynes asserted that "no government dares" bankrupt multis because of the ensuing economic consequences (2). This was blatant nonsense. There is ample evidence to prove that during the last 30 years numerous governments have dared to behave in a beastly fashion toward many MNCs. Yet the gospel that Haynes and the other three preached with such passion was generally received with (often uncritical) acclaim by the foes and friends of multis—and still has adherents today.

For the purpose of this book it often matters little whether multis are loved or hated—what is decisive is whether they are treated as powerful giants. I shall be arguing that most of the ostensibly mighty MNCs are in fact fragile, strife-ridden entities.

There are advantages to being listed among *Fortune*'s top companies. The CEO of GM is received by the president of the United States at short notice and Gianni Agnelli of Fiat can easily obtain an appointment at 10 Downing Street. But if mammoth turnover figures and the size of the international labor force are cast aside as measuring rods and, instead, return-on-capital is selected as the supreme criterion, large companies in general and TNCs in particular do not head the profitability league. Diverse elements account for this. Recent disclosures testify to the intracorporate clashes between International Telephone and Telegraph's (ITT) various national subsidiaries, which impeded the profit growth of this complex TNC; costly bickerings between German and British executives have for years plagued Ford's European activities. It has been said of the Belgian TNC Union Minière that it was

torn by its own internal dissensions, as is bound to happen in an amorphous, overgrown multinational conglomerate. These dissensions were further complicated by the need to reconcile the interests of all its disparate shareholders and different internal pressure groups. The result was a hesitancy and confusion of aims which made the company taken as a whole the most unreliable of allies and the feeblest of enemies (109).

MNCs, unlike medium-sized national firms, are constantly in the limelight of world opinion. As a result they are under pressure to accommodate themselves to (nonstatutory) social pressures; they must also take heed of nonpastoral pronouncements by trendy bishops. Large international firms find it difficult to bribe lavishly because if they are found out, the consequences can be very damaging. The bigger the corporation, the more likely it will face extortionate demands from host countries that originally wooed it to invest. Nowadays, even in the face of the expropriation of their assets and the kidnapping of their executives for ransom, TNCs can expect little comfort from the governments of their home countries. These are certainly not prepared to send gunboats!

When the Hymer-Perlmutter-Levinson-Haynes declarations on the supremacy of MNCs were launched, which were then the most infamous global corporations? What MNCs were then mentioned most frequently in "progressive" journals as excelling in perniciousness? UFCO (United Fruit Company) was the most savage of all the bêtes noires. It richly deserved the name of *El Pulpo*, the octopus that strangled all it touched. There is no dispute about its past wickedness and might. Yet the tide of nationalism in Latin America, and the abhorrence for untrammelled economic imperialism which has engulfed modern U.S. public opinion, took the teeth out of UFCO. Who has cause today to denounce this once powerful monster? Since its founding in 1898, UFCO unashamedly had bought politicians and manipulated governments in Latin America without meeting severe reprimands at home. Yet, in the changed atmosphere of the 1970s, the president of United Brands, of which the despised UFCO had become a constituent company, committed suicide because of commercial mishaps and revelations of corrupt practices in some of UFCO's foreign operations. Some of the other highly politicized, infamous TNCs—ITT is perhaps the most prominent example—have only survived by radically altering their modi operandi. They have been rewarded in that they no longer appear as prominently in the anti-MNC literature as in the good old days. The depraved oil companies—especially the Seven Sisters, which, at the time, were BP, Chevron, Esso, Gulf, Mobil, Shell, and Texaco—were widely cited to illuminate the popular belief that omnipotent MNCs can successfully trample on national susceptibilities and are able to force sovereign governments to lick the boots of profitable MNCs. Recent history has demonstrated that the oil producers were the weakest of the MNC species. Many of their foreign assets were expropriated and even small LDCs—among others, Peru, Bolivia, and the Gulf States—kicked them out mercilessly. The oil executives bowed in submission and begged for some kind of compensation. How are the mighty fallen!

An amazing medley of fanatically pious persons from the right and the left, atheists and assorted religious believers, business executives, and politicians have portrayed the MNCs as awesome, unassailable, commanding corporations. Clearly, their inspirations were disparate.

1. The chiefs of many global businesses have been eager to emphasize that their companies are not just profit-making entities but also effective instruments for molding a new, integrated world. To enhance their credibility they embroider the might of their MNCs.

2. Numerous, avowedly well-meaning, individuals have perceived TNCs to be a more weighty and pervasive force for evil than racism, nuclear power, and vivisection. Preposterous embellishments of the misdeeds of MNCs are to be found in a variety of religious publications, such as those emanating from

Catholic 'liberation' theologists, the Church of England, the Methodists, and the vehement, Geneva-based, WCC (World Council of Churches). The WCC did not suffer gladly Christian bodies that failed to subscribe to its wild condemnations of MNCs. Such reluctance is churlishly attributed to the fact that "they have funds invested in TNCs or have influential business executives as part of their constituencies" (5).

3. The clamor for supranational supervision arose because MNCs were perceived to be beyond national control. The UN apparatus—avid for new responsibilities—was eager to fill this perceived vacuum. The majority of MNCs rejected the need for the projected controls. Others, however, actively cooperated in the erection of the gallows. They helped to establish the UN Centre on Transnational Corporations because they implicitly agreed with their adversaries that MNCs are potentially dangerous: world corporations should be kept in check by an international police force.

4. In the Western world socialists of different hues view MNCs of the OECD as a contemporary form of 'monopoly capitalism.' In the COMECON they are featured as the apostles of modern imperialism; they are termed abusively "international monopolies" (4).

5. Politicians who have reason to attack MNCs find it expedient to magnify their corporate influence. When the rulers of LDCs default on loans or steal the assets of foreign investors, they naturally depict their prey as vile and powerful. Jimmy Carter, in his presidential campaign, played to the gallery by castigating the MNCs of his own country. This sort of exercise comes in handy, especially when a politician seeks an alibi to explain away his own failure. He then attempts to present himself as David who has been smitten by the sturdy Goliath. In 1970 the British electorate deposed the Wilson government, which had been in power since 1964. Relegated to leading his party in opposition, Harold Wilson whined that individuals were becoming increasingly helpless against the ruthless and remote economic power of TNCs. Why did his administration not carry out all the things that had been promised? Its good intentions had been frustrated because the Labour party had failed to recognize the "growth of irresponsible multi national organisations" (6).

One of the men Wilson had brought into his government, Tony Benn, was obsessed with MNCs both in and out of office. When he was in charge of the Department of Energy some comrades thought that he was not doing enough to overthrow the bourgeoisie. To expose the ignorance of his critics, Benn told an interviewer that there were forces in the world which

have got far greater power to decide what is to happen in any country than its parliament has. Multinational business is a very powerful influence and the oil companies come to see me in the very room where we are sitting. I am very well aware that I am like a parish councillor meeting the emperor, enormous power—moving their capital, moving their technology (7).

6. For reasons of self-interest, trade unions and/or companies operating mainly within a national context may inspire denunciations of MNCs which arraign them for being stronger than they actually are.

For some three decades, I have been involved in different capacities with TNCs. They have provided my family with ample bread and butter. In addition, I have had the opportunity to meet a large number of TNC executives when I made presentations at closed, intracorporate conferences (from Seoul to Vancouver, from Helsinki to Tokyo). Between 1964 and 1981 I was the Senior Economist in Europe of BINCO (Business International Corporation), which enrolled MNCs from five continents. Though BINCO is no longer an independent company, I shall be writing about it at some length because, uniquely, it once sought to furnish the academic MNC ideology with nuts and bolts. (The reason why this failed is closely linked with the central theme of this book.) I was lucky that BINCO afforded me insight into the workings of the higher echelons of major international corporations.

I have put to good advantage personal experiences and encounters with corporate decision-makers. Many of them can obviously not be identified. A number of MNCs and individuals are mentioned by name—even when they were once my clients—because what they have said or done has become public knowledge and/or is recorded in non-private documents. Some original, hitherto unpublished, material is presented and I have drawn on the findings of many researchers, who are acknowledged in the listed sources. While I hope that the descriptive substance will prove of interest, the book is essentially a disquisition that sets out to challenge the current consensus view on the character of multinational corporations. Judith, my wife, friend, and ruthless critic, must be blamed (or praised) that the text now before the reader is less polemical than was originally planned.

Following a diversionary chapter on some world conspiracies, the text is divided into three sections. Part I deals with the concepts of the multinational company as formulated by idealistic advocates, hate-filled adversaries, and sanctimonious preachers. Part II dwells on the prosaic practices of TNCs. Part III examines the revised strategies of Western megacompanies pertaining to overseas investments and concludes that the legend of the mighty MNCs is on the wane.

PART I

THEORIES,
FANTASIES,
DENIGRATIONS

FOUR WORLD
CONSPIRACIES

The poor nations . . . are exploited by the great multinational corporations which dominate a growing proportion of the economic
and social life of the Third World. They are the gunboats and soldiers
of the new economic style of imperialism.

Paul Harrison

TRILATERALISM

The Trilateral Commission was founded in 1973 as a loose body which
was "joined" by some 300 prominent individuals from business, unions,
universities and politics. They shared the woolly belief in a close partnership between Japan, North America, and Western Europe. The trilateralists have been depicted as members of a cabal who form a "shadow
world government." Enlisted in their ranks were President Carter and
the head of the UAW (United Automobile Workers), Leonard Woodcock;
Henry Kissinger and Andrew Young; Prime Ministers Raymond Barre,
Garret Fitzgerald, Edward Heath, and Helmut Schmidt; Gianni Agnelli,
and Coca Cola's chairman, Paul Austin. Among the UK conspirators

were Foreign Secretary Lord Carrington, Chancellor of the Exchequer Denis Healey, the political editor of *Independent TV News*, Alastair Burnet, and the chairman of the merchant bank Warburg, Lord Eric Roll. Japanese notables included the chairman of Mitsui, Yashizo Ikeda, professor of law, Masataka Kosaka, and the TV commentator Kazushige Hirasawa.

In essence the Commission was an intellectual workshop at which members met—albeit infrequently—to discuss wordly affairs. Certain research was initiated and a number of reports were composed; some of them were published. Clearly, these important busy people who had lent their names to the Trilateral Commission did not have time to attend many of the scheduled seminars. There was no way of enforcing decisions or implementing the many suggestions that were aired.

Trilateralism has been denounced as "the creed of an international ruling class." According to Holly Sklar, a fanatic U.S. critic, trilateralists believe that "the people, governments and economies of all nations must serve the needs of multinational banks and corporations." The chairman of Chase Manhattan, David Rockefeller—singled out as the "cabalist-in-chief" and the "most conspicuous representative of a multinational fraternity of men who shape the global economy"—has sought to put the record straight. In an article in the *Wall Street Journal* (April 30, 1980) he rejected the charge that he is leading a nefarious plot. His readers were implored to believe that although the meetings of the Commission are not open to the public, it is not true that they are a "coterie of international conspirators with designs on covertly ruling the world." What a wasted effort! The audiences Rockefeller addressed, like the sane readers of this book, have never believed for a moment that the trilateralists are world conspirators. This notion, however, has fallen on fertile ground in the LDCs where leftist intellectuals have been disseminating details of this conspiracy. In the Soviet Union too there are publications that describe the serious threat to humanity posed by the existence of the Commission (4).

But there is also extant in the West reading material that attests to systematic propaganda directed against the trilateralists. Two extreme right-wing authors have denounced the conspiratorial features of the Trilateral Commission in a bestseller that was meant to curdle the blood of a frightened American public (187). Barry Goldwater accused the trilateralists of grooming Carter for the presidency. He would have it that the Commission represents a coordinated effort to seize control of the centers of power and aims at an "international economy managed and controlled by international monetary groups through the mechanism of international conglomerate manufacturing and business enterprise" (136). The anthology compiled by Holly Sklar has assembled 25 contributions from anthropologists, journalists, lawyers, and university teachers in the United States and Canada (10): "Generous contributions from the National Council of Churches (Division of Overseas Ministries), the Board of Global Ministries and the Women's Division of the Methodist Church . . . defrayed the many expenses incurred in researching and compiling the manuscript." The cited anthology spells out the intricacies of the fabled trilateralist conspiracy. Here are a few morsels:

- The Trilateral Commission is a small, powerful, self-appointed group making plans for the rest of the world.
- The goal of trilateral food policy is to transform the basic human need for food into a source of economic gain and social control. Indeed, economic gain and social control are inseparable goals of trilateralism.
- Trilateral interest in world hunger comes from a desire to maximize profits in the long run.
- The owners and managers of global corporations view the entire world as their factory, farm, supermarket, and playground. The Trilateral Commission is seeking to strengthen and rationalize the world economy in their interest.
- Trilateralists are pragmatic, not fanatically ideological, in the defense of their class interests. . . . Thus the trilateralists see trade unions as an important tool of their own class rule.
- In their grandiose attempt to manage world events . . . trilateralists are opposed by capitalists with different material interests, the rival Soviet superpower, and the growing forces of national and popular liberation.
- Trilateralism will not roll over and play dead or drop dead from a case of acute contradictions. Its opponents need a viable counterstrategy.

THE JEWS

Until the French Revolution Jews suffered persecution mainly on religious grounds, as infidels and the putative murderers of Jesus. In the nineteenth century, secular antisemitism—which was to culminate in Hitler's racial Nuremberg edicts—came to the fore. In many countries zealots propounded that the Jews, irrespective of their religious convictions, were plotting to dominate the world. (Some have asserted that the Jews made use of the machinations of servile Freemasons.) The Jewish conspiracy is said to have been orchestrated jointly by men of the left and the right, the atheists Karl Marx and Leon Trotsky, the Rothschilds, and the German industrialist Walter Rathenau. Even the baptized Benjamin Disraeli is mentioned as a participant in the Jewish plotting.

Sergey Nilus, a mystical writer in Czarist Russia, published the surreptitious *Protocols of the Meetings of the Learned Elders of Zion* in 1905 (13). He boasted that he "had obtained them from the secret archives of the Central Chancellery of Zion which is in France." According to Nilus, these minutes serve as guidelines to action. They were amended whenever the Elders convened global conferences to further the Jewish domination over the gentiles. One such convention was said to have met in Switzerland in 1897.

Nilus's book was originally distributed mainly in Russia where it fanned the flames of the pogroms. After 1919 this conspiratorial story gained worldwide circulation. It was acclaimed in influential circles after *The Morning Post* (the organ of Britain's diehard Conservatives) had publicized the *Protocols* with approbation. The authority and wealth of Henry Ford ensured a mass sale for the U.S. edition, which he helped to finance. The Detroit magnate insisted that Nilus's revelations were authentic because they told the truth about the past and the current situation. The *Protocols* were later proven to be a crude forgery but this did not shake the faith of the believers in an international Jewish conspiracy.

The preface to the 1922 London edition asserted that though the leaders of the Zionist movement (Theodor Herzl and Chaim Weizman) knew the identity of the Elders, the intrigues described in the book were not linked to the movement, which strove to establish a Jewish state:

The desire for a 'National Home' in Palestine is only camouflage and an infinitesimal part of the Jews' real object. It proves that the Jews have no intention of settling in Palestine or any separate country, and that their annual prayer that they may all meet 'Next Year in Jerusalem' is merely a piece of their characteristic make-believe. It also demonstrates that the Jews are now a world menace.

Nilus would have it that the aim of the Jewish conspiracy was to establish a super-government. One day the "King of the Jews will be the real Pope of the Universe." Which wily ruses do the Jews employ? The *Protocols* explain:

The aristocracy of the goyim [gentiles] can still be harmful to us from the fact that they are self-sufficing in the resources upon which they live. It is essential therefore for us at whatever cost to deprive them of their land. This object will be best obtained by increasing the burden upon landed property—in loading lands with debts.

What we want is that industry should drain off from the land both labour and capital and by means of speculation transfer into our hands all the money of the world and thereby throw all the goyim into the ranks of the proletariat. Then the goyim will bow down before us.

To complete the ruin of the goyim we shall raise the rate of wages which, however, will not bring any advantage to the workers, for, at the same time, we shall produce a rise in prices of the first necessaries of life.

We shall further undermine artfully and deeply sources of production by accustoming the workers to anarchy and to drunkenness and side by side therewith taking all measure to extirpate from the face of the earth all the educated forces of the goyim.

We shall not overtly lay a finger on existing churches, but we shall fight against them by criticism calculated to produce schism.

The Holocaust and the birth of the state of Israel have not shattered the faith of rabid antisemites in the fables of a global Jewish conspiracy. The Protocols were still a bestseller in the 1980s. The Iranian embassy in Brazil actively distributed a Portugese edition. The Protocols were sold in Arabic throughout the Middle East. (Foreign correspondents report from Ryadh that the information services of Saudi Arabia also make available an English-language edition.) Most surprising is the wide dissemination of the *Protocols*, together with other antisemitic literature, in Japan—a country with hardly any Jews.

THE MASONIC FRATERNITY

The perennial and universal charge against Freemasons is that they are members of a secret organization that metes out heavy penalties for breaching the oath. Anti-masonry societies have attacked the rituals as a worship of the devil. More balanced critics would have it that the masonic lodges harbour "men of rank, wealth, office and talent" who assist one another (15). The accusations, centering on jobs for the boys, string-pulling, and favored treatment for fellow Masons, undoubtedly contain an element of truth. To concede this does not entail subscribing to wild charges, such as the allegation that British justice in the second half of the twentieth century is seriously perverted because of pernicious ties between Masonic judges, lawyers, and police officers. It is paranoiac to assert that Giscard d'Estaing only won the French presidential election in 1974 because he had become a Freemason at the last moment. Equally fatuous is the attribution of Mitterrand's victory in 1981 to the decisive influence of the brotherhood (14).

The majority of the Masonic fraternities are akin to snobbish, mysterious clubs. Their members usually favor social reforms and delight in performing charitable deeds. On balance, Freemasons have abhorred political and racial bigotry. The Masonic lodges are inclined to reject religious fundamentalism, which has not endeared them to the Roman Catholic Church and orthodox rabbis (16).

Most of the Masonic conspiracy theories are formulated within a national context. But at different times and in various countries there has also been widespread support for the more pernicious insinuation that the secret machinations of Freemasonry are directed globally from one command center. The elite Masters of the fraternities in each country are expected to place their loyalty to this center above their patriotic

duties. The authoritative Nazi publication on the Masonic world conspiracy concludes that—like the Roman Catholic Church, Jewry, and
Marxism—Freemasonry is a supranational body (17).

The first 'serious' anti-masonry publication, which highlighted the
international dimensions, was a book published in 1797 by John Robison,
professor at the University of Edinburgh, entitled *Proofs of a Conspiracy
Against All Religions and Governments of Europe Carried on in the Secret
Meeting of the Free Masons* (18). The banner was unfurled by Jedediah
Morse, a Congregational minister in Boston. He proclaimed that the
foreign Freemasons, who had been the driving force behind the French
revolution, were now seeking to control also the United States and other
countries. The organizer of this world conspiracy was said to be Adam
Weishaupt, a professor of canon law in Bavaria, who had formed the
order of Illuminati which became a higher order of Freemasons. Morse
contended that the Illuminati doctrines ridiculed the being of God, pronounced the possession of property to be robbery, and taught that adul-
tery, assassination, and poisoning are virtuous actions. There are more
of such absurdities. It is significant that the pros and cons of the Illuminati conspiracy were discussed earnestly and in depth, especially in
the United States.

In the twentieth century stories of another type of Masonic world
conspiracy were prevalent. Mussolini declared in 1925 that there can be
no compromise with the Masonic conspirators: "Freemasonry must be
fought by the Fascists because it is an international organization which
acts in Italy in accordance with orders received from abroad." Hitler
wrote in *Mein Kampf* of his violent opposition to the destructive forces
of Freemasonry, which he associated with the hated Jews. The race
theoretician of the Nazis, Alfred Rosenberg, composed diatribes on Freemasons, dwelling on their global maneuvers ("Freimaurerische Welt-
politik" and "Der Weltkampf"). In 1938 the Nazi party published its
considered attack on the Masonic world conspiracy, claiming that in-
criminating material had been found in secret police archives. Reinhard
Heydrich, an Obergruppenführer of the SS, wrote the introduction. The
book is important because it explicates the fantasies—current not only
in Germany but also in other countries—concerning the impact of Freemasonry on history.

According to Nazi revelations, the conspiracy was directed by the
Association Maconnique Internationale, headquartered in Geneva; this
was alleged to be the focal point for the Masonic elitists from the Supreme
Conseils of 36 different countries. They were accused explicitly of pursuing cross-border policies without the knowledge of the national governments affected. We are told that the movement that led to the
American War of Independence "was almost exclusively" in the hands
of Freemasons. "Nowadays nobody disputes" that the French revolution

was instigated by Freemasonry. The global conspirators are rebuked for helping to overthrow authoritarian governments by disseminating the creed of liberty, equality, and fraternity. Freemasonry is denounced for kindling the fires of revolution in order to help establish liberal-democratic regimes. The Nazis also blamed the Masonic conspirators for the birth of the accursed League of Nations.

THE MNCs

The sketches of the Trilateralist, Jewish, and Freemason conspiracies form a background to the allegations that MNCs—for good or for evil—unite for common purposes. In his evidence at the UN, before the Group of Eminent Persons, Ralph Nader attributed near-divine powers to MNCs for "the way they manipulate or play off nations, governments and rulers against each other" (27). There is ample evidence that the enemies of MNCs find it expedient to exaggerate the strength of individual international corporations and sometimes underline their accusations by claiming that MNCs (of a given nationality or of several nationalities) secretly work together. There was once populist clamor for the U.S. Congress to probe U.S. MNCs, as a group—they were blamed for a drastic fall in the value of the dollar. (In the absence of any proof, the investigation was never started.) At its 1975 Nairobi assembly, the WCC elucidated the nature of the MNC conspiracy: these capitalist forces "join together to oppress the poor and keep them under domination" (19).

The MNC brotherhood is examined in Chapter 10, which also instances the advocacy of conspiratorial actions by the founder of BINCO. Eldridge Haynes, chanting the same tune as Nader, embroidered the might of TNCs: "Their economic leverage is so great that no nation can afford not to listen to their collective voice" (2). Some individuals and groups have indeed striven to organize global MNC intrigues, but their fanciful designs were not followed through.

NOTORIOUS BUGABOOS

Geologists, vegetarians, osteopaths, and nudists regularly confer with their peers at international conventions. They may pass resolutions that implore the world to listen to their tidings. They may warn of impending dangers. They may even threaten. But this is harmless stuff, and even journalists with imagination cannot turn these events into demonic conspiracies.

To arouse paranoiac apprehensions of an unpleasant worldwide conspiracy, a number of elements must coexist. The links between the conspirators must appear to be firm and the plots should be hatched at secret gatherings. Not by chance did a firm enemy of MNCs describe them as "invisible empires" (a term frequently used to characterize the Ku Klux Klan) (20). The TUC (the British Trades Union Congress) had no doubt that TNCs were powerful and evil: "Nobody knows much about how they operate" (25).

I like to think that it is not offensive to surmise that the names of the delegates assembled at the conventions of the geologists, vegetarians, osteopaths, and nudists mean little to the man in the street. To arouse populist fears the conspirators must be distinguished individuals or executives of renowned corporations—fame, wealth, and power are vital ingredients! Holly Sklar's virulent attack on Trilateralism contained an impressive roll-call of elitists who were accused of planning to manage the world; because the names of the celebrities rang a bell they made plausible the alleged conspiracy. It is commonly thought that if you are rich or influential you can easily escape the rigor of the law. The Council of the Churches in the Netherlands has given prominence to the "elusive powers" of the MNCs, which are said "to have more influence on the course of events than the governments and parliaments of independent nations" (19). The Dutch theologians called up images of GM, ICI, and Philips, which made their (unfounded) generalization sound more credible.

It is a laborious, and frequently ineffective, task to expose tales of legendary conspiracies by factual analysis. Unscrupulous political and religious leaders know this.

2

DEFINITIONS DO MATTER

To be big and to be loved seems to be against nature.
Ernest Woodroofe, *chairman of Unilever*

A CATALOGUE OF NAMES

David Lilienthal, the first director of the Tennessee Valley Authority and the first chairman of the (U.S.) Atomic Energy Commission, submitted a paper to a 1960 symposium at the Carnegie Institute of Technology on economic life 25 years hence. On that occasion he coined a new term. Portraying certain businesses, he said: "I would like to define [them] as multinational corporations" (21). Since then many synonymous appellations have appeared in the voluminous literature on MNCs.

Aggregate-national firm

Anational company

Cosmocorporation (Cosmocorp)

Crossnational corporation

Global conglomerate

Global firm

Globalkonzern

(La) Grande Unité Interterritoriale

(La) Grande Unité Pluriterritoriale

International corporate group

International firm

International monopoly

Many-national firm

Mega-corporation

Multilocal company

Multinational bee

Multinational company (MNC)

Multinational enterprise (MNE)

Multinational family group

Nationless company

Neutral corporation

Plurinational company

Supranational enterprise

Transnational corporation (TNC)

Transnational enterprise (TNE)

Trans-international company

Weltunternehmen

World company

Worldwide enterprise

There is a crop of informal designations. Stephen Hymer called the MNC "the beast" (22). Another detractor spoke of "new leviathans." A leading French politician chose the derisive term "corporate monsters." But when Simon Short referred to "monster companies," he actually intended this to be a flattering description. Giruan wrote disparagingly of "corporate imperialists." The authors of a book on TNCs entitled it, tendentiously, *The New Sovereigns.* The British union leader Victor Feather abused the international companies as "juggernauts." The AFL-CIO published a pamphlet on "modern-day dinosaurs" (which devour the jobs of American workers) while the TUC chose a more figurative phrase, "the firms who follow no flag." John Plender irreverently pictured MNCs as "hoof-loose Trojan horses." In the United Kingdom's Upper House, Lord Davies of Leek chose the connotation of "rogue elephants."

I first came across "multi" on a banner carried in a German trade union demonstration: *Nieder mit den Multis!* (down with the multis). This convenient term is used interchangeably with MNCs and TNCs throughout this book. "Home country" is shorthand for the national location of the multi's head office and its top management. The foreign territories in which subsidiaries and affiliates operate are designated as "host countries."

A NARROW DEFINITION

In the social sciences definitions are rarely right or wrong—they are more likely to be subjective. The exposition below is no exception. It largely corresponds with the parameters of the multinational corporation set out by the four founding fathers.

MULTIS ARE PROFIT-ORIENTED ORGANIZATIONS WITH CENTRALISED CONTROL OVER DOMESTIC AND FOREIGN SUBSIDIARIES/BRANCHES/AFFILIATES. MOST OF THEIR WEALTH-CREATION CENTRES ON PHYSICAL PRODUCTION (e.g., extracting oil, growing bananas, melting ore, manufacturing automobiles). MULTIS ATTEMPT TO MAXIMIZE INTRACORPORATE FLOWS OF RESOURCES (which betoken the transfer of finance across frontiers, the global application of innovations and technical-cum-marketing knowhow, the crossborder movements of senior and specialist personnel).

Does size matter? My definition has not been formulated so as to cover only mammoth corporations. Others would not agree. Stephen Hymer defined the beast as a corporate vehicle which was "large in size." Howard Perlmutter envisaged that the supergiants at the end of this century would be "monsters in size and power.... [T]he million-employee firm will not be unusual" (26). In 1977 the UN estimated that 11,000 multis existed. However, it merely highlighted the operations of the 430 biggest corporations because only these were deemed mighty enough to warrant the imposition of supranational controls. The British delegation at the UN observed that the size of a corporation does not determine its qualitative importance or influence. However, it was the opposing ideological standpoint of the Soviet Union that prevailed. The Soviet spokesman denounced transnational corporations because they violate national sovereignty, support racist regimes, are guilty of economic robbery, destroy cultural values, and so on. He argued that such evil deeds can be performed effectively only by "certain large corporations which are powerful enough to engender all those problems."

Several types of internationally active companies are excluded by the definition above. Fortnum & Mason is a famous firm in Piccadilly, London with a distinctly global commercial outlook: it imports delicacies from a hundred countries. Yet, as these are trading activities, Fortnum & Mason cannot describe itself as an MNC. The gigantic Boeing Corporation of Seattle, Washington views the whole world as its market and sells more planes abroad than at home but Boeing too is not qualified to wear the multi badge. Japan's huge general trading companies—the Sogo Shosha (Mitsui, Marubeni, and Itoh among them)—are sometimes dubbed multinationals. Essentially, however, they are import-export merchants and therefore should not be allowed to join the multi club. The same rule applies to the Communist multinationals that are the foreign trading, marketing, financial, and servicing subsidiaries of COMECON trusts and do no or little manufacturing; they therefore cannot be treated as 'pure' multis.

In the days when Haynes, Hymer, Levinson, and Perlmutter were still regarded with deferential reverence, service companies were automatically barred from membership of the multi fraternity. The ban was imposed despite the fact that many accountancy partnerships, banks, advertising agencies, law firms, transport businesses, and leisure corporations were represented throughout the world. This debarment is now meeting with resistance. The UN Economic and Social Council, in its dissemination of antimulti propaganda, draws attention to the nefarious work of worldwide advertising agencies. These not only help to sell products in the LDCs but are also engaged in "changing attitudes and building images" favorable to their MNC clients—hence the need to treat these devils as MNCs in their own right and curb their activities even though they do not actually manufacture goods themselves! The Big Eight accountancy partnerships, employing some 150,000 staff in 2,500 offices in more than a hundred national economies, have been described as some of the most influential powers on earth (28). (Until 1989, the Big Eight referred to the accountancy firms Arthur Andersen, Arthur Young, Coopers & Lybrand, Deloitte Haskins & Sells, Ernst & Whinney, Peat, Marwick, Mitchell, Price Waterhouse, and Touche Ross.) In my appraisal, transnational servicing corporations are not orthodox MNCs; they are the handmaidens of the large international manufacturing companies. At best, they are second-class MNCs.

My specification focuses on *profit-oriented* industrial companies to differentiate them from international bodies such as the Roman Catholic Church, the International Labour Office, and the Red Cross. The WCC, which relies on "spiritual messages" to sustain its antimulti convictions, implicitly blesses this definition: the wicked MNCs must be fought because their target is to "increase profit through economic activities on an international scale" (5). A strong body of opinion, however, would have it that making a profit ought not to be the decisive criterion. Some assert that it matters more who owns the equity capital. President Mitterrand nationalized in the 1980s the private-sector TNCs, Saint-Gobain and Rhone-Poulenc. As state-owned corporations they continued to make acquisitions abroad and generally conformed to the sort of behavior that antimulti partisans condemn. The Communist ideologues were willing to accept that these two companies had remained French MNCs even though their profits accrued to the state. However, they would not concede that the foreign operations of organizations controlled from within the COMECON economies were on par with the foreign subsidiaries of Western multis, irrespective of whether the latter had parents in the private or the public sector.

In the 1970s the Soviet Union, its allies and satellites, successfully lobbied for the establishment of a UN Centre on Transnational Corporations. They had surmised correctly that this would create a prestigious forum from which the OECD countries could be castigated for utilizing their TNCs as neo-colonialist instruments in the exploitation of LDCs. The Centre's first task was to prepare a disciplinarian code that would regulate the conduct of MNCs. However, the members of the working party could not agree on a definition of what constitutes a MNC. The representatives of the Western powers urged that all relevant international companies should be drawn into the net. But, without blushing, the Communist delegates objected. They maintained that as the COMECON multis were not concerned to generate profits for private shareholders, they were qualitatively different from TNCs with parents in OECD countries. The centrally planned economics insisted that the UN had no right to monitor Communist multinationals for these did not oppress LDCs (145, 161). Notwithstanding the sophistry that enveloped the construction of the UN code, my definition does not distinguish betwen private and socialist profit-making.

THE KARL MARX CONNECTION

Christian fundamentalists discern a living thread between the Bible and current affairs. The Church of England has propounded that there is "theological justification" for the Church's program against MNCs (29). On parallel lines, exegetists have sought to establish a link between the homilies in the sacred writs of the nineteenth-century fathers of socialism and the corporate world at the end of the twentieth century: "We draw attention to the continuity of a process of reflection which connects the early Marxist tradition of political thought with recent efforts to evaluate the impact of the multinational corporation" (30). This is significant for, among the vocal adversaries of TNCs, there are many socialists who are inspired by the writings of Marx and Engels and their immediate followers. The COMECON's political scientists subscribe to the ingenuous proposition that the iniquity of modern international corporations is but an extension of the evils of imperialism that had been condemned in the works of Nikolai Bukharin, Rudolf Hilferding, John Hobson, Karl Kautsky, Vladimir Lenin, and Rosa Luxemburg (32).

Karl Marx predicted that capitalists in the advanced countries would set their sights on what the *Communist Manifesto* described as the "world market." His disciples specified the targets of imperialism: gaining access to raw materials abroad; exporting manufactured goods to the colonies; and most importantly, exporting capital that had been accumulated by squeezing surplus value out of suffering proletarians who were destined to become ever more impoverished. Thus economic imperialism was buttressed by "finance capitalism." The three listed targets have little relevance to the ventures of today's TNCs. International companies, which used to extract and process raw materials, have long since had their foreign assets expropriated or, at best, have had their profitable wings clipped by hostile host countries—only a few foolhardy MNCs continue today with such activities. The exporting of manufactured goods to the colonies (under favored conditions) is also a matter of the past. The hallmark of multis is the manufacture of goods in several national locations. The Marxists, who before World War I wrote at length on the nature of economic imperialism, did not anticipate such a development. Bukharin went out of his way to praise a German economist who had opined in 1907 that the creation of "international companies with centralised management of production appears unlikely" (31).

Marx forecast a steady decline in the profitability of domestic investments in the major industrialized economies. The hypothesized drop in the interest rate was the starting point for the theories on economic imperialism. Hilferding went on to predict that "the concentration of all idle money capital in the hands of the banks leads to a planned organisation of capital exports" (33). The funds were destined to be transferred abroad to foreign governments, municipalities, and enterprises engaged in the extraction of raw materials and the building of railways. International manufacturing corporations, which flourish at the end of the twentieth century, have nothing in common with "finance capitalism." There are indeed investment trusts and mutual funds in the Western economies that specialize in channeling domestic savings to foreign countries. But these, and financial institutions in general, are not deemed to be MNCs. One (albeit temporary) illustration of modern finance capitalism was furnished by the Organization of Petroleum-Exporting Countries (OPEC) after 1973. The oil states suddenly came into possession of billions of petrodollars and were forced to invest most of them outside their borders. Unwittingly, they acted as economic imperialists (in accordance with the old Marxist tenets) because they could not earn interest on their petrodollars at home and lacked viable manufacturing multis of their own. The treasurers of OPEC had become purveyors of money to foreign governments, municipalities, and large corporations. Overwhelmingly, their money was invested anonymously.

In the Soviet Union MNCs are given the anomalous name tag of "International Monopolies." The COMECON propagandists and the Western Marxists who assail the exploiting imperialist multis present their campaigns as a sacred crusade. Be that as it may; however, they ought not to attempt to legitimize this holy war by sanctifying it through copious citations from the anti-imperialist writings of the fathers of socialism. The MNCs, about to enter the twenty-first century, are playing an entirely new ball game. Attacks on them will not sustain comparison with what appeared in *Das Kapital*.

3

THE IMAGE OF THE BEAST

> Militarism, monetarism and multinational capitalism are the greatest
> threats on the world scene today.
>
> Stuart Holland

The first part of this chapter mentions cursorily some of the good things
attributed to multis while the second part lists succinctly many of their
putatively horrible deeds. The following pages are overloaded with
quotes, many of which excel in absurdity, tendentiousness, mendaciousness, oversimplification, or (at best) ingenuousness. Surveys on the merits and demerits of global corporations frequently lack objectivity—and
deliberately so. Silly and exaggerated images of multis are tossed about;
they do not advance a serious study of MNCs. Yet these hyperboles are
significant and deserve to be reported for in this field it matters greatly
what the average person thinks.

Business managers are not always eager to mention profit-seeking as
their principal aim. In the seventeenth century the (London-based) East
India Company euphemistically called its overseas branches "outposts
of progress." Is it not pathetic that the president of Toyota, Shoichiro
Toyoda, felt the urge to proclaim publicly that the objective of his MNC

was to become a "caring" corporation? Ryuzaburo Kaku, president of the Japanese multi Canon, was not satisfied with praising the quality of his products. His publicity advisers prepared for him a solemn declaration that stressed Canon's yearning for "global prosperity . . . generating great benefits for the host countries . . . being a premier corporate citizen and contributing to the development of the host country." Yet Kaku is no more farcical than the left-wing propagandist who spouted that multis "constitute a growing threat to the cause of peace and detente. . . . [T]hey directly whip up the arms race, block the peace initiatives made by the socialist countries."

HALOES

A list of glowing tributes for transnational corporations follows.

- A sweeping song of glory by Orville Freeman, BINCO's CEO:

  The multinational corporation is today the single most powerful force to put the world together. . . . [W]ith its capacity to move resources it makes an indispensable contribution in many LDCs. . . . [A]s an economic workhorse of the world it makes it possible that a decent standard of living might be attained for a world population that will reach 6 billion by the year 2000. . . . [N]o other institution has the skills and innovative strength to raise the world's production to the level needed to meet the demands of an expanding population (34).

- Multis are extolled for their antinationalist strategies. This appeals particularly to the protagonists of a world government. According to one admirer, MNCs are building a global economy in which "the constraints of geography have yielded to the logic of efficiency." Another enthusiast argues that "to the international corporation, borders between states are a hindrance." The chairman of the UK's largest manufacturing MNC, ICI, expressed his sentiments in language appropriate to lyric poetry: "In the multinational company people of every colour, creed and race work together for the achievement of a common end. It is one of the very few institutions where the shared goals overcome nationalist or racialist considerations" (188).

- Some executives of multis boast indelicately that they generate peace. According to the chairman of U.S. Steel, TNCs "bring the people of nations together for peaceful purposes . . . to bind nations together . . . in man's pursuit of peace" (35). Mertz titled his panegyric *Peace and Affluence through the Multinational Corporations*.

- MNCs have commercial reasons to condemn wars, for these interfere with shipments of raw materials and finished products and generally disrupt the international flow of trade. A similar puerile theme on armed conflicts among nations in the twentieth century is found in H. Perlmutter's writings. He is adamant that multis could conceivably make war less likely because the "bombing of customers, suppliers and employees is in nobody's interest" (36). When he was treasurer of GM, David Collier made a remarkable political pronouncement: "Multinational companies help promote world peace and stability. . . . By transcending national boundaries, they are a source of hope to the world."

- Why are MNCs in a stronger position than corporations that depend largely on the domestic market? They enjoy greater stability because, when the home market becomes sluggish, output can be diverted to foreign markets.They can carry through acquisitions more efficaciously because of their ability to raise capital with relative ease. Many banks accord multis a high credit rating; being international monster firms, they can "sustain large losses and still survive." Global corporations are also in a better position to recruit the best technicians and managers because they enlist on a worldwide basis—the prospect of foreign job assignments is an added attraction for certain individuals.

- LDCs that host subsidiaries of foreign multis benefit greatly from the 'free' transfer of technology and managerial know-how.

- Developed economies gain from hosting the subsidiaries of technologically advanced foreign TNCs which manufacture side by side with indigenous firms. The latter will be under pressure to modernize their working methods because it is only by reducing the efficiency gap that they will survive.

- The impact of multis on international trade is crowned with a double halo. LDCs have reason to welcome the establishment of factories by foreign corporations which have facilities to export through their global organizations. Apologists for MNCs claim that, simultaneously, the home countries also record enhanced exports: "investment abroad has a pull effect on exports."

- When seeking approval for manufacturing subsidiaries in host countries, multis promise to create additional jobs. A parallel blessing is also said to be showered upon the home country. The U.S. food multi, CPC, told a Congressional committee that by heightening foreign demand for U.S. goods, "investment abroad often generates jobs in the United States" (3). The president of BINCO proclaimed in Washington that research among his members had revealed "a very strong relationship between the intensity of investment abroad and job creation in the United States" (37).

- Sometimes haloes are bestowed on MNCs by host countries that beg to be 'exploited.' The Scottish Council for Development and Industry once lauded U.S. manufacturers for their prodigious contributions to Scottish industry. Acclaiming them as "welcome invaders," the Council asked for more U.S. companies to come. Florid compliments were scattered by President Ahmed Sekou Toure of Guinea when he addressed some 80 international businessmen in New York under the tutelage of Chase Manhattan's David Rockefeller. Hitherto, his country had been extremely hostile to Western multis but in 1982 expediency dictated a new public face: "Your creative genius . . . your pragmatic approach, your open-mindedness, and your understanding, combined with our ability to give you highly profitable investment outlets, constitute the major reason that led me to come here." In July 1989 the French minister of industry visited Tokyo to woo potential Japanese investors. He gracefully flattered his hosts, who recalled unpleasant anti-multi experiences in France. Envious of Japanese capital flows to the UK, he remarked: "Mrs. Thatcher is beautiful but Mr. Mitterrand is still more beautiful." Did this impress them?

BRICKBATS

General Abuse

Before dealing with specific accusations, it is appropriate to savor some of the juicy epithets—which are not intended to be funny—that are hurled at multis by politicians and religious leaders. Lord Davies of Leek attempted to persuade his fellow parliamentarians that British sovereignty ought not to be sacrificed to a group that "has no international responsibility apart from a worship of the God Mammon" (24). This view is consonant with the thesis advanced in a book produced by a Russian state publishing company in 1985, which asserts that multis are not worried by legal or moral considerations "in their pursuit of maximum profits. Their only councillor is the Golden Calf" (1). Emeric Blum, one of the Group of Eminent Persons (a UN advisory body), took up the cudgels for the LDCs because the neo-colonialist transnational corporations "aggravate their position in the world economy, reduce their share in world trade, lever the disproportionate outflow of their financial resources, pose a ceaseless and real threat to their economic independence and [are] often an instrument of gross interference in their internal affairs" (40). Congressman James Burke, the sworn opponent of direct foreign investments undertaken by U.S. companies, was of course a compassionate man. He opposed employing a "ten-year old child in Korea and paying him 6 cents or a woman 8 cents an hour, and have them work ten hours a day, six days a week. Our multinationals . . . enjoy the tremendous profits they receive as a result of that exploitation" (39). Britain's Liberal party voted overwhelmingly for a decisive antimulti resolution at its 1979 assembly after a delegate had received thundering applause for asserting that "multinationals have no loyalty to any country, no ethics except growth, no answerability and no masters. Corruption, blackmail, bribery and threats are their business skills."

Do academics employ more moderate language? Probably the most popular textbook on TNCs in English-language universities is that by R. J. Barnet and R. E. Müller: *Global Reach* (38). The authors explain to their students that the policies of the TNCs "have contributed more to the exacerbation of world poverty, world unemployment, and world inequality than to their solution." Though the publishers of the Oxford University Press usually demand scholarly restraint, Michael Kidron was not censured for his wild statement that "the multinational companies are the major polluters of the environment of our planet" (41).

It is the churches that take the lead in venomous abuse. Below are some choice scraps from the poisonous nonsense that is on record. The Canadian Conference of Catholic Bishops sparked front-page news with talk of the "moral disorder" mentality of transnational corporations which violates the "value, meaning and dignity of human labour." The Methodist anti-multi world campaign was instituted because "many thousands must go hungry so that the MNCs can make real profits." The Methodists accused global corporations of ravaging the resources of the LDCs, exploiting black people, and undermining the culture of the host countries. How is this done? Products that attack family life and the community spirit are marketed: "senseless violence, promiscuity, acquisitiveness and blind materialism" (42) are generated. The WCC has outlined an ecumenical program to fight TNCs and published with obvious approbation the declaration of an Anglican priest from Sri Lanka: "Transnational corporations are intrinsically evil because their unconstrained, unaccountable power is integral to their nature and can never effectively become subject to social control" (5). At its 1975 Nairobi assembly, the WCC arrived at a similar conclusion. It was implied that the executives of multis are beyond repentance: "They join together to oppress the poor and keep them under domination. Measures to check their activities . . . are now under discussion but . . . it is very difficult to envisage any effective measure which will eradicate their innate exploitative patterns" (19). In 1967 the Pope condemned the double standard of TNCs that evince some social sensitivity in rich countries but apply rugged and inhuman individualism in poor economies. The U.S. Catholic Conference felt that the Pope was "not optimistic about the willingness of MNCs to initiate reforms." Hence the Conference advocated that international corporations should be compelled to change their stance by congressional action and supranational regulations (39).

Improper Transfer Pricing

It was not a firebrand of the left but the staid president of the AFL-CIO, George Meany, who told the U.S. Senate that multis "can juggle their bookkeeping and their prices and their taxes" (50). This is the most sustained and substantive charge against MNCs. Their head offices strive to maximize post-tax global profits and for this purpose are often ready to manipulate the accounts of subsidiaries. Transfer pricing irregularities are frequently not a criminal offence for they do not necessarily entail drawing up fraudulent documents. In any case comprehensive laws, which set out what mark-ups are mandatory, have rarely been enacted. Under-invoicing and over-invoicing are the order of the day. Tax evasion or avoidance is of course the main purpose but there are also other motives. When exchange controls limit profit-remittances, some imaginative accounting helps to counter the law. In countries with statutory profit-sharing and/or powerful unions, TNCs find it expedient to scale down the profits earned by certain subsidiaries.

Complaints in the Home Countries

When Ford Motor Company declared in Detroit, "We don't consider ourselves basically an American company. . . . [W]e are a multinational company. . . . [W]e carry a lot of flags," its lack of patriotism was denounced. Multis that act as good and lawful corporate citizens of host countries, harboring their subsidiaries, are frequently deemed to have betrayed the national interest of the country in which the parent is domiciled.

Multis have been attacked for exporting technological expertise from the home country (49). Certain totalitarian societies restrict the emigration of their nationals on the ground that the state has financed their acquisition of professional expertise. A parallel proposition was put to the U.S. Congress: "When a multi-national corporation licenses a product abroad, it gives away the technology created by Americans educated at public expense" (51).

In addition, multis deprive the home country's treasury of tax revenue which is diverted to the host countries of their foreign operations.

The accusation that MNCs cause unemployment in the home countries has been voiced since the first multi opened up a manufacturing operation abroad. Unilever's biographer relates that its founder shrugged off cries that 'English workers are being robbed of work' and refused to be intimidated (52). Unilever and other Western MNCs were abused for organizing "runaway corporations," many of which have been given a name different from that of the parent—the intent, of course, is sinful! If the subsidiaries supply primarily foreign markets, the parent is still condemned for making people jobless at home through foregone exports. The detractors of the modern multis regard it as particularly pernicious when goods manufactured by foreign subsidiaries are exported to the home country. One critic points out that astute advertising agencies help to hoodwink the consumers by camouflaging the national origin of the branded goods (50).

Union leaders in the home countries often excel in their vociferous attacks on corporations that invest overseas. The passage below is extracted from a bleak AFL-CIO submission to the United States' senior legislators (54).

Proud countries are losing the power to shape their own destinies, to guide their economies, to collect their taxes, to better the lives of their people. They are increasingly at the mercy of stateless, soulless, anonymous multinational corporations. . . . The great exodus of American production to overseas plants has led economists, labor leaders and even enlightened businessmen to wonder whether we are witnessing the dimming of America. This greatest industrial power in the world's history is in danger of becoming nothing more than a nation of hamburger stands . . . a country stripped of industrial capacity and meaningful work . . . a service economy . . . a nation of citizens busily buying and selling cheeseburgers and root beer floats.

The chairman of White Consolidated Industries, Edward Reddig, commented that "when all manufacturing is done overseas, I'm going to be a cheese salesman." The spokesman of the AFL-CIO was scornful: "Unfortunately, when all manufacturing is done overseas, American workers are going to be employed, and Mr. Reddig will have no one to buy his cheese."

TNCs are accused of weakening the national currency by exporting capital, thereby generating BoP deficits and raising domestic interest rates.

While multis are especially prone to bullying host countries, they are also accused of blackmailing the governments of the home countries. If the authorities do not award them liberal subsidies and other favors, international corporations will "threaten to locate their next major project abroad or even close down home production" (53).

The Political Impact on Host-Countries

Multis are rebuked for depriving nation–states of their political sovereignty. Cheryl Payer has discovered that they are "the natural enemies of Third World independence and can usually mobilise the resources to crush it" (43). A British trade union leader convinced himself that multis "bring to naught all efforts by governments to check inflation" (44). This theme was also elaborated upon in an official document of the British Labour party which attributed to MNCs the ability to undermine the effectiveness of fiscal, monetary, and devaluation strategies of host countries (53). The Brandt Report noted similarly that international corporations are "out of reach of effective controls by nation–states" (45). The Pope too has observed that TNCs have the means to "conduct autonomous strategies which are largely independent of the national political powers" (39). If MNCs find that politicians in the LDCs resist their plans (on how the host country should be run), and bribes will not change their minds, they are overthrown by insurrections financed from abroad, and replaced with other, compliant politicians.

The more sober adversaries of multis do not claim that MNCs are intent on interfering in the internal affairs of the host countries. Their criticism centers on the fact that the real decision-making in foreign subsidiaries takes place—far away—in the head office of the parent. Multis seek to disguise this cosmetically. For the purposes of public relations, and to assuage national susceptibilities, certain managerial positions are reserved for natives; this of course does not mean that they wield the power suggested by their functional titles. Another form of window-dressing is seen when multis appoint an individual from the host country to be formally in charge of labor relations while his deputy is a citizen of the home country; it is the latter who receives instructions from the parent company and is truly in command. When Cummins Engines announced the closure of one of its foreign plants, the union leaders travelled from the host country to the United States to plead their case with the CEO of the multi; they did so because the local managers allegedly lacked authority to conclude a meaningful settlement.

The Impact on the Labor Market in Host Countries

The Methodists, among others, despise multis for causing unemployment in the LDCs; the resultant jobless masses have to be looked after by the governments of the poor countries while, in the rich economies, the shareholders of the guilty international corporations "rake in dividends" (42). A more temperate accusation would have it that no new jobs are created by multis. The establishment of subsidiaries appears to generate additional employment in the host countries, but this "does not necessarily mean that the employment would not have been generated without the presence of foreign investment" (46). Some critics of MNCs, who concede that new jobs are brought into existence, say that these are not permanent jobs. Employment with multis is volatile because subsidiaries are liquidated whenever the parent company finds reason to move to a new location.

Clerical adversaries of MNCs emphasize the deleterious consequences that flow from "a preference for capital-intensive technology which aggravates the unemployment problem." The Exxon Corporation seemed to be substantiating this contention in its evidence to the Group of Eminent Persons. The oil multi agreed that by introducing "labor-saving technology when unemployment exists or by making some national [indigenous] enterprises non-competitive," MNCs could be viewed as "disruptive." It is frequently alleged that multis do not train the workers of their foreign subsidiaries but steal them from native employers (35). MNCs are criticized for their anti-union stance; in Europe Kodak and IBM have been singled out.

The cornerstone of the Levinson thesis would have it that a multi can successfully defeat strikers in the subsidiary of country A by increasing output in the non-striking subsidiary of country B, thus breaking the strike of A through imports from B.

"MNCs . . . scour the world for the cheapest labor"—this, many assert, is the chief motivation for manufacturing in the host countries. Yet another stigma blights the good name of MNCs: they pay high wages, which—according to the TUC—leads to the "creation of enclaves of highly paid native employees who earn five, ten or a hundred times more than local people." This crime is fully documented in company biographies and the published memoirs of multi executives. Unilever has been found guilty. Gulf Oil has admitted to paying in Angola more than the union rates, but it cried "mea culpa": "As a multinational company we have the obligation not to upset the apple cart for other residents of a nation" (48). Multis investing in Sweden have been criticized because their relatively higher emoluments have militated against the equality ideology of the Swedish unions and annoyed Swedish industrialists. California's Kaiser-Frazer ran into trouble when it opened an assembly plant in Holland. Naively, the parent imagined that it could neutralize incipient trade union resistance—and generally earn good will—by formulating wage rates that were 30 percent above the union scales. The Dutch metal workers federation castigated Kaiser-Frazer and compelled it to be less generous (55). Vic Feather, at one time the United Kingdom's top union leader, told British audiences how the horrible U.S. TNCs were ravaging the UK economy. He related a story to indicate their wickedness and illustrate his own prowess in challenging them. It appears that a U.S. company, which opened an office in Cornwall, had been so depraved as to pay the locally recruited shorthand typists considerably more than the norm prevailing in this English county. Wielding the heavy stick of the TUC, the U.S. multi was told to stop such a bad labor practice. Gripped with fear, this foreign employer complied and cut wages.

MNCs and their Exports from Host Countries

Many LDCs woo the despised multis because they hope to reap benefits that would strengthen their BoP. When these expectations are not fulfilled, multis are rebuked for failing to export in sufficient quantities. Frequently, they are accused of having deliberately deceived the host country. They are said to have failed to implement explicit export undertakings which they had originally given; without them, their direct investments would not have been sanctioned (and in some cases the companies would not have been able to collect state subsidies). Host countries often discover belatedly that the parents of multis impose restrictions on exports from certain of their foreign manufacturing subsidiaries lest these compete with exports from the home country or encroach upon markets supplied by their other foreign subsidiaries. When the native authorities finally learn of these rules, they have been known to scream loudly.

Side by side with reproaches that MNCs do not export enough, many foreign-owned subsidiaries are chided for exporting too much. In 1959 Brazil was nasty to the German multi Volkswagen, refusing its subsidiary a license to export 300 vehicles to the United States. Hostile press comments drove home the message: "Why should Brazil export cars to accommodate Americans when it cannot satisfy its own Brazilian customers at home?" (56). MNCs eager to discharge their export obligations to the satisfaction of the government of the host nation may find themselves attacked as export-maniacs from other quarters. They will be charged with causing harmful changes to the economic structure of the host country. This accusation is amplified when they have been encouraged to invest in agriculture. Barbara Ward, a distinguished Western adversary of TNCs, gave public vent to her anger. She had uncovered that meat from Central America did not end up in Latin American stomachs but as hamburgers in franchised restaurants in North America. This, Barabara Ward considered, was disgustingly antisocial conduct by TNCs! Del Monte was named a guilty corporation by virtue of its ownership of farms, fisheries, and canneries in two dozen countries (57). Andrew Chetley sought to make his readers' blood boil: "Brazil exports 97.5% of its orange crop—much of it to the Coca-Cola company which in turn imports Fanta orange soft drink into Brazil. Fanta, however, contains no orange juice" (58).

Adherents of the *dependencia* school inveigh against the "modernization" role of multis in Latin America and India. They stress that direct investments by Western TNCs tend to uplift the international trade involvement of the host economies. The *dependencia* academics deplore the behaviour of TNCs which hoist the volume of exports. They regard this as objectively unsuitable and undesirable for LDCs. As good nationalists they are upset when export-oriented enterprises (controlled by parents in foreign lands) are mollycoddled by governments. Many intellectual brickbats have been hurled at Western multis for diverting scarce resources, which could have been utilized to fill vital domestic economic needs, to production for exports (81).

Miscellaneous Criticism

Multis use their material wealth to control the global spread of information and are thus able "to create myths and to obscure the truth." The Church of England's Board for Social Responsibility has blamed the iniquitous MNCs for "empty consumerism"; they are villains because they manufacture products "ill-designed to meet the basic needs of the masses of the people and they sometimes create false needs and then cater for them for the sake of their own quick profit." Not to be outdone, the Methodists have joined in to deplore the dissemination of dishonest advertising by multis. This leads to the eclipse of local products; the duped masses buy instead "magic food," Coca-Cola, and cigarettes.

The Church of England draws attention to the power of international corporations to "remould the culture and its values in the interests of industry and business." The Group of Eminent Persons refers to the transplanting of "business culture," which can threaten the "very cultural identity and the entire social fabric" of countries in which MNCs have subsidiaries. A tendentious UN publication tells of a special kind of misfortune that overtakes countries that host multis: "The ostentatious styles of foreign personnel as compared with those of domestic employees are a source both of envy and resentment. Styles of management directed towards efficiency but insensitive to local cultural values may appear to people in the host country as arrogant and dehumanizing." What if the multis give native workers good technical training? That too is a bad thing, for the 'victims' will be "unduly influenced by alien values" (79).

MNCs are widely cursed for "seeking pollution havens to dodge anti-pollution legislation [in the home countries]" (44). The WCC is adamant about the vile impact of TNC production on the environment of the LDCs. In addition, the Western enterprises of some international corporations are exposed for shipping toxic waste to the Third World. Multis are also abused for exporting to the LDCs products, ranging from contraceptives to pesticides to baby pacifiers, that have been banned as unsafe in the home countries (47).

The WCC has maligned global corporations as "accomplices of racism." The Methodists, eager to echo this denigration, point out that "support for racist regimes" by TNCs is not confined to South Africa. The investments of multis in other parts of the globe are also accompanied by the exploitation of black people, who are given more menial jobs and fewer opportunities for leisure, education, and medical treatment than whites. The WCC has told its Christian affiliates that multis are not only racists but also sexists: they "exploit women" (78). 'Progressive' church leaders explain that "women workers offer special advantages," which is why TNCs "prefer female to male labour." According to the journal *Multinational Monitor*, founded by Ralph Nader, "around the globe multinationals use women to keep labor costs down and profits up." The UN agrees: "By employing a very young, unorganised female labour force, TNCs benefit to a large extent from the deep-rooted socio-economic patterns of gender discrimination (186).

Research and development (R&D) is not carried out by multis in host countries and for this the multis are frequently condemned. But MNCs are also vilified when they do undertake research in the countries where they have located subsidiaries. Do such nefarious activities not prove that they are clearly intent on stealing the innovative ideas of foreigners? Are MNCs not encouraging indirectly a brain drain from the poorer parts of the world for the benefit of Western-based global operations?

Finally, I present a quotation from a book on transnational corporations promoted by the Soviet Union. The author is said to be in no doubt that the majority of TNCs have "a direct vested interest in the intensified militarisation of the capitalist economy. Many of them take either an indirect or direct part in the implementation of large-scale arms programmes and reap enormous profits from this" (1).

4

THEIR COMBINED MIGHT

The fact is that Henry Ford is a head of state, and the turnover of his world-wide empire is of the same order in money terms as the whole National Budget of India. . . . In dealing with Mr. Ford, the British Government is dealing with someone who has the same resources—and possibly more personal power—than Mrs. Gandhi.

Tony Benn

STATISTICAL SOOTHSAYERS

Writers of such pretentious books as *Multinationals Take Over Australia* (76) and *Als Wär's der Liebe Gott* (77) describe in general terms the manner in which indigenous and foreign multis emasculate the national sovereignty of developed countries. Others purvey the same message by aggregating numerically the powers of MNCs; the oppressive might of multis is then laid bare in truly frightening colors. Arithmetic data on the combined weight of international corporations are lapped up avidly by those who feed the myth on the supranational conspiracy of TNCs.

The Table that follows records an eclectic sample of 14 forecasts re-

The MNC Domination of the Globe

SOURCE	PROPHETS	ATTRIBUTION	YEAR OF PROPHESY	TARGET DATE	NUMBER OF MULTIS	CONTROLLING PERCENTAGE	TOUCHSTONE
60	BINCO	"some scholars"	1967	within two decades	-300	50+	(WORLD) GNP
67	UNION OF INTERNATIONAL ASSOCIATIONS	"the estimate"	1969	within the next decade	300	75	(WORLD) PRODUCTIVE CAPACITY
65	NAT WEINBERG (AFL-CIO)	Richard Barnet	1970	1980	300	75	(WORLD) MANUFACTURING ASSETS
64	CHARLES LEVINSON	...	1970	1980	200	75	(WESTERN WORLD) CAPITAL ASSETS
24	LORD SELSDON	"there are people who claim"	1971	1985	300	50	(WORLD) PRODUCTION
24	LORD SELSDON	"other people say"	1971	2000	200	80	(WORLD) PRODUCTION
63	JAMES LINDSAY (HENLEY COLLEGE)	"a professional prediction"	1971	within a generation	300	50	(WORLD) BUSINESS
62	E.G. WOODROOFE (UNILEVER)	"a well-aired statistic"	1972	1985	300	75+	(WESTERN WORLD) CAPITAL ASSETS
68	CORPORATE INFORMATION CENTER	"it is predicted"	1973	2000	300	90	(WORLD) PRODUCTION & SERVICES
23	LORD BANKS	"it has been estimated"	1975	1980	300	75	(WORLD) MANUFACTURING ASSETS
44	BOB EDWARDS (UK CHEMICAL WORKERS UNION)	...	1977	within a decade	...	50	(WORLD) TOTAL PRODUCTION
66	R. DESATNIK & M. BENNETT	"well-informed observers"	1977	2000	250	50	(WORLD) OUTPUT
42	METHODIST WORLD DEVELOPMENT ACTION	...	1979	2000	200	80	(NON-COMMUNIST WORLD) TRADE & INDUSTRY
61	RALPH NADER	...	1980	end of this century	200	70	(WESTERN WORLD) ECONOMIC OUTPUT

lating to the quantitative influence of big multis. They convey an awful message: 200–300 corporate colossuses will rule over 50–90 percent of the global economy (measured by varying economic benchmarks). When the small print is read, substantive differences between the seemingly similar predictions can be discerned. A few forecasters say of multis that they will collectively "own" something or other while most of the prophets employ the verbs "control," "account for," or "dominate." MNCs will have a stranglehold—but over what? Quite different points of references are mentioned: GNP, output, productive capacity, capital assets, manufacturing assets, and so forth. There is not even agreement on the geography of the measured standards: the world? the Western world? the non-Communist world?

Howard Perlmutter, hero of the next chapter, was the first individual to quantify the combined future might of TNCs. With hindsight it is easy to comprehend that his methodology was faulty and his prophetic judgment wrong. Nevertheless, he was an intellectual innovator and the first to evaluate the tribe of international corporations in a numerate context. In the 1960s, after "some rather intensive research" (26), Perlmutter felt able to predict that by 1985 some 200—on other occasions he refers to 200–300, 300, and 300–400—supergiants would have the whip hand over the economy of the free world. Alas, Perlmutter does not seem to have been always consistent because his gospel has also been quoted as alluding to "60–70% of the world's industrial output," "the greater part of the world's output," and "80% of all productive assets of the non-Communist world."

At first Perlmutter's conjectures were presented at private forums but in 1968 he went public. He mentioned his predictions in several lectures, interviews, and articles. As the target date of 1985 approached Perlmutter did not renege on his comprehensive multi theories but chose not to repeat the grandiose pronostications. The fact that he has demonstrably failed to forecast meaningfully has not stopped others from using (often without attribution) the discredited projections made in 1967–68. He was plagiarized in many languages by outstanding religious, political, and trade union dignitaries. Demagogues and simpletons circulated Perlmutter's quantifications without the caveats that the pioneer had attached to his predictions.

HOW NOT TO ADD UP

Value-added

The economic influence of individual multis is gauged almost invariably by turnover, (gross) output values, and/or sales figures. As these benchmarks incorporate the value of inputs bought from outside the company, they differ radically from net output, that is, value-added, which is the appropriate indicator of a business's importance in the economy. Net output is frequently half the value of gross output and in some cases, for example, General Motors and Ford, as little as one-third. It is particularly incongruous to compare the sales of a corporation with a country's GDP or GNP; national accounts are carefully computed to avoid double-counting and, essentially, represent the value-added of a national economy.

Only the Foreign Share

If one seeks to quantify the role of multis in host countries, only the non-domestic activities of the global corporations ought to be aggregated. In 1977–78—midway between the date of Perlmutter's prognostications and his target year—J. M. Stopford and his colleagues (74) prepared an international directory of MNCs that had minimum annual sales of one billion dollars. Excluding the oil companies, there then existed only 50 private sector multis where the foreign subsidiaries accounted for more than half of the global output of these corporations. In those days left-wing propaganda equated MNCs with companies nurtured by Yankee imperialism. Yet in this directory only eight (non-oil) U.S. firms (of the total of 50) were awarded the accolade of being truly multinational corporations. Firms such as Union Carbide, Ford, du Pont, General Electric, Caterpillar, Monsanto, Texas Instruments, Motorola, Dresser, and Bendix, which were singled out for abuse in the anti-multi literature (unscrupulous! oppressive! rapacious!) produced abroad less than half of their total output. GM's proportion was about one-third. The parents of MNCs par excellence were headquartered in small countries. Switzerland's Nestle, Sweden's SKF, the Netherland's Philips, Canada's Massey-Ferguson, Belgium's Solvay had only very limited opportunities to sell in the home country—hence the foreign share of their global sales was in the range of 85–97 percent.

Poor Vienna!

Were the world ruled by one government it might perhaps make sense to compare the world's GNP with the total value-added generated by the supergiant firms. Today this is a nonsensical exercise. It is even more disingenuous and dishonest to juxtapose the globally consolidated accounts of an individual multi with the national accounts of a single country. Very 'respectable' practitioners make tendentious use of global turnover figures relating to a given multi and ought to be put to shame.

In the anti-MNC agitational literature GM occupies a prominent place. The company is described pejoratively as a "political state" with a foreign policy of its own. Why? "Its sales figures are larger than the GNP of all but fourteen members of the United Nations in 1967" (75)—the year of Perlmutter's first numerate forecasts on the world power of multis. The same demagogic assertion appears in different guises: the sales of GM are said to make it a world political force because they exceed the GNP of 130 countries (65).

Austria is a small Western country which, until recently, had been largely deprived of direct investments by American multis. To the chagrin of the managers and trade unions of its German subsidiary, the U.S. parent of GM chose in 1980 to locate a components factory in the vicinity of Vienna. Detroit and the welcoming Austrian government knew that this enterprise, even if expanded, would employ less than half of one percent of GM's total labor force. Nevertheless, there were those who maintained that this was a dangerous threat to the country's sovereignty. They had been indoctrinated to believe that "many multinationals are more powerful and wealthier than their host country" (73)—did this not also apply to Austria? Coincidentally, from London came soft-spoken support. The Church of England's synod made no explicit reference to the imminent GM exploitation of the Viennese proletariat. But in one of its pamphlets, readers were given the 'relevant' facts: in 1978 GM had global sales of more than $63 billion while in the same period little Austria's GNP was only $56 billion. Let the faithful draw their own conclusions! A group of Austrian left-wingers felt conscience-bound to warn their fellow citizens that if GM were allowed to proceed with its nefarious project, this would be the first step in the subjugation of Austria by U.S. multis (72).

Heterogeneous MNCs

Notwithstanding the MNC model constructed by the four founding fathers, most of the very large international corporations are not fully integrated entities. Chapter 13 illustrates that particular national subsidiaries are known to conduct their activities in an independent fashion that affects adversely other subsidiaries of the same corporation. For this reason host countries can often afford to take action against one national segment of a multi without necessarily provoking retaliatory action from other national segments, some of which may in fact chuckle with *schadenfreude*.

On yet another plane the supergiant firms frequently fail to perform according to Perlmutter's percepts. Most of them are multiproduct corporations, the parent of which acts as an umbrella for a number of smaller autonomous multis. This means that within the jurisdiction of host country X there may be operating several subsidiaries of one powerful TNC. These subsidiaries do not necessarily work in concert, for each of them is a constituent of a separate international framework. There are many cases on record in which the government of X has acted in a beastly manner toward one of these subsidiaries without inducing bellicose reactions from subsidiaries (of the same multi) which belong to other product divisions.

CANADA'S GAY BANKERS

To summarize the two basic propositions of this chapter: it is absurd to compare the global sales figures of one MNC, especially of a multi-product corporation, with the GNP of one country. It is equally ridiculous to aggregate the global sales figures—and, implicitly, the putative might—of all multis and then to contrast the bottom line with the total output of the world. The projections in Table 4.1 have turned out to be factually inaccurate. But what if they reflected genuinely the combined quantitative output of all TNCs? Would this have validated the thesis on the domination of the globe by mammoth corporations which actively combine to pursue the same goals?

In two, obviously far-fetched, similes it will be hypothesized that researchers have collated some startling facts that became publically known. The first concerns Canadian bankers, 12.8 percent of whom were found to have been in 1985 homosexuals or bisexuals. The second set of figures is even more bizarre and relates to Brazil: non-Catholic executives were said to have been responsible for 23.4 percent of all Brazilian exports in the 1979–82 period. What ominous inferences, if any, could be drawn from such reports on the putative power of gays on Canada's financial scene and the influence allegedly exercised by atheists, Jews, and Protestants on Catholic Brazil's international trade? Clearly, anyone who chooses to disseminate such spurious statistics is a charlatan. But if this were to happen, serious commentators ought not to concentrate their wrath on challenging the numerical accuracy of figures that are not backed by substantive evidence. It would be more productive if, instead, they pointed out the specious purport of such arithmetic aggregations. Even if the data were authentic, what would it prove? Is it suggested that there is a policymaking club of homosexual bankers in Canada? What sane person would suspect that there exists in Brazil a secret society of non-Catholic export managers? Homosexual bankers from Montreal and bisexual bankers from Vancouver are not members of a professional fraternity but merciless commercial competitors. The non-Catholic Brazilian export executives are rivals, bitter rivals. Whoever depicts them as members of a unified group, out to employ their combined might to oppress Catholic Brazilians, deserves to be locked up in a lunatic asylum. Mutatis mutandis, only the believers in the legend of powerful multis are comforted by the summation of the global sales figures of large MNCs.

I have argued that the game of calculating the combined numerate might of the world's multinationals is a deceitful exercise. Nevertheless, it may prove intellectually wholesome when some appropriate data are cited from the anti-multi stable of the UN. Perhaps these will debunk the fantasies underlying the figures set out in the preceding Table.

Global direct employment by TNCs [are estimated] at a minimum of some 65 million in the world's market economy countries. Of this approximately 43 million are in the home countries . . . and 22 million are employed abroad, of which . . . 7 million are likely to be in LDCs. . . . Thus, the direct employment by TNCs accounts for only 3 percent of the world's economically active population. In the developing world . . . TNCs represent much less than 1 percent (186).

5

HOWARD'S PERFECT MULTIS

I like to think of the whole world as a production floor, and what is best is to go where production can most readily be achieved—the cheapest and the best.

Thorton Bradshaw, *chairman of RCA*

Howard Perlmutter's academic title was "Professor of Social Architecture." In business history he is likely to be immortalized as the high priest of the multi ideology, the doyen of the founding fathers. Like many religious prophets throughout the ages he has constructed models of purity and perfection. Nevertheless, at times Perlmutter was also a shamefaced pragmatist. Corporations found guilty of operating in a manner that offended his orthodox tenets were not always excommunicated. Near-perfection was sometimes tolerated. I once shared a platform with Perlmutter and Britain's pious left-winger Tony Benn. Our brief was to debate the merits of MNCs. Benn then no longer held political office because the Labour party had just lost the election. Someone in the audience reproved him because, when cabinet minister, he had stopped Chrysler from acquiring 100 percent of the equity of the (UK) Rootes company; the U.S. raider had also been forced to acquiesce in a mandatory representation of UK directors on the board of its British subsidiary. All eyes turned to Perlmutter, who was known to look upon 100 percent ownership of foreign subsidiaries as one of the attributes of a true multi. Though he did not want to be beastly to Benn, he acknowledged that Chrysler's capitulation to the dictates of the then British government had been sinful. But, grudgingly, he offered absolution to companies (like Chrysler) that are raped by nationalist-minded host countries: "We live in a real world and frequently we must put up with something less than . . . 100 percent ownership" (70).

INTERNATIONALISM

In his homilies Perlmutter warned that by virtue of extensive exports and/or the ownership of several foreign manufacturing subsidiaries, corporations do not gain automatic access to the select group of MNCs that are destined to survive into the twenty-first century. He maintained that this could only be achieved if the top decision-makers act as true internationalists. They must conduct themselves as citizens of the world in charge of a globally oriented company. If they are the CEOs of a U.S.-based parent they must disdain U.S. patriotism. Perlmutter spelt out his derision for the "home country executives [who] feel the obligation to show loyalty to the interests of the home country—as, for instance, when U.S.-owned firms are asked that investments overseas be limited for U.S. balance of payments reasons" (26). According to Perlmutter and several of his disciples, only executives who have abandoned thinking in terms of "what is good for my country" and concentrate on "what is good for my multi" are deemed to have embraced the true faith.

The professor from the Wharton School has not hesitated to give practical advice. He recommended that multis, headquartered among powerful nations, should change their domicile and settle in some remote place in a small country—a "nation of low national identification," such as Switzerland—where the temptation to act chauvinistically is muted. (In this Perlmutter differed from Stephen Hymer, who predicted that the head offices of MNCs, located in small countries or in middle-sized urban centers amid large national economies, would in the course of time congregate in a few key cities such as New York, Paris, and London.)

There are ideological differences between Howard Perlmutter, Stephen Hymer, Jacques Maisonrouge, George Ball, and David Lilienthal. They do, however, agree on the gist of global management: resources are to be shifted across borders when it is worthwhile; this must be done unemotionally and without regard to the outdated notion of the national interest. Technology, managers, capital, and physical and intellectual assets of all kinds must be moved around remorselessly on the world's chessboard. Maisonrouge repudiated the anti-establishment aims of the youngsters who manned the barricades in the 1968 Paris University conflict. But he insisted on praising the revolutionary students for one of their slogans: "Down with borders!" (38).

The international mobility game is usually played without breaking the letter of national laws. The German subsidiary of Royal Dutch Shell once commissioned tankers for its fleet from British shipyards while the British subsidiary of Shell commissioned tankers for its fleet from Germany. From the vantage point of the parent's stockholders, the swapping exercise maximized the receipt of subsidies and minimized the payment of taxes (81). Ralph Nader reports that

unions are especially frustrated by this playing-off of nations. . . . [S]triking an ITT subsidiary in Spain simply means that ITT increases production elsewhere or lets the strikers cool their heels while its empire suffers little (27).

This grandiloquence ignores the fact that MNCs are rarely able to conduct their affairs in this manner. Yet Nader is implicitly right in assuming that Perlmutter and his followers heartily applaud the sort of behavior that he finds reprehensible. Hyster (the largest Western forklift manufacturer, headquartered in Oregon, with 14 plants in eight countries) became a ruthless disciple of Perlmutter. In contradistinction to most MNCs, which implement their cross-border mobility quietly and without seeking to attract too much attention, Hyster in the 1980s showed that it cared little for a benevolent public relations image. The U.S. corporation publicized the tenor of its negotiations with a number of government departments in European countries where it was already established or was promising/threatening to set up shop. Among others, the authorities of the Netherlands, Belgium, Northern Ireland, the Republic of Ireland, and Scotland were told bluntly of the radical policy of this U.S. multi, which was ready to close down plants at short notice and transfer production to other national locations where more lucrative subsidies and grants were made available. Hyster proved that it meant what it said—it was indeed a genuine MNC in the Perlmutter mould.

TNCs with head offices in small countries, do not expect the executives in their foreign subsidiaries to learn the language of the home country. Why, according to the Perlmutter gospel, are the Netherlands' Philips and Sweden's Atlas Copco imbued with the spirit of authentic internationalism? For many purposes they have renounced the use of Dutch and Swedish and instead employ English as the linguistic medium for internal, worldwide company communications.

A large number of the top U.S. corporations are guilty of wearing social compassion on their sleeves. They demonstratively select women, blacks, Jews, Catholics, priests, and ecologists as non-executive directors. "Tokenism" is the pejorative designation for appointments that are not dictated by the merits of the individuals. Perlmutter has reserved some of his most acidic contempt for the tokenist practices of corporations that have attained undeserved fame as true international companies. He sneers at the window-dressing carried out by these corporate giants which invite (and pay handsomely) nationals from host countries to become members of local boards of directors and call some of them to sit on the parent's board. "Appointing a number of incompetent 'foreigners' to key positions" is often intended to convey a spurious impression. The high priest of the multi ideology has no truck with such dissimulation, which may cloak the innate nationalist disposition of a corporation with an attractive internationalist outlook. An ability to converse in a foreign tongue or the appointment of a few non-nationals to senior posts cannot buy admission to Perlmutter's elitist club of globally oriented MNCs.

THREE STAGES

Some regard it as quibbling when detailed criteria are formulated according to which international companies are awarded certificates of approval which testify to their bona fide TNC credentials. To Perlmutter, ostensibly petty distinctions matter a great deal. He has consigned all mammoth corporations with foreign involvements to three compartments (described below): in line with Perlmutter's standards, only the corporate entity C represents an authentic multi—those in compartments A and B are impostors.

The Ethnocentric Firm A does not authorize the managers of its foreign subsidiaries to make important decisions; detailed instructions are issued by the head office. Activities abroad are looked upon as adjuncts of operations in the home country. In Perlmutter's words, the parent of this kind of MNC considers foreigners, that is, nationals of the host countries, to be less reliable and trustworthy than nationals of the home country. For this reason only the latter are given the key jobs at home and abroad; they are also paid higher emoluments than the native executives. If a foreigner wishes to advance in a U.S. corporation of this type, he is well advised to tell his superiors that he would be prepared to apply for U.S. citizenship.

The Polycentric Firm B is a corporate vehicle that groups together (largely autonomous) companies in various national locations. The parent body is akin to a roof organization. The corporate structure is such that resources cannot be shifted on a worldwide basis, as Perlmutter expects the head office of a genuine multi to do. The managers of the assorted companies are supposed to maximize the profits of their national bailiwicks and to conduct themselves as good citizens of their respective countries. Assignments of nationals from the home county to the foreign subsidiaries are kept to a minimum. Consequently, the companies abroad employ, with very few exceptions, only native staff. Their advancement is not tuned to the global dimensions of the MNC but restricted to the opportunities present within each national subsidiary. There are generally no intracorporate ladders.

Not surprisingly, some polycentric firms have gone out of their way to decry Perlmutter's economic-political philosophy. They have said that they do not want to be members of the multi club if this requires adherence to Perlmutter's guidelines. The company philosophy of Rio Tinto-Zinc (RTZ)—especially pronounced when Val Duncan was the CEO between 1950 and 1975—strongly favored local equity participation in its overseas subsidiaries. RTZ was vitally concerned to gain the approbation of the politicians of the host countries. In public statements this London-based corporation stressed that, unlike other international companies, it paid sympathetic attention to the national interests of its overseas subsidiaries. They were not subordinated to a global strategy orchestrated by the parent. RTZ's CEO drubbed Perlmutter by boasting that his company's head office was content to be merely a coordinator of "inter-dependent—but in themselves mainly autonomous—companies."

Under the leadership of Duncan Oppenheim, the British-American Tobacco Company (BAT) had a similar corporate blueprint. Its board insisted that a great deal of real effective authority over each national subsidiary should be delegated to indigenous shareholders and local managers. BAT even advocated joint ventures with native partners in host countries—anathema to Perlmutter (82). BAT was emphatic that it should not be called a multinational corporation and demanded to be described as an "international group."

Woolworth used to be an exemplary polycentric corporation. The head office in the home country intervened very little in the commercial affairs of the overseas companies, where the national CEOs were in complete charge of procurements. The parent was only interested in the bottom line, the profits earned in each host country.

The Geocentric Firm C is organized as a "stateless supergiant corporation." The parent is not wedded to the fortunes of any single division or national subsidiary. The managers are educated to place the worldwide objectives of their multi above sectional interests. This makes it necessary to devise a system in which the emoluments of all responsible executives are linked to the global fortunes of the TNC. Only if this is done can executives belittle the significance of the profits/losses of the product divisions or national subsidiaries with which they happen to be associated at a given point of time.

George Ball, the Democratic politician who was once under-secretary of state and later chairman of the Wall Street firm Lehman Brothers, was an early enthusiastic supporter of geocentric firms. He welcomed their evolution with relish: "For the first time corporations are beginning to use the world's resources with maximum efficiency." Jacques Maisonrouge, the French-born chief of IBM's international division, was equally euphoric: "I strongly believe that the future belongs to geocentric companies. . . . [T]he first step to a geocentric organisation is to realise the need to mobilise its resources on a world scale."

In the coming chapters the implications ensuing from geocentric MNCs are discussed in detail. Eldridge Haynes planned to organize the genuine multis; Charles Levinson wanted to pressure them into signing worldwide labour contracts. Their vaunted statelessness led to requests for UN intervention, and joint ventures became unfashionable. Some of the consequential pressures rebounded on the people who were being recruited for the executive functions of geocentric multis. Only exceptional individuals with a special outlook on life could be considered, and there were problems with their wives and children.

6

ONE HUNDRED PERCENT

We at Ford look at the world map without any boundaries. We don't consider ourselves basically an American company. We are a multinational company.

Robert Stevenson

The path to the idyllic geocentric firm is beset with many obstacles. Unless the total equity of all (or at least most) of the subsidiaries is owned by the parent, the cross-border switching of resources cannot be maximized. A multi that aims to operate effectively as a global business cannot afford to be distracted by outsiders who lay claim to the ownership of shares in constituent companies. In the absence of the 100 percent equity ownership there are serious restraints on the parent's capability to hire and fire, retain profits rather than distribute dividends, recruit finance, minimize corporate disclosures, and prevent trade secrets from falling into the wrong hands.

The transfer pricing of MNCs is decided arbitrarily by the head office. It is codswallop to assert, as apologists for multis do, that intracorporate cross-border transactions are carried out at arm's length. Indigenous equity holdings in foreign subsidiaries may curb the execution of astute transfer pricing. If, nevertheless, the head office engages in "constructive invoicing," this can be unfair to the local minority shareholders, or at least appear so.

STATUTORY EMBARGOES

Immediately after World War II LDCs were not as uncompromising about 100 percent investments by foreigners as many are today. In those days governments merely stretched their wings to impress upon potential MNC investors the desirability of enlisting indigenous partners. Even when LDCs were officially opposed to 100 percent-owned subsidiaries, it was frequently possible to appease the authorities with a vague promise that in the future the multi would sell locally shares of its subsidiary. In any case, consent to establish a wholly-owned operation was almost always granted when multinational firms offered something unique and vital *and* were able to convince the native politicians that, as a matter of principle, the investment would not proceed without 100 percent authorization. (For many years Japan had repelled all foreigners who wanted to manufacture without a Japanese partner. Nevertheless, IBM was given a special dispensation.) Some weak MNCs, unable to resist the pressure from host governments, abandoned 100 percent-equity ownership but employed a stratagem whereby 'suitable natives' were given an opportunity to acquire shares which, ordinarily, were not traded on a bourse. They were held firmly by senior employees, suppliers, the subsidiary's local bankers, or other friendly individuals who were expected to come to the AGM in order to cheer and vote for the proposals tabled by the parent company.

Since the 1970s a growing number of LDCs have allowed for no exceptions. They treat the 100 percent condition of TNCs as an imperialist affront to their sovereignty. It has become a symbol of national virility to record a high proportion of indigenous shareholdings in companies affiliated to foreign MNCs. Neither bribery nor the acknowledged importance of the multis' products can nowadays sway the bureaucratic decision-makers who are obliged, by unequivocal rules, to turn down MNCs that wish to act in accordance with the Perlmutter gospel. OECD-based multis have learned to accept as a fact of life that if they wish to be directly represented in certain parts of the world, they cannot do so with 100 percent control. Some MNCs have quietly drawn the conclusion that under those circumstances they would rather forego their planned investments in obstinate LDCs. Others, which had previously regarded wholly-owned subsidiaries as sacrosanct, have conceded defeat and said so: "Moving into new areas [has] required Norton to abandon past shibboleths about total control." The U.S. company reluctantly went over to licensing in the COMECON and took a minority stake in an Indian enterprise (87).

Many host countries have waged their war against 100 percent-owned subsidiaries not only with reference to new investments but also with regard to subsidiaries that were established when native shareholdings were not a requirement. Most multis have complied with retroactive legislation, for the alternative was and is expropriation. However, not all of them are succumbing to these edicts with the serenity that they evince in public. Several MNCs have formally acquiesced and sold shares to natives while their head offices are scheming to run down these subsidiaries. In the interim period there will of course be no new investments; technical innovations, developed by the parent, will be withheld.

Two celebrated feats of resistance are reported from India, where the (retroactive) law, laying down a 60 percent minimum of native-shareholding, is religiously enforced. When Coca-Cola first commenced its operations in India, Prime Minister Nehru was delighted to be photographed sipping this foreign beverage. In 1977 Delhi insisted on immediate compliance with two demands: the U.S. parent was to own no more than 40 percent of its Indian subsidiary, and the know-how of the concentrate was to be disclosed to the local company, which would be majority-controlled by natives. Coca-Cola actually considered agreeing to the first demand but refused adamantly to hand over its proprietary secrets to foreign outsiders. The Indian government thought that bullying tactics would win the day: it held back import licenses, but after a few months Coca-Cola left India.

IBM set up its Bombay factory in 1951 at the specific invitation of Prime Minister Nehru. Ever since 1966 the authorities in Delhi had pressed it to dilute the U.S.-owned shareholdings of its Indian subsidiary. In 1975 the host government lost patience: "Sell 60 percent at once or out you go!" In 1977 IBM liquidated its Indian operations though two weaker competitors, ICL of Britain and Burroughs of the United States, caved in to similar official requests. Throughout the world IBM has steadfastly adhered to the 100 percent principle. It has consistently reiterated that "100 percent ownership is the appropriate way to operate in our industry. . . . This remains our belief." (89).

VOLUNTARY RESOLUTIONS

The hostility of host countries to 100 percent-equity ownership is not the only reason that international companies have foreign subsidiaries with indigenous shareholders. Reference has already been made to corporate giants, such as BAT and RTZ, that are intent on distancing themselves from multis in the Perlmutter mold; for ideological reasons they are therefore very happy to sell shares to natives.

Polycentric corporations, such as Woolworth, are confederations of independently managed companies in several national locations. They do not shift resources from one company to another and the 100 percent canon is breached with impunity.

Many multis have sought native partners in order to enhance their commercial standing in countries where, they believe, it is a distinct disadvantage to operate through companies that are wholly owned by aliens. The public relations ploy of turning a 100 percent subsidiary into a half-native affiliate is intended to ward off populist resentment. But corporate strategists often have concrete matters in mind. GM has been one of Venezuela's largest foreign investors. When in 1988 it voluntarily sold, at a bargain price, 51 percent of its local assets to a native entrepreneurial group, the Mendozas, the parent in Detroit hoped to please the Venezuelan authorities. In the same year the pharmaceutical multi Merck announced a joint venture in Brazil. The company did not pretend that the local partner was needed for his money or expertise. This was a pre-emptive strike to counteract the anti-MNC policies of the Brazilian government, which were directed against wholly-owned foreign enterprises. Once again no compulsion was applied but Merck expected to escape from hostile measures against 100 percent-owned subsidiaries.

Mira Wilkins has a bizarre story to tell of the Kennecott Copper company, which had initiated negotiations with the Chilean government. Of its own volition, the U.S. multi was eager to relinquish 100 percent ownership of its local operations. The Chilean authorities were implored to take over 51 percent of the equity. Kennecott hoped that a mixed-venture status would lead to improved labor relations and less onerous taxes (93). Though ITT regarded 100 percent as an article of faith, it nevertheless sold shares of its wholly-owned British telecommunications subsidiary on the London stock exchange. The scarcely disguised aim was to heighten its chances to sell equipment to the (then) nationalized telephone company. Some observers believed that ITT was wrong in assuming that having local UK shareholders would, by itself, be of benefit to the company. But whether the advantages accruing from abandoning 100 percent-ownership are real or imagined, the considerations that moved GM, Merck, Kennecott, and ITT have indeed proved to be an important motivation.

Some MNCs take in foreign partners because they are not financially strong enough. Thomas Fahey, a senior executive of General Tire, has explained that his company was introduced to the "joint-venture posture" during its first foreign operation when the company could not raise sufficient funds to go it alone (27). Even when multis have ample resources, they may still prefer to enter a partnership with native capitalists if they wish to unload some of the political risks. When multis based in OECD economies were impeded by exchange controls from expanding abroad, they often offered minority equity stakes in their foreign subsidiaries in order to recruit (foreign currency) capital.

THE PROOF OF THE PUDDING

In 1964 Chrysler, anxious to emulate Ford and GM with their wholly-owned subsidiaries in Europe, was eager to buy all the equity of Rootes, a UK automobile manufacturer. The Conservative Chancellor of the Exchequer Reginald Maulding could not stop this outright because there were no legal limitations on foreign-held equity. Employing a subterfuge, the Bank of England's exchange controllers vetoed the takeover proposal. Chrysler was then so resolved to obtained a foothold in Britain that it agreed to limit its acquisition to 50 percent of the voting shares. An undertaking was given not to purchase any Rootes shares above this ceiling without official permission. Detroit soon learned that the partly-owned company could not be integrated fully in Chrysler's global network. In the meantime the Labour party had come to power and the responsible minister was now Tony Benn. Chrysler's head office informed him in 1967 that unless more shares could be bought to give the U.S. multi a controlling majority, Chrysler would sell its holdings and abandon manufacturing in the British Isles. Though the Labour government grumbled that it was being raped, the original undertaking was rescinded. To save political face, the 100 percent principle was still not conceded: the U.S. stake was lifted only to 73 percent and (at a later stage) to 85 percent. In 1972 the then Conservative administration finally bestowed upon Chrysler the right to buy up the remaining shares. Heath's government pooh-poohed the idea that multis could be controlled effectively by host countries through mandatory native minority shareholdings.

The Chrysler case had been an idiosyncratic exception to the British practice. Apart from restrictions on the ownership of financial institutions and public utilities by foreigners, 100 percent subsidiaries were not only permitted but actually encouraged. Several thousand such subsidiaries flourish today in Britain. Many of them had originally been joint ventures and/or had native shareholders; a number of UK subsidiaries of foreign multis used to be traded actively on the London stock exchange. As the message spread that the British authorities do not penalize foreign multis for buying out their indigenous shareholdings, practically all TNCs (with head offices in the United States, Germany, France, Sweden, the Netherlands, and Canada) took advantage of this rare liberal stance, which had few parallels in the world. This happened between 1951 and 1985. At the end of that period only a handful of subsidiaries were still quoted on the London stock exchange. If proof has to be delivered that most multis prefer 100%-owned subsidiaries, then Britain provides evidence attested to by the behavior of hundreds of multis. To pave the way for total control, almost all of them offered generous compensation to their minority shareholders. Heinz, Hoechst, Lafarge, Philips, and Union Carbide—among many others—knew what was good for them!

The British multis that were saddled with minority shareholders in their non-British enterprises also strove to act in a manner that would please Perlmutter. In one typical example, the tiny Canadian subsidiary of Marks & Spencer used to have 45 percent native shareholdings. When, in 1986, the new management at the helm of this prestigious UK retail chain planned to expand operations in North America, expediency dictated that the Canadian shareholders should first be bought out. In July 1986 Australia's rules on mandatory indigenous shareholdings in the subsidiaries of foreign multis were eased and the door was opened to 100 percent bids. Within one month Reckitt & Colman, the British food multi, made an offer to buy out its Australian minority. This was clearly not a fluke but company policy: "All our main subsidiaries around the world are wholly owned and Australia was an anomaly." Cadbury, Courtaulds, Unilever, Thorn, and other MNCs followed suit.

As Philips of Eindhoven built an empire it acquired native shareholders in many of its 60 foreign subsidiaries. These proved onerous impediments in the commercial battles with globally integrated competitors. Philips, at some undisclosed date, changed the design of its master plan. Whenever possible, it opted for 100 percent control. The vast U.S. economy, however, was deemed to merit a subsidiary with wide autonomous powers and local shareholders. In 1987 that bastion too fell. Offering some $600 million to buy out the natives, Eindhoven proclaimed: "We will now be one unified company and once more able to compete on a global basis."

The first postwar foreign ventures of Japanese manufacturers had been in LDCs where they were happy to partner local entrepreneurs. In the 1970s they were spreading into the OECD economies. This story is told by a British consultant who has advised several Japanese firms on direct investments in the EEC.

On my first assignment in Tokyo I caught on that even large corporations fervently believed that they would only be able to establish successful manufacturing operations in the *developed* countries if they did so in conjunction with native, private or public, companies. They were convinced that the supposed hostility of the Western world to their projects could only be deflected if they did not press for 100 percent equity ownership. I tried to disabuse them of this idée fixe. I attempted to persuade them that Her Majesty's Government will like their subsidiaries no more and no less whether they were 60 percent or 100 percent owned by Japanese parents. My clients were too polite to say to my face that they did not believe this. (Other consultants have had similar experiences.) In the course of time Japanese multinational corporations perceived what MNCs of other countries had already digested: if 100 percent ownership is feasible, then it is the ideal arrangement. I have observed that while Japanese executives are not prepared to confess that their previous policies were wrong, they nevertheless learn quickly and are ready to carry out U-turns. The majority of Japanese subsidiaries, founded in the U.S. and the UK during the 1980s, have no native shareholders and the men in charge of the international divisions are no longer self-conscious about it. They have ceased to apologise.

TWO U.S. TNCS

Crown Cork & Seal, a Philadelphia-based corporation, deserves a tiny niche in the history of the City of London. Because individual shareholders were "completely impotent," J. M. Keynes had suggested in 1928 cooperative action by institutional investors to make their views and wishes felt. The UK investment trusts, pension funds, insurance offices, and so on took note and several "protection committees" were formed. These made their opinions known privately to company chairmen. In turn the committees were often consulted prior to the tabling of some extraordinary proposal at an AGM. In accordance with an unwritten rule, the institutions did not appear as a collective force at AGMs. They feared that this might convey the impression—it would of course have been a correct impression—that institutional investors had a dominant stake in Britain's corporate sector.

In May 1964 tradition was breached with a vengeance, sparked off by the announced intention of Crown Cork's British subsidiary not to pay the annual dividend. Its U.S. parent owned 71.5 percent of its equity while the remainder was traded on the London stock exchange. The company's profits were flourishing and its liquidity position was so healthy that a few months previously the low-interest preference shares had all been redeemed. The company had no net debts. Passing a dividend meant that the shares lost their trustee status and thus certain institutions could no longer hold them. The U.S. parent gave a reason for not distributing to shareholders some of the large profits: the intention was to use all the profits and cash reserves to finance the manufacture of aerosols. The Association of Investment Trusts and the British Insurance Association overcame their dislike for publicity. They were ready to blemish their carefully nursed image of being merely passive investors. A bus was hired to bring representatives of the City to the AGM in a suburb of London.

As an observer at the meeting, I was struck by the arrogance of the directors and the emissary of the Philadelphia head office who had specially flown in. Shareholders were told that if they did not like it, they could sell their shares. Though a majority of those present rejected the board's proposals, the voting strength of the parent company proved decisive when the proxies were counted.

The matter was raised in parliament and rarely can a multi have had such a bad press in Britain as Crown Cork: They browbeat the minority.... Unfair.... Crown Cork is not going to be allowed to get away scot-free with its shabby treatment of minority shareholders.... It is a dire warning to shareholders in companies who contemplate partial deals with U.S. firms.... American company steamrollers its plan through.... Not a very edifying example of American business methods of dealing with minority interests.... I have never seen such bulldozing tactics used in this country before.

From the standpoint of the U.S. parent, the decision not to pay a dividend was probably a sound one. At the time no British newspaper chose to publish the rumor that was circulating in the City, which would have it that the parent hoped to attain 100 percent ownership of the subsidiary. The share price had already dropped some 50 percent over the preceding two years and the detractors of the Philadelphia multi whispered that the no-dividend policy was aimed at giving the parent an opportunity to pick up cheaply the outstanding shares. This outraged the institutional investors, but of course no proof was ever documented. Almost one-quarter of a century later the chairman of Crown Cork's British company—it had of course become a wholly-owned subsidiary— revealed the prosaic truth: "The remaining minority shares held around 1964/5 were progressively bought in by the parent company following a declaration of 'no dividend' policy" (150).

Hoover, the Ohio-based multi, faced a different kind of problem. In any case, Hoover's management showed a concern that distinguished it from the callous behavior of Crown Cork. Hoover did not want to be chastised as unfair to its minority British shareholders because this might damage the reputation of its brand name and harm sales in Britain. Once again, in terms of public relations, it mattered little whether the charge against this U.S. multi was justified or not. In the absence of total disclosure of the internal accounts of this foreign MNC, rumors and suspicions fell on fertile ground. Having foreign minority shareholders can bring forth unpleasant experiences even when the head office goes out of its way to be fair.

Hoover's British subsidiary was quoted on the London bourse: 45 percent of its equity was not owned by the parent. A Dutch trading company engaged mainly in selling UK-made Hoover products was owned 50:50 by the Ohio parent and the British subsidiary. A City broker investigated this Dutch firm and subsequently advised his clients of a clash of interest between the U.S. and UK partners, with the latter losing out badly. These findings were publicized widely in the British financial press. *The Investors Chronicle* recommended that until Ohio had clarified the situation, UK investors should sell their holdings in Hoover's British subsidiary.

The broker's bill of complaint was based on the arithmetic notion that the parent company benefited from generating profits in the Dutch company at the expense of its British subsidiary. A $100 profit of the British subsidiary yielded attributable profits of $55 to the parent while a $100 profit of the Dutch Hoover company yielded $77.50 ($50 plus 55 percent of $50). Hoover's Ohio parent flooded the British press with long denials of the warped transfer pricing of which it had implicitly been accused. It rejected strenuously the allegation that the profits of Hoover's Dutch company were being inflated by the artificially low invoice price that was set for goods supplied by Hoover's British subsidiary. The denials were published but critics in the City reiterated that a potential conflict of interest would remain until either Hoover's Dutch company was owned wholly by Hoover's British subsidiary or the Ohio parent had bought out the minority UK shareholders. Today Hoover's British company is a 100 percent-owned subsidiary.

7

EXECUTIVES SANS PATRIE

> In recent years much has been written about the international corporation but little about the international man.
>
> Thomas Aitken

Fully-fledged multis are managed by elitist cadres. BINCO emphasized that these have a specific "state of mind." They are dedicated to a supranational society: "The true international business manager is a renaissance individual who stands astride continents" (71). Howard Perlmutter asserted that "the geocentric enterprise depends on having an adequate supply of men who are geocentrically oriented." (36) Swidler, the firm of management consultants, published an advertisement in March 1988 which commenced: "Seeking true internationalist for truly international corporation—from its Canadian base, this company spans the world." Feminists will note that these heroes are almost invariably men though women also have a role to play because MNCs expect their senior executives to have (married) heterosexual partners. The author of a book on this stateless, male species refers to his spouse as "Barbara, a truly multinational woman" (83).

The children are often the main sufferers. Lilienthal—it will be recalled that he is the etymological father of the MNC—wanted corporations to think in terms of "multinational families." He compared their offspring with the children of missionaries. Like human packages, they are educated here and there as the parents change residence. I have met several such adolescents who were multilingual experts on the layout of airports but had failed to secure scholastic credits for admission to a higher place of learning in their home country. Perlmutter wanted to remedy this tragic situation by forming a non-national University of the World with a curriculum of subjects attuned to a global outlook on life. Paris was his favored location. Unfortunately, neither the gypsy executives nor their children liked the idea. BINCO dolefully confirmed this.

A recent phenomenon plaguing international corporations . . . is the reluctance . . . of employees to take on international assignments. . . . Employees are placing their children's education and spouses' careers ahead of the work ethic and the 'organisation first' attitude of their predecessors.

Reading between the lines one senses that BINCO regarded these culprits, who refuse to sacrifice their children's future on the altar of their employers, as renegades.

The numbers involved are but a very small proportion of the total labor force. A multi, employing globally 100,000 people, is likely to have a nomadic corps of fewer than one thousand individuals. This travelling fraternity, which is prepared to be shoved from country to country, does not include those employees who accept transfers to a foreign location where they are expected to stay for the rest of their working life. The accolade of being a truly international executive is also not awarded to the many who make occasional trips to conferences abroad. There are other restrictions on membership of this exclusive club of roaming managers. They have to be ready to operate in any part of the world. The young man who is willing to have a stint in the French or Argentinian subsidiaries but is not agreeable to work in Ghana or Peru is clearly not the sort of man Perlmutter and BINCO had in mind. Honeywell boasted that it was "alert to weed out those candidates who feel they are primarily interested in a Cook's tour abroad."

It is compatible with the ethos of a multi for its manual and clerical work force, plus the middle managers, to remain stationary. But when people reach the higher echelons, a refusal to move on may be treated as an unacceptable corporate crime. A celebrated U.S. TNC had appointed a British manager chief of its UK subsidiary. He turned it into the most profitable foreign operation of his employers. The head office appreciated his talents. One day he was told that his wife and he were to come to the United States to select a suitable house because he was being transferred to take charge of the international division. It would have made him the first non-U.S. director on this multi's main board. His wife did not like the United States and she mattered more to him than the glittering promotion prospects. He thanked his superiors profusely but asked to remain at his post in London. This was not to be. His attitude had proved that he did not merit being the CEO of a weighty national subsidiary. He was dismissed unceremoniously.

What sort of person is fit to reach the icy summits of geocentric multis? The president of the U.S. TNC National Cash Register recounted this illuminating story which helps to provide an answer:

Our office in Paris was on the line of march when Hitler's Wehrmacht rumbled into the ancient city and along the Champs Elysees. Suddenly, one of the tanks swerved out of line and headed straight for it. The tank came to a halt and disgorged a German soldier, who thundered on the door and made it plain he wanted to come in. Come in he did, and there he stood in enemy uniform, with a gun on his hip and a grim look on his face. Our French employees had a bad moment—until the German soldier suddenly smiled and said: "I am from the National Cash Register Company in Berlin. I'm sorry I can't stay very long, but I was wondering—did you make your quota last year?" (93)

To require executives to migrate from one national location to another is not just a prosaic exercise in management training. It also has ideological undertones: managers must be taught to shed national associations that could influence their decision-making. The AFL-CIO has reasons of its own to deride multis that behave as if they were functioning in a world that had buried the sovereignty of nation–states. It has denounced by name the executives of U.S. MNCs who foolishly stated in public that a multi ought to be led by those whose loyalty is to the shareholders of the parent company—if necessary, at the expense of the national interest of the countries in which the corporation operates. The AFL-CIO concludes: "A good multinational manager must ignore any feeling of patriotism or responsibility to the citizens of his country" (54). The public relations agencies of TNCs will not propagate such sentimentality. Yet despite the tarnished source, the above quotation represents faithfully the beliefs of the adherents to the Perlmutter creed. They recruit those youngsters as management trainees who strike them as potentially sound converts to their religion.

THE BREEDING OF GLOBAL EXECUTIVES

There are sensitive, intelligent university graduates in the affluent countries who disdain to work for big corporations. Some object on principle to employment with multis headquartered in their own country because of the evil things they might be called upon to do abroad. They register even stronger disapproval for jobs with foreign-based multis.

When IBM's Jacques Masionrouge found a (surprising) unwillingness on the part of Harvard graduates to join international businesses, he inferred that this was due to the misconceptions that universities teach about the nature of MNCs. In some societies a stigma is still attached to employment with an alien company. In the late 1960s a Japanese executive once poured out his heart to me. He spoke of the great sacrifice that he had made by accepting a U.S. company's assignment to organize, and later to manage, its Japanese subsidiary. His fate was now sealed, he said, because he could no longer expect to be offered a responsible position by any of the indigenous prestigious companies. Perhaps he exaggerated when he claimed to have been ostracized for life.

Such individuals apart, multis have a magnetic pull precisely because they are able to tempt graduates with the prospective membership of an elite in a powerful corporation. This is so attractive that the initial salaries of renowned MNCs are often lower than those dangled before recruits by smaller, national companies. 'Join us and see the world' is frequently a juicy carrot. Global promotion prospects are especially of interest to native managers in the LDCs. Employment with a subsidiary of a foreign multi can sometimes provide an opportunity to emigrate through a posting within the framework of the international company—it is an elegant escape route.

A survey on the international management development (IMD) schedules of OECD-based multis has shown that some German companies exclude from their international training programmes specialists such as scientists, engineers, marketing managers, and accountants. This is contrary to the practices of Anglo-Saxon countries in which all youngsters, who have the recognized attributes to climb to the top, are regarded as suitable candidates for IMD. They have to be ready to change from time to time their functional roles. The purpose of the program is to beget executives with all-round managerial experience. In the days when Dunlop was a burgeoning MNC, its expensive IMD was not targeted to make managers or technicians more proficient in specific jobs; neither was it meant to prepare individuals for work in one given national location. Dunlop's IMD focused on grooming trainees to take charge of the company's multinational and multiproduct activities—that is why they had to agree to be switched on the corporate chessboard. The most senior management positions at the head office of Philips in Eindhoven have in recent years been offered only to individuals who had previously completed at least two stints in foreign subsidiaries. The articles of association of the most famous Dutch multi used to provide that Dutch nationals alone could be directors. This restrictive covenant was abrogated to give Philip's executives throughout the world a chance to be elevated to the parent's main board.

Before the theory of a geocentric firm had been formulated, Dunlop had already anticipated Perlmutter's prescriptions. A young manager from its Dublin operations was promoted to chief engineer in Britain. Then he became a works manager in Japan and was later appointed managing director of the German subsidiary. ICI has proudly publicized the biography of one of the stars of its IMD, John York, who graduated from Cambridge with a degree in French language and literature. Britain's illustrious chemical multi thought that his educational qualifications were ideal and paid him to become a commercial trainee. He showed a readiness to go "anywhere in the world in search of business" and for this reason he was made marketing manager of the General Chemical Group. In quick succession he worked as a divisional manager and then as distribution manager before he was elevated to be a Commercial Services director. Later he was promoted to manage ICI Brazil. This was followed by an assignment which meant that he had to live in the United States, where he ran the Latin American Group within ICI Americas. Contrary to the somber tales of Lilienthal, John York has allowed himself to be quoted that his wife and three teen-aged daughters "have enjoyed their postings abroad." This confession probably contributed to his nomination in 1981, not to a UK post but to the coveted position of general manager of ICI Europa. From there he moved on to become CEO of European Vinyl Corporation, a joint venture of ICI and Enichem of Italy located in Brussels.

Roger Enrico is a U.S. citizen who became president and CEO of Pepsi-Cola USA after he had been moved around for years like a pawn on the corporate chessboard. He started in Frito-Lay, a food division of Pepsico in Texas, where he rose from associate brand manager to brand manager to marketing director. He was then promoted to president of Pepsico Foods in Japan. This was followed by a term as area vice-president, relating to the drinks activities of Pepsico, in Brazil. And so it went on until he reached the top.

One of the things that used to be true about Pepsi was that it churned executives; just when you'd begun to understand your job and figured out how to find your way around that strange city you'd be moved; the company offered you a different job in a different business in another country. I had obviously been tabbed as one of the people who had a chance to make it big at Pepsico. I didn't know it at the time, of course, but . . . Pepsico management did. For them it was a way to see me operate in a lot of different situations, under different pressures, handling different problems (192).

Since the turn of the century various institutions have organized courses to which companies send staff who are about to go on protracted work assignments abroad. However meritorious such training, it has little in common with IMD, which seeks to mold the "true international business manager." The pioneering management schools which have sponsored this ethos are the Lausanne-based IMEDE (founded in 1956 by Nestle) and the Geneva-based IMI (set up in 1946 by Alcan). Multis from all over the world have registered their bright executives—usually in the 28–40 age group—at these two Swiss centers to let them imbibe there the spirit and practice of global management. Perlmutter first vented his ideas on the ethnocentric, polycentric, and geocentric firms when he taught at IMEDE.

In 1971 I lectured at an IMI seminar which dealt mainly with IMD. All of the students had already had managerial experiences in the corporations that paid for their attendance in Geneva. Some of them told me that they had deliberately chosen to work for MNCs because they personally regarded nationalist loyalties with scorn. One of the IMI students was a Paris-born executive of a German manufacturing company that had been taken over by a famous U.S. multi. He said with some passion that though he and his family travelled on French passports, he considered himself to be "sans patrie." Ever since, without attribution, I have made use of this pertinent characterization.

To switch executives from one national subsidiary to another is an essential ingredient of IMD, but the program also serves other purposes. Carborondum's president laid down this edict: "Having managers indigenous to the country where you are located is not multinational management" (54). This suggests a corporate strategy similar to the policy of newspapers which are endowed with sufficient funds to maintain full-time correspondents in foreign locations. If feasible, they choose not to be represented by native journalists. Non-native correspondents are more expensive, may encounter serious language difficulties and, at the beginning at least, lack sound background knowledge. Yet these handicaps are deemed to be of less weight than the correspondents' superior objectivity. Why do most editors favour assignments of only three to five years? After a few years the expatriate correspondent may indeed have become very knowledgeable and perhaps even mastered the local language. But there is reason to fear that his (initial) dispassionate detachment may have been eroded as he identifies himself increasingly with the joys and tribulations of the host country. Mutatis mutandis, the head offices of MNCs want to ensure that the important managers of their subsidiaries are not tempted to fall in love with one country. Frequent mobility is an effective prophylactic.

In the good old days when the international trading companies and the civil services of imperial powers awarded youngsters long-term appointments in one foreign country, it certainly made sense to encourage them to study the language of the land in which they would reside during most of their working life. Multis today, especially those with head offices in English-speaking countries, are often hostile to the notion that their mobile executives should be burdened with the task of learning the language of a country in which they are likely to spend only a few years. While MNCs are generous about relocation expenses, some of them object, on principle, to paying for language tuition. Several companies, questioned on the role of foreign languages in their IMD programs, replied that while language qualifications may be commendable, they are "not a consideration." One U.S. automobile manufacturer was adamant that "language ability is not of major importance in choosing men for foreign assignments." When the head office decides which executives should have a decisive say in the running of foreign subsidiaries, these elitists are expected to be able to do their jobs without being fluent in the local language. In any case, goodwill is not necessarily generated when foreign managers communicate in faulty Portugese or Chinese. An American who is in charge of a factory outside his country is not loved because he can converse in the native tongue, but neither is he hated if he can only speak English. For social reasons it is obviously an advantage to know the language of the country because the expatriate executive will then be able to make smoother contact with the natives. But does this pleasing drawing-room attractiveness raise corporate profitability?

INTERNATIONAL MANAGERS ARE EXPENSIVE

The considerable IMD costs of formal training, such as attendance at business schools and the relocation expenses incurred in frequent transfers, are on the whole ascertainable. No price tag, however, can be attached to many intangible IMD costs. For example, there is a stiff bill to pay for the sustenance of the elite's esprit de corps. The managers sans patrie are rewarded generously for their supranational loyalty to the parent; this may entail treading on the toes of the non-mobile staff.

The Perlmutter guidelines governing the remuneration of the mobile elite are unambiguous. The nominal (often arbitrarily determined) profit-and-loss accounts of the individual divisions and subsidiaries of a multi should not serve as yardsticks with which to assess the attainments of international executives. The decisive criterion for the compensation of top managers is the furtherance of global profits. Similarly, promotions for these gypsy executives are not to be decided within the divisions and subsidiaries in which the individuals happen to be active at a given point of time: they ought to be the concern of a special committee at head office.

Mobile executives are either citizens of the multi's home country or third country nationals, for example, Australians who work for the Dutch subsidiary of a Canadian MNC. In some respects they are not equals. This is one of several impediments encountered by corporations that seek to translate Perlmutter's theory into practice. Ideally, the head office has a master schedule that does not discriminate between those employed in country C and country D, between the holders of Peruvian and French passports, between pensioners who have retired in their native lands and those who have chosen to end their days in other countries. But such equitable plans are upset by the horrible reality of nation–states. Diverging company laws, varying tax considerations, diverse state controls on permissible salary increases, differing statutory restrictions on the exercise of stock options in the parent's equity, the vexed cross-border transferability of pension annuities—all these, and other reflections too, provide bread and jam for a host of specialists who advise TNCs on fringe benefits for nomadic executives.

MNCs generally aspire to conduct their affairs in compliance with the law. Nevertheless, they do not hesitate to perpetrate illegalities to bolster the morale of the global cadres. Subterfuges are resorted to so that emoluments can be paid even-handedly. The technique of split salaries, that is, the transfer of part of an executive's salary into a banking account outside the country in which he is employed, is widespread. If outrageously high personal tax demands cannot be avoided, the roving staff may be compensated surreptitiously by the head office. International managers frequently enjoy "deferred benefits"—a tax dodge—which they collect on retirement.

Prevarications, deceptive tricks, and breaches of the law can have disastrous consequences when the non-mobile staff discover them. It is, for example, expedient to offer hardship allowances to executives who are transferred to dangerous or climatically unpleasant locations. Habitually, this is kept a secret because the native managers might be offended if they probed the implications of this specific fringe benefit to which they, of course, are not entitled. Members of the mobile elite who work in foreign subsidiaries are obliged to conceal from their colleagues the various hidden subventions that they receive in addition to their declared salaries. To tell the whole truth would create resentment. Sometimes it might also expose the expatriate managers and/or the company to prosecution for contravening local regulations.

Maybe things will be different in the 1990s but hitherto Japanese TNCs have not had to face many of the mentioned problems because non-Japanese employees rarely benefit from their IMD schedules. Of course, many non-Japanese managers and technicians are employed by the foreign subsidiaries of Japanese TNCs. Some of these individuals are indeed invited to visit the parent's operations in Japan, both to learn and to instruct. But the notion that a non-Japanese employee of a Japanese MNC should be groomed to become one day the CEO of the parent company is a pipedream. Japanese multis have not even bothered to camouflage their policy of reserving the important decision-making jobs in their subsidiaries for Japanese expatriates who are being promoted by standards set in the head office. This has ruffled the feathers of many native managers and technicians.

In the United States, where litigation flourishes, Japanese MNCs (such as Sumitomo) have been hauled before the courts for violating the employment rules of some states and the Federal Civil Rights Act by not engaging enough women, members of ethnic minorities, and so on. After such experiences Japanese multis quickly mend their ways and change the hiring practices appertaining to non-mobile staff. But, understandably, they do not adjust the IMD procedures that focus on Japanese who serve abroad for periods of three to four years. Their salaries and fringe benefits—semi-annual bonuses, education awards for the children, automobiles, pensions, and so on—continue to be determined in accordance with the individual's status in the global hierarchy of the corporation. Itoh, one of Japan's largest trading conglomerates, has had to defend itself in protracted U.S. lawsuits against indigenous employees who complained that their Japanese colleagues on temporary assignment in New York were being paid more than they. Japan's corporate giants still have to learn how to disguise effectively the actual value of the emoluments made available to expatriate staff. Itoh also encountered another serious accusation. It was said that 29 of its top 30 U.S. jobs were being held by Japanese nationals. The lawsuit alleged that this was racial discrimination!

The most extravagant aspect of IMD expenditure has still to be spelled out. Multis acquaint management trainees with the multifaceted aspects of their business. They are also given an opportunity to work in several foreign locations in order to widen their horizon and become good internationalists. Lacking in gratitude and sometimes breaking outright explicit undertakings, some of the IMD initiates refuse to climb the last steps of the stairs that lead to the top mobile managerial group. A considerable number actually leave their employer in order to join another corporation. The concept that IMD engenders executives who stay all their working lives with the company that has lavishly spent money on their training is an expensive illusion.

When corporations send staff to business schools, they almost invariably pay the requisite fees; these mature students remain of course on the payroll. In connection with my book on IMD I spoke at length to the dour CEO of an idiosyncratic Swedish MNC which paid neither the fees nor the salaries. He explained that an individual who made out a good case for attending an external course was given unpaid leave and, in special circumstances, his corporation might lend him some money. The wise Swede opined that if formal training at a business school is truly useful, then budding senior executives will want to invest their own money to improve themselves for surely at a later stage they will be able to recoup these investments by earning lucrative promotions.

Attempts have been made to tie IMD candidates contractually. GM made an English employee sign a promissory note for some £4,500 to be paid if he left the company within two years of completing a training course. When this undertaking was breached—during the proscribed period the man went to work for another employer at a higher salary—the U.S. multi sued. The High Court in London in 1987 ruled in its favor, compelling the employee to discharge his financial obligations to GM. The court upheld the company's view that this amount was only a fraction of the overall cost of training. Most corporations, however, regard this type of arrangement as unpalatable because it is rarely prudent to keep an individual against his will. This is just one of the burdens that corporations must bear stoically. Headhunters may be the enemies of IMD but they are a fact of life.

MULTIS PAY RANSOM

In Part II of this book reference is made to the harassment of MNCs, especially in LDCs, by hostile governments, unions, and commercial competitors. Today most multis are wise enough to subdue their anger. Even when threatened with the expropriation of their assets, foreign-based MNCs rarely take off the gloves to fight dirty. On the grounds of expediency, and to shore up a 'progressive' public relations image, international companies, having registered their protests, nowadays turn the other cheek and meekly cut their losses. When Italian anti-multi partisans burned down warehouses of ITT and Honeywell, the companies suffered heavy damages. They did not like it but saw no reason to withdraw from Italy because of such hostile acts (84).

Things are different when enemies of foreign MNCs kidnap executives, vowing to kill them unless certain extortionate demands are met. The corporations are then not restrained by any law-abiding sentimentaility; they will in practice do everything, dirty and illegal, to free the captives. Argentina's ERP, the Trotskyist People's Revolutionary Army, is the best-known left-wing group that has been collecting "revolutionary taxes" from foreign corporate enemies. The plague is a global one and has spread to countries of varied political complexions: Venezuela, Lebanon, the Republic of Ireland, and France. Though a government may itself be hostile to foreign multis, it invariably opposes kidnapping because the perpetrators are also intent on undermining the regime in their own country. MNCs lie unashamedly when they conceal their negotiations with these guerillas who are denounced as terrorists. Unwilling to defy host countries when their property is challenged, multis pugnaciously break the law to free their own executives.

In the 1970s and 1980s scores of managers of foreign subsidiaries were abducted. Among the many companies involved were Acrow Steel, AKZO, AMOCO, Bank of Italy, BAT, Citibank, Coca-Cola, EXXON, Fiat, Firestone, Ford, Kodak, Lloyds Bank, Mercedes-Benz, Owens-Illinois, Pepsico, and Peugeot. Some of the victims stayed in captivity for a long time; the record is believed to be held by Bill Niehous of the Toledo-based glass multi Owens-Illinois who spent almost three and a half years as a hostage in the jungles of Venezuela. A number were murdered because the kidnapping was bungled, the police closed in on the captors, or the ransom was not paid in time.

It must be stressed that political gangsters are rarely motivated to enrich themselves personally. Neither are the abductions primarily revolutionary deeds to extort money from the rich. Subversive forces in Germany and Italy have indeed been guilty of dastardly exploits directed against the native bourgeoisie. The anti-multi revolutionaries, however, have a specific alternative target. The Revolutionary Command of Venezuela, as reported by *The Times* (London), once expounded why an American executive had been kidnapped: the objective was to hit "the many multinationals that plunder the country and submit the working class to overt exploitation." Several hundred millions of dollars are estimated to have been spent by MNCs on ransom; there were both open and undisclosed payments. It appears that kidnappers do not usually take less than one million dollars per victim. The highest amount chronicled is $14.2 million, handed over to free EXXON's Victor Samuelson (85).

Not all the extortion demands are designed to acquire cash for the coffers of the revolutionary groups. Corporations are usually presented with a package of demands that must be complied with to obtain the release of the captive. Host governments do not generally object when foreign corporations respond positively to seemingly innocuous parts of the ultimata. Thus multis are allowed to meet extortionate demands to increase wages, rehire laid-off workers, and 'donate' ambulances, toys, and food for the poor. There are exceptions to this unwritten rule. The Argentine government once forbade ESSO (as EXXON then was) to supply $4.2 million of aid-in-kind for flood victims. Having bargained for 144 days with the captors, who held the general manager of ESSO's Argentinian subsidiary, it had been agreed that there would be a cash payment of $10 million plus $4.2 million of goods. The ERP had intended to distribute the 'donated' goods. The authorities feared that if this happened, ESSO would unintentionally be enhancing the prestige of the guerillas among the masses. ESSO was able to convince the ERP to accept $4.2 million cash in lieu.

Sometimes the package contains an item that urges the company to publish advertisements, formulated by the kidnappers, in the native press and foreign journals. Corporations are often unable to induce the indigenous newspaper publishers to insert, for payment, advertisements that are not only hostile to the multis but also denounce the government. The publishers fear reprisals. Thus ESSO was only able to persuade three out of 12 Buenos Aires newspapers to reproduce the ERP declaration, but this partial success was enough to help release the captive. Mercedes-Benz was compelled by an extremist Peronist group, which had abducted its local industrial director, to publish advertisements in Europe, Mexico, and the United States denouncing the "economic imperialism" of TNCs in developing nations. Owens-Illinois, despite the host country's explicit disapproval, published (as requested) the kidnappers' manifesto in London, Paris, and New York newspapers.

Most host governments have been adamant that multis shall not accede to the payment of ransom in cash. It is said to be treacherous for foreign corporations—admittedly under duress—to furnish revolutionaries with the wherewithal to overthrow the government of their host country. When ERP had collected its $14.2 million, it brazenly announced that $5 million was being transferred to Uruguayan, Chilean, and Bolivian insurgent groups by way of the Junta de Coordinacion, which had been formed to direct the joint struggle against multis in five Latin American countries. Observers have commented that "paradoxically, one of the world's largest multinational corporations may thus have provided start-up financing for one of the world's largest multinational terrorist networks" (88).

When Owens-Illinois was told of the abduction of one of its executives in Venezuela, it hastened to agree at once to some of the demands by the political gangsters. This multi was ordered to award a bonus of $166 to each of the 1,600 employees of its Venezuelan subsidiary and to distribute food and toys. This it did. The government, however, explicitly forbade compliance with the ransom demands, which varied between $2 million and $5 million. The company in turn declared that it was ready "to donate to any charity named by the kidnappers to obtain the release of Niehous." There have been reports that a ransom of $1.25 million was in fact handed over but the multi has denied this strenuously. The official story would have it that the executive was "rescued accidentally by two policemen and two farmers looking for cattle rustlers." Owens-Illinois maintains that it had openly defied the Venezuelan government in only one respect. Though the authorities had prohibited it, Owens-Illinois—to please the kidnappers—published their manifesto in three foreign newspapers. The kidnappers identified themselves as a Marxist-Leninist party which greeted the heroic people of Vietnam; supported the just cause of the Palestine Arab people who decidely oppose Yankee imperalism and its lance point, Zionism; firmly opposed Soviet revisionism; and exposed the corruption of the Venezuelan administration by the multinationals and the native bourgeoisie. The U.S. glass TNC is accused in this long manifesto of many crimes: inter alia, it has pressured the government to suspend the import of a certain type of glass. The corporation was also guilty of "guiding" the Association of Architects "towards the design of surfaces with large windows." The dissemination abroad of this fatuous declaration was not appreciated by the government in Caracas. In 1976 it announced that Owens-Illinois would be punished to ward off disobedience from other multis: its local assets would be sequestrated. After a new president had taken over in 1979 the threat was not carried out. However, it was a close shave (86).

In 1972 the ERP kidnapped Oberdan Sallustro, the chief executive of Fiat's Argentinian subsidiary. His corporation was attacked for "pillaging the country, monopolistic activity against small local industry, interventions in the political life of the country," and so on. Among the several demands was the payment of one million dollars for school supplies and children's clothing. The multi's head office in Turin publicized Fiat's willingness to negotiate with the kidnappers. Lanusse, the president of Argentina, responded that his country would not permit anybody, and certainly not a foreign corporation, to deal with "common criminals." In fact, Fiat had already started to bargain with them, promised to hand over the money, and—as a first sign of goodwill—had rehired, as requested, certain past employees. President Lanusse complained to his Italian counterpart, President Leone, that foreigners (Fiat) were interfering with the internal security of a sovereign state. A few days later Buenos Aires revealed that Oberdan Sallustro had been murdered by his captors as the police were closing in on them. The Pope declared that the killing was an "unqualified act of barbarism." According to some reports, Fiat's top managers, who had been reluctant to flout the edict of the host government, now had doubts whether the company had acted wisely. In 1977, when the managing director of Fiat's French subsidiary was abducted by the Committee for Socialist Revolutionary Unity, the Turin head office moved with less regard for the feelings of the host nation. After three months of haggling, the original $30 million ransom was reduced to $2 million. The police of the three countries involved insisted that no money be paid to the criminals.

The efforts of the French, Swiss, and Italian police were deliberately thwarted by activities of the family, its intermediaries and Fiat. From experience in Italy and Argentina, Fiat had learnt to run such matters its own way. Communications with the gang were conducted through small ads, Swiss bankers and secret meetings. One day in July, by the lakeside in the middle of Geneva, a man from

Credit Suisse handed over the money to a 'passer-by' who jumped into a moving car and took off. Three days later, policemen found the kidnapped executive sitting on a park bench in Versailles (88).

One must not romanticize the apparent disregard of multis for property and profits and their contrasting obsession with saving the lives of abducted executives. Salaried individuals, however exalted, are expendable in large organizations. However, MNCs are concerned for the well-being of managers who serve them in dangerous locations because they contemplate the daunting repercussions that would ensue if a fatality occurred. They fear that the news of a murdered executive may have a disastrous impact upon the morale of the mobile managerial elite. When Bill Niehous returned to the United States after more than 40 months in Venezuelan captivity, he was asked whether his attitude to Owens-Illinois had changed. He said on record that he was no longer "sure if climbing the corporate ladder was what he wanted." This was an ominous signal.

A spokesman of the ERP has suggested that "all the big foreign companies have already figured ransom demands into their budgets." This is partly irrelevant because events in Argentina have demonstrated that corporations are not prepared over a long period to compel or allow their executives to remain exposed to a real danger of being murdered. Even in 'normal' times, executives and their families had had armed bodyguards, had travelled in bullet-proof cars, and had lived withdrawn in compounds. The attendant anxieties could not be compensated by danger money. In 1973 and 1974 a host of multis moved their expatriates out of Argentina.

The attitude of MNCs toward kidnapped executives highlights the fact that the expensive managerial elites are considered to deserve special (costly) treatment. To induce them to roam as nomadic executives, and accept assignments in dangerous places, self-confidence must be boosted constantly. They must be reassured that if they are kidnapped, their employers will spend millions to save them—and do so in the teeth of opposition from host nations. In more than one sense, the top executives of MNCs are a valuable breed.

8

CHARLES LEVINSON

The Communists are...reproached with supposedly desiring to abolish fatherland and nationality. The working men have no country. We cannot take from them what they have not got.

Communist Manifesto

The global transfers of technology, profits, tax liabilities, finance, and goods embody the raison d'être of the geocentric multi. Humans are generally not a mobile factor. The preceding chapter dealt with a small managerial elite that flitted across borders. Proletarians, however, are supposed to stay put within their national domiciles. They were the constituency of Charles (Chip) Levinson.

For more than a decade, from the mid–1960s to the mid–1970s, Levinson was mentioned frequently in the financial and commercial columns read by business managers. His picture appeared in scores of journals. Books and articles from his pen were published in many languages. He lectured in the major cities of the non-Communist world. Journalists eagerly sought to interview him and television producers (particularly in Europe) felt privileged if he deigned to accept their invitations. Levinson's utterances heralded an innovative approach to trade unionism.

Serious attention was given to his original prophesies and, at first, his bombastic descriptions of MNCs bolstered the legend on the might of multis. A *Financial Times* profile described him as a modest person. Maybe he was in his youth but at the height of his fame several union leaders, who did not like being outshone, had come to sneer at his superciliousness. The media discarded him when his forecasts did not come true and he could not deliver on his promise of cross-border strikes.

Hans-Goeran Myrdal, a director of the Swedish Employers Confederation, opined that the differences between Swedish employers and trade unions were "insignificant in comparison with the gulf which divides the latter from Charles Levinson." His fellow citizens were warned of this strong, but implicitly dangerous, man. Myrdal wrote in 1973: "He occupies a unique position among trade union leaders and is really a remarkable combination of . . . economist, ideologist, preacher and PR-man. No one like him has contributed so much to the creation in mass media of the popular notion of 'the multinational threat' " (80).

Levinson had to endure personal attacks from trade union leaders whom he had eclipsed. This ebullient Canadian, living in comfortable conditions in Switzerland, also became the butt of a double-barrelled smear campaign. He was accused of working at the behest of the CIA. This claim was sedulously sustained by the European Communist parties which actively obstructed several of his multinational actions. Others denounced him for being a Marxist agitator—if not an actual KGB agent.

GEOCENTRIC BARGAINING

The ideas that Levinson propagated were not new. When David Lilienthal coined the term 'multinational company,' he had already prognosticated that in the 1980s "collective bargaining contracts for worldwide operations may be the job of a corporate vice-president for industrial relations" (21). Howard Perlmutter, spreading the gospel among Western union leaders, told them that the bosses of TNCs have to choose between the ethnocentric, polycentric, and geocentric orientations. When corporations opt for geocentrism, unions ought to follow suit and organize along parallel lines. In one of his books, Levinson revealed himself a confrere of Perlmutter. Imploring the comrades to adopt a geocentric outlook, he pleaded with them to create a "global counterforce" (90).

Levinson viewed the class enemy, the captains of MNCs, through bifocal spectacles. They were of course his adversaries but many of them were also his intellectual allies: jointly, they subscribed to the belief that the future of the world economy belongs to multis. BINCO, which was to regret it later for commercial reasons, helped to put Levinson on the map by promoting him in their publications. In seminars and conferences on both sides of the Atlantic he was introduced as a glamorous star. In BINCO's publicity, Levinson was a "unique and enormously charismatic individual who represents the new breed of internationally-minded labor leader. . . . [H]e is also a pretty potent guy" (91). At Cerromar Beach in Puerto Rico BINCO convened a four-day round table for the CEOs of leading multis. Among the many speakers, Levinson was the only one who was considered formidable enough to make two presentations. He returned the compliment in kind by asking an American director of BINCO to address a meeting of union delegates in Switzerland that he was organising. (Many of the comrades did not like it and BINCO's standing was impaired when some of its clients learned of this strange bonhomie.) Richard Conlon is reported to have told the delegates that patriotism counted very little with multis. He stressed the importance of Levinson's international campaign and applauded his host's efforts to create a "countervailing force" which he regarded as both necessary and salutary (94).

Levinson flew with the Royal Canadian Air Force during World War II, attained university degrees at Toronto and Paris, and then became immersed in various activities pertaining to vocational training and trade unions. He started on the road to world fame when, in 1964, he became secretary general of the Geneva-based International Federation of Chemical and General Workers' Unions (ICF) which also covered the glass and rubber industries. This was one of 15 International Trade Secretariats (ITSs), the majority of which were headquartered in neutral Switzerland. On paper they represented tens of millions of workers, but in practice they were fraternal organizations with unexciting officials in dusty offices. They were maintained by subscriptions from affiliated trade unions. Until Levinson appeared on the scene they were mostly slumbering giants that did not merit much mention in the media. The old ITSs provided merely forums for occasional international meetings. The participating national union leaders were happy to travel abroad and, incidentally, exchange information about their industries with colleagues from other countries. For our story the most important two ITSs—apart from ICF—are the International Metalworkers Federation (IMF) and the International Union of Food and Allied Workers Associations (IUF).

The new leader of the ICF paid scant regard to trade unions with autonomous branches. He also looked disdainfully upon nation-wide bargaining between unions and employers (of all sizes) within a given industry. In so far as they remained passive umbrella organizations, Levinson had no quarrel with federations such as the AFL-CIO, TUC, and DGB. He was, however, strongly opposed to associations of trade unions—a prominent specimen was Sweden's LO—that negotiated, within a national context, the wages and conditions of employees in diverse industries. Levinson raised the flag of international action against *individual* multis. The other ITSs sought to emulate the spectacular meta-morphosis of the IFC. They too became more daring and buoyant though their leaders had to suppress their envy at the superior public relations skill of Levinson.

The secretary general of the IFC advocated that ITSs should be sub-divided into world councils of given industries, for example, automobiles, tobacco, rubber, and so on. Each such council should in turn attempt to organize company councils, which were to consist of delegates from the national subsidiaries of individual multis. About one hundred of such company councils were formed, among them Ford, GM, Volkswagen, Pilkington, ICI, Philips, IBM, Hoechst, Shell, Good-year, ITT, Nestle, Oetker, Union Carbide, Unilever, Firestone, CIBA, and Siemens. Levinson might not have achieved the wide publicity that stood him in good stead when he confronted fearful CEOs and suspicious union leaders had he not scored an early success that seemed to usher in a new age. In 1969 he no longer had to be satisfied with paraphrasing the ideas of Lilienthal-BINCO-Perlmutter. He could point to a concrete achievement: the world council of Saint Gobain, under the aegis of the ICF, had made history by negotiating wage demands on a global scale. The concept of a union body bargaining with the parent of a multi for simultaneous wage increases in a number of its national subsidiaries had hitherto been only an academic concept. Levinson—so it seemed at the time—had proved it a reality!

The ICF had struck it lucky. The board of the glass multi Saint Gobain was in some disarray following the news that an unwelcome bid was in the offing. In several countries the unions thought it a propitious moment to press for higher wages. Levinson coordinated these claims and presented them jointly to the parent company, backed by the implied threat of a multinational strike. The company's top echelon was impressed and instructed the managers of the various national subsidiaries to surrender. Negotiations in France, where the biggest Saint Gobain union was in the hands of the Communist CGT, were conducted separately. The workers employed by the parent company settled for a lower increase than that effected in the joint negotiations. The Communist union leaders had demonstrated that they would have no truck with the internationalist stance of Levinson (119).

SIX FACETS

Levinson judged that before he could even think of planning international campaigns, he had to gain respect as a serious contestant. MNCs had to recognize that he was capable of negotiating from strength, that they could not afford to ignore the ICF and the other ITSs. Initially, it did not matter much to the advocates of cross-border union actions whether they were loved or hated—they wanted corporations to acknowledge their existence. The tactics employed often bordered on mendaciousness. The ICF told journalists that it had been involved in talks with Monsanto concerning the closure of some of its European plants. Monsanto furiously pursued those journals that reproduced this 'sensational' news that proved to be untrue. One German TNC reported the unexpected arrival of delegates from the Swiss-based IFU at its head office. They had no appointment but asked to see the company's senior labor relations officer. He was not available but a junior official received them courteously and regaled them with coffee. A few days later an IUF communique stated this German corporation "had been talking" to it. Like Levinson, the officials of the various ITSs knew how vital it was to have a foot in the door—and for the world press to say so.

Some MNCs such as Chrysler, Ford, and GM were openly contemptuous of the IMF's attempts to establish formal contact with them. The old-fashioned but wise Unilever company, a century-old multi, politely laughed when the IUF announced the formation of a Unilever world council: "We cannot negotiate internationally. . . . [There] is no question of international collective bargaining." A number of MNCs, however, earnestly debated in their boardrooms whether to talk to ITSs. Not infrequently, there were clashes between the top brass and the labor relations executives. Many of the former believed that global wage ngotiations were a logical inference from operating as a global company. Few of the personnel officers in the national subsidiaries had read about geocentrism. But while their superiors saw the specter of Levinson haunting MNCs, they grasped that all this talk of international solidarity was ridiculous.

The three most enterprising ITSs flooded the business press with news of multis lining up to commence negotiations. Pilkington, Hoechst, Monsanto, Oetker, Nestle, SKF, Volvo, Brown Boveri, AKZO, Rothman, Philips, BSN, and Continental Can were frequently mentioned. Some of the reports were completely divorced from the truth. In other cases the denials by the maligned multis were hollow. Some felt betrayed. Naively, they had imagined that their confidential contacts with representatives of the ITSs would remain undisclosed. There is now sufficient evidence to state emphatically that several MNCs did protest too much in the 1970s (122). Some Swedish multis undoubtedly had preliminary talks. Volvo has never denied that its CEO, Pehr Gillenhammar, had met the IMF to discuss the impact of corporate investment and production plans on employment. It is now confirmed that while Philips had not entered into official negotiations, it had participated in "informal and informative meetings." Today it is also established that the South

African TNC Rothman, the U.S. MNC Continental Can, and the Swiss multis Nestle and Brown Boveri did have "exploratory contracts." Almost certainly there were others.

Having become recognized, Levinson dreamed of reaching the Perlmutter millenium stage by stage, by marching along six routes.

1. Calls of solidarity to rally *all* employees of an MNC when one subsidiary is involved in a dispute. Money is to be collected and goods to and from the affected subsidiary are to be blocked. Short sympathy strikes will drive home the message to the parent that its global involvements make it expedient to yield.

2. Levinson knew in his bones that claims for equal wage rates throughout the company were as yet unrealistic. For this reason he preferred, at first, to formulate global demands on specific non-wage matters, for example, the introduction of identical health and safety standards in all subsidiaries.

3. Levinson labored hard to convince multis that representatives of the apposite ITS should sit on the board of the parent company as a symbolic steward of the MNC's international labor force—so far without success.

4. The coordinated presentation of wage demands to the parent. On the Saint Gobain model the level of the simultaneous claims can vary as between one national subsidiary and another.

5. The ICF has proclaimed that international labor action would be directed at halting disinvestments. Also, multis were only to be permitted to make new cross-border investments under certain conditions. Levinson went on record: "Traditional wage bargaining is just arguing about sharing the pie. We want a voice in baking the pie" (88). The Du Pont world council met for three days in London in 1974 and requested that Levinson tell the press: "We no longer intend to allow Du Pont to expand internationally if it continues its anti-union policies." The IUF noted that tobacco companies were divesting themselves of tobacco-manufacturing assets, planning to use the proceeds to diversify into other industries. The Swiss-based IUF wanted this stopped and the available funds utilized for increased wages. In 1973 unions from 12 countries were represented at the Paris meeting of the Michelin world council. This French multi had announced plans to spend $200 million on a new plant in Carolina. The enterprising Levinson somehow managed to bring a representative of the U.S. building workers to this conference. He was asked to persuade the U.S. trade unionists to boycott the construction of this factory. The ICF promised to call a worldwide strike, with or without the support of the U.S. building workers, if the parent went ahead with this investment. It was explained that this direct investment in the United States would endanger the jobs of 5,000 employees of the Italian subsidiary of Michelin.

6. The final, and highest, stage will be reached when the world council of each particular multi puts in a claim for worldwide wage parity. Levison was of course fully aware that the U.S. affiliates of the ITSs would love to see their employers, the U.S.-based multis, pay equal wages throughout the world.

The unions in the LDCs, however, were opposing the advent of this Golden Age. Hence, Levinson was biding his time.

THEY REALLY FEARED HIM

Today, when Charles Levinson is but a footnote in labor history, it is difficult to recall the hysterical atmosphere which enveloped this man and the ideas for which he stood. With hindsight it is easy to scorn the fears that were expressed by powerful industrialists. Nowadays, the fatuous and simplistic concepts espoused by Levinson arouse hilarity. Yet many of those in charge of mighty MNCs during the 1970s did not laugh when the ITSs announced that they were waging a global battle against them. They trembled. What made them think that Levinson represented a concrete threat?

The facts relating to the 1969 Saint Gobain affair have now been determined. At the time, however, Levinson was able to exaggerate the glory of his international campaign without being challenged. The strong alliance, which he had seemingly forged between various national glass unions, was more brittle than the ICF's public relations machine would have it. Yet for several years after 1969, it was largely irrelevant whether Levinson had indeed gained a victory of weighty dimensions. The ICF boasted that he did and it was generally believed. Multis feared that having succeeded in humiliating a prestigious French multi, Levinson and the ITSs would be capable of striking again. In the 20 years that have elapsed since, neither the ICF nor any other ITS has been able to stage a repeat performance of what appeared at the time to be a plausible forerunner of widespread multinational labor bargaining. Saint Gobain proved to be a fluke.

When did the business pages of the American press first give due notice to doubting CEOs that the ITSs, though based in a foreign land, could interfere with wage negotiations in the United States itself? The occasion was the invitation extended by U.S. unions to the IMF to send to the United States representatives who would sit in as observers at the collective bargaining sessions with General Electric and Westinghouse.

Philips of Eindhoven had a magic name as an eminent MNC, hence the shock waves when the IMF released a statement that proclaimed the capitulation of the Netherland's most renowned multi. After years of refusing to bargain internationally, Philips was now said to be willing to do so. Though the company denied this strongly, the news had a prolonged impact on the internal deliberations of many TNCs.

Another portentous report from the Netherlands—this time a true one—helped to shake the self-confidence of those U.S. multis that were then questioning the viability of their direct investments in Europe.

Between 1972 and 1977 AKZO was engaged in closing fiber plants in Switzerland, the Netherlands, Belgium, and Germany. Levinson personally took charge of a cross-border coalition of chemical unions. He insisted that the negotiations should be conducted within an international framework. AKZO did not agree with this approach. Then came the bombshell. Netherland's Prime Minister Joop den Uyl publicly called upon AKZO to accept the ICF as its partner. Never since has the head of any government openly declared his support for Charles Levinson in such a blatant manner. Though AKZO did not obey its government and still won the day, the intervention of the prime minister frightened foreign multis with European subsidiaries. Several of them opined that they, as good corporate citizens, could not have refused to comply with such a crude instruction. AKZO denounced the Dutch government's "emotional distrust of international companies," played up some of the smaller unions against the ICF, and carried out the plant closures through separate national negotiations (88, 120).

In 1973 Levinson gained an unprecedented spate of publicity in the United States. The United Rubber Workers Union was meeting in Cincinnati and the secretary general of the ICF was invited to speak at their convention. The U.S. union was making a lot of noise about industrial action against the U.S. plants of Uniroyal, Goodrich, Firestone, and Goodyear. Levinson had not come from Geneva to deliver just a fraternal greeting. He told the astonished (but delighted) delegates that if the union was serious about its willingness to pursue an industrial dispute with the rubber multis, he in turn would make them a promise: led by the ICF, the workers in the European subsidiaries would be called out on solidarity strikes. The idea was startling and the charismatic speaker was cheered. The ICF undertaking was repeated on television. Levinson froze the blood of the horrified directors of the four named TNCs. Whatever the survivors of those boardrooms may say in 1990, there is evidence that they treated seriously Levinson's intimidating warning. Few bothered to ask whether Levinson had been mandated by the European workers to declare that they would be willing to lose pay in order to help the rich U.S. rubber workers to become even richer.

The executives of some renowned multis nurtured a love-hate relationship with (as they would have it) the ogre Levinson. Even those who feared him were curious to see the man in the flesh. Thanks to my active participation at a round table meeting in the Hotel des Bergues, facing the Lake of Geneva, I can personally testify to this voyeurism. The seminar had been convened by BINCO to acquaint its client firms with Charles Levinson. The proceedings were to be behind closed doors and Levinson had given an explicit undertaking not to talk to the press about this meeting. To the consternation of BINCO, several of its established clients phoned to say that they would not be attending. Although the meeting was to be a secret one, several multis were worried that if the news of their attendance leaked, it might be considered an implicit recognition of the ICF. Other MNCs were more blunt: they expressed their consternation that BINCO was promoting Levinson. One of them wrote that "the less he is encouraged, the better." Some corporations actually threatened to leave the BINCO club. This was of weighty concern to a profit-making organization that depended for its material fortunes on not annoying wealthy clients. The organizers of the meeting had to go back to the drawing-board. A revised invitation was drawn up which clarified that the Levinson appearances had an educational purpose and did not mean that BINCO commended him to its members. One specific concession was made. At BINCO meetings it was customary to disseminate a comprehensive list of the attending corporations and short biographies of the executives who represented them. Identification tabs were routinely affixed to the lapels of all the male participants, giving the names of both the individual and his employer, for example, John Smith, World Metals. On this occasion, however, the tabs were to be marked only with the name of the executive and would not state his association with a particular multi. The format of the traditional list, which was distributed to all the participants, was also changed. It now recorded the attending corporations and, on a separate sheet, catalogued alphabetically those who were present without giving a hint as to their employer. An outsider could therefore not identify the corporate affiliation of any participant who might speak in the discussion or ask questions of Charles Levinson. A childish exercise? Not at all. It was symptomatic of how people groped in the dark as they contemplated a future in which multinational labour action would be the rule. Chapter 14 will elucidate why and how things worked out differently.

9

BUSINESS INTERNATIONAL CORPORATION

> A new kind of man is appearing and his numbers are multiplying
> rapidly. He is the international man. His forerunners were the great
> religious leaders. They were later joined by scholars and historians.
> Today they are joined by scientists all over the world, by doctors,
> educators, millions of students, some political leaders and—signif-
> icantly executives of multinational corporations. Of all these
> groups, perhaps the executives are the most important.
>
> Eldridge Haynes

Rajiv Gandhi, the leader of a country with rabid anti-multi traditions,
yearned to tell Western MNCs that he favored foreign investments.
Hence the Indian government blessed BINCO's New Delhi round table
meeting in January 1986. The prime minister participated in person and
chaired one session. Little did he know that a few months later many
of his guests were to be hosted by Pieter Willem Botha. South Africa's
president was delighted to see the anti-apartheid campaign deflated by
BINCO arranging for its client-members to meet in his country and
debate the merits of direct investments in this controversial economy.
The South African round table was also a lucrative venture for BINCO.

As the chiefs of its New York head office flew in to add luster to the event, they were handed ominous telexes. These announced that the *Economist* Newspaper Group intended to buy the equity of their company in a contested raid. The executive directors were of course displeased. It was unclear why the prestigious London-based bidder hankered after this modest information business—publisher of several (subscription only) journals, vendor of research, and organizer of seminars—which was in no way remarkable except for its past. The target company was then plagued by financial and personnel problems. Many shareholders were eager to sell their stock to any buyer at any price. *The Economist* paid over $8 million for the acquisition, and this effectively ended the 33-year life of Business International Corporation. All this would not have been worth mentioning were it not for the imaginative blueprints designed by BINCO's originators. By the time the company was sold, it had become a wholly non-political vehicle that was certainly not what Eldridge Haynes, the principal founder and Orville Freeman, his successor, had had in mind. To them the bread-and-butter activities were subordinate to the political campaigns that they expected BINCO to wage. Despite an early, apparently temporary, link with the CIA, Haynes and Freeman were distinctly left-of-center; they were earnest enthusiasts for a world government. Their intention was to present the collective voice of MNCs. Many large corporations became client-members because they preferred to have advocacy lobbying carried out by an external body. The former heads of BINCO had hoped to organize a global trade union—or trade association—of international companies. While for many years they managed to purvey information services at a profit, their real aim, engraved on their hearts, was never realized. Because this protracted failure tells much about the nature of TNCs, BINCO's architects deserve a niche in any comprehensive discussion on the international company.

ELDRIDGE HAYNES

BINCO came into existence in 1954 after Haynes—an advertising salesman, reporter, and publisher with little money of his own—had rounded up capital from private backers who either shared his ideals or were enchanted by glittering financial prospects. Before the word "multi" had been invented, the perceptive Haynes had already concluded that companies with global manufacturing operations would proliferate. He was the first to service this new market by the provision of information on the perils and attractions of overseas investments. Both intellectually and commercially, Haynes was an innovative entrepreneur. He commenced by publishing a weekly journal with the revealing title *Business International*. But Haynes's ambition was not confined to being a publisher. He created "the big-corporation club" with BINCO publicized as "the most expensive club in the world." Under the promise of secrecy executives met at round table meetings and seminars to exchange views on their foreign adventures and experiences in mysterious Bolivia and awkward Sweden. Membership was confined to suitable corporations which were charged variable annual fees that sometimes exceeded $100,000, and, in addition there were all sorts of extras to pay as a result of membership.

After initially recruiting exclusively U.S. corporations, Haynes took his gospel abroad. Pilkington, the UK glass multi, was the first non-U.S. company to join. Regional offices were opened to accommodate the 500 corporate giants that at one time or other were members or associate clients. On the impressive list were Toyota, Hitachi, Sony, General Electric, GM, IBM, Kodak, Pepsico, Du Pont, Monsanto, Union Carbide, Philips, Shell, Kone, Volvo, SKF, Alfa-Laval, Olivetti, Fiat, Hoechst, Heineken, Saint Gobain, Pioneer Concrete, Wormald, CRA, Lucky, Samsung, ICI, BOC, Glaxo, Massey-Ferguson, Alcan, Nestle, Sandoz, Brown-Boveri, and many others. Though BINCO was prepared to enlist in its ranks Communist multis, only one mackerel was caught: Energoinvest, based in Yugoslavia. Great care was taken not to offend clients by allowing undesirable corporations into the club. Once a celebrated U.S. corporation was signed up whose CEO was unacceptable to some existing client-firms; these threatened to resign. BINCO's principals had political aspirations but they also loved money. Thus they cancelled the stipulated membership of the disputed corporation.

Haynes was at first adamant that non-manufacturing international corporations should not be admitted because they were not pure multis. Later he compromised and reluctantly allowed several servicing giants to enter: Arthur Andersen, Arthur Young, Price Waterhouse, Chase Manhattan Bank, Midland Bank, Bank of America, Dai Itchi, and Manpower. Their membership dues were of course received gladly though they were not true TNCs.

The highlights of BINCO's program were the top-level government round table meetings to which only the highest ranking executives of the member-firms were supposed to be invited. For almost a quarter of a century Haynes and Freeman were respected as the putative spokesmen of the world's mightiest multis. The organizers of their round tables approached governments to deliver a pithy message:

Individual MNCs are powerful. The trade union of multis is even more influential so that you cannot afford to antagonize us. We are more or less doing you a favor by proposing to organize a series of meetings between your politicians, senior civil servants, heads of industry, trade union leaders, and the CEOs of famous global corporations. Only if you undertake that your prime minister and/or president will attend, shall we proceed.

With hindsight one can debate which was the more remarkable, the superciliousness of BINCO or the naivete of the leaders of rich sovereign nations. In those days the conspiratorial legend surrounding multis still had many adherents which in turn raised the reputation of BINCO. One nation–state showed that it did not fear the might of the self-appointed spokesman of TNCs. Shortly before the scheduled 1971 round table with Prime Minister Pierre Trudeau and 21 of his cabinet colleagues, the Canadian press learnt that BINCO had sent a message to the potential participants urging them to use this opportunity to lobby the Canadian government concerning its forthcoming restrictions on direct foreign investments. This attempt by aliens to influence the government on a delicate issue caused an uproar and the forcible cancellation of the round table.

The impressive government round table meetings, lasting three to five days, were the biggest achievement of BINCO's old guard. The pièce de résistance were the meetings and discussions with, among others, Generals Franco and Pinochet; Prime Ministers Pompidou and Barre; Indian Prime Ministers Nehru, Desai, and Rajiv Ghandi; Federal Chancellors Brandt and Schmidt; Presidents Marcos, Tito, Castro, Suharto, Houphouet-Boigny (of the Ivory Coast), and Sadat; Prime Minister Pearson, Japanese Prime Ministers Kishi and Sato; Prime Minister Palme; and nine prime ministers of Australia, Italy, and Britain.

Eldridge Haynes's political orientation and commercial acumen led to the organizing of the 1964 and 1971 Moscow round tables during the Cold War with the personal participation of Brezhnev, Mikoyan, Kosygin, and Gromyko. These were followed by round tables in Romania, Hungary, the German Democratic Republic (GDR), Poland. In each case these were attended by the top Communist leader: President Ceausescu, Prime Minister Fock, Chairman Sinderman, and Prime Minister Jaroszevicz. The meeting in Berlin dominated the front pages of the GDR's newspapers for days. Haynes and Freeman preached the virtues of freer East–West trade and advocated more licensing of technology by the West. They also probed opportunities for direct investments by MNCs in the COMECON. At the round tables the hated multis were feted while the Communist parties in the LDCs and the home countries of MNCs described them as the scourge of humanity. Charles Levinson frowned upon this collaboration between Communist state organizations and multis; he described it, offensively, as "Vodka Cola."

BINCO's biggest and most luxurious round table meeting was with the government of the Kingdom of Saudi Arabia. No fewer than 190 selected executives of 100 MNCs came in 1980 to Ryadh. BINCO scored a huge financial success though expensive Australian apple juice had to be imported for the banquets. There was one jarring note. The Swiss (female) secretaries, who had been specially flown in, were not allowed to enter the meeting rooms.

Conservative Prime Ministers Harold Macmillan and Edward Heath were happy to attend the UK round tables in 1961 and 1972, respectively. An extraordinarily hearty welcome was extended to BINCO's 1966 London round table by the Labour Prime Minister Harold Wilson, who appeared to have had an exaggerated view of the might of multis. As he was eager to attract foreign investments to Britain, he was advised to woo MNCs and court their trade union. Consequently, when the proposal for a BINCO round table meeting was mooted, Wilson endorsed it enthusiastically. He 'suggested' to the senior members of his cabinet that they should attend. Only one important individual, who could not square this with his socialist conscience, refused demonstratively. Harold Wilson chose to flatter the representatives of the omnipotent multis who were assembled in Britain's capital by inviting them to his official abode at 10 Downing Street. There he permitted himself to be questioned in a two-hour session.

As the CEO of BINCO, Eldridge Haynes had to walk a tightrope. Many of his clients were right-wing individuals who were proud, patriotic citizens of their own country. Most of them cared more for the profits of their corporation than for the good of humanity. Haynes clearly could not afford to ignore their political susceptibilities because BINCO's shareholders loved dividends. Yet he did not always disguise his own extreme views and at times ventilated them openly though it was not in his commercial interest to do so. His philosophy was popularized in *The Mission of Business International* (118). Though akin to the 39 Articles of the Church of England, neither the CEOs of member-companies nor his employees were forced to declaim them regularly in public. Nobody had to take an oath of allegiance but Haynes let it be known that he expected his clients and his staff to abide by the golden rules that he had formulated. Indeed, corporations that rejected the basic contents of *The Mission* sooner or later left the club of their own volition. Employees who were disdainful of Haynes's religious principles were tolerated as dissidents in the organization; they were kept on for their technical expertise but excluded from the inner circle of the true believers. *The Mission* averred that profits were on the whole a good thing but "we do not regard the profit system as an end in itself. . . . Capitalism is not an end in itself." To assert this (in a by no means secret document), and yet to retain many powerful capitalist business organizations as paymasters, is a tribute to the magnetic appeal of Eldridge Haynes. *The Mission* proclaimed that BINCO stood for free trade, the abolition of exchange controls, and the removal of tariffs and import restrictions. It demanded the free cross-border movement of all people (not just of managers). Inflation was of course denounced as an evil, while aid to the LDCs was praised wholeheartedly. Perlmutter's precepts for the radical internationalization of globally operating companies were supported fully. *The Mission* concluded with the pious sentiment that the policies outlined would serve the self-interest of MNCs and, simultaneously, keep faith with the "need of mankind." Chapter 10 outlines the most outrageous feature of Haynes's political penchant. This was not disclosed in *The Mission* for it would have aroused too much ridicule.

The non-commercial aspirations of Haynes ceased to be 'marketed' by BINCO's executives years before the company was actually sold. Many of his ideas were dropped because life had stamped them as unrealistic. In any case, many of the important multis, which formed the original core of members, had left disillusioned. Governments were recognizing belatedly the vacuousness of BINCO's claim to be a meaningful trade association of MNCs. Nevertheless, the energetic and charismatic Eldridge Haynes will be remembered as the apostle who first unfurled the publicity banner of multis, travelling the world to extol the virtues of the international company to all and sundry.

ORVILLE FREEMAN

Eldridge Haynes retired in 1970 to be succeeded by Orville Freeman, who was an even more political animal than he. Freeman, after performing brilliantly at university, became a Marine officer. A bullet shattered his face as he led a patrol behind Japanese lines in the Pacific. Having relearned speech after his war wounds healed, the veteran practiced law before being elected the youngest-ever governor of Minnesota. He was reelected twice. In 1960 Freeman nominated J. F. Kennedy for the presidency. Kennedy had assured him that he would be his vice-presidential nominee. Hubert Humphrey, Freeman's mentor, had warned him not to rely on this promise. Kennedy, for strategic reasons, reneged on his undertaking and chose L. B. Johnson instead. After Kennedy's assassination some of Freeman's detractors unkindly dubbed him "the politician who-almost-became-president." Kennedy rewarded the former governor of Minnesota by naming him Secretary of Agriculture and he retained this appointment for eight years, serving also under President Johnson.

In a frank interview, before he retired as CEO of BINCO in 1981, Freeman admitted that as a left-wing Democrat, he had found it somewhat difficult to be accepted by many of the Republican presidents and chairmen of the U.S. multis. Some actually reminded him that he had cut his political teeth helping Hubert Humphrey establish Minnesota's Democratic-Farmer-Labor party. While Freeman attempted to shrug off the incongruity of his appointment ("Oh sure, some businessmen tease me about being a Democrat"), the *New York Times* commented appositely that "he might seem out of his element in the generally conservative corporate environment."

After Eldridge Haynes had anointed his successor, the latter announced that he was pleased with the new post because it gave him an opportunity to take charge of a commercial undertaking with manifest political overtones. None of the clients could attack Freeman for lacking in patriotism, but several of them noted with horror that his left-of-center views came to the forefront, for example, when he sponsored the resumption of trade links with Communist Cuba. He attacked unions for their protectionist stance and informed the emerging Japanese and Korean multis that BINCO would fight against import restrictions pertaining to their merchandise exports. He conceded that his convictions, favoring supranationalism, were seen to be "tantamount to pie-in-the-sky" but nevertheless pressed on with his campaigns advocating the abrogation of national sovereignty. He declared his faith in "One World."

Freeman was an enthusiastic and expert lobbyist in Washington. Thanks to his political connections and his good name as an honest former politician, he was frequently summoned to give evidence at congressional hearings. He did so as the president of BINCO. On Capitol Hill they welcomed him as the unofficial spokesman of an association of U.S. multis. When testifying, he gave implicit credence to this appellation. However, once Freeman was abroad at conventions and round table meetings, he emphasized that BINCO was a sort of trade union for MNCs of all nationalities. He had good reason to do so. When *The Economist* acquired Business International Corporation, almost half the client-companies were headquartered outside the United States.

THE CIA EPISODE

Until the 1970s much of the anti-multi propaganda, particularly that emanating from the Soviet Union and its satellites, used to equate MNCs with global corporations headquartered in the United States. It was therefore not suprising that certain adversaries of multis should publicly have given vent to their suspicion that BINCO was a covert agency of the CIA and/or the recipient of subventions from Washington. Those who had an opportunity to discuss politics with Eldridge Haynes could not have nursed any doubts that this left-wing liberal genuinely detested the CIA and its putative misdeeds. Before anti-CIA sentiments became popular in the United States, Haynes had already voiced them strongly, albeit only in private sessions. As an employer he laid down one strict rule governing the conduct of BINCO's staff. While the fiddling of expense accounts and drunkenness were not encouraged, they did not lead to instant dismissal. This punishment was reserved for any employee who was found to be working for, or channelling information to, the CIA.

Great was the shock to clients, staff, and governments (which had hosted round table meetings) when the *New York Times* broke the news in December 1977—Eldridge Haynes had died the previous year—that BINCO and other named organizations had had links with the CIA between 1955 and 1960. Eldridge's son, Elliott Haynes, junior co-founder of BINCO, confirmed the astounding revelation: "When quizzed about this by the *Times*, I decided to admit the truth." It appears that when the journal *Business International* was launched, Eldridge Haynes wanted to be able to say that he had correspondents in foreign lands who were providing original, significant information. He could, however, not afford to hire any. Hence—at least in the version of Haynes's family—he colluded with the CIA "to arrange cover" for four of its agents in Europe by providing them with journalistic credentials. What the CIA gave in return has not been disclosed though its agents are said to have sent valuable dispatches to the BINCO journal.

Officially the arrangement came to an end in 1960. Perhaps by then Haynes did not need the CIA money any more, for his company was established on a sound financial basis. Perhaps the CIA did not need BINCO any more. In 1977–78 Orville Freeman had to pick up the pieces and seek to limit the damage that this exposure was causing. It would perhaps have been swept under the carpet more quickly were it not for one senior employee, Melbourne-born Ken Gott, the editor of *Business International* in New York. For some reason BINCO had been subjected to protracted virulent attacks in Australia. A weekly paper actually wrote that this so-called U.S. information company was in fact an agency of the CIA. BINCO did not sue for libel but Ken Gott, BINCO's erstwhile senior representative in Australia, stated publicly on several occasions that these accusations were untrue; he denounced them as smears. Gott is a respected supporter of the Australian Labor party and genuinely believed in what he said. His political principles were such that he would never have accepted employment with BINCO had he known that it was surreptitiously subsidized by the CIA. In January 1978 he resigned and issued a mild statement in which he disassociated himself from any involvement in CIA activities. Ken Gott aimed at persuading his personal and political friends that he had unwittingly misled them by denying his employer's link with the CIA. BINCO did not like his resignation and he was treated harshly. When you seek to build a new, supranational world, the scruples of one individual do not count for much.

FLIRTATIONS WITH THE LEFT

When I first met Eldridge Haynes and listened to his 'progressive' ideas, I was skeptical. It was amazing to hear, at a tête-à-tête luncheon, that he admired Herbert Marcuse, the dreaded guru of the student revolutionaries. When Haynes intimated that, were he living in England, he would be supporting the Labour party, I began to doubt his sincerity. I wondered what could be his ulterior motives in relating these tales to me. I was wrong. Eldridge Haynes—and the same applies, albeit to a lesser extent, to Orville Freeman—genuinely espoused leftist causes. It took me some time to comprehend how someone with Eldridge's political opinions could be the active CEO of a club that was financed largely by diehard Republican company presidents. It was also not easy to disabuse myself of the notion, reiterated in much of the anti-multi propaganda, that all the heads of MNCs are hoary, reactionary devils. I discovered that some, though certainly only a minority, were inclined to share the viewpoint of Harry Heltzer, the chairman of 3M, that the CEOs of international corporations are this generation's "real radicals" (38).

In 1968 students in Britain, France, Germany, and the United States— led by cadres of the ultra-left—demonstrated, sometimes violently. The disturbances alarmed the chiefs of all the Western-based multis, irrespective of their political affiliations. The top echelon of BINCO in New York sought out the leaders of the student revolutionaries in the United States who were organized in the radical SDS (Students for a Democratic Society). The aim was to commence a dialogue that might lead to a strategic alliance. Elliott Haynes and his confreres prided themselves on their initiative, yet they had a sound motive not to publicize their efforts. If disclosed, they were bound to antagonize many client-companies. After these approaches ended in failure, there was then even more reason to keep quiet. In 1970, however, a colorful account by one of the revolutionary students was published and confirmed my own information about BINCO's proselytizing ventures. The "college revolutionary" (as he described himself) wrote about a conference held at Columbia University:

A kid was giving a report on an SDS convention. He said that J. Edgar Hoover had said that we were as big a threat as the Communist Party. This evoked peals of laughter, as we consider the C.P. to be a stodgy old group who are no threat at all compared to us. . . . Also at the convention, men from Business International Roundtables—the meetings sponsored by *Business International* for their client groups and heads of government—tried to buy up a few radicals.

These men are the world's leading industrialists and they convene to decide how our lives are going to go. . . . They're the left-wing of the ruling class (117).

Eldridge Haynes was always flattered when left-wing student groups invited him to address them. Some of his speeches were recorded. He argued consistently that multis are a revolutionary force in modern society; they are a powerful instrument pressing for accommodation with the Communist world; anti-militarist if not actually pacifist; and the true internationalists of our age.

BINCO could justly point out in the late 1960s that it was agitating for normal economic relations with Communist China. Eldridge Haynes used to stress that MNCs were set upon increasing the volume of all cross-border trade. In particular they strove to remove the existing economic barriers between COMECON and the West. He gave prominence to his round table meeting in Moscow in 1964: MNCs need freedom to trade and trade is the harbinger of improved political relations.

Eldridge Haynes sneered at those who taught youth that "it is noble to die for God and country and God is always on the side of our own nation–state" (2). He exploited astutely the anti-Vietnam sentiments in the United States and asserted repeatedly that the attacks on multis, stigmatizing them as warmongers, were unfounded: in fact MNCs favor a reduction in arms expenditure. According to Haynes, TNCs are truly pacifists.

The multinational corporation is not primarily engaged in making weapons for if it were, its own government would severely curb its freedom to produce abroad and it could hardly be multinational. . . . The multinational corporation . . . needs peace to move people, money and information about the globe speedily and without danger or interruption. It does much better with its customers at home than in foxholes. It must have workers skilled in production, distribution and finance—not in killing.

Perlmutter sang in an even shriller voice when he addressed BINCO's Bermuda round table meeting in January 1968. He was obsessed with the strength of multis and forecast that war would not come about when there is much international trade and MNCs have subsidiaries all over the world: "Since monster firms will be represented in all countries, war will not be possible" (26).

Eldridge and Elliott Haynes addressed themselves, energetically and passionately, to the reputed internationalism of the anti-establishment groups in the United States. Raising the banner of multis, the father-and-son team averred that global corporations would be happy to see the surrender of national sovereignty. It was conceded that few CEOs of multis knew the words of the Communist hymn, the *Internationale*. But, BINCO maintained, many were disinclined to sing the national anthem of their home countries. The revolutionary students were challenged to probe the authenticity of the internationalism of the leaders of the AFL-CIO and of the trade union chieftains in the rest of the OECD. Did not their utterances and conduct stamp them as rabid nationalists? Were they not in the forefront of protectionism? BINCO repeatedly claimed that multis are genuine internationalists, working effectively to achieve world government. One of Fiat's directors, Aurelio Peccei, who was closely associated with BINCO's leaders, affirmed this message. He shouted from the Italian rooftops that the TNC "is the most powerful agent for the internationalization of human society."

BINCO's vain endeavors to impress the revolutionary students with the progessive credentials of multis were followed by equally ineffectual dialogues with the leaders of the Third World and anti-establishment clergy. In January 1972 the CEOs of a number of multis affiliated to BINCO came together during a five-day convention in Trinidad under the tutelage of Orville Freeman. A local paper reported that the "world's brains met at the Hilton . . . the biggest gathering of millionaires and multi-millionaires in Trinidad at any time." When not in working sessions, the participants were treated to cocktail parties, steel band music, a gala rendezvous fiesta, and an elegant banquet. They also had the opportunity to swim, sun, play golf and tennis, or just stroll in the botanical gardens. Facing the bosses of mighty MNCs were a number of critics. They were not invited on the principle of "learn to know your enemy": BINCO considered them potential allies of MNCs. At considerable expense, radical churchmen, German and U.S. trade union dignitaries, representatives of the UN and the LDCs, and others were flown in. The organizers promised the attendance of "Joseph Rhodes, representing youth" and also of the neo-Marxist Stephen Hymer—one of the four founding fathers—who was designated as the spokesman of "leftist intellectuals."

From the other side of the Atlantic arrived Tony Benn. Whatever induced him to come, it was not the modest fee which he collected for his lecture. His arrival raised some eyebrows because he was an outspoken enemy of MNCs. His consent to attend the Trinidad convention made the naive principals of BINCO think that he was really a friend and admirer of multis. At home Tony Benn's main aim was to replace the reactionary command of Britain's Labour party with new leaders, headed by himself, who would be imbued with the true spirit of socialism. Benn had already learned from Perlmutter about the multis that would soon dominate the world. Though some of his comrades thought it incongruous for him to fraternize with the enemy, Benn brushed aside such unworthy reproaches. He was very pleased to have a chance to enter the lion's den. Tony Benn came and went. Orville Freeman and his advisers suffered from the illusion that he had been won over to their cause. Subsequently, they pursued him with ingenuous requests to explain the praiseworthy mission of BINCO to fellow socialists. Benn ignored them. Just as Eldridge and Elliott Haynes had returned emptyhanded from their evangelist dialogues with the revolutionary students, so Orville Freeman had to recognize finally that Tony Benn shunned BINCO and had never intended to be its friend. His visit to the Trinidad Hilton served him well because he could now imply that his abhorrence for multis had been fortified. He met the monsters in person and this qualified him to warn the labor movement to beware of the dangerous and evil international corporations.

Only when his diaries were published was it revealed that though Benn had been glad to have had "access to the collective thinking of the multinationals," their most famous 'friend' on the ultra-left had never been taken in by BINCO's flirtations with the anti-establishment forces. He describes at length his attendance at the Trinidad convention.

I went to the plenary session. . . . The more they listened to some of the criticisms that were being made—notably from me—the more frightened they seemed to become and there was a motion that after the conference no papers of proceedings be published. . . . I had to leave just before the end and I took my papers with me; but Richard Conlon came specially to my hotel room to get them back. He was embarrassed and I was cross. . . . Orville Freeman came up to me and he was also embarrassed. . . . I told him I felt as if I had dropped into a meeting of the Central Committee of the Communist Party in the Kremlin and had only been discovered at the end (194).

10

THE MULTI
BROTHERHOOD

Had Thy Lord willed, He would have made mankind one nation.
The Koran

Do U.S., Swedish, and Korean MNCs have long-term, substantive common interests? The founders of BINCO, striving to create a trade union of (ultimately) all MNCs, naturally answered in the affirmative. They would dearly have loved to inscribe on the masthead of their literature: "Multis of the World, Unite!" Eldridge Haynes was a happy man when his organization was described in *The Times* (London) as the "transnationals' trade association." Chapter 12 finds fault with the notion of the multis' "common interest." Even global companies of the same nationality are not necessarily loving brothers. The present chapter cites several concrete instances of MNCs joining forces, chronicles proposals to call into being worldwide organizations of TNCs, and tells of dreamers who envisaged a stateless homeland for multis.

A FEW PRAGMATIC SPECIMENS

Many have attempted to unearth joint machinations by MNCs but no momentous examples have been brought to life. The Steuer commission, examining the UK scene, reported that a number of large U.S.-based multis had established informal contacts. They met at dinner parties to discuss problems arising from their British operations. ("For what it is worth, the existence of any such grouping was denied by some of the members.") The dreaded anti-trust laws, however, cast their shadow even over U.S. corporations abroad. Ford and GM were not invited simultaneously to the same functions. The Steuer commission struck a blow at the multi conspiracy theory by asserting that, despite the dinner parties, competition among U.S. MNCs was more significant than their common concerns (35).

In the 1970s I came across an association which, if it had not met in secret, would have brought grist to the mill of the multi conspiracy. Membership was confined to U.S. citizens who were employed as senior industrial relations executives in the European subsidiaries of U.S. multis. They convened three or four times a year in different towns. I was asked to address them for a handsome fee. This enables me to relate that the putative conspirators indeed ate extremely well and, I must add regretfully, drank large quantities of alcoholic beverages. There were no traces of transnational plots to oppress the proletariat of Europe. The discussion, which I initiated, on "Codetermination in Germany" did not disclose collusive sharp practices by a multinational cabal. Yet I understood why they sought no publicity.

The Council of the Americas is a loose umbrella organization of U.S. corporations with direct investments in Latin America. Outsiders might be misled into thinking that they constitute an effective pressure group. The Council does indeed voice the opinions of many multis but, lacking powers to back them, it is purely a consultative body.

The "informal club," founded in Paris in 1983 by 17 European MNCs under the chairmanship of Volvo's Pehr Gyllenhammar, is a dignified talking-shop. Among its original members are Nestle, Unilever, Thyssen, ICI, and Olivetti. Their aim was to stimulate collaboration between European multis in order to resist the competitive might of Japanese and U.S. MNCs. Since 1983 other corporations have joined. Nowadays the CEOs mostly meet in small committees to discuss matters of wider interest. Though they do not publish the results of their deliberations, it is surely an innocuous association. No one was frightened when Gyllenhammar boasted that "never before has such a group been assembled."

In 1978 two left-wing organizations reviled the large Swiss multis (including Ciba-Geigy, Sulzer, Sandoz, Nestle, HLR, and Brown-Boveri) because they had formed a secret committee. This had the specific task of warding off the threat that the UN Group of Eminent Persons might make proposals that would adversely affect MNCs in general and Swiss corporations in particular. If the accusations of these anti-multi groups, which distributed copies of documents purportedly supporting their charges, are correct, then the corporate conspirators succeeded: the harsh recommendations to the UN, which the Group of Eminent Persons had originally intended to make, were toned down (116).

An instance of cooperative action by the subsidiaries of multis in an LDC was reported from Karachi at the end of the 1960s. Twenty-five German, British, French, and U.S. pharmaceutical companies, operating in Pakistan, abandoned their traditional private lobbying and instead issued a public ultimatum to the host government: unless they were granted a 30 percent price increase to compensate them for the fall in the value of the rupee, they would induce the retail distributors of their products to strike by not handling their goods. This aggressive behavior paid off and the authorities relented. It was a significant victory though it is equally noteworthy that three pharmaceutical giants (Glaxo, HLR, and Ciba-Geigy) had not joined the common front.

Multis have combined on several occasions to counter the imposition of unjust taxes on their subsidiaries and/or expatriate staff. Concerted pressure by U.S. multis on the German government, to modify the fiscal law which double-taxed profits generated by the subsidiaries of American MNCs, was unsuccessful. Action in Britain—this time by international corporations of different nationalities—led to a resounding success. When Britain's Chancellor of the Exchequer, Denis Healey, presented the 1974 budget, he spiced it with pejorative references to MNCs. He said that the foreign employees, working for them in Britain, often do not discharge properly their personal tax liabilities. His proposal to tax, on a global basis, all the earnings of non-UK citizens was not really draconian because it was meant to apply only to those foreigners who chose to reside continuously in Britain for more than five years. An alliance of Greek shipping companies, U.S. banks and manufacturing MNCs from continental Europe organized a unique lobby which underlined the warnings to close down operations in Britain and transfer them to a more hospitable country. Callaghan's Labour government surrendered very quickly; the original 'harsh' tax arrangement was amended radically.

Some 23 states of the United States have at one time or other toyed with 'unitary' taxation. This is a technique by which, in the case of multinationals, states do not tax the profits generated within their boundaries at arm's length. Instead, they ascertain the worldwide profits of the corporations and tax a proportion of the whole. The relevant ratios are calculated by juxtaposing the company's turnover, payroll, and fixed assets within the state with the MNC's global turnover, payroll, and fixed assets. This technique is applied to U.S. multis with overseas subsidiaries and to non-U.S. multis with U.S. subsidiaries. The preparation of the concomitant bookkeeping is costly, but this is a minor matter.

Multis do not like it when loss-making subsidiaries are assessed to state taxes because the corporation, overall, is profitable. The unitary system is a bone of contention that has forged an ad hoc international fraternity of MNCs. U.S. multis clasped the hands of their foreign confreres. Companies such as BAT, which do not usually enjoy rubbing shoulders with Perlmutter-type MNCs, joined the herd. Particularly significant were the vociferous contributions from usually low-profile Japanese multis. They bullied California's legislature, threatening the state politicians that they would no longer invest in California and might close down existing facilities. Nowadays it is rare for governments to take up the cudgels for oppressed multis but this issue has proved an exception. The British Treasury did all sorts of naughty things to persuade Washington that it should prevail on the states to abolish unitary taxation. Chancellor of the Exchequer Nigel Lawson actually made public his intent to consider retaliatory steps. The U.S. federal authorities were indeed firmly opposed to unitary taxes, but were powerless to act after the Supreme Court ruled them valid. Hence Washington was engaged in the perverse game of encouraging foreign multis to cajole the guilty states. Sony's founder complained to Secretary of State George Shultz. To his surprise he was told that the State Department agreed with him. Shultz advised Sony that when next planning a U.S. investment, it should "just go to a state where there is none" (115). In 1990, the issue of 'unitary taxation' in the U.S. is still unresolved. But the protracted campaign to abrogate it is is the most outstanding example of a well-endowed international conspiracy by multinationals.

IDEOLOGICAL MOTIVES

George Ball has never been an overt or covert member of any anarchist group. Yet he denounces the "archaic nation–state" and expresses delight that "stateless" MNCs have global loyalties that supersede political allegiance to their home countries. Tom Clausen, the famous CEO of the Bank of America, has gone on record to express his hope that in his view international corporations should "shed all national identity." Samuel Pisar, an attorney specializing in the affairs of U.S.-based multis, says of his clients that they have "detached themselves from their American moorings and have taken off on the high seas. Now they are stateless" (54).

If these sentiments were truly representative of how the decision-makers of global corporations view the world, then the formation of an international trade union of multis would have been a natural consequence. Yet only few have ventured to step on to this minefield. H. Mertz was one of them. He prepared a rough blueprint for a World Association of the Multinational Corporations which, he suggested, should be charged with regulating the behavior of MNCs. It ought to impose restraints lest the unacceptable behavior of some corporations damaged the interests of all TNCs. Mertz's plans, like those of others with similar ideas, have remained words on paper (114).

In a letter to Orville Freeman, James Hodgson, secretary of labor in the Nixon administration, grumbled that there was "no *concerted* effort" on the part of TNCs to defend themselves. He opined that humanity would suffer because there was no organized effective defense. Hence he pleaded with BINCO to fill this void: "The world would be better for it."

If economic historians in the twenty-first century find it worthwhile to dissect the, by then, burned out legend of the multi conspiracy, they are bound to mention the founders of BINCO. Eldridge Haynes repeatedly called for "*collective* action by multinational corporations" but he did more than just theorize. Haynes founded an organization that, he hoped, would one day be transformed into a recognized negotiating body of TNCs. The concept was so alluring that some observers jumped the gun and related to BINCO as if it was an established viable trade association. The organ of the Confederation of British Industry said of "Business International, the big-corporation club" that it already performed some of the functions of a world body that could guide governments and is ready to berate MNCs if their actions are restrictive, disruptive, or unjust.

Eldridge Haynes definitely did not want all international corporations to join his trade union. He summoned only those who were ready to

place the global interest ahead of national and regional interests. Membership would consist of companies that are truly international in character and mentality. . . . [T]hey will not be alone. Undoubtedly, such a group . . . could wield significant influence, for they would have the power of an idea whose time has come. . . . Individually, the multinational organisation has little influence . . . Collectively, no one could accuse them of conspiring to benefit people in one country or of being agents of a particular nation–state (71,1).

WE WANT AN ISLAND

Most of the zealots who prided themselves on the statelessness of their multinational corporations were barren rhetoricians. Apart from using extravagant language, what could they do on this earth? At best they were able to move the domicile of the parent company to another country; this is what, for example, International Nickel did when its head office was transferred from the United States to Canada. Legal and taxation impediments, however, make it nearly impossible for the majority of MNCs to change their national abode. All sorts of gimmicks have been suggested to give TNCs an international look. A German critic of multis wanted each parent company to install a Council of Host Countries to be staffed by government representatives of those countries in which the foreign subsidiaries are located. The Council was supposed to receive confidential information in order to participate in the "internal decision-making processes of the TNC."

The UN is brought into play by several of those who stress the state-lessness of multis. Tony Benn favored the registration of all large international corporations with the UN. They would be required to supply information about their activities. Tony Benn envisaged that in turn the UN would offer some protection for "their legitimate interests if these were improperly threatened" (113). BINCO too flirted with the UN. In view of later events, its unequivocal pronouncement sounds rather hollow today: "The United Nations has no greater friend than multinational corporations." Eldridge Haynes dreamed of the day that his trade union was recognized by the UN as a non-governmental organization that would be consulted formally. He visualized that in due course it would post ambassadors in selected capitals (2).

These tame recommendations did not set out to transform the legal environment of multis. Each global company would continue to be incorporated in one given country. After deduction of the taxes paid in the host countries, all the profits of its worldwide operations would accrue to the home country. There was no escaping the accursed nation–state. Only political extraterritoriality could put into practice what the visionaries were preaching. As early as 1967 George Ball had proposed a supranational authority, established by treaty with the large industrialized nations. (Ball thought the UN too unwieldy an organization. Also, for this purpose it was unnecessary to enlist all the countries of the world as signatories.) This body would provide for the incorporation of multis; they would be granted a charter recognized by the parties to the treaty. Global companies would be free from national interference because the supranational company law (which was to bind them) would take precedence over the relevant national laws. The supranational authority was also to enforce rules governing the conduct of MNCs in host states, and simultaneously prescribe the limits within which host governments were allowed to intrude in the affairs of multis. According to Ball, this would turn TNCs into "citizens of the world" (110, 112).

Carl Gerstacker, when chairman of Dow Chemical, presented a paper at a White House conference in 1972. A few sentences from it ensured his fame:

I have long dreamed of buying an island owned by no nation, and of establishing the World Headquarters of the Dow company on the truly neutral ground of such an island, beholden to no nation or society. If we were located on such truly neutral ground we could then really operate in the United States as U.S. citizens, in Japan as Japanese citizens, and in Brazil as Brazilians, rather than being governed in prime by the laws of the United States. . . . We could even pay any natives handsomely to move elsewhere (111).

Asked why he had not already moved his "nationless" company to an obscure island, Gerstacker responded: "We have not done it simply because the tax problem is insurmountable." Dow is nowadays embarrassed when asked about this declaration of its former CEO. The company's public relations executives would have liked to disavow him or perhaps even to deny that such remarks were ever made. Unfortunately for them, Gerstacker's declaration was published and disseminated widely at the expense of Dow's shareholders. The present incumbents of Dow's top echelon are particularly fearful that his derisive reference to "any natives" might bruise the image of the corporation.

In 1971 BINCO publicly came out in favor of the island idea. The occasion was the launching of a documentary film, "The Reluctant Death of National Sovereignty," which centered on a discussion with the historian Arnold Toynbee, Aurelio Peccei (a top executive of Olivetti and Fiat), Eldridge Haynes, and Orville Freeman. The world premiere was held at Westminster under the auspices of the Parliamentary Group for World Government. Some excerpts were later printed in the *Hansard* of the House of Lords.

Peccei: I know of one step one small step that seems to me may lead toward something: it is to give the multinational corporation an international charter. It may be located in a real or symbolic territory, but it will give it a non-national identity.

Freeman: Why not an island somewhere that could be the *situs* for the multi national corporation?

Haynes: The Caribbean.

Freeman: I'll buy that. This would be comparable to the situation in the United States in which most corporations are chartered by the State of Delaware for pragmatic reasons. I think this is exciting because it would do two things: it would constantly remind multinational corporate management that they really are world-wide, and that they should act and think so, even more than they do; it would remind the countries in which they do business and where most of their people come from, that they are international and must think and act in that fashion. And thirdly, it would tend to meet this religious fervour—the tension of whole world—by dramatising the basic concept that here's a little island somewhere which these great corporations call their home. It might even be a member of the United Nations family, and it might even, in the long run, begin to provide independent revenue to the United Nations.

Toynbee: [He turned down the suggestion by Eldridge Haynes that Switzerland should be considered as a possible location.] I prefer an island; there are

some ex-colonial islands that have become independent and don't know what
to do about it. I think one of them might be persuaded to lend itself as a kind
of Vatican City as a seat for the world's multinational corporations (24).

Twelve months later Eldridge Haynes developed this theme in an
address to a closed session of CEOs from corporations affiliated to
BINCO. He proposed that nation–states should abandon their taxation
of income earned by MNCs outside the home country, in favor of allowing the UN to collect the same amount directly from multis. The
nation–states, surrendering this revenue, would be allowed to reduce
their contribution to the UN by the same amount.

I can also imagine . . . raising some money for the purchase of an uninhabited
island—perhaps in the Caribbean—and arranging with whatever nation–state
has been claiming sovereignty of that island to relinquish that sovereignty to
the United Nations—and hoisting the United Nations flag over it. The island
could be used as the headquarters for studies of international cooperation initially. Perhaps in due course it could become the symbolic home of the multinational corporations that may be chartered by the United Nations—a sort of
international Delaware, so to speak. This island would also be a symbol of hope
for mankind—a hope for one peaceful world (2).

R. J. Barnet and R. E. Müller have written of their visit to Gerstacker.
They called on him to ascertain whether this island notion of his had
been a joke but found that "he was deadly serious" (38). In fact, a group
had offered him the Minerva atoll near the Fijis in the Pacific. He declined
because he "thought this particular group had too conservative a mission." When I was first apprised of Haynes's plan for an island, I was
extremely distrustful. At my first opportunity I tackled him about further
details though, to my shame, I did so with tongue in cheek. Like Gerstacker, Haynes replied solemnly; he was quite unconcerned that some
regarded his proposal as frivolous. He said that he had found some
backers: "bankers and like-minded CEOs of multinational corporations."
Together they had approached the UN. He would not give me the name
but stated emphatically that they had been received by a "very senior
official." The most striking disclosure was that the group had already a
specific location in mind. Haynes's backers had hired a boat and together
they had "encircled the island" to inspect whether it might prove suitable
for their purpose. I was assured that the idea had by no means been
rejected by the UN: "It is still under consideration." After Eldridge
Haynes's death his island idea was dropped abruptly. BINCO's sales
executives were disconcerted when clients recalled the fantasy of the
company's founder.

PART II

THE HARSH
REALITY

11

THE BIRTH OF MULTIS

In Australia U.S. firms frequently sought to take on a national guise—to have the man-on-the-street consider them an Australian organization.

Mira Wilkins

This historical summary reviews the reasons why, during the last hundred years, companies became TNCs and why they chose particular foreign locations. Some of the reasons are no longer valid today. The current back-pedalling by conventional multis is discussed in Part III. After some general points to clear the decks, three main causes and a number of less momentous motives are enumerated; at the end some bizarre and seemingly illogical stimuli are recorded.

According to Karl Marx's disciples, the gestation of the modern international corporation was linked to the growth of finance capitalism. If that were so, the nominal return on capital invested by the parent company in overseas subsidiaries would have been an important consideration. Actually, the strategists of multis concern themselves with more sophisticated calculations. They pay heed, for example, to the risk of expropriation and the public relations handicap of investing in politically sensitive countries. The actual transfer of funds from the home country is often irrelevant to MNCs and sometimes also to the host countries. At one stage Northern Ireland was so intent on attracting foreign companies to set up plants in its high-unemployment areas that the authorities were willing to supply up to 100 percent of the capital. (This wild wooing of multis led to cheating and the formation of non-viable businesses.) IBM evaluates the profit-and-loss performances of its national subsidiaries by various criteria—the earnings on investment dollars remitted from the United States are not regarded as significant. In the three decades following World War II, British-based MNCs expanded vastly their manufacturing operations overseas. Until 1979 exchange controls and Britain's sick balance of payments meant that the majority of these investments could not be financed by conveying foreign currency from London to the host countries: most of the needed capital was in fact borrowed abroad against the security of the foreign assets about to be acquired by the expanding MNCs. During the heyday of their economic conquest of Europe, U.S. corporations suffered from no such restrictions and yet frequently raised most of their required capital in the host countries. Only one-quarter of the financial resources backing the overseas operations of U.S.-based TNCs have emanated from the United States (147). Anti-multi German critics have been known to shoot with a double-barrelled gun. They have denounced U.S. companies for "buying the whole of German industry" and also complained that these predators are not transferring capital from home to execute their plans. The 3M company is an often quoted example. With an initial capital outlay of $1.7 million in 1954, it laid the financial foundations for operating one manufacturing plant. The ensuing profits were used to buy up existing German businesses and ten years later 3M had six plants in the country—Germany and not the United States had provided most of the financial wherewithal.

It is unhelpful to cast around for a correlation between the explosive expansion of TNCs and the growing dimensions of international trade. While intracorporate cross-border flows of goods by multis account for a rising proportion of international trade, it does not follow that MNCs invariably have a vested interest in free trade. Very often the opposite is true: the raison d'être of many multis is to manufacture in national locations where weighty import restrictions are in force.

Perusing the memoirs of industrialists who presided over the multinational escalation of national companies, one is struck by the frequently adduced explanation: "We had no choice, we were forced to do so." Externalities of various kinds have impelled reluctant company directors to organize manufacturing operations outside their home country. In many—though clearly not in all—instances national companies would have preferred to serve the world market by exporting output manufactured in the home country. I call upon two witnesses. In 1934 the then head of ICI, Lord Melchett, told his shareholders of the dilemma facing the company. Most of the overseas plants were "bascially uneconomic but that was immaterial because overseas governments were determined to have them and the cost factor, except in very extreme cases, is in no way decisive" (107). Thomas Murphy, vice chairman of GM, told a congressional hearing in 1973 that his company manufactured overseas, even in locations where the cost of producing vehicles was greater than the price of vehicles imported from the United States. Were they not to do so,

multinational firms based in other countries would be alert and quick to fill the need. . . . The origin of General Motors as a multinational manufacturer can be traced back to the competitive necessity to establish overseas assembly facilities in order to maintain an export business. It became quickly apparent, however, that General Motors could not rely solely on the export-overseas assembly approach. . . . As a result General Motors took its first tentative steps to manufacture components in Europe and acquire two overseas manufacturing facilities. . . . Our decisions have not involved a choice between exporting from the United States or manufacturing abroad. . . . Tariff barriers, reflecting deep-rooted national policies . . . have generally foreclosed the export opportunity (54).

In relation to their strength, the Japanese and German manufacturing giants were not properly represented in the world economy as powerful multis until after 1975. There are non-economic explanations for this backwardness. For more than two decades after the end of the war, the Japanese authorities were not eager for their corporations to set up wholly owned manufacturing subsidiaries in OECD countries. Tokyo feared that if this were allowed to happen, the host countries "would then demand similar rights in Japan." Cultural handicaps were also a vital reason that Japanese firms with advanced technological products used to be so circumspect about manufacturing abroad. Japanese executives were not yet sure of their ability to manage a production facility in a Western industrial society; they particularly doubted their competence to handle foreign workers. As pressures mounted and threats to their exports grew—the embryonic Japanese multis were compelled to put up foreign manufacturing plants. Lack of self-confidence (and not financial considerations) provided a strong impetus for entering into joint ventures with local entrepreneurs. In the 1980s the need to manufacture abroad had become paramount and Japanese corporations had gained sufficient self-assurance to opt for 100 percent-owned operations; some of them commenced to buy out their former partners in joint-venture enterprises.

Nicholas Faith (106) has set forth an interesting thesis to explain why, post–1945, most of Germany's world-famous firms evolved only tardily as MNCs. He has attributed this to "ancestral fears" that German manufacturing assets abroad might one day be subject to a third wave of confiscation. Older people remembered that during the two world wars, the pioneering German multis were dispossessed of many of their foreign subsidiaries, particularly in the United States. It took considerable time for German industrialists to gain the certitude that this was not likely to recur—at least not in the world of the OECD.

Some huge corporations point to special circumstances to explain why they cannot become TNCs. Others assert that they have no such ambition. The president of Mitsubishi Heavy Industries declared:

There are simply many things that cannot be produced overseas. Customers equate the words made-in-Japan with quality and trying to maintain the high level of quality in locations abroad is not always possible, no matter how strong the yen becomes nor how cheap costs are in those countries.

Some corporations, usually unwilling to say so in public, disdain manufacturing abroad because of the high risk that their technological secrets would become known to competitors in the host countries. There are firms which, on principle, are unwilling to become MNCs. One of Britain's mammoth construction concerns, Wates, turned down lucrative offers to open branches in the Middle East with the financial assistance of the British government: "We don't wish to become a multinational company and neither do we want growth for growth's sake." It ought to be stressed that Wates's policy declaration is not consonant with the ethos of the overwhelming majority of Western corporations. Perhaps not many, but there are companies such as Wates.

THREE STRAPPING MIDWIVES

Vertical Integration

The hankering after secure and cheap supplies of raw materials and basic inputs, to be shipped to the parent company's plants in the home country, led to the birth of the early multis. Backward integration was a factor that used to weigh heavily in the globalization of national companies. U.S. tire manufacturers could not cultivate rubber plants in Ohio; this fact induced Goodyear and Firestone to invest in Liberia. England's Quaker chocolate producers needed a tropical climate to harvest cocoa beans—hence their direct investments in what is now Ghana. Unilever's founder was concerned that his soap and margarine factories in Europe might one day suffer from a shortage of fats, and for this reason he carved plantations out of jungles and saddled his heirs with the albatross of the United Africa Company (104). In 1910 UFCO, the dreaded *El Pulpo*, set up a subsidiary in Honduras. Instead of purchasing the bulk of its bananas on the open market, the American food multi bought land and grew its own supplies. Similarly, Bowater, the English paper manufacturer, planned foreign ventures to advance its vertical corporate integration. Pulp was produced in Canada and then in the southern parts of the United States because of the suitable climate, ample supplies of wood, and abundant water.

Protectionism

Unilever's multinational roots had many shoots. Apart from the search for secure raw materials already cited, it became "one of the great practitioners of tariff jumping" (41). The import duties that foreigners imposed on his exports from England gave William Lever a strong incentive to build plants in continental Europe and North America. His patriotism was impugned but he defended himself vigorously: "When the import duty exceeds the cost of separate managers and separate plant, then it will be an economy to erect works in the ['protected'] country so that our customers can be more cheaply supplied from them" (52).

Until, say, 1950 tariffs acted as a busy midwife of MNCs; thereafter their influence receded. The Japanese demonstrated that truly efficient and cunning manufacturers could penetrate foreign markets despite onerous tariffs. Exporters from LDCs also proved that high import duties cannot always shield outmoded producers in the old industrialized countries. As a result, protectionists, particularly in Latin America and Asia, ceased to rely on the tariff weapon and opted for import controls and quotas. Most members of the OECD were also not slow to restrict exports from Japan and the LDCs by non-tariff barriers. These have proved more effective than high tariffs in causing the birth rate of TNCs to soar.

Tariff areas (free-trade regions) offer multis a certain latitude in that they can tariff-jump into several foreign markets by establishing one manufacturing subsidiary. The Imperial Preferential Tariff was a protectionist device that gave a distinct advantage to UK-located manufacturers who exported to the Empire (and later the Commonwealth). U.S. corporations established plants in Britain to benefit from this arrangement. One U.S. MNC set up a manufacturing subsidiary in Scotland; some of its output was marketed in Canada, thus replacing exports from the parent's factories. This seeming absurdity was replicated when Grundig established a manufacturing subsidiary in Belfast. At the time Austria and Britain were members of the European Free Trade Association (EFTA), while Grundig's head office and most of its production facilities were situated in the EC. Grundig had found the existing UK tariff oppressive and consequently built a factory in Belfast that could supply (tariff-free) the whole of Britain. It was also worthwhile to export from this EFTA base to Austria rather than supply this market from the parent's factories in neighboring Germany. After Britain joined the EC, the UK subsidiary of Grundig was gradually wound up.

Member-states of free-trade regions vie with each other to attract MNC subsidiaries that produce for the whole of the region. When the Hungarian-based TNC Tungsram sought a backdoor, tariff-free entry for its products into the lucrative EC markets, it looked around to find where the most luscious subsidies were handed out. On that account, Tungsram, with no commercial interest in its meager domestic market, chose the Republic of Ireland as a manufacturing location within the EC tariff walls. Some commissioners of the EC and vocal industrialists in Germany and France have not disguised their annoyance with Britain for showering gifts and subventions upon Japanese MNCs to induce them to build plants in Britain from which to export (generally without hindrance) to the rest of the EC. Britain is castigated for practicing unethical midwifery and the Japanese subsidiaries are called Trojan horses.

Enticing Conditions

It was noted earlier that if corporations were intent on owning and controlling the supply of basic inputs, they often had no alternative but to organize foreign subsidiaries. U.S., UK, and German food multis found that pineapples could not be grown in Chicago, Glasgow, and Berlin, thus they had to make direct investments in the Philippines and Brazil. The Dutch TNC Shell did not discover much oil in the home country and therefore had to explore in those foreign lands which the Deity had selected as a vast repository for oil. Backward vertical integration of that kind has a logic of its own, one which is not on par with the behavior of embryonic MNCs that abandon production at home in order to manufacture in low-cost locations abroad. Radios and shoes are not like pineapples and oil. There are no geological, climatic, or other physical reasons why radios and shoes are produced in foreign subsidiaries.

During the 1960s and 1970s numerous electronic multis—among them Philco, RCA, Westinghouse, and Zenith—closed down some of their U.S. production facilities. With the trade names unchanged, they promoted throughout the world the sale of goods that were manufactured in their newly created subsidiaries in Hong Kong, South Korea, Taiwan, and other 'attractive' places. By the beginning of the 1980s Asia was losing some of its pull and many TNCs had become enamored of Mexico. It was estimated in 1988 that 1,000 small and big multis were manufacturing near the Mexican border with the United States; most had U.S. parents, but Japan and other OECD countries were also represented.

Low wages in LCDs are reinforced by the absence of fringe benefits—especially pensions, paid holidays, and vacations—on a scale that is customary in the developed countries. The administrators of the Yucatan region in Mexico advertised boldly that not only are its direct wage costs lower than in other parts of Mexico but that its turnover is negligible and absenteeism as low as 1–2 percent per annum. Some MNCs are especially enticed by no-strike promises and the prospect of not having to negotiate with unions (or at least not with powerful unions). The South Korean authorities once publicized an undertaking to MNCs that build factories in the Masan Free Trade Zone: they will benefit from a special law that "restrains workers" from striking (81).

U.S. corporations, relinquishing domestic production to the tune of billions of dollars, did not have to go into liquidation because they were kept busy marketing imported goods from their low-cost subsidiaries (3). Some of these new multis have argued persuasively that while, admittedly, there were no physical reasons for manufacturing abroad, they had no economic alternative but to organize foreign subsidiaries: "Essentially we are no better and no worse than those U.S. companies which grow bananas in foreign locations." There is substance to this apologia. Over a period of years one North American shoe manufacturer after another has closed down domestic production facilities and gone over to the marketing of imported shoes. The cost differential between shoes made in Haiti and those made in North America is so vast that any company that continues to mass-produce shoes in the United States is either owned by a lunatic or a magnanimous millionaire.

The anti-multi lobby would have it that multis have been and are predominantly motivated by the opportunity to employ cheap labor in their foreign subsidiaries. Undoubtedly, this was an important factor in the past and the above examples indicate that it was still of significance to a number of MNCs in the 1980s. This old-fashioned midwife, however, has never been as popular as is generally believed and is certainly finding it difficult now to make a good living. GM has recorded that the birth of its manufacturing subsidiaries was induced only by market opportunities and not affected "by the availability of hourly labor costs lower than those in the U.S." (105). 'Progressive' bishops will reject this as specious talk by a guilty multi, but GM was and is not alone in rejecting the cheap-labor factor as a determinant reason for putting up a foreign plant.

An increasing number of TNCs have burned their fingers in LDCs and now shun them. MNCs ought to allow themselves to be enticed by low wages only if they have highly labor-intensive work for their foreign factories. The recruited labor force must consist primarily of unskilled people who need no more than short-period training and subsequently demand inexpensive supervision. (Skilled workers in LDCs are in short supply and, consequently, are paid relatively high emoluments.) Such subsidiaries can be established very quickly, for no complicated capital goods are likely to be installed. If these conditions are fulfilled, it follows that the manufacturing subsidiaries can be liquidated by the parent at short notice. Even if the host country were to confiscate the assets (or native Luddites smashed up the machinery), the material damage to the MNC would not be great. These stipulations are clearly not apposite for the majority of multis. IBM can be denounced as the "scourge of mankind" till the cows come home, but no one can assert that cheap labor has ever motivated it when selecting the location of its overseas production facilities.

'Enticing conditions' is a notion that is not restricted to the employment of cheap labor and does not always represent a corporate motivation that is confined to manufacturing in LDCs. Though mentioned in neither the religious nor the secular anti-multi literature, long-term modifications of exchange rates may impel MNCs to usher in new foreign subsidiaries. Since the early 1970s the more or less continuous decline of the U.S. dollar, vis-à-vis the currencies of the stronger members of OECD, has given birth in the United States to hundreds of manufacturing subsidiaries with foreign parents. (The 1976 decision of Volkswagen to build a plant in North America was only implemented after the German unions had given their blessing: they accepted that there was no alternative if the company intended to continue selling in the affluent markets across the Atlantic.) It opened the U.S. gates to a flood of direct investments and the takeover of existing manufacturing companies. The cheap dollar was a more proficient midwife in the proliferation of multis than the cheap labor of Mexico.

ADDITIONAL SPURS

Certain MNCs have switched from exporting to manufacturing overseas because of the transport factor. This includes shipping charges; special packaging costs incurred when goods are dispatched on long sea journeys; additional insurance to cover the concomitant pilferage; and the expenses associated with the time span of exporting merchandise to a distant market. GM, explaining why it set up operations in Europe, has related that in 1928 the transport costs of sending two fully-assembled Chevrolets equalled those incurred in dispatching kits of nine unassembled Chevrolets (54).

Selling foreign-made goods to consumers in the private sector is beset with obstacles, some of which can be circumvented by offering cheaper and better-quality articles. Tariff walls can be climbed and import quotas may be breached by various illegal means, including smuggling. However, the sale of imported merchandise to the public sector is sometimes frustrated by obstructions that cannot be overcome by price and quality. This accounts for an often neglected impetus in the development of

MNCs. Many procurement agencies are under instruction not to buy foreign-sourced goods and this injunction is frequently backed by considerations of national security. At times recipients of funds from the public purse are also bullied to buy only domestically manufactured goods. Harold Wilson's government told the universities—so proud of their academic freedom!—that as the state provides them with grants for their research, they must comply with the edict to procure computers, optical instruments, and so on only from local firms. The Swedish TNC Ericsson, manufacturer of communications equipment, has admitted that producing its goods in foreign subsidiaries has little economic rationale and is certainly not done to benefit from cheap labor (123). Ericsson says of itself that it is a reluctant—but realistic—multi. In its files are ultimata from a number of governments: 'Either you issue a license to an indigenous company or you build up a manufacturing facility in our country. If you do neither, we shall buy from your rival, ITT, which manufactures in foreign locations to be able to tender as a native firm for public sector contracts.'

The small-sized home markets of Sweden, Switzerland, and Holland furnish an obvious explanation of why, pro rata, these small economies harbor a record number of industrial companies that have invested in manufacturing subsidiaries abroad. The same reasoning also applies to those national companies in large economies that have saturated the domestic market and cannot therefore expand except by penetrating foreign markets. YKK, the zip fastener corporation, was one of the first Japanese MNCs because it already dominated the home market.

In many OECD economies some national companies are perforce turned into multis not because they have already saturated the local market, but because further domestic expansion would meet with the disapproval of the watch-dogs supervising monopolies. In 1986 Germany's Bertelsmann became an important communications MNC by acquiring the U.S. firms RCA Records and Doubleday. The company explained this branching out into foreign lands by mentioning the gut feelings of its board. If, instead, Bertelsmann had sought to take over German competitors, the Kartellamt would not have approved.

Large manufacturing corporations maintain close links with a pack of suppliers. Many of the latter initially became MNCs because (like camp-followers) they had to pitch their tents near the foreign plants of the former. When the U.S. automobile TNCs commenced to assemble abroad, their traditional suppliers—the manufacturers of radiators, motors, tires, beltings, electrical accessories, and machine tools as well as banks, accountancy firms, and advertising agencies—pursued them and also set up foreign subsidiaries. In the 1980s a similar process is taking place in the wake of Japanese direct investments. The Japanese automobile manufacturers would have preferred to be supplied from their traditional home-based sources. But, apart from the fact that it is convenient to have access to supplies from a nearby factory, there is a more important reason why it is not feasible for the managers of the new foreign ventures to procure most of their inputs from factories in Japan. The Japanese TNCs must prove to the host governments that they are complying with the prescribed local-content regulations. Nippon Seiko, a Japanese ball-bearings producer, established a manufacturing subsidiary in North England which sold some of its input to Nissan's British assembly plant that was then able to claim that it had purchased UK-made inputs. This is a powerful spur to turn national components makers into global manufacturers.

Unilever's company biographer mentions a third dimension—in addition to the search for secure raw materials and the need to jump tariff walls—which gave birth to the corporation's multinationalism. William Lever was fully aware that the man in the street was a xenophobe; hence the inducement to build factories abroad that would have native names and be managed by indigenous executives, thus disguising the nationality of the parent company. When his sales agents in the Benelux markets reported on sales resistance due to Lever's Englishness, he called them together and undertook to put up works in their countries: you will then be able to say that "this soap is made in Belgium for Belgians and this soap is made in Holland for Dutch people" (52). To make Unilever's German operations appear truly German, he appointed Ludwig Stollwerck chairman of the subsidiary. Xenophobia also influenced Alfred Sloan, the architect of GM's international activities; he said that the German firm of Opel had been acquired in order to give the U.S. TNC a "German background instead of having to operate as foreigners" (105).

If the identical product can be sold in all parts of the world, then economies of scale may deliver an impressive argument in favor of concentrating manufacturing in one location. But if there is no such uniform global demand, MNCs ponder the merits of producing in several locations. The automobile giants of Detroit found that as against the U.S. consumer's preference for large vehicles, the European buyer opted for smaller cars. Supplying Europe through exports from the United States would have involved the companies in a radical redesign of models and necessitated separate assembly lines. Detroit was driven to the conclusion that under those circumstances, and motivated also by other factors, it was worthwhile to build plants abroad that catered predominately for the specific demands of the native customers (54) (124). After some tribulations William Lever also became convinced that the nature of his products must be varied so as to satisfy national or regional tastes. His researchers had demonstrated that in most parts of Germany there was no demand for hard soap of the kind manufactured in English factories for the British public. Germans generally favored potash soap. In the United States there were distinct ethnic preferences for different types of soap and reports spoke of "violent prejudice against the smell of Lifebuoy" (Unilever's popular English brand). The recognition that it made commercial sense to pamper the local population stimulated Unilever and many other embryonic MNCs to build factories abroad (52).

For almost a century MNCs have been known to locate manufacturing subsidiaries in countries in which they have received implicit or explicit undertakings that the host government would exclude competing manufacturing multis and restrain (or forbid altogether) damaging imports. The first such attempt is reported to have been made in Czarist Russia. According to the company biographer of International Harvester, the authorities were delighted when in 1909 the corporation announced its intention to build a factory in Russia. International Harvester suggested that the government might wish to show its appreciation by imposing onerous tariffs on the harvesting machinery of certain competitors so that the projected venture could prosper unimpeded in the vast market of Russia. The ploy failed for a variety of reasons that have nothing to do with morality. Since then a number of LDCs have actually concluded collusive pacts of this kind with Western MNCs; neither the governments nor the companies are eager to publicize them.

Critics of MNCs accuse them of not doing enough R&D in the host countries and some governments pressure their corporate guests to do so. Paradoxically, MNCs are sometimes tempted to buy foreign companies (especially in OECD economies) because they are specifically interested in acquiring the know-how and R&D facilities of their targets. Prompted by the same consideration, multis have started up foreign subsidiaries in both developed and developing countries to provide a working environment for suitable indigenous staff who are recruited to carry out research of which the parent can make use throughout its global network. The consequent R&D costs are lower than if the scientists and technicians had been lured to emigrate in order to perform in the laboratories of the parent's home country.

Ralph Nader put his finger on a sensitive issue that was to plague the ITSs in their global fights against the multis: "I don't go along with exporting dangerous industries—loose laws abroad are an incentive to produce abroad" (61). This was and is an important reason for chemical and pharamaceutical concerns to manufacture abroad, especially in LDCs. The unions in the rich economies obviously want to halt them in their tracks. One of Levinson's vocal supporters, the union leader of Britain's chemical workers, put it colorfully: "The multinationals are now seeking pollution havens to dodge anti-pollution legislation" (44). In a year of full employment the Hamburg municipality prohibited a French MNC from manufacturing an obnoxious product; the authorities insisted on radical modifications and the introduction of safeguards that would have made production economically nonviable. The French firm was advised to close its Hamburg factory and relocate in an underdeveloped country where the compunctions of Hamburg citizens did not prevail. In another example, a famous Swiss pharmaceutical TNC had invented a new product and proposed manufacturing it in existing plants in its home country. The board of directors was compelled to reconsider this decision after the domestic environmentalist lobby had intimated that it would stir up trouble. Hence a specially constructed plant was set up in a European country that wooed foreign investors. In 1984 the Council of Churches in the Netherlands confronted a number of Dutch MNCs; they were asked to justify foreign investments which the Council had censured on environmental grounds. All of the corporations pointed out that the host nations had welcomed them with open arms. The union leaders in the LDCs were especially happy that they had brought productive work to poor regions even though there were some physical dangers. The church leaders stridently disagreed: MNCs ought to ignore invitations from foreign governments to manufacture in their lands if such production would have been condemned at home as environmentally deleterious. Philips, one of the TNCs that had incurred the displeasure of the churches, replied that it was extremely hesitant about big business making political judgments. Shell defended its establishment of subsidiaries in LDCs on two levels. First, it argued that certain chemical operations that were dangerous in densely populated areas (such as the Netherlands) were acceptable in countries where the inhabitants lived in less crowded conditions and the climate was more tolerable. Second, it rejected the notion that "business should be expected to act like missionaries or like the army" (19).

In countries with full employment, national companies expand output by poaching labor from other employers and/or by importing temporary *Gastarbeiter* (guest workers). Some corporations have chosen a third avenue: they have opened manufacturing subsidiaries in foreign territories with a surplus of labor. German and Swedish companies, among others, have established production facilities abroad for this reason. Multis, having agreed in principle to manufacture in a given geographical region outside their home country, are known to select particular towns or areas by reference to suitable labor resources. When Britain had full employment during many of the postwar years, the development authorities of Northern Ireland and of the Republic of Ireland referred to it as a potent argument to persuade TNCs, eyeing the markets of the British Isles, to build factories in their domains which had pockets of unemployed. GM, having decided to place a new plant in the Benelux countries, opted for Antwerp, saying that the availability of labor in that town had been the "biggest factor" (46).

Governments court foreign entrepreneurs with a variety of strikingly luscious subsidies. Some host countries cloak their deficiencies by offering bountiful grants, long-term cheap loans, factories at nominal rents, and so on. Contrary to a general belief that these inducements ensnare multis, they actually play only a minor role in determining the location of projected manufacturing subsidiaries. There are of course exceptions. National companies, which would have liked to expand at home but could not raise the money, have been infatuated with the prospect of receiving capital provided they manufactured in a given foreign location. Few serious investors are swayed by such appealing gifts. Many MNCs, however, are guilty of playing up one potential host country against another in order to collect the maximum amount of subventions from the authorities of a country/region/town in which they had already decided to establish themselves irrespective of the level of subsidization. The engagement of an efficient public relations agency is a prerequisite. This was understood by a prosperous global UK-based firm that appeared unable to persuade the authorities in the home country to mollycoddle it with some extraordinary capital gifts. The news was trumpeted to the press that this company had received an attractive offer from the Netherlands. Consequently, production was to be transferred to a newly constructed factory in this benevolent host country. The British government took fright and the firm was provided with commensurate British presents to expand locally. The company stayed. Even gigantic TNCs take part in these unsavory competitions and many OECD governments, which ought to know better, allow themselves to be blackmailed.

Tax considerations are not as important a factor in the evolution of TNCs as anti-multi literature would have it. Corporations naturally shun setting up subsidiaries in countries with high taxes and obviously avoid economies with punitive taxes on the profits of global firms and their expatriate staff. It does not follow, however, that a low tax regime is necessarily a magnet that pulls in foreign corporations. Wise decision-makers comprehend that low taxes today can become heavy taxes tomorrow, that benefits accruing from low taxes can be more than offset by burdensome disadvantages. Taxes do, however, carry much weight in the location of assembly plants and labor-intensive factories. The free-trade zones in Latin America and Asian LDCs, which exempt foreign manufacturers from taxes on exports, have proved alluring.

Multis will frequently try to minimize their global tax liabilities by skillful transfer pricing, but this is rarely a raison d'être for planning capital-intensive, long-term investments in foreign lands. Screwdriver plants, however, which need little capital are sui generis. Switzerland used to house thousands of mailbox companies, dummy subsidiaries of foreign parents, which played around with invoices of international trade transactions though no goods were actually imported into and exported from Switzerland. This was transfer pricing at its most convenient, with the ensuing profits piling up in Switzerland. Manufacturing MNCs, making use of such Swiss facilities, are increasingly treated with suspicion by customs and tax authorities. Hence many have forsaken Switzerland and opted for an alternative, albeit more complex, subterfuge that dresses up transfer pricing in more respectable garbs. They build screwdriver factories, which import virtually all the inputs and merely assemble them for sale in other countries; sometimes they only repackage goods. Hundreds of foreign multis have been enticed to establish subsidiaries in the Republic of Ireland for the sole purpose of defrauding other countries. Dublin does not reprimand its foreign corporate guests provided Irish law is not breached. (Other countries have tried and failed to emulate efficient Ireland.) The triangular stratagem works as follows: the multi exports from its factories in the home country to the Irish subsidiary at deflated prices (possibly even at below production costs). Having assembled or repackaged the imported goods in Ireland, they are exported at inflated prices to various sales subsidiaries of the multi. The aim is to manipulate prices so that the parent company and the (non-Irish) sales subsidiaries are seen to make no or only minimal profits. The global gains accrue to the Irish subsidiary which is privileged to pay no, or only low, taxes. An Irish economist has observed that the Irish people are not too upset by the supernormal profits generated by the screwdriver subsidiaries of foreign multis because "they would typically be at the expense of foreign rather than domestic consumers." (125).

Illegal designs underline the evolution of some MNCs headquartered in LDCs. India, among others, provides a number of examples. Several of its national companies have set up branches and subsidiaries abroad and the authorities in Delhi have declared their pride in the proliferation of newborn Indian multis. Unfortunately, the motives of a number of entrepreneurs who turned LDC companies into MNCs were not noble. By means of subsidiaries abroad they hope to evade exchange controls and the payment of taxes. To smuggle funds out of the country by making the 'right' bookkeeping entries is more satisfactory than passing through customs with suitcases stuffed with banknotes.

THE IRRELEVANCE OF ECONOMETRICS

There is no conventional rationality in the corporate investment judgments that are touched upon in the following potpourri. Nevertheless, such outlandish decisions deserve to be listed. It can, however, be perilous to enumerate these seeming absurdities—even when they are genuine causal factors in the expansion of certain multis. The credibility of the compiler is in danger of being eroded when, for example, personal prejudices of the CEO or family associations of the major shareholders are adduced to explain why a certain foreign location was chosen to build a new factory.

Powerful multis invariably have an economics department. To derive vicarious prestige it is sometimes headed by a famous academic luminary or even a former minister of finance. Alas, most global companies do not accord their in-house economists much scope to influence decision-making, however illuminating the memoranda that they are requested to prepare.

Outsiders, in contact with the ICIs, Sonys, and Du Ponts of our age, are overawed by the strength of such mega-sized corporations. Is it not cogent to assume that when such mammoth organizations evaluate overseas projects, they hire the best brains to assess political risks, pay handsomely for advice from reputable location experts, and engage experienced market researchers? Having digested the commissioned analyses, the corporate captains are then assumed to be in a position to pronounce authoritatively which of several alternative investment plans will prove the most profitable. This perception accords with the legend of the mighty multis that has helped to build up a mental picture of highly paid CEOs who pray to the god Mammon. These cool, unemotional, hard, and decisive men—they are rarely women—drive their corporations to maximize global profits. It is not easy to invalidate convincingly this populist conception. Yet plausible or not, many important corporate resolutions have been arrived at because of superficial impressions, gained by the responsible directors from reading newspapers and paying cursory visits to potential host countries. The president of a U.S. TNC with five operating subsidiaries in Britain flew to London to finalize the takeover of another British manufacturer. The company's office was on the fifth floor and his heart was not very good. The elevator was not functioning because of a strike. Perforce the president climbed the stairs. Chairing the meeting, he denounced Britain as "decadent," "full of lazy people," "the worst country of the EEC." The outraged CEO opposed the investment in an economy in which there can be no assurance that the elevator works. Ridiculous? Puerile? Those who write books on the merits and demerits of MNCs will shrug off this outburst—to which I was a witness—as irrelevant.

In the 1970s the majority of U.S. manufacturing corporations with a listing on the Big Board (of the New York Stock Exchange) were multis. Among the minority was a company, the directors of which felt that their corporation was losing out in the virility contest because all of its manufacturing operations were domestic. The board discussed this defect. A consultancy firm was commissioned to recommend what products the company might manufacture in Europe and Latin America, respectively, and to suggest suitable locations. Reputed prestige mattered!

The former principal of McKinsey's Swiss branch expounded in Geneva that while most MNCs "have been motivated by logical reasons," in his experience "some companies have moved overseas for purely emotional reasons" (127). He added what professors of economics surely do not tell their students: "A few [corporate presidents] have even built plants next to their favorite resorts." Decision-making based on the idiosyncracies of autocratic, self-opinionated company presidents is well known to those who deal with real people in real multis. *Fortune* once related that one U.S. corporation had "picked a village in Scotland for its factory because the president's wife, who was with him on an [exploratory] trip, remembered the lovely roses in front of the cottages as a rare bit of sun burst forth." Myles Mace, professor of Business Administration at Harvard, cited the confessions of two American executives:

We went into Latin America blind, and I guess the main reason for our decision to invest was a desire by the president to include in our annual report that, as part of our annual efforts to employ the company resources profitably, we have created manufacturing and sales subsidiaries in Peru, Mexico and Colombia. In response to a question as to why a factory was constructed in Spain, the president of [another] company said: my wife speaks Spanish, loves Spain, and now we are able to make several trips a year to visit the operation.

In 1984 Ford's assembly plant in Cork was closed down. There had never been any rationale for this factory, which was meant to serve the tiny domestic market of the Republic of Ireland. Why had it been built in 1917? Apparently Henry Ford wanted to honor his father William, an emigrant from Cork to the United States in 1847. The Good Book indeed says: "Honor thy father and thy mother that thy days may be long"— and if you are the CEO of a mighty TNC, the corporation is bound to be helpful.

The Japanese government helped to pay for research to ascertain where budding Japanese TNCs should place their European regional head offices. It was thought desirable to agree on one town in Western Europe so that support facilities (banks, schools, leisure activities) could service a large number of Japanese expatriates and their families. London was ruled out because at that time Japanese businessmen treated Britain as a declining country—and in any case it was riddled with strikes. Brussels was a hot favorite but was only dropped when Tokyo no longer believed that it would become the capital of Europe. Düsseldorf was finally selected. As institutions and head offices gradually moved into specially constructed buildings, the town became known as the "Japanese Center of the EC." Though it had all been planned methodically, several Japanese companies quickly abandoned the Düsseldorf location and most new arrivals on the European scene did not even consider it. Although it should not really have been significant, the executives of Japan's international companies had found German a difficult language to master. Most of them were in Düsseldorf only on temporary assignments. They questioned whether it was worthwhile to make the effort to learn German. Of what use would be their laboriously acquired knowledge of the German language, once they had been transferred from Düsseldorf? It is for that reason that in the end London became the Mecca of the European head offices—and this process began before Margaret Thatcher had revived the economic fortunes of Britain. When the first Japanese manufacturing subsidiaries were opened in Europe, Germany was also a favorite location. However, by the end of the 1980s Japanese employers had more people on their payroll in Britain than in any other European economy. The language factor again played an important role. In 1985 the French initiated a special campaign directed at Japanese multis to persuade them to make direct investments in France or, at the very least, to locate their regional European head offices in Paris. Money was spent to investigate why the Japanese, with some exceptions, had avoided France. Many of the answers pointed to bureaucratic obstacles, but the single biggest barrier was the French tongue. The respondents pointed out that Japanese schoolchildren learn English as their first foreign language. Whatever economic benefits Paris's magnanimous government might wish to bestow upon prospective Japanese investors, the resistance to learning yet another foreign language was formidable. "For those Japanese who have struggled all their lives to half-master English, French is simply too much to tackle" (126).

Public relations practitioners are called upon to resolve a host of problems faced by introspective multis. The experts' advice is targeted to maximize universal love and respect for the corporation and to minimize worldwide attacks on its performance and integrity. CEOs are pleased when their company is acclaimed as a benevolent corporate vehicle and hate investigative journalists who drag it through the mud. But the public relations considerations also serve a more material purpose: to be loved means that more of one's products can be sold profitably, while scandals betoken lost markets and lower dividends. Hence it is necessary to take a stand on what products shall, and which ones shall not, be manufactured. In what countries is it expedient to manufacture, sell, or procure and which are taboo? Above all, the image of the corporation matters—is it kind to animals, women, trade unionists, members of ethnic minorities, small businesses, young people? More of this in Chapter 17.

In 1989 Chile, Israel, and South Africa headed the list of countries in which it was undesirable to have a subsidiary; multis were counselled not to be seen even to trade with them. For the sake of being loved in other parts of the world, scores of MNCs have divested themselves of assets in those countries at considerable cost. Only the Japanese MNCs were out of step. They used to have no compunction about breaching the trade embargoes on Southern Rhodesia. During the 1980s they also did not seem to care that, by deliberately supplanting other multis in South Africa, their image might be blemished. Unashamedly, they stepped up exports to the country of apartheid and proved singularly insensitive.

The wish of certain host countries to accommodate the subsidiaries of MNCs vastly exceeds their supply. In order not to offend these countries, which might otherwise proscribe the import of their goods, some multis have established "ornamental subsidiaries." Unlike screwdriver plants, these do generate considerable value-added. Nevertheless, they are best described as sops thrown to foreign governments, because were it not for tactical considerations these manufacturing subsidiaries would not have come into existence. "Ornamental factories" have been built since the first big MNCs evolved. ICI's authorized company biography recounts what happened when the head office sent an emissary to Brazil in 1934. He returned to say that various European, North American, and Japanese exporters to Latin America—including ICI—were unpopular and the authorities were considering the imposition of selective import restrictions. The clever man in charge of ICI's Brazilian subsidiary had an idea:

Importations are looked upon as a drain on the national economy . . . I consider it, therefore, expedient that we establish a small vested interest in Brazil, so as to create the impression in official quarters that we are interested in the country's industrial development (107).

This public relations need to be considered a good corporate citizen is not confined to LDCs. A famous U.S. multi had reasons to ingratiate itself with Harold Wilson's administration. To bribe influential individuals or make contributions to the Labour party would have desecrated the ethos of the corporation and was also not the way to do business in Britain. An astute political adviser counselled this multi to set up a financially well-endowed research establishment in one of Britain's distressed areas. The laboratories were given real R&D assignments and in that sense the investment was genuine. But if the corporation were to have located such a research station in accordance with sound economic criteria, it would never have chosen the wretched town it did.

One of IBM's biographers asserts that while the corporation builds its main plants in politically acceptable countries, it has also established a presence in 130 other economies. The author, Robert Sobel, calls them "token plants," for they have no direct commercial raison d'être (129). IBM has hinted on many occasions that its international procurement strategy takes account of the public relations need to place orders in as many countries as is feasible.

Sony's chairman, Akio Morita, does not say so explicitly, but from his public utterances one learns that he prefers PR advice to the admonitions of economists. Morita recognized at an early stage in the internationalization of his company that there are solid non-economic reasons for building a larger number of manufacturing subsidiaries than is justified by economic calculations, and that the location of plants is frequently determined by politics. Sony's planners in Tokyo have had no difficulty in outlining the cost-logic of concentrating most of their manufacturing in the home country and/or a cheap-labor economy of Southeast Asia. Yet several production ventures have been deliberately located in Europe: "Once we produce in one regional market, we get the right to import as well as to export. . . . It's economics versus politics" (128).

The PR machine is also called upon to repair the damage caused when a multi opens a manufacturing subsidiary in country A and thereby appears to be slapping the faces of politicians in the alternative host countries B, C, and D. From a PR standpoint it is particularly troublesome if the parent company puts out to tender the location of a new factory, inviting various nation–states to participate in an open competition. The top prize accrues to the country offering the most acceptable package— the (relative) size of the subventions is only one relevant factor. Ford's parent company was highly conscious of the susceptibilities of European governments when it announced in 1977 that it was looking for a site to build an engine plant. After receiving a number of detailed proposals, Ford selected Wales. The then British prime minister labored hard to achieve this. (Incidentally, or perhaps not so incidentally, he represented a Welsh constituency in the House of Commons.) Fanfares were sounded in Britain and the prime minister proclaimed the dawn of a new age, now that the famous multi Ford had chosen Britain in preference to other countries. Ford was embarrassed by this publicity though it understood that the ruling British politicians relished their triumph which—in part—had, of course, been bought by promising abundant help from the taxpayers. Lest the choice of Wales slight the national honor of the rejected European countries, Ford beat no drums during the low-key launching of its new manufacturing venture. The company's spokesman confirmed the facts but prudently said no more.

Many business schools in OECD countries play the game. Students are taught the 'scientific' way to assess the risks associated with investing in a given country. One particularly sophisticated model was so constructed as to facilitate the appraisal of 100 national economies by gauging elaborately 100 factors (GDP growth, indigenous supply of fuel,

social harmony, student unrest, the size of the public debt, racial conflicts, personal taxes, strikes, and so on). Variable arithmetic weights
were attached arbitrarily to the 100 factors. Each country was awarded
the number of points that the players considered it had earned. By
definition, the more points scored, the more idyllic the investment climate! The beautiful points system thus enabled analysts to grade the
100 economies in accordance with their putative merits as host countries.
The United States rarely topped the league in these contests; in one year
it was listed as ranking fourteenth in the matrix prepared by a famous
consultancy group that charged dearly for its risk assessment expertise.
Are students at business schools told that while MNCs often subscribe
to several risk assessment services, they take no blind notice of them?
This can be demonstrated convincingly by examining the statistics on
the locations in which multis actually make direct foreign investments.

Numerous national companies have been transformed into global corporations because their CEOs disliked the political climate at home. They
sought to have manufacturing investments abroad 'in case something
goes radically wrong'—the relative profit returns of the foreign subsidiaries were not a decisive element. The fear of being nationalized has
given a powerful impetus to the building of branch factories abroad. In
the 1980s Germany was almost invariably at the top of the risk assessment tables while, according to the weighted points, the United States
lagged behind badly. Yet during that decade, Germany was at the receiving end of few direct investments by foreign TNCs. Most large German companies acted like their counterparts in the majority of the OECD
countries: they flocked to open new manufacturing subsidiaries in the
United States. The farther the ranking of the United States slipped down
the tabulated scales, the longer was the line of foreign corporations eager
to invest there. There were of course a number of straight economic
causes to explain this, but towering above them all was a non-economic
stimulus: the United States was seen as the 'last bastion of secure capitalism.' The United States became attractive by default and in this fashion helped to activate the growth of (non-U.S.) TNCs.

One Swedish multi confessed diffidently why it had built a plant in
the United States. There were no import restrictions and it was in fact
cheaper to produce at home than in the newly created manufacturing
subsidiary in North America. Yet the board was apprehensive that the
Soviet Union might one day advance into Europe and occupy Sweden.
If this were to occur, supplies to the corporation's customers in the non-
Communist world might then be cut off. Even worse, there could be
problems in servicing machinery and supplying spare parts. This strange
motivation set in motion the establishment of a U.S. subsidiary. The
extra costs ensuing from manufacturing in the United States were treated
by the board of this MNC as a political insurance premium (123).

12

AN INTERNECINE FRATERNITY

> The other oil companies . . . went into paroxysms of rage, claiming
> that I had sold them out and betrayed them. . . . My answer . . . is
> simple: I survived, they didn't. . . . I had to protect the investment
> of our shareholders.
>
> Armand Hammer, *president of OXY*

A bright executive of BINCO had an original idea to counter the AFL-
CIO attacks that charged MNCs with exporting U.S. jobs by setting up
foreign plants. He persuaded a number of corporations to finance the
gathering of data to substantiate the thesis that the more a multi expands
abroad, the more people it employs additionally at home. The results
were published in glossy volumes which, notwithstanding their tendentious contents, pleased the sponsors and ingenuous readers. Orville
Freeman, not satisfied with BINCO's commercial success, recited the
tale on the employment record of U.S. MNCs in his testimony before a
congressional committee. Senator Ribicoff was impressed so favorably
with these findings that he asked Freeman whether the figures could
be examined by outsiders and "be made part of the [committee's] record." This request was turned down because, it was explained to the

senator, the information had been supplied on a confidential basis and each corporate respondent to BINCO's questionnaire would have to give his permission. Freeman envisaged a sound reason why individual corporations would not want to divulge their data.

They do have some problems, particularly in other countries where they operate, where they are sometimes accused, you see, of not contributing to the well-being of the country where they operate and merely contributing to the well-being of the United States. So as of now, the figures are confidential (50).

This episode helps to negate the view that MNCs, irrespective of their national domicile, belong to one closely-knit international brotherhood. In reality U.S. multis have often flourished at the expense of their foreign confreres. Neither are U.S. multis members of a warm-hearted, amiable U.S. fraternity—there is no love lost between them when their commercial interests clash. Freeman unintentionally revealed something about the dilemma faced by the PR tacticians of TNCs. When a U.S.-based corporation ceases to export to, say, Australia because it has opened a manufacturing subsidiary there, who benefits in terms of employment? In the United States the public is told that U.S. labor is the beneficiary, while in the host country the local unions are told that they are reaping the advantage. In a very few situations both assertions are true, but in the majority of cases this is clearly not so.

Not only do TNCs have no collective targets (or ideals), they also do not agree among themselves on how to fight their common enemies. When the UN arranged hearings before the Group of Eminent Persons to advise on the mechanics of regulating the conduct of TNCs, the potential victims were unable to organize a united front. Some thought it expedient to give evidence and fulminate against UN controls; many preferred to boycott the hearings. Others chose to flatter the anti-multi fanatics in the Group of Eminent Persons by cooperating and voluntarily putting their corporate heads in a noose. There is little, if anything, that binds the world's TNCs. Fratricide in the multi brotherhood occurs on two levels: Stop your rival from exporting to a foreign market that you already supply! Stop your rival from constructing a factory that would compete with your manufacturing subsidiary in the host country!

FREE TRADE

"Transnationals have a vested interest in the removal of trade barriers. . . . Anything which reduces friction in the movement of resources from territory to territory should be to the benefit of transnationals," Michael Shanks asserted in *The Times* of London. Though Shanks was not a blind admirer of multis, he—as many others—subscribed to the fallacious belief that TNCs champion Adam Smith's doctrine on free trade. Some years ago a conference of European multis in Brussels listened to barbed attacks on the nation–state by spokesmen of global Swedish companies. They implied that MNCs with head offices in Sweden were more internationally minded than those from other European countries. The anticlimax came to pass when a Swedish participant stood up and said in perfect English: "My corporation is wholeheartedly in favour of free trade except in relation to the unfair export of Japanese ballbearings." He came from Goeteborg. I was present and still nurse today my astonishment that no one had burst out laughing. Was it because the other multis present were equally guilty of incongruous conduct? For decades Siemens and Philips have publicly advocated free trade. Yet they barefacedly formulated demands to restrict the European sales of their U.S. competitor IBM. They have expressed disappointment that the EC taxpayers made only a small subsidy available to EC-based computer firms "to help fight IBM." Monsanto and Du Pont were the sworn enemies of U.S. protectionism, except when they pressured Washington to erect barriers against certain textile imports into the United States. Britain's ICI thinks it wicked that international trade should be distorted by the payment of overt or covert state subsidies to manufacturers. ICI is clearly on the side of the angels, except when its chairman entreated the British government to subsidize the fuel bill of factories located in Britain so that, with consequently lowered production costs, British chemical MNCs could compete more efficiently in world markets.

The Japanese concede privately that the crown of free trade hypocrisy belongs to them. Before establishing manufacturing subsidiaries abroad, the growth of many large Japanese corporations depended heavily on exports. For this reason the representatives of incipient Japanese TNCs became such vocal advocates of Adam Smith's philosophy, which promises bliss on earth after the removal of all trade barriers. How did the captains of Japan's mammoth corporations interpret free trade? There ought to be no restrictions on the sale of Japanese goods in foreign countries while, at the same time, the authorities in Tokyo will see to it that—legally or not—few foreign-made goods are marketed in Japan. If this disposition has changed progressively since the mid–1970s, it is in part due to the retaliatory measures adopted by those developed and developing economies that chose to act in restraint of Japanese exports. Many free traders in the OECD have pointed to the import restrictions prevailing in Japan to justify the imposition of special punitive limitations on the import of Japanese goods. Japan's international corporations have let it be known that they now favor the inflow of goods into Japan, particularly from those economies that do not discriminate against Japanese exports. Employing PR agencies, Sony has publicized its willingness to market foreign-made goods in Japan through its domestic network. The press officers of Mitsui have impressed upon Western cynics that its joint venture with Tokyo's largest department store, Mis-koshi, is aimed at bringing in foreign merchandise. When Japan's prime minister called on Margaret Thatcher in 1984, he was taken aback because his countrymen were reproached for not importing enough. His spokes-man disclosed the startling news that the reaction of the visiting premier had been to instruct his son to buy a Burberry raincoat! Such distasteful gimmicks were not considered funny and certainly did not enhance Japan's prestige. When the yen soared in the late 1980s and the Japanese balance of payments recorded a gigantic surplus on current account, Japanese MNCs continued to indulge in sentimental talk on the merits of free trade. Yet the authorities in Tokyo still obstructed the import of some goods that competed with local products. A favorite excuse was the need for 'safety.' For that spurious reason difficulties were placed in the way of, for example, foreign ski equipment; this was deemed to be dangerous for Japanese consumers because Japanese "snow is par-ticularly wet."

When an MNC supplies a given national market or region with goods manufactured in the parent's factories, it resents the protectionists who wish to impede such imports. Once, however, exports cease because a manufacturing subsidiary has been established in that national market or region, the MNC's enthusiasm for free trade is on the wane. There are numerous instances from many countries to demonstrate that the managements of such new subsidiaries—sometimes with the blessing of their head office—join local manufacturers in clamoring for import restrictions. This was blatantly so in Canada, where the subsidiaries of U.S. parents generally supported a high-tariff policy that was directed at manufacturers in the United States. According to the U.S. trade jour-nal *Electronic News,* "multinational companies, supposedly avid free trad-ers, often become protectionists overseas where they have plants flourishing behind foreign trade barriers." Some perverse news ema-nated in 1975 from GM's Australian subsidiary. Its chiefs had persuaded the authorities to let them import duty-free components from Japan to ensure that their vehicles would remain competitive and that GM "could thus avoid firing its Australian car workers." At the same time GM goaded the Australian government into fixing tight import quotas for automobiles manufactured in Japan (132).

DOWN WITH DIRECT INVESTORS!

The well-wishers of TNCs say of them that they espouse free trade and the right to make direct cross-border investments. The following chapters will illustrate that investments overseas are being circumscribed in home countries and challenged by hostile elements in host countries.

But there are also other enemies! MNCs with head offices in country A show virulent animosity to competing foreign MNCs that seek to open a manufacturing subsidiary, or take over an existing producer, in country A. (The MNCs of country A of course want to retain their own right to establish subsidiaries abroad.) The most ridiculous—and some would say nauseating—resistance to direct investments stems from TNCs which, having already fought their way into a given host country, instruct their established subsidiary to join with indigenous producers to frustrate the entry of other foreign manufacturers.

ICI laid plans for a mega-investment in Wilhelmshaven. The angry trade association of German producers of synthetic materials, dominated by three gigantic TNCs—BASF, Bayer, and Hoechst—joined with the apposite union, IG Chemie, in lobbying Bonn to stop the threatened invasion by a British competitor. When three UK chemical producers—ICI, BP, and Shell—heard that a foreign MNC, Dow, intended to invest in a mammoth ethylene Scotish venture, they attempted to persuade the authorities in London that the project of this alien corporation ought to be foiled. In yet another example, the French government was pleased when Nissan asked for permission to make a direct investment in France. Strong opposition, however, was organized against the intended establishment of a Nissan subsidiary, designated to produce car radios. The campaign was not waged by French MNCs but by the French subsidiaries of foreign MNCs, Bosch of Germany and Philips of Holland.

A U.S. multi is not in violation of U.S. antitrust laws if it pays bribes abroad for the purpose of furthering its foreign interests at the expense of a non-U.S. competitor. Payoffs to prevent another U.S. company from obtaining a share of the market are, however, deemed to be an unfair method of competition within the purview of the Federal Trade Commission Act (189). Despite all the talk of the brotherhood of multis (and of U.S. multis in particular), details of several such cases have been described. Bribery is not the only weapon wielded by multis to prevent a competing TNC from putting into effect direct manufacturing investments. In 1989 Coca-Cola let it be known that it was willing to return to India. Its projected operations met with opposition in some official quarters. Indian and Western press reports are agreed that the existing subsidiary of Pepsico is actively fighting the plans of its global rival to regain access to the Indian market.

General Foods already had an important subsidiary in England when it proposed to bid for Rowntree, a UK chocolate MNC headquartered in the ancient town of York. The British government did not dislike the idea and the suggested terms were such that a majority of the institutional and personal shareholders would gladly have accepted the bid. The board of directors did not like being taken over but, being at the helm of a British-based international company, could not personally rally the troops behind a xenophobic flag. This ignoble mission was performed by three charitable trusts, established by the Quaker founders of the target company, which owned 56 percent of the total equity. The trustees turned down the General Foods proposition, implying that whatever the financial value of the bid, they would reject it because of "non-financial considerations." Translated into English, this meant that, on principle, they ruled out a U.S. company. The charities had their way and the board then set about enhancing the multinational spread of Rowntree, buying up companies in several countries. Multis are not always consistent in their xenophobia. In any case, Rowntree's management thought that an English multi was particularly suited to control subsidiaries in the United States. Consequently, a number of such acquisitions were made, culminating in a successful $230 million bid in 1986 for the Missouri-based Sunmark company.

If ever a corporate story can shed light on the humbug of the multi brotherhood, it is that relating to Hitachi. This Japanese TNC had the impudence in 1977 to lay the foundation for a small assembly plant in Britain, an investment of a mere £5 million to build color television sets. Those were the days when unsavory campaigns in the West were in full swing against embryonic Japanese multis. A British television channel screened a program, ostensibly to document the alleged anti-Japanese sentiments of U.S. consumers. There were flashes of Americans wearing T-shirts with the motto: "Sony—from the people who gave you Pearl Harbor." (It was later admitted that as the producers could not actually find such consumers, shirts were especially prepared with this offensive phrase and two Americans volunteered to be photographed wearing them.) The UK anti-Hitachi movement was directed by gentlemen. It was conducted under the aegis of a trade association. Five of its prominent member-firms were MNCs: the indigenous GEC, Rank, Thorn, and the British manufacturing subsidiaries of ITT and Philips. The trade union of the electricians was enlisted and, if rumors are to be believed, played a not insignificant role in making Hitachi turn back. Lord Thorneycroft, the head of the trade association, had been a chancellor of the exchequer and at the time was chairman of the Conservative party. Thorneycroft successfully challenged the right of foreign corporations to establish manufacturing subsidiaries on British soil. He intervened so vehemently because he was also the chairman of the British subsidiary of the foreign MNC Philips. This company had published its decisive views on these matters. It advocated free trade but justified selective discrimination to halt imports. It opposed the setting up of a factory, if the foreign party was suspected of engaging in unreasonable trade practices. Philips, a foreign company that itself had climbed over the walls surrounding Britain and was manufacturing there in several plants, delivered a sermon to the British government: "Sadly, there are also examples of foreign investments in UK industry being damaging to the economy and to the existing UK industry's future" (162). Hitachi only set into motion its UK initiative after the British authorities had said explicitly that the projected venture was very welcome. When the five multis forced Hitachi to retreat, Prime Minister Callaghan repeated that he would have liked this Japanese project to proceed but was powerless against the mighty lobby of an influential trade association. There is a postscript. While not very pertinent, it is at least piquant. Almost a year to the day after the Japanese TNC was chased away, one of the five multis broke rank and asked Hitachi to join in a 50:50 venture to produce television sets in Wales. GEC it was! Having failed in this field, GEC was now prepared to pay Hitachi to benefit from its superior production know-how and technology. The two multis combined forces and manufactured in one of GEC's underused factories. Sixty-three months later this joint venture folded because it had satisfied neither of the two partners. GEC sold its 50 percent stake to Hitachi which thus, circuitously, became the owner of a wholly-owned manufacturing facility in Wales (131).

Direct investors headquartered in the United States, Australia, and South Africa have not always been greeted with a hearty handshake in the EC but they have certainly had to endure less bloodymindedness and pinpricking than Japanese multis. European (continental and British) TNCs used to be afraid of Japanese-sourced imports; the intention of many Japanese industrialists to establish manufacturing subsidiaries within the EC gripped them with more fear. The apprehensive CEOs of European MNCs could not very well revive the previous populist animosity against the yellow peril. But the governments of some member-states of the EC, and the Commission in Brussels, succumbed to corporate demands that Japanese international companies be singled out for special treatment. In particular, the "local contents" rules were interpreted more harshly than in relation to many non-EC multis. In 1981 Nissan announced that it would build a plant in the UK; the output would embody 60 percent (and ultimately up to 80 percent) of EC-generated value-added. Nissan's British assembly lines turned out the first cars in 1986, signalling the end of six years of agitation and united lobbying by the EC-based automobile TNCs, BL, Fiat, Peugeot, Renault, and Volkswagen. It was not for lack of trying that they had failed to put skids under the biggest direct Japanese investment in Europe. In Britain the anti-Nissan campaign was notably unseemly because more than 80 percent of all UK-produced automobiles were then manufactured or assembled in plants owned by continental European and U.S. TNCs. The most consistent and vocal opponent of the Nissan venture was Ford, which itself was a foreign corporate guest in the EC. Ford led the fight—backed by all sorts of threats—to stop Nissan competing with other foreign TNCs behind the tariff walls of the EC.

SCABS

The behavior of TNCs has at times been "downright illegal or morally repugnant with easily uncovered shenanigans backfiring and soiling the entire landscape of international business" (88). True or not—why are the misdeeds of individual large corporations discovered more frequently than the bad things done by smaller companies? There are several explanations. One of them has to do with the inclination of individual MNCs, eager to grab business from their competitors, to denounce other MNCs to host governments. In India a minister once asserted that a U.S. aircraft manufacturer had forwarded to him the photostat of a letter, allegedly sent by a competing company, which contained the offer of a bribe to an Indian official. The Damascus Boycott Office has for decades maintained files on Jewish firms and Zionist sympathizers; ordinarily, suspect companies are refused permission to invest in, or sell to, the participating Arab member-states and placed on the official boycott register. Where does Damascus obtain its information? Perhaps one day the files will reveal the truth or some official may publish his memoirs. It will then come to light that to eliminate competitors in the Middle East, TNCs have informed against other members of their brotherhood for trading surreptitiously with the Israeli enemy! Sometimes the information is deliberately false but in any case the Damascus Boycott Office is not sent an official letter from the chairman of the accusing corporation—there are more subtle ways.

When host countries pursue extreme anti-multi policies, they rarely commence by driving out all foreign corporations at one stroke. More likely they will focus on one firm, expelling it or confiscating its assets. There is enough historical evidence to prove that it is not usual for the other corporate guests to participate in fraternal resistance; in some cases they have actually been delighted to see a competitor removed from the scene. Astute host governments have learned that solidarity is not a concept dear to TNCs. They are therefore not worried even when a united front of affected multis has been formed. Two instances, from Libya and Chile, will exemplify this.

The powerful constellation of the Seven Sisters, the mightiest of the oil TNCs, has been blackened by investigative journalists. In theory the Seven Sisters are agreed that they must fight together against the common enemy, the host countries where the oil is extracted, and they have pledged to support one another loyally. Armand Hammer, the enigmatic chief of Occidental Petroleum (OXY), has contributed to the demise of this cosy, elitist club. Hammer's international oil explorations have had a chequered history. His assets in Venezuela were expropriated without compensation after accusations of bribery, which OXY denies (130). When the Peruvians confiscated the property of Standard Oil in New Jersey, the victimized oil multi was unable to dissuade other U.S. companies from investing in that country. Only days after the initial seizure, OXY went so far as to offer to help Peru develop the expropriated properties. But it was in Libya that the Seven Sisters suffered most grievously from Hammer's enterprise. Within months of Qadhafi coming to power all the oil producers were told to pay greatly increased royalties. In unison, they refused. OXY, the weakest oil company, was the first to be picked on. OXY was told it would be driven out if it remained faithful to the united front. Hammer went to see ESSO and averred that he would remain loyal if in turn the big TNCs would protect him. They would not, whereupon OXY paid up. One oil producer after another followed suit. Libya was the first domino to fall and soon other oil-producing host countries had learned how to squeeze more money out of the Seven Sisters. One year after Quadhafi's demands had been met, Libya set a new ultimatum. This induced 23 oil producers to meet secretly in New York to agree on a joint strategy. Once again the oil multis swore to keep their nerves and to aid any company that was harassed selectively by the host country. Their pathetic declaration assumed that united they were strong while the LDC Libya was weak. But once again the Libyans won—and laid the foundations for subsequent victories by other LDCs. OXY agreed to the new, enhanced demands and managed to survive. Others too paid up ultimately but had to accept more onerous terms. The more stubborn multis were nationalized outright. Hammer knew that they called him a scab, but he did not seem to mind. After all, the Seven Sisters were not faithful to one another.

In the days when it was led by the dynamic Harold Geneen, ITT was the bête noire of the U.S. TNCs. This global corporation has been immortalized as the symbol of wickedness. Perhaps its most publicized misdeed was its attempt in Chile to prevent Allende from coming to power. ITT money was spent to no avail. After the Marxist revolutionaries had assumed power, Geneen contacted several TNCs with subsidiaries in Chile to plan a joint campaign that would frustrate the expropriation of their assets. ITT wanted U.S. corporations to disrupt the Chilean economy, hoping that this would encourage the military to overthrow Allende. Internal ITT documents name several U.S. TNCs and banks, in New York and California, that were approached repeatedly but would not cooperate with ITT. When various corporations were later called to give evidence before a congressional committee, they confirmed the ITT approach but also affirmed their own innocence— ITT had failed in its efforts to recruit them.

Once Allende was firmly in the saddle and the confiscation of the assets of the large U.S. multis was in the offing, an unofficial common front came into being with Washington's blessing. All the affected U.S. multis agreed to resist Allende jointly, though not by violent means. ITT was of course one of the parties that promised not to have any private dealings with the Chilean government. This infamous multi had had much experience in dealing with Latin American regimes that coveted the properties of foreign corporations and Geneen had no compunction about supping with the devil. Secret meetings were arranged with the top men of the Marxist government and a compromise was discussed that would have safeguarded ITT's continued presence in Chile. The new administration had a paramount commercial interest to make concessions to ITT which it did not find necessary to offer to other, less vital, U.S. multis. ITT, the arch-enemy of Allende, was willing to betray the other U.S. TNCs and to frustrate Washington's efforts to put pressure on Chile through the united efforts of all corporations concerned. According to Sampson, ITT's duplicity almost bore fruit: Allende personally favored the draft arrangement but was overruled by the ultra-leftists in his government (133). In the context of this chapter, ITT's underhanded interventions in the politics of a host country (which had seized forcibly one of its subsidiaries) are perhaps less remarkable than the intended double-crossing of the other U.S. TNCs.

13

THE CLAY FEET OF THE CORPORATE DINOSAURS

> ICI is so big and so decentralized. I've long believed the macho chairman, who decides everything, is rubbish. So therefore there are only a few things you can influence.
>
> Denys Henderson, *chairman of ICI*

There are textbooks that explain why corporations can make two plus two equal five. Maybe there are such cases. However, the structure and global dispersion of most multis give rise to countervailing factors that trigger off a (relative) drop in the profitability: $2 + 2 = 3$.

Large corporations are fragile.

Large multiproduct corporations are more fragile.

Large multiproduct multinational corporations are the most fragile.

Some of the internal clashes that weaken the profit-making capacity of TNCs are discussed in this chapter: autonomous product divisions often destroy the overall loyalty of decision-makers to the corporation; there is a sharp conflict between exporting and manufacturing abroad; parent companies frequently find it difficult to overcome the harmful aspirations to self-rule on the part of national subsidiaries; the global profitability of a given multi may be seriously damaged when those in charge of production in country A scheme to succeed at the expense of their colleagues in country B.

THE INTERNATIONAL DIVISION

When a national business, that is, a company manufacturing in one country only, takes an interest in overseas markets and develops exports on a large scale, it will most likely set up an export division. In time this may become an international division, especially if manufacturing subsidiaries are established abroad. GM's Overseas Operating Division was in charge of manufacturing, assembling, and warehousing outside North America *and* of exports from the home country (105). IBM had a similar structure: all its foreign interests were concentrated in the World Trade Corporation. No love was lost between the stewards of the domestic and the overseas activities. Initially, the controllers of the two sectors were headquartered together in Manhattan. To accentuate the differences, the offices of the former were moved to Armonk while the latter stayed behind in New York City. A decade later, World Trade was also transferred to Armonk, accommodated in a specially constructed W-shaped building. At first, the accounts of IBM's domestic and foreign activities were kept on a separate basis; they were consolidated only in 1963.

There are those who maintain that the organizational separation of domestic and non-domestic affairs is part and parcel of a corporate philosophy that regards activities outside the home country as being of secondary importance. Though often true, this is not always the explanation. In a few instances political considerations are determinant. Prescient Philips of Eindhoven created a trust before 1939 to which it transferred the assets of a large number of its subsidiaries on the American continent and in the British Commonwealth. The board envisaged that the Germans might occupy the Netherlands. If the foreign subsidiaries were held directly by the parent company, the invaders would have the legal authority to control them. This subterfuge, to own the foreign subsidiaries through the medium of a trust, proved successful (134). In 1948 the board of the British TNC Metal Box initiated the transfer of most of its foreign corporate assets to an intermediary body, a holding company named Metal Box Overseas (135). The directors had been apprised of the intention of the ruling Labour party to nationalize Metal Box. They hoped that if that calamity were to occur, the damage would be limited because only the UK assets were then liable to be nationalized while the foreign assets in Metal Box Overseas would be spared. Actually, the parent company of Metal Box was never nationalized. However, several of the putatively safe subsidiaries in various parts of the former empire were effectively expropriated: Metal Box's London head office learned to give up 'voluntarily' the ownership and/or control of established subsidiaries in a number of LDCs.

Together with the majority of U.S. multis, GM and IBM have retained their dichotomous corporate structure through the 1980s. (Just as British-based multis often treat the Republic of Ireland as part of their domestic activities, so U.S.-based multis ordinarily exclude Canada—and sometimes even Mexico—from the orbit of their international divisions.) A formidable stumbling-block is erected when a bureaucratic buffer is interposed between the foreign subsidiaries and the TNC's top decision-makers. While the bosses of the various domestic sections have direct access to the CEO, the managers of the foreign subsidiaries have to contact him through the international division. During the annual global carve-up of finance for expansion, a foreign subsidiary may not be able to present its own case directly but may have to rely on the head of the international division to plead on its behalf. The influence of foreign subsidiaries is weakened further when the international division is subdivided into regional organizations, each with its own head office. This is usually, but not always, located within the geographic bailiwick. (Multis of different nationalities have placed their Latin American regional offices in New York and Miami.) Having regional offices used to be justified on the ground that the national subsidiaries within a given region have vital interests in common. In practice they have augmented ill will in so far as they constitute an additional hurdle, barring the direct access of foreign subsidiaries to the TNC's head office. The chiefs of large subsidiaries have always been irritated because they had to report via the international division. They become even angrier when the formation of regional offices extend their line of communication. In an age of the jet airplane and electronic mail, regional organizations are on the decline and many are being disbanded.

The grandmother approach, however, is still being pursued. This arouses resentment because the managers of the foreign national operations concerned are made to feel very remote from the corporation's decision-makers. Grandmother Ford in Detroit once asked one of her daughters, the Canadian subsidiary, to own the shares of Ford's Australian company, which was thus treated as a granddaughter (93). On a larger scale, American Home Products of New York arranged for a UK subsidiary, Prestige Products, to own a host of granddaughters, subsidiaries in Europe, Australasia, and South Africa. The most extreme instance of a grandmother arrangement is that operated by the Danish corporation Sophus Behrendsen, which used its British, majority-owned subsidiary Rentokill to build a multinational empire in five continents—from Australia to Uganda, from Cyprus to the United States. Rentokill's numerous daughters, that is, Behrendsen's granddaughters, are of course all controlled, albeit circuitously, by Copenhagen. Ironically, the British subsidiary set up also a wholly-owned subsidiary, A/S Rentokill of Denmark, in the home country! Ninety-five percent of the total assets, beneficially owned by the Danish TNC, were registered in the name of Rentokill and her daughters. Nowadays, greatgranddaughters are in vogue. In 1986 the South African TNC Barlow Rand sought to acquire an American check-printing company, Interchecks. Probably on grounds of political expediency, Interchecks became a greatgranddaughter. Its equity was bought by Princeton Babbington, the U.S. subsidiary of Liverpool-based Bibby, which was a UK subsidiary of Barlow Rand.

A very persuasive argument against the concept of the international division relates to the second-class status of the executives within this fortress. Take a native of Finland, who excels in his work in the Finnish subsidiary and deserves to be promoted. As a third-country national he could be moved to top positions in, say, the Argentine and French subsidiaries. If he is truly brilliant, the TNC may bestow upon him the accolade of a job at the head office of the international division. Its supremo is ordinarily a national from the TNC's home country, but if our Finnish friend is as talented as IBM's French-born Jacques Maisonrouge, he could rise to the summit and head the international division. In a corporation, which compartmentalizes strictly domestic and foreign activities, that must be the end of the line for him.

Despite the formidable caveats above, the institutional set-up of the international division has played a positive role in the historical evolution of the modern TNC. Its executives were charged with examining dispassionately the markets outside the home country, to weigh up whether these were served best by exports or manufacturing subsidiaries. As was noted, the top echelon of IBM encouraged its domestic and international activities to be controlled by competing head offices and at one stage thought it helpful if they were located in different towns. Other TNCs have arrived at similar conclusions, though few went so far as Cummins Engine of Columbus, Indiana, which in 1970 moved its head office, responsible for most of its foreign facilities, out of the United States. The London-based international division—under the command of sound U.S. executives—was to supervise production in eight countries (including plants in Japan, Mexico, and Australia, some of which were located nearer to the parent's head office than to London); sales and servicing representations in 129 countries; a joint venture in India; a licensing agreement with Krupp; and more. Cummins was planning to build a factory in England to produce diesel engines and it intended to export a good proportion of the output to North America.

There are good reasons for having an international division with overriding authority. Those in charge of manufacturing in the home country, self-servingly do not favor manufacturing abroad. They are fanatic advocates of exporting—if necessary, at a loss. Each foreign project needs to be examined on its merits. Will the gains from producing abroad exceed the ensuing losses caused by foregone exports? When the international division judges the answer to be in the affirmative, it must have powers to slap down those executives in the corporation whose horizon is confined to manufacturing at home. Opening up manufacturing facilities abroad will almost certainly curtail domestic production destined for exports. Sometimes the evolution of foreign subsidiaries entails the total closure of production lines at home because the domestic market is to be supplied from the new factories abroad. Would executives with responsibility for domestic operations take such drastic decisions (involving redundancies in the home country) with the same certitude that one could expect from an independent international division?

THE PRODUCT MODEL

Perlmutter, BINCO, Charles Levinson (by implication) and other adulators of the geocentric corporation have regarded the notion of the international division as anathema. They would have it that a truly multinational firm ought not countenance the nationalist attitude of partitioning the global economy into the home country plus the rest of the world. Most TNCs have not responded to this ideological message and changed their company structure accordingly. If, nevertheless, the all-embracing international division is being abandoned by certain multis, this is because of two pragmatic, non-ideological factors: the proportional decline of the home market and the proliferation of multiproduct MNCs. Three American multis—Kellogg, Kraft, and Nabisco—have obstinately refused to follow Perlmutter's exhortations to dissolve their international division; they thought it expedient to continue in the old way because their main business was transacted in the United States. Across the ocean, in the Netherlands and Switzerland, food multis treat the world as one market. No administrative curtain separates sales and manufacturing in the home country from operations in the rest of the world. Three percent of Nestle's total sales are made in Switzerland. A globally integrated structure is clearly suitable for multis domiciled in small economies.

A completely unrelated predicament has compelled numerous TNCs, even those with domestic sales accounting for a majority of their total sales, to give up the ordinary international division. As large corporations diversify—sometimes into unrelated branches—products and not geography determine the pattern of the new corporate organization charts. A French multi, a worldwide manufacturer of margarine and socks, is likely to have two subsidiaries in, say, Canada. Both have the same parent and generate dividends for the same set of shareholders but, despite their consanguinity, there is not much they have in common in producing and marketing their disparate output. In a one-product MNC, the international division acts as a postbox to link the managers and technicians of the domestic and foreign plants. The larger the number of foreign subsidiaries, and the greater the number of product groups, the clumsier are the workings of the international division. If technology is to flow between the home country and the foreign subsidiaries, it makes sense to encourage direct and speedy cross-border communications, especially between the managers and technicians of the same industrial branch. This requirement frequently brings into being several head offices within the sphere of the TNC's headquarters, each of which supervises the domestic and foreign activities of product groups.

Norton's company biographer (87) relates that the company's board of directors debated whether they should follow the example of other MNCs and abandon their international division. They decided that so long as Norton remained basically a one-product corporation (abrasives), they would not change. On the other hand, a TNC like ITT—with interests in cosmetics, hotels, insurance, defense technology, telecommunications, natural resources, electronic components, and a myriad of other things—could not possibly have operated with one international division. Friends and foes have described ITT as one mighty multi but in practice it was but a framework within which co-existed a series of smaller-sized multis. Similarly, RCA remodelled its corporation in 1970 by establishing 17 autonomous product groups, each of which had global responsibilities (134). The American TNC United Shoe Machinery (USM) had once been a one-product company but by the end of the 1960s less than 30 percent of its worldwide output was connected with the specialized equipment implied by its name. Before it carried out its radical reorganization, USM had some 100 subsidiaries and affiliates, fabricating a variety of products. Plant managers abroad complained of long and unwieldy lines of communication. USM not only adopted the concept of independent product division, but actually moved the head offices of two newly created mini-multis out of the United States. The headquarters of the (global) Bostic Chemical Group was positioned in Switzerland. The headquarters of the fastener division, located in England, ruled over 12 subsidiaries (in this product line) which were scattered across Asia, Europe, and the United States. Some companies—3M was one of them—relished the demise of the comprehensive international division and actually encouraged competition between the product divisions.

While the CEOs of many TNCs regretted it, they conceded that perforce a great deal of freedom of action had to be given to the new breed of mini-multis. They also recognized that the advent of product divisions made it pointless—except perhaps for decorative purposes—to maintain offices in foreign countries or regions that coordinated all the activities of the TNC. Some MNCs, however, sought to have their cake and eat it. When several disparate manufacturing facilities were functioning within one foreign country (or region), their managers were expected to manifest a dual loyalty: to the head offices of the respective product division, and to the chiefs of the national or regional organization who insisted on having a decisive say as geographical controllers. The result was a criss-crossed grid structure that looked nice on paper. In practice this was often ignored but, if adhered to, impeded the smooth running of the complex global corporation. Some MNCs went so far as to lay down rules that obliged subsidiary A, belonging to one product division, to buy from subsidiary B which was within the orbit of another product division. Such rules could be innocuous or inherently dangerous. Not much harm was done when ITT bullied the executives of all its divisions to stay at Sheraton hotels, but when the manager of plant A had to buy inputs at inflated prices from plant B, resentment and factional in-fighting ensued.

Having dismantled the welded structure of their TNC, granting effective independence to product divisions, the bosses in the top echelon of the home country then labored to display a (contrived) unified face to the world. To drive home that point, scores of mega-corporations in the 1980s placed large sums of money at the disposal of image-building PR agencies; the funds were not to be spent extolling the merits of the clients' merchandise.

In 1949 ICI debated at the highest corporate level the possible division of the corporation into several independent companies, because "if we are not careful . . . ICI will grow too big to be manageable" (107). It was not to be. Yet 40 years later this has in fact happened and ICI is today a corporate vehicle that oversees a series of international businesses. This became so obvious that it was thought necessary to spend money hiring external specialists who could devise a PR campaign that would highlight the group's corporate identity. The chairman, Denys Henderson, was said to be "aware of the need to present a more coherent and understandable image to the world." Whether indeed such a "need" existed is a moot issue. However, the directors of ICI were determined that their company should be perceived as one distinct global corporation, in a class by itself and with a soul of its own.

I was slightly involved in two corporate communications programs, both orchestrated by U.S. TNCs. The first was initiated by a mammoth organization known by a three-letter acronym. A PR adviser had discovered that the public and most of the customers did not know what the acronym stood for. Even more depressing was the ignorance of the majority of the employees. This seemingly disgraceful plight was particularly rampant in the host countries. The corporation's London office was manned by a solitary executive who savored this sinecure to the full. He sent occasional reports about the British Isles to the TNC's head offices but had no say in the running of the nine UK subsidiaries, each of which reported to the head office of its product division. The ambitious PR adviser made the London representative call a meeting of 17 managers from these subsidiaries. They were then addressed—and later dined and wined—by the top brass that had flown in from the United States. The essential message was: "You are all part of one family." A newly designed logo was exhibited and the acronym of the TNC was decoded. Since then no further collective meetings of representatives from the nine UK manufacturing subsidiaries have taken place.

A few months later I participated at a similar, but more elaborate and expensive, gathering in Spain. This was organized by a corporation that had diversified in an unplanned manner, engendering a medley of unconnected businesses. Over the years the parent had bought various European companies with manufacturing facilities for 21 different product groups. As a matter of policy the subsidiaries had retained the original appellation of the acquired companies. Only one of the 21 subsidiaries bore the name of the parent which was quoted on New York's Big Board. Many of the European participants did not know one another. Prior to this convention a few were even unaware that the parent owned some of the companies represented. I mentioned this to the chairman of the TNC who, together with other directors, had come to the celebration. He replied in a playful mood:

Of course all the people here will enjoy your lecture on the 'World Economy in 1990.' My colleagues and I will also be making speeches. But surely you are not under the illusion that this is the purpose of the exercise. The day-by-day problems of our 21 European subsidiaries have few features in common, which is why we have not instituted a proper regional headquarter. It is therefore the more urgent that we should have such a get-together. Would it really matter if our managers were to spend the whole time here drinking in one another's company? At work they all operate under different names but we frantically want them to feel they really belong to the same global outfit.

MANAGERIAL DOGFIGHTS

In 1974–77 disclosures, brought to light by several investigating committees in Washington, named the CEOs of a number of U.S.-based multis who had initiated, approved, and/or personally carried out acts of deception, corruption, and fraud (176). The economic and moral aspects of their misdeeds were highlighted in sensationalist tabloids. Less attention was focused on the baffling puzzle of why these rich and powerful men chose to violate the law. It became apparent that the majority had been motivated by the lust for corporate power rather than by straight material self-interest. The individuals expected to receive no, or only derisorily small, financial rewards for themselves. With incredulity one attempted to understand what had made a high-ranking director, the legal executive of a famous oil company, launder his corporation's money and in person carry the dirty funds across national borders without aiming to gain a single cent for himself. The self-evident conclusion pointed to a perplexing state of affairs: some top executives of mammoth companies were ready to execute external crimes—cheating tax authorities, bribing politicians, evading exchange controls—in order to aggrandize and enrich their employers.

Very little publicity has been given to the internal deceptions practiced in large TNCs by the heads of departments, controllers of product divisions, and managers of subsidiaries. These submit to the global head office tendentious, mendacious, and sometimes falsified data relating to their domains. They lie about sales and present fanciful profit projections so that, during the annual planning deliberations, disproportionately more resources are allotted to R&D, investments, acquisitions, and so on in their realms. Armed with knives and intrigue in their hearts, successful executives must destroy their rivals within the corporation to grab the most succulent plums from the global budget.

Simpletons believe that the directors of GM are constantly plotting to outshine Ford and Nissan. In real life the acrimonious conflicts within GM devour more time and energy of the corporation's decision-makers than the open competitive struggle with Ford and Nissan. The most bitter adversarial clashes have in the past been those between the Chevrolet and the Pontiac divisions. GM's international division is constantly scheming to increase the corporation's share of the European market. Yet the executives of Vauxhall and Opel (the British and German subsidiaries) do not always cooperate in promoting GM because they are too busy fighting one another. A pivotal aim of this book is to debunk the legend that multis are strong, well-coordinated giants—frequently, they are weak corporate vehicles. Behind the PR facade the vanity and personal ambitions of the managerial elites play a significant, albeit underreported, role. The story of Pepsico illustrates this theme.

Starting in 1978 irregularities occurred in a few subsidiaries of Pepsico (137). These were uncovered only at the end of 1982 when they were found to be very serious. The company announced that it had become necessary to restate its reported earnings and, in consequence, reduce its previously stated net global income by more than $92 million, equal to 6.6 percent. In addition, special audits made it incumbent to write down the value of the net assets of the foreign bottling plants by almost $80 million. The accounting irregularities of the Mexican and Philippine operations were cloaked by the collusive commission of assorted deceptions. Elaborate and sophisticated schemes were concocted to overstate the profits of these subsidiaries. The responsible managers inflated the receivables, failed to recognize bad debts and obsolete inventories, and deferred the recording of legitimate expenses. Layers of false documents were prepared to cover up these falsifications and hoodwink the financial controllers of the parent. When the chairman disclosed all this to the stockholders, he was concerned primarily to find an answer to the question: "What financial controls were we lacking?" He was stunned and agonized over the fact that individuals, some of whom he had known personally, had been guilty of "a fraud of such proportions" that served their short-term aims. He concluded that when key managers—trusted employees—conspired to evade and override financial controls, there was little, if anything, that "could have been done to prevent the irregularities." This was clearly an internal scandal and the criminal law was not transgressed. A statement issued jointly by the chairman and president hinted at a possible motivation. They let it be known that these falsifications were made by the top executives of the relevant foreign subsidiaries in order "to improve the apparent performance of their operations. These misrepresentations were not designed to divert company funds to personal, improper or illegal use." The culprits were of course dismissed but presumably they knew beforehand that this was a risk that they had to bear. It is much easier for corporations to detect thieving executives who cheat to line their own pockets than to unveil tactics that are targeted to make a national bailiwick look more attractive than it actually is. Self-glorification is something many frail, egotistical executives of multis are guilty of. This makes international operations more vexatious than Perlmutter allowed for when he constructed his simple model of the TNC.

ACCOUNTING PROCEDURES

C. Tugendhat, a perceptive writer on multis before their putative might became legendary, has recounted accurately the fact that subsidiaries are supposed to put the wider interests of the MNC as a whole above their own (138). However, he was wrong to deduce that "the managers know that their own future and promotion prospects depend on the good opinion of the top men at head office." In very small multis the CEO can be in touch with the senior decision-makers and personal impressions carry great weight. Hence the loyal executive is bound to be rewarded when he contrives that his foreign subsidiary records nominal losses for the greater glory of the parent company. Such self-sacrificing behavior will surely earn him promotion! But in complex mammoth MNCs the allocation of resources and the advancement of individual executives cannot depend on "the good opinion of the top men." Objective criteria are needed such as profit and loss (P&L) accounts of profit centers, divisions, subsidiaries, product groups, functional activities, and so on.

TNCs prepare separate accounts for every national subsidiary. If there are several subsidiaries within one country, several P&L statements may be prepared. The information gained is meant primarily to enlighten the creditors and shareholders. Company laws do not stipulate that data should be provided so as to enable the CEO to infer which activity has been the most profitable and which executives were the most successful in advancing the global interests of the corporation.

Most shareholders of TNCs bother only to examine the consolidated global account. This cannot be arrived at just by adding up the figures in the various company accounts of the group. They have to be translated into a one-currency language, which almost always is that of the country of the parent's domicile. A properly consolidated account ought to aim at consistency and uniformity. Accountancy guidelines on the presentation of consolidated accounts differ in the various economies which harbor the headquarters of TNCs. Sometimes the parent company's accountants are expected to summarize unaltered the items appearing in the accounts of the foreign subsidiaries. Occasionally the consolidated accounts may be prepared by recasting the accounts of the foreign subsidiaries so as to apply universally the rules prevalent (or legally binding) in the home country. Depreciation rates, for example, vary widely and it may be decided to 'rewrite' the foreign P&L statements by using uniformly the rates of the home country. When the P&L statements generated in several countries are agglomerated by the accountancy rules of one country (and expressed in terms of the currency of that country), perverse results may ensue. The recorded big profit of the Venezuelan subsidiary (calculated by the standards of the Venezuelan company law) could be transformed into a small profit. A rise in the asset values of the Finnish subsidiary measured in the local currency is turned into a fall when translated into the buoyant currency of the parent's country.

Do the bottom lines of the consolidated accounts render intelligible the profit performances of a TNC's constituent enterprises? If they do, the CEO could identify the unsuccessful undertakings and transfer resources to the successful ventures; he could measure quantitatively the comparative achievements and shortcomings of the disparate activities within the group. To acquire such knowledge from the consolidated accounts is very difficult indeed when the company is a multiproduct business that operates within only one national context. The stumbling blocks are more formidable still when the chief executive orchestrates a multiproduct and multinational corporation. Of course, if the CEO of a corporation with worldwide manufacturing facilities is satisfied to perform as if he headed an investment trust, his task is relatively easy. Each foreign subsidiary is then treated as if it were one shareholding of a global portfolio. The relative performances of the subsidiaries and their responsible executives are then judged simply in relation to the P&L statements and asset valuations that have been incorporated within the consolidated accounts. In a genuine MNC, however, less significance can and should be attached to the nominal accounts presented by individual subsidiaries. The very raison d'être of a multi is to juggle losses and gains in different parts of the world in order to augment the overall profits of the corporation. The CEO instructs the managers of the product divisions, national subsidiaries, and so on how and when to move resources around. They are told explicitly that they ought not to target such exercises to maximize the profits of their own bailiwick. If executives are to be treated as heroes because—for the higher good—they turn their profitable enterprises into loss-making ones, one cannot very well judge relative success and failure by the accounts that have been prepared to comply with the national company law.

Below are a few instances that illustrate why the nominal accounts of individual subsidiaries of a complex multi sometimes represent only inconsequential numerate caricatures.

1. The head offices of TNCs initiate, at arbitrary prices, intracorporate buying and selling transactions. Often 'managed' transfer pricing is intended to minimize the global tax liability of the TNC.

2. By extending credit and/or borrowing funds, the financial officers of subsidiaries can play around with the volumes of their receivables and debts. If the multi's head office curtails this functional autonomy by instituting globally directed financial manipulations, the reported earnings of some individual profit centers are likely to be reduced. In extreme cases, actual gains are turned into reported losses. It also means treading on the toes of senior executives. Nevertheless, from the vantage point of the parent, there is much to be said for international cash management. A bank—probably one located in the parent's country—is designated as the main operator. Cutting across the demarcation lines that separate the various product groups and national subsidiaries, excess cash positions and borrowing requirements are offset by electronic transfers through a 'box.' (The cross-border pooling of money within the corporation can encounter legal restrictions in certain parts of the world and this system is sometimes feasible only on a regional basis.) The senior managers of the profit centers do not like the arrangement. If an autocratic CEO is able to overcome their dislike, he will incidentally distort further the true profit picture that is conveyed by the nominal P&L statements submitted by the integrant divisions of the MNC.

3. Some parent companies have taken over global control of the foreign currency decisions that formerly used to be made by the national sub-

sidiaries. A special functional section in the head office formulates the multi's worldwide perspective on the strength and weakness of major currencies. This section is authorized to make binding decisions on behalf of some, many, or all of the national subsidiaries. No longer can these arrange to hedge currency risks after applying their own judgment. They are instructed in which currency to denominate their import/export transactions and must obey dictates on cross-border credits. The managers divested of decision-making in this field are especially annoyed when this central planning implicitly deprives their subsidiaries of foreign currency gains. One oil TNC established such a functional section in the 1970s and the whiz-kids in charge delighted the CEO when they enriched the parent company's accounts by tens of millions of dollars. It was achieved by bullying the marketing and financial officers of the foreign subsidiaries. Despite this success the section was dissolved after two years. As a result of the global manipulations, one national subsidiary had been forced to record a heavy (artificial) loss while in fact it made a hefty profit. The top executives concerned felt that they had been made to look foolish and threatened to resign. The CEO staved off the impending revolt by returning this decision-making function to the national subsidiaries.

4. Many multis sanctimoniously subscribe to the policy declaration of Philips that each profit center is free to acquire its components from the most suitable supplier and sell its output to the most appropriate customer: there is no obligation to give preferential treatment to consanguineous companies within the corporate family. This is fine in theory, but what if an important manufacturing plant is in danger of collapsing? The CEO will almost certainly order companies within the group to breach the stated principle. Alternatively, executives in charge of prosperous subsidiaries, who wish to endear themselves to the head office, may respond to winks and nods and 'voluntarily' rescue the endangered factory, even though their P&L statements are affected adversely.

5. The way in which the head office places patents and the fruits of central R&D at the disposal of national subsidiaries can affect the comparative (reported) returns on capital. Foreign subsidiaries operating in some Latin American countries are not allowed to pay any royalties to their parent. Most other countries impose selective restrictions. In a number of OECD economies there are no limitations and all reasonable royalties are treated as an allowable expenditure. Some TNCs, for example, Ericsson (123), invoice their subsidiaries at differential prices for the use of the parent-owned patents. (All these charges, however, are usually lower than the payments demanded of external licensees.)

6. It was noted already that TNCs such as IBM choose to locate token plants in certain territories in order to show the flag or to curry favor with the authorities (129). Head offices judge the performance of these

unorthodox enterprises in relation to the PR consideration that led to their establishment. The nominal accounts are therefore of little interest per se; nobody will be upset if they record a loss. Sometimes the P&L statements of token plants actually register a profit. Only insiders would know how misleading this can be if it is due to covert subsidies by means of 'massaged' transactions with other subsidiaries.

7. Multis make their profit centers pay a portion of the expenses involved in running the global headquarters. Most tax authorities accept this as a valid tax-deductible item. It is often the managers of the subsidiaries who are outraged that they are expected to pay for services that they do not regard as value for money. Ordinarily, multis charge pro rata to turnover, profits, and so on, but sometimes the apportionment is highly selective. The prosperous subsidiaries are expected to contribute disproportionately more.

8. For a variety of reasons, the head office may decide that subsidiary A shall cease to supply a given market and that subsidiary B shall take its place. There may be good overriding factors to justify such an edict but this is not always acknowledged when, subsequently, subsidiary A reports a loss and the seemingly enterprising subsidiary B boasts of extraordinary profits. During the Rhodesian crisis many countries had pledged themselves to implement a trade boycott. A well-known Swedish multi was conscious of the possible PR damage should it be revealed that one of its factories in the home country was continuing to supply Rhodesia. The manager in charge was told to transfer this business to a foreign subsidiary that was better placed to breach the boycott with impunity. The domestic profit center, which had been instructed to give up its sales to Rhodesia, regarded this as a necessary subterfuge. For this reason it pressed the head office to assign to it the chance profits earned by the profit center that was helping out temporarily.

9. What is the estimated damage that would be suffered by an MNC if given foreign subsidiaries were expropriated? The question features an indeterminate, unpaid cost factor that ought to be significant when comparing the P&L accounts of different national subsidiaries. It is not unreasonable to assume that the implicit danger is very much more pronounced in Peru than in Switzerland. Before measuring the relative performances of national subsidiaries, one ought to know something about the variable, notional insurance premiums to cover the MNC against expropriation and other unpleasant things befalling its subsidiaries. Were this information available, the Swiss profit center that reported a 4 percent return on capital might be deemed to be trading more profitably than the Peruvian subsidiary with a 10 percent return.

Faced as CEOs are with highly arbitrary P&L statements, how can they make wise comparative judgments on the allocation of resources within their corporation? Intuitively, the cornershop grocer perceives that it is more rewarding to promote sardines than tuna fish. There are top executives who imagine that they too are competent to make decisions based on gut feelings, but this is not a generally commendable solution. The goal is to ascertain, without too much guesswork, the genuine P&L of profit centers. A number of MNCs have considered composing a notional set of accounts to aid the CEO in his decision-making. Some corporations have actually devised such a tool, named the "memo accounting system." Credits and debits are handed out to profit centers in relation to the 'uneconomic' steps they have had to take to comply with orders from the head office. The official accounts of subsidiaries cannot of course be amended to allow for dodges and artifices, but the notional statements—prepared for internal, confidential use only—can be manipulated. The technique is employed to cut down to size the artificially high profits of subsidiaries by saddling them with financial penalties. Subsidiaries that received (and carried out) loss-making instructions are awarded offsetting compensation. In a typical instance, the head office will reduce the extraordinarily high profits of subsidiary A, knowing that in part these have been generated because other companies in the group were coerced to buy its expensive products. The nominally lean profits of subsidiary B are uplifted because its managing director, a loyal executive of the global corporation, had foregone certain gains by selling below cost to another subsidiary that was kept solvent by this covert procedure.

This is a marvellous system, in theory. On the one hand, the TNC's top echelon can move resources around on the world's chessboard without having to worry unduly about the impact on the nominal P&L of the individual companies in the group. On the other hand, the memo accounting system provides the multi's CEO with a refined tool to verify when it is both expedient and fair to brandish the sword and when to parcel out incentive carrots. It presents an intellectually stimulating challenge but hardly offers a practical solution. The ensuing administrative nightmare would demand intensive time and effort by the top managerial elite, for the confidential character of the exercise will not allow it to be delegated. Conceptually, the system is an improvement on the nominal accounts but the size of the allotted credits and debits would still depend largely on discretionary rulings. While the composition of in-house notional accounts is not illegal per se, it would be perilous if the contents were leaked. The manipulative skills of the head office would be exposed and many people at home and abroad would be asking awkward questions.

The memo accounting system is meant to convey to the executives sans patrie that carrying out 'uneconomic' instructions will not disadvantage them during the annual assessments. Alas, executives are a cynical breed. In many cases the CEO will tell them to do certain things without spelling out why and how this is for the good of the corporation. But when they are told why the seemingly incongruous instructions, which they are asked to carry out obediently, are logical and even when they are promised explicitly that sham loss-making can be a virtuous deed, their credulity is still strained. What if the CEO forgets his promises or deliberately reneges on them? What if he is replaced? Are the notional accounts really fair? Consequently, senior managers may prefer to rely on the conventional accounts that record in black and white the profits they have attained for their bailiwick. It follows that they do not always obediently carry out 'uneconomic' instructions: they withhold relevant information that should reach the head office, falsify data, and in the last resort collude with outsiders (including government authorities) to sabotage orders from the CEO that would make the official accounts of their operations appear less glamorous.

MACHO CHIEF EXECUTIVES

The most famous, highly centralized, international institutions—the Moscow-based Communist International and the Rome-based Catholic Church—have tolerated patriotic affirmations by the faithful rank and file. In the top hierarchies, however, individuals were expected to surmount any latent allegiances to a nation–state and abide by supranational, ideological, and theological doctrines. Not all of the cardinals and Marxist chieftains have lived up to their international calling and national rivalries have played a role in the history of the Comintern and the Catholic Church. Multis find themselves in a somewhat analogous predicament. In the next chapter the manual and clerical employees of MNCs are shown to lack faith in internationalism. The four founding fathers were not surprised that lower-rank employees love the nation–state. But to their disappointment (and astonishment), many senior executives of MNCs are also guilty of the same heinous inclination. They relate personally to the fortunes of the national subsidiary in which they hold a leading managerial position.

It is a helpful symbol to have a true internationalist at the helm of the multi. The Irish rugby star Tony O'Reilly, who was appointed Heinz's CEO by its U.S. board of directors, clearly filled such a bill. So did Richard Giordano, who headed a U.S. company that was taken over by the UK-based BOC; he later became the chairman of the foreign raider, one of Britain's successful TNCs. Harold Geneen, the accountant born in Bournemouth, England, made the journey in the reverse direction. This erstwhile foreigner captained ITT, perhaps the most hated US multi of our days. He wanted his staff to know that he was a devout internationalist. On his frequent journeys abroad he made it a point to leave his watch unadjusted, thus impressing upon the managers of the foreign subsidiaries that it was the time prevailing at ITT's head office in the United States that mattered to him—and therefore ought to matter to them! Henry Ford II also laid bare his multinational soul. He scored over other CEOs in that he had effective control over his MNC and could afford to behave as an autocrat. If the occasion warranted it, he openly favored one national subsidiary at the expense of another. PR considerations were not allowed to interfere with his vocal condemnation of countries that hosted Ford subsidiaries but did not behave to his liking. During the perennial quarrels between the German and British operations, Henry Ford II came out brutally in favor of Cologne. At a press conference he described the British subsidiary as "a cesspool of the world" and denounced the quality of the UK-made Ford vehicles. Proclaiming that U.S. consumers would not want to buy the British product, he commended German-made Ford cars.

The bugbear of managerial disunity, often along national lines, is difficult to document. Those who know the truth are used to meeting outsiders, besotted by the image of strong and united multis, to whom such revelations appear implausible. But some internal evidence has been divulged. Giordano saw it as the task of the CEO to curb the managers' "crude inclinations" to climb up the slippery pole. In his experience, executives plot to "screw their associates." Giordano preached that while "aggressive tough guys" were needed, "you want them to fight in a team spirit." An enlightened sermon! But what to do with the recalcitrant bosses of profit centers in an age in which chief executives can no longer conduct themselves like Henry Ford II? Leaving the watch unadjusted is not a substitute for the machismo necessary to coerce all senior executives to behave as if they were stateless. The infighting between the various subsidiaries reaches its climax when the global cake is cut during the annual budget sessions. But clashes on national lines are also routine occurrences throughout the year, as the following items illustrate.

Though it seems that R&D is an obvious corporate function to be carried out on a supranational basis, strong subsidiaries can frustrate this objective. When an executive of Lorenz, ITT's biggest German manufacturing operation, was asked whether his national company shared information and knowledge with consanguineous subsidiaries, such as those located in Spain and Britain, he smiled and answered: "Of course not." R. Sobel says of Geneen (ITT's outstanding dictator) that it had been his ambition to unite the research capabilities of the Paris laboratories, the development expertise and marketing skills of (U.S.-based) Bell Telephone, and the manufacturing facilities in Germany and Britain. Geneen's "attempts failed, dashed on the rocks of nationalism, the peculiarities of the markets, and tradition" (139). IBM's biographer relates that the "decision on whether a new research facility should be constructed in Japan, Britain or France was far more difficult than one involving the location of a plant in New York, California or Texas" (129). When the Swedish ballbearing MNC SKF sought to concentrate in one place all the R&D conducted in various facilities at home and abroad, it faced the reality of nationalism. If, as first intended, the existing Goeteborg R&D center (in the home country) was expanded for this purpose, it would have made the company look even more Swedish than it was; however, SKF wanted to appear as an internationally oriented corporation. To locate the global R&D in one of its big subsidiaries would have aroused national resentment from the other big subsidiaries. Though the Swedish trade unions screamed that this was a national betrayal and the Swedish government was also displeased, a neutral country was selected, one in which SKF had hitherto done very little business. The Swedish MNC's R&D was to be centralized in specially built premises in the Netherlands. Some of the scientists and engineers who had hitherto worked on the R&D of national subsidiaries and in the Goeteborg laboratory were transferred to the new establishment. In a way it was a cowardly solution, but one that implicitly recognized the necessity to compromise because of potent national jealousies.

Obvious cultural difficulties must be solved when a TNC assigns a national of the home country to take charge of a foreign subsidiary. Most of the staff, however, accept that while working for a multi, they have to put up with a foreign boss. But there are real troubles ahead when the head office appoints a third-country national. IBM's subsidiary in Stuttgart was and is a formidable company in its own right. Yet the German executives treated it as a fact of life that their superiors came from the United States. They were outraged and voiced their national resentment when IBM's head office nominated in 1959 a French citizen, Jacques Maisonrouge, as chief of European operations in the regional headquarters in Place Vendomes, Paris.

In the previous sections I have mentioned that multis can pool efficiently their financial resources through international cash management. BINCO, interviewing member-firms, was told that while this was a very attractive idea, it had "met with organisational obstacles." The euphemistic phrase alluded to the refusal of financial officers in strong national subsidiaries to cooperate in the implementations of such schemes that the head offices tried to force upon them.

In the days when most OECD countries still had exchange controls on capital movements, the CEO of a U.S. chemical multi came across rebellious conduct by some of his senior executives. The matter was so delicate that the saboteurs could not be dismissed instantly. The story began when the global head office decreed that two of the European subsidiaries, Y and Z, were to be expanded; most of the funds were to be drawn from the very profitable subsidiary X, which had accumulated large cash resources. The financial officers of X were instructed to request permission from the authorities to transfer funds to Y and Z. X's directors went through the motion of filing such an application and then reported to the head office that consent was refused. A letter to this effect was in fact received but did not convey the whole truth. X's executives had not overtly colluded with the officials of the host country but they had nevertheless dropped enough hints to convince the exchange controllers that it would not be in the country's interest to sanction this transfer. Why this disloyal behavior? The bosses of X were aggrieved that Y and Z, rather than their own bailiwick, had been selected for expansion. As they had concluded that this decision could not be reversed, they wanted at least to keep their profits in reserve for future investments within the orbit of X. Significantly, they called these funds "our money." The CEO, however, treated X's unremitted profits as the multi's money, which could be moved around at his discretion. He sent two senior people from the head office to see the exchange controllers, bypassing X's financial officers. It is not known what arguments were deployed, but the original decision was rescinded! The profits of X could be used to pay for the machinery, installed in Y and Z.

The nationalist intracorporate squabbles among Ford's European subsidiaries antedate World War II. Mira Wilkins cites material from the Ford archives to testify to the long-standing intense personal rivalry between the managements of Ford's German and French subsidiaries. After 1940 both came under the control of Hitler's war machine. The Frenchman who was in charge of Ford-France discovered that, when forced to cooperate with the Germans, he got a better reception from Nazi government officials in Berlin than from the German management of Ford-Cologne (93). Some decades later Ford-Germany and Ford-UK were frequently at loggerheads. When Detroit planned to transfer work from Britain to Germany, the management of the Dagenham plant unofficially tolerated the public display of its unfriendly attitude to Cologne. Some British technicians were resolved not to talk to their German colleagues. When a technician phoned from Cologne to discuss corporate matters, an English voice would reply: "We are not prepared to discuss business." This conduct was extremely silly and significant only because the managements of the two subsidiaries allowed such an atmosphere to prevail.

What happens when the reasoning that led to the founding of given foreign subsidiaries is no longer valid? It has happened that the distressed top executives will not want to see them closed. They are prepared to fight for their continued existence even though this runs counter to the overall global interests of the TNC. Nicholas Faith found that Dutch, German, and Swiss companies had established dye subsidiaries in the United States largely because of the onerous tariffs that had frustrated exports from their European plants. (The U.S. customs assessed duties on certain chemicals in accordance with the ASP American Selling Price—rather than the price prevailing in the country of origin.) Outside the United States, chemical MNCs agitated for a change in the infamous ASP system and they were joined by free-trade protagonists within the United States. When the U.S. free trade lobby approached the U.S. subsidiaries of foreign multis—Ciba, Geigy, and Sandos are mentioned by name—these did not agree to support the campaign, aimed at softening U.S. tariffs on chemical imports. Why should they do so? The U.S. subsidiaries of foreign multis were prospering, together with the indigenous U.S. manufacturers, under the umbrella that kept out foreign-made chemicals. If the pressure from the U.S. free traders and the chemical MNCs of Europe brought about lower U.S. duties, the European multis might find it economically feasible to renew exports to the United States. This could threaten the profitability, if not the very existence, of the U.S. subsidiaries that would then have lost their raison d'être (106).

When a new CEO comes in, he may have good cause to throw out the old guard and, for public consumption, paint a dreary picture of the corporation he is about to govern. The worse the situation he is inheriting, the greater could be his potential achievement. A rare opportunity to peer into the sanctum of a global corporation was provided when Black & Decker's new chief executive, Laurence Farley, a 48-year-old tough guy ("Those who do not share Farley's vision usually do not stay around long; last year he fired all of his European managers.") expediently opened his heart to *Fortune* magazine. In the process he told of the nationalist in-fighting that he wanted to end.

When Farley became president in 1982 Black & Decker operated 25 plants in 13 countries on six continents. It was divided into three operating groups—plus the headquarter group—each with its own corporate staff. Below that, individual companies operated autonomously in each of more than 50 countries where Black & Decker did business. In this setup not only did the twain never meet, they didn't even say hello: peer-to-peer communciation between Black & Decker of West Germany and Black & Decker USA . . . was practically verboten. Managers of these international fiefdoms had complete control over their operations, under the assumption that they knew their country and could best judge which products would succeed. Chauvinism, however, produced some curious decisions. Dustbuster, the cordless vacuum cleaner that has been a runaway seller in the U.S. since 1979, was not available in Australia until 1983. And at one point Black & Decker's eight design centers produced 260 different motor sizes, even though the company needs fewer than ten. The European managers refused to sell Black & Decker housewares. They maintained that the products were strictly for Americans. . . . Farley underlined his rough-and-tumble reputation by firing 25 European managers and then closing the [regional] Brussels headquarters (140).

In 1986 the still young Farley retired. His successor praised him: "We are most grateful to him for his vision of globalization."

14

WORKERS HAVE A MOTHERLAND

> The multinational firm could team up with world-wide unions to further neutralise the nation–state.
>
> Howard Perlmutter

In 1960 David Lilienthal made the pioneering suggestion-cum-forecast that in future international unions should and would sign worldwide collective bargaining contracts with TNCs. He envisaged the global parity of emoluments. When a U.S. canning company commences tuna catching in Ghana, "it will not be many years before the local operators bargain toward the same rates of pay and fringe benefits as American operators receive" (21). Not for lack of trying has this come to naught. Even Levinson, secretary general of the ICF since 1964, could not report meaningful progress.

Seemingly, Canada was an exception. By the end of the 1960s it was still the only industrialized country to lack a strong, independent trade union movement of its own. The majority of the organized Canadian employees were in U.S.-based unions which were often accused of placing the interests of their U.S. members before those of the Canadian members. It was also widely believed that the U.S. unions collected more dues in Canada than they returned in benefits or strike pay. In the 1970s a groundswell of national resentment paved the way for an upsurge of independent Canadian union activities. Despite the close links between the United States and Canada, most U.S. unions (with Canadian affiliates) do not bargain on a cross-border basis; only a minority of unions sign contracts that lay down more or less identical wages and conditions for the whole of North America.

SELFISH MOTIVATIONS

When a union in one country assists a union in another country, does this signify genuine international working-class solidarity? Perhaps sometimes it does, but prudent analysts look gift horses in the mouth. When in the 1870s the British glass manufacturer—today an important MNC—Pilkington cut wages drastically, a number of its employees left for the United States. This emigration was encouraged by the U.S. glass companies that were trying to seduce others into crossing the Atlantic. Consequently, Pilkington found it expedient to raise wages in 1880. It hoped to cause the potential emigrants to "turn a deaf ear to the temptation" (141). The British workers not only emigrated but apparently were ready to work in the United States below the current rates. The glassmakers union, a section of the Knights of Labor headquartered in Pittsburgh, adopted drastic and expensive measures to halt this influx of foreign workers. They sent two delegates to Europe "to ascertain why glass workers came to America . . . and, if possible, to have the European workers form and establish a closer communication between America and the old country, in order to protect the interests of all glass workers." The year 1884 was significant on three counts. Branches of the Knights were founded in England (Sunderland and St. Helens) in order to enroll workers of Pilkington. In that year the U.S. union supported financially the Belgian glassworkers who were striking for higher wages. Most remarkable was the establishment of the Universal Federation of Glass Workers at a conference in Charleroi—a nineteenth-century precursor of the modern ITSs. During the 1880s the U.S. glassmakers union convened three Universal Conventions; delegates from the United States, Britain, Belgium, France, and Italy attended. The meetings took place in St. Helens, and Pilkington dismissed those of its employees who participated. The chief constable was asked to keep a close watch on the Conventions and on the firm's factories. By the beginning of the 1890s this "defensive" solidarity, financed by the Knights, had come to an end.

BL (British Leyland) used to operate several plants in foreign countries. In the summer of 1973 the news agencies transmitted a piquant item: BL's UK employees told management that they might take proxy action to obtain redress for the suspension of the labor force at BL's Authi factory in Pamplona. To comply with a request of the IMF, the shop stewards were immediately blacking the dispatch of components destined for Pamplona. Why were British workers ready to sacrifice wages to help foreign workers? A very idealistic explanation was given. Those were the days when Franco was still alive and the law prevented Spanish workers from striking—hence the solidarity action by BL's British workers who were living in a society in which strikers were not sent to prison. This was a delightful story,though few bothered to read the elucidative statement by the chairman of BL's Combined Shop Stewards' Committee. This honest document ought to be deposited in the archives of the international labor movement! Eddie McGarry revealed that the UK shop stewards had learned of their employer's plan to expand substantially the Spanish subsidiary. McGarry wasted no time on denouncing Franco's repressive regime. Instead, he came straight to the point. The comrades felt concern that work would "be transferred from Britain to Spain because the Spanish workers are paid lower wages. . . . By offering support to our Spanish colleagues at this early date we want to ensure that they receive a proper wage as soon as possible."

No doubt inspired by the publicized solidarity of BL's workers for their Spanish comrades, the employees of Innocenti, BL's Italian subsidiary, hoped for some similar fraternal gesture. (The Italians were not to know that the selfish motivations of the British shop stewards had nothing to do with genuine solidarity relating to foreigners who worked for the same employer.) Since 1972 Innocenti workers had developed bonds with BL's shop stewards in Britain. When in 1977 the head office of the British multi unilaterally threatened to close down Innocenti unless its labor force was cut by one-third, the Italian unions inveighed against BL's colonialist behavior. They sent a delegation to London to enlist the support of the British unions. Their disappointment was great. Grunberg later interviewed two Italian union representatives who maintained that if the situation had been reversed, they would have gone on strike to help the workers in BL's home country. Be that as it may, the shop stewards in Britain did not organize a strike. They did not even send money. How then could they demonstrate their sympathies with the aggrieved workers of Innocenti? "The only concrete result was a telegram" (142).

In 1980 there was a glut of steel on the world markets. In all industrialized countries many steel workers were being laid off while others were kept in employment only by state subsidies. It was at this point that the employees of the nationalized British Steel Corporation chose to go on a protracted strike. They were not left in the lurch. The IMF remitted a £60,000 check to the comrades in Britain, a first token of solidarity from the Swedish, German, and Japanese steel unions. This was accompanied by another morale-booster: the strikers were asked to "rest assured that there will be sufficient financial support forthcoming from the steelworkers of the world." The IMF press release mentioned specifically that unions in Europe and the United States were organizing collections. Some cynical tongues were wagging in Britain, intimating that these donations—if they helped to keep the British strike alive—were a wise investment by non-UK steel unions determined to safeguard the endangered jobs of their members.

Some examples of cynical international solidarity come from the stables of the AFL-CIO with particular reference to the UAW (United Automobile Workers). In the immediate postwar years U.S. technology and labor productivity were so superior that few U.S. unions felt it necessary to spend their members' dues on protectionist causes. By the mid–1960s the situation, as perceived by the AFL-CIO, was changing radically. The constituent unions were encouraged to join, and financially bolster, the dormant ITSs. Walter Reuther, UAW's president, did not just lend his union's prestige to the new-look automobile section of the IMF but took an active part in the development of the world councils of Chrysler, Ford, and GM. U.S. trade unions saw jobs in Detroit threatened by imports from both LDCs and those industrialized countries that were learning to produce good-quality, and relatively inexpensive, goods. The AFL-CIO raised the flag of international labor solidarity, on par with the onslaught of the Knights of Labor on Pilkington in the previous century. Unlike their confreres abroad, the leaders of the various U.S. unions—now appearing regularly at the deliberations of the various ITSs—were hard-boiled and highly paid protagonists of capitalism. Was it then not incongruous when they joined in the chorus for global company bargaining? Actually, this apparent madness made sense. Walter Reuther plotted to attack on two fronts. He strove to whet the appetite of the non-U.S. workers by dangling before them the good wages and conditions that the U.S. multis were bestowing upon their employees in the home country. Simultaneously, during (domestic) collective bargaining sessions with the Big Three, the UAW attempted to press the employers to upgrade the wages paid by their foreign subsidiaries. With hindsight the UAW is known to have wasted its money on this Machiavellian strategy: Chrysler, Ford, and GM did not fall into the trap.

THE BIG THREE

Chrysler, Ford, and GM had this in common: confronted with highly publicized and well-endowed IMF company councils, which brought together representatives of their manufacturing operations throughout the world, they consistently refused to deal with them. The CEOs of the Big Three rejected outright global bargaining. Unlike many other multis, the U.S. automobile corporations never feared that the IMF, backed though it was by the UAW, could implement damaging effective multinational labor action. History proved them right.

General Motors

The Detroit headquarters of the UAW are located in a building named "Solidarity House." I presume that when this appellation was chosen, it symbolized solidarity in North America but now that the UAW has become wedded to multinational labor action it is probably meant to signify international solidarity. In 1970 the UAW called out on strike 350,000 of its members in order to pressure GM into signing an improved collective agreement covering its factories at home. The union obviously considered that this was the moment to test whether its investments in the IMF were paying dividends. Victor Reuther (the brother of the late Walter Reuther), director of the UAW's International Affairs Department, rushed off to Europe to enlist substantive support in the pay strike against GM; his most important calls were made to the heads of the German and British engineering unions. Press reports indicate that he was received warmly in both countries. No real help—which would have made a serious impact on the dispute in the United States—was extended but all the unions concerned publicly proclaimed their solidarity with the strikers. The German and British unions promised that they would not handle any work transferred from the strike-bound U.S. plants. Though GM had never toyed with this idea, it helped to save the UAW's face. Sympathy strikes were quickly ruled out but there was a proposal on the table that the German and British employees of GM should at least impose an overtime ban for the duration of the U.S. dispute. Reuther was regretfully told that the rank-and-file European trade unionists were not internationally minded enough to make this sacrifice.

Charles Levinson, secretary general of the ICF, had of course no locus standi in this automobile strike. Reputations, however, are boosted by lots of publicity and telegrams are not expensive. Hence the world was told that the ICF, in the name of its many members, had sent a message of solidarity. Alas, the UAW could only garner such morsels. From Leonard Woodcock, the UAW's president, came this pathetic reply in a letter dated November 11, 1970:

Your message comes at the right psychological moment: it helps to raise the morale of our strikers; it forces GM to become more keenly aware that our support extends far beyond the frontiers of the U.S. and Canada; all the while it helps to lay realistic foundations for a truly effective world-wide trade union movement.

With your determination to use every practical form of international labor unity and solidarity in support of our justifiable demands and with the militancy of our striking UAW members, we will bring this giant monopoly to accept some social responsibilities.

Please convey to your officers and members our deepest appreciation for your splendid support.

Chrysler

David Blake surveyed in depth the views of Chrysler's Canadian employees (143). (The majority were members of the UAW, headquartered in the United States.) They were asked about their willingness to support fellow Chrysler employees outside Canada. While 53 percent said that they would be ready to go on strike in support of a dispute in the United States, only 10 percent and 9 percent respectively were inclined to demonstrate corresponding solidarity for Chrysler strikers in England and Mexico. However, 71 percent and 62 percent were prepared to give "moral support" to their striking brothers in England and Mexico! The willingness of Canadian trade unionists to suffer materially in order to assist non-Canadians employed by their common multinational employer has been tested at length in the two decades that have passed since this survey was made. It proves that respondents who strike a valiant posture when filling in questionnaires do not necessarily behave as heroes when it comes to the crunch. While the 53 percent answer is not to be taken seriously, the survey is nevertheless significant because in their answers relating to England and Mexico, the UAW members appear to have replied candidly. The honest figures of 10 percent and 9 percent have been recited widely in Europe by those union bosses who wanted to warn their members not to be taken in by promises of international solidarity. The TUC once called a convention devoted exclusively to the cross-border struggle against the MNCs. Secretary General Vic Feather said that it did not matter greatly whether this conference voted for multinational strikes or not because in real situations British workers would not respond affirmatively. He then quoted from the Blake survey and added that a similar pattern would apply in Britain if there were calls for solidarity strikes to support workers in other countries. That was in 1970.

Those who are enslaved by outmoded doctrines have short memories and in the process delude themselves and others. In 1975 Chrysler ordered the managers of its British subsidiary to shed one-third of the 25,000-strong labor force; if this proved impossible, the multi threatened to liquidate all the UK operations. Recalling previous declarations of international solidarity by Leonard Woodcock, the UAW's president, Jack Jones, leader of the union representing the majority of Chrysler workers in Britain, appealed to him to intercede on behalf of the British workers with Chrysler's top echelon. Jack Jones' message must have been well received because Woodcock sent back an emotional dispatch offering help. Woodcock's deputy, Douglas Fraser, was even more forthcoming. In an interview at his office in Detroit he promised that U.S. Chrysler workers would strike, if necessary, to support the employees of British Chrysler. He spelt it out: their support could range from petitioning the Chrysler head office to stopping work on Chrysler's U.S. assembly lines. Other, smaller, British unions jumped on the bandwagon, telling their members that they too were seeking to establish a multinational alliance. They held out the prospect of help from the unions at Chrysler's plants in continental Europe and the United States to stave off the impending calamity. A few months later the talking stopped. Apart from "moral support," the UAW did not send over one cent and not one Chrysler worker in the United States or elsewhere lost one hour's wage on account of sympathy strikes. One-third of the workers, employed by Chrysler UK, were dismissed. Less than three years later Chrysler UK was sold to Peugeot,which closed the Scottish plant and, in time, dismissed one-half of the employees it had inherited from Chrysler. On that occasion the UAW did not even send condolences.

Ford Europe

This company's many plants are more integrated than those of other automobile multis. Industrial stoppages affecting some of Ford's factories can quickly lead to short-time working or even lay-offs in others. In theory, this opens up wide opportunity for fruitful cross-border trade union activities. When the IMF created the Ford world council to represent the manual workers in the multi's worldwide operations, it had little reason to expect effective global action. But there were ambitious plans to coordinate union efforts relating to Ford's 150,000 European employees. There has been plenty of talk but this did not lead to any important joint actions. Numerous IMF-sponsored conferences and ad hoc meetings—confined to the European scene—have taken place since 1964. There have also been unofficial cross-border contacts between the shop stewards of the European subsidiaries. Yet these endeavours have not been crowned with success. Pay parity and equal fringe benefits were frequently discussed but at the end of the day these goals were always relegated to the distant future. At one stage it seemed that Europe-wide agreement might be reached on a relatively simple matter that would have enabled all the unions to "take on Ford Europe at one fell swoop," to quote Moss Evans, the chief union negotiator at Ford UK. The proposal was that all national agreements should end at the same point of time, thus removing a barrier which had allegedly impeded

Ford workers in the whole of Europe from acting in concert. First raised at a meeting in Geneva in 1972, it is still on the drawingboard.

Among all of Ford's European subsidiaries, Ford UK probably holds the (pro rata) record for strikes. The British union leaders have thick files—actually they are kept in cartons—that testify to the fraternal messages that have been showered upon them from their European colleagues and from non-European unions, especially the UAW. Before the ten-week strike in the spring of 1971 is mentioned, it is relevant to go back to 1968, when the 6,500 striking Flemish workers at Ford's Genk subsidiary sent a delegation to Dagenham and Cologne asking their foreign co-workers to block work switched from Belgium. They returned from Britain announcing that they had received specific commitments from their British counterparts. One UK union leader at once denied that any arrangements had been made. Another, the chairman of the union side of Ford's National Joint Negotiating Committee, even chose to be offensive: "I know they were over here, but there has been no talk of an agreement. We've got problems enough of our own."

Coincidentally, a conference of the automobile section of the IMF met in London in March 1971, when the workers of Ford UK happened once again to be on strike. The UAW president delivered a routine speech about the natural propensity of multis to play off workers against workers, governments against governments. He pleaded for coordinated collective bargaining with multis. The conference, with the UAW delegation cheering loudly, naturally highlighted its solidarity with the striking Ford workers and promised to assist. Most of the continental European unions undertook specifically not to accept work transferred from Britain and not do overtime to enable Ford to fill the vacuum created by the British dispute. The workers at Genk, however, reminded the striking British workers that as Dagenham did not help them in their struggle, the Belgians would only send a message.

These monotonous pledges not to tolerate international strike-breaking bored the British union leaders. Having experienced many Ford strikes, they knew that, while occasionally something was done which slightly inconvenienced Ford, the major promises were mostly not kept. Leonard Woodcock and Victor Reuther promised that Ford U.S. would not be doing any work that was ordinarily performed in the UK plants— a meaningless statement, for nobody had contemplated this. As was their wont, the UAW leaders pledged financial support should the strike drag on. What rankled most, however, with the UK union leaders was the conduct of the German metal workers union. Their leaders conceded that the only thing that would really help to defeat Ford UK was an unlimited sympathy strike in Cologne (Ford's most important factory on the continent). A delegation of IG Metal specially flew into London to explain that because of their valid contract with Ford Germany, such a strike was out of the question. But, they said privately and later publicly, IG Metal offered a lot of money to the British unions. Moss Evans was furious. With tongue in cheek he expressed his pleasure at hearing of this generous announcement. But, he pointed out, the British unions had millions of pounds in their coffers and had canvassed no financial help. He implied that if foreign unions did not want to extend effective help, which demanded real sacrifices from their members, he was not going to salve their conscience by accepting their money.

CHARITABLE IMPULSES

Not all multinational labor campaigns have selfish motivations and not all declarations of global fraternity are empty words. There are also deeds propelled by genuinely charitable impulses which are not motivated by material rewards. Such expressions of international solidarity may be good for the soul but generally they are not efficacious, though the resulting publicity may help the cause. Dockers and stevedores have halted imports and exports that they (or their leaders) considered undesirable. History records that attempts were made to stop weapons reaching the insurgents who strove to topple the Communist regime in the Soviet Union, prevent oil supplies reaching Italy during its invasion of Ethiopia, and impede the sale of Californian vegetables to aid the farmworkers union of Cesar Chavez. By chance, most of Britain's car workers and dockers are members of the same union. When Ford UK was on strike in 1978, the Ford workers on the continent were requested not to erode the strike by exporting cars to Britain. This they promised to do, but cars made in continental European factories continued to flood into Britain. The British dockers were called upon not to unload them. They played their part successfully. Once again dockers had used their functional position of power to demonstrate working-class solidarity— only in this case it was not for an international cause!

Financial help is frequently extended to support trade unions in countries where they are proscribed or restricted. Political donations are made available for worthy causes. These are rarely collected by means of voluntary offerings from rank and file members but, more usually, are drawn from existing union funds. Having previously mentioned some selfish motivations of the AFL-CIO, it ought to be underlined that in the immediate postwar years, the American unions—for charitable reasons—provided finance to help rebuild foreign, war-ravaged unions. In Italy and other countries money was spent by the AFL-CIO to counter the threatened takeover of the European labor movement by the Communists. Some assistance, although compassionate, is tinged with an unsavory flavor. During the 13-month UK coalminers strike in 1984–85, the Marxist union leader, Arthur Scargill, personally beseeched foreign

union leaders and the main COMECON coal-exporters to display concrete solidarity. Above all, he wanted no foreign coal to breach the
blockade of the steel mills that the National Union of Miners was frantically seeking to close down by starving them of indigenous coal. In
fact COMECON coal exports to Britain flourished. Simultaneously, the
foreign Communist parties wholeheartedly supported the British miners. As a practical gesture children from deprived British mining families
were being entertained in several countries of the COMECON. Was it
not natural that they and their hosts should appear on television?

The instances above, however laudable, have nothing to do with intracorporate labor solidarity. It has already been noted that no significant
global strikes have occurred within the orbit of given multis. Neither
have there been protracted sympathy strikes in one subsidiary to support
employees of the same multi in another national subsidiary. What about
other sympathy action? The striking workers at Singer's Glasgow subsidiary complained in 1911 that the head office of their multi was cowing
them by exporting U.S.-made sewing machines to Britain: "British labour
is being defeated by American labour." Since those days, striking employees in country A have always appealed to their fellow employees
in countries B and C not to become scabs. In reality most multis are so
structured that there is not much scope for the switching of finished
goods from one market to another at short notice if this is intended for
a limited period only. Even when this is physically feasible, many MNCs
will choose not to do so lest it exacerbate the situation. In any case, to
employ the resources of B and C to smash a strike in A only makes
sense if the industrial dispute is anticipated to last many months. If a
multi seriously wants to undermine the strike in A, it can often use
sophisticated subterfuges without the workers in B and C becoming
aware that they are in fact assisting management to break the strike in
A. It may take unions a long time to discover how goods are routed to
reach the market of A. The employees in B and C may be happy to do
overtime after receiving assurances that the extra output is not destined
for A: such promises, rarely given in writing, are not always kept.

Set out in the communications of the ITSs are hundreds of authentic
examples of benevolent feats by trade unionists. These indicators of
intracorporate, cross-border solidarity have three common features.
First, the participants, whether they are individuals or unions, are not
breaking any contract that could lend them in court. (Sometimes they
are indeed doing something illegal, but there is good reason to assume
that no one will be prosecuted.) Second, though the multis concerned
may be inconvenienced slightly, there is no question of anyone being
dismissed for showing sympathy with comrades in another national
subsidiary. Third, the expressions of solidarity cost the unions and/or
individual union members either no money or involve them only in a
minimal loss of wages.

The head office of the U.S. food corporation Nabisco is annoyed when reminded of the IUF boast that employees in its European subsidiaries had once gone on strike to show their active sympathy with striking employees in the MNC's home country. This strike took place in 1969. The wage earners in Nabisco's Italian subsidiary stopped work for one hour to give vent to feelings of solidarity with their fellow employees in the United States.

The French TNC Peugeot was involved in a dispute with the manual workers in its Argentine subsidiary and suspended 1,000 of them. The employees in the factories of the home country threatened that if the Argentinians were not reinstated, they would come out on a 15-minute stoppage!

Several instances are on record in which unions that are recognized bargaining agents for the workers in the multi's home country have beneficently 'put in a good word' with the top echelon for employees in LDC subsidiaries. If wise counsel prevails, the head office takes into account that—in relatively unimportant matters—it is expedient to pay heed to such representations. This is what happened when the German chemical multi Hoechst had some labor problems in Turkey, where the local union was financially and legally restrained from pressing its case effectively. IG Chemie sent a senior official to Turkey to assist the Turkish union and later had friendly talks at the head office in Frankfurt to help settle the matter. It is doubtful whether the rank-and-file German trade unionists at Hoechst were even aware of the altruistic things that were accomplished in their name (94).

The IUF disseminated a pompous press release: "Unilever workers throughout the world are either going on strike or taking other action this month." The world company council announced that 24 national subsidiaries had responded positively though only seven would actually organize stoppages. The intention was to pressure the British-Dutch TNC into recognizing an IUF affiliate with black members in South Africa. This was clearly a humanitarian undertaking by individuals, mainly in developed countries, who had nothing to gain from it personally. The *Financial Times* investigated the nature of the sacrifices: "900 workers at Unilever plants in Sweden and Finland stopped work for two hours; in the Netherlands senior union men met for an 'information week' though production was not interrupted; in Denmark and Germany leaflets were distributed."

SOLIDARITY—BUT NOT FOREVER!

Why has geocentric wage bargaining failed to get off the ground despite the optimistic noises made at the time of the Saint Gobain affair? Why has the agitation for a 'world wage' turned out to be an academic joke? There are a host of answers—a number are discussed below—which all point in the same direction.

Karl Marx's devotees have mythicized 'the workers.' They are said to be brothers and sisters of a defined group, who share common interests and are ready to help one another. Working-class comradeship is to some extent a function of geography. It is most developed when employees live in close proximity in a company town or a mining village. Though members of the same union and sharing a common employer, workers feel less ready to sacrifice themselves for the welfare of comrades who live hundreds of miles away. Companies have been threatened with strikes when they strove to transfer work between plants within the same country. There are few self-sacrificing trade unionists in an international context. Except in Marxist literature, the wage slaves of Düsseldorf feel no affinity for the oppressed masses in Nicaragua. German trade unionists may sullenly put up with leaders who donate money on their behalf to causes in far-off lands, but it is a political hallucination to envisage that they would voluntarily lower their living standards at the behest of a foreign-based ITS. In March 1985 the (IMF's) Ford world council met in Liverpool. The chairman reported rumors of overcapacity and expressed his fears that Ford might close one or more of its plants. What practical global solidarity campaign did the chairman recommend? He proposed that the burden of the problem should be shared among the employees of all Ford's factories: they would be asked to reduce working hours worldwide. Even if Ford's management had agreed, only residents in cloud-cuckoo-land could believe that the prosperous workers of this automobile multi could have been driven by the union bosses to support such an egalitarian, selfless solution. Indeed, the IMF quickly dropped the proposal.

Multinational strikes are illegal in some countries and many unions are not prepared to be penalized for breaking the law. Neither are they ready to breach a valid contract with an employer at the behest of an ITS in Geneva. Otto Brenner, the former leader of IG Metal, said it all: "We cannot strike in sympathy with our British colleagues because our laws prevent that" (144). Efforts to achieve wage parity among different national subsidiaries of an international corporation could encounter insuperable legal difficulties. To take only one instance, the wage controls that many governments in their wisdom choose to impose may indeed be a foolish measure, but if the controls are statutory, global agreements could only be honored by overtly breaking the law.

The ineffectiveness of the ITSs is cited as a reason that global bargaining has not advanced. Vic Feather explicitly mentioned "personality and political problems" as decisive negative factors. It is a fact that Charles Levinson's flamboyant, publicity-seeking behavior has not endeared him to all unions officials. The destructive role of the Communist parties, which have often opposed cross-border labor campaigns, has also not been helpful. But these are peripheral to the serious tensions between the chiefs of the ITSs and the senior leaders of the national unions. By definition, global wage bargaining means that the latter are subordinated to those who would confront the multis on behalf of the workers in all the various subsidiaries. The bosses of the constituent unions of the ITSs are not enraptured! This functional enmity is not always kept under wraps. On one occasion the IUF had cause to be angry because its global campaign against Unilever had been sabotaged by the three British unions involved. They were accused publicly of paying lip-service to international solidarity but failing to initiate effective action. Such open censuring of constituent unions is not only rare but also dangerous for the ITSs because it means biting the hand that feeds them.

The ITSs, and those who would be the coordinators of global wage demands, face the xenophobic antagonism of rank-and-file members and top union leaders: these do not like taking orders from a center abroad, irrespective of whether the foreigners are inspired by charitable impulses or selfish motivations. When the UAW formulated a North American strike threat to achieve wage parity for its Canadian members, the proposal was by no means welcomed in Canada, where the paternalism of the Detroit-based union leaders was treated with suspicion. The *New York Times* acknowledged that this "is a type of economic imperialism no country can welcome" (143). How much more vehemently would the employees of the Finnish and Bolivian subsidiaries of a U.S. TNC resent labor bargainers from Switzerland who claimed to speak on their behalf during global negotiations at the head office?

Even within the orbit of the OECD economies, there is a clash between the interests of workers employed in different national operations of a given multi. The resulting conflicts cannot be accounted for just by the xenophobia of workers. The good fortune of subsidiary A may actually depend on the projected decline of subsidiary B. Hence there can often be no raison d'être for cross-border bargaining in the furtherance of groups of workers with disparate aims.

To the fury of UK trade unionists, Ford's head office cancelled in the spring of 1988 its plans to construct an electronics plant in Scotland. Did the workers on the continent send messages of sympathy? No! They were too busy celebrating. Austria, Germany, and Spain pressured Detroit to locate the factory in their country instead.

Those who dream of multinational bargaining at GM may wish to absorb the implications of the following two unrelated episodes. GM did not have an easy passage when it built a factory near Vienna. The fury of the managers of its German subsidiary and of IG Metal was great because workers and bosses alike felt that instead of manufacturing in

Austria, the U.S. MNC ought to have taken on unemployed German workers and expanded the operations of Opel. In another example, to save jobs in Britain, the shop stewards at GM's British subsidiary Vauxhall told the head office that they would boycott the import of components made in continental European GM plants.

Because of its international ramifications, the French automobile multi Renault was often browbeaten by the CGT, which had enrolled many Renault workers employed in the home country. The union leaders argued that its members were adversely affected by Renault's foreign subsidiaries, which had caused the export of French-made cars to decline sharply. In 1985 the CGT demanded that Renault's production in Spain be scaled down. To ensure that their message was understood, they held up loads of components destined for the Renault plant in Palencia and blocked the Champs Elysees with cars made in Spain that were intended for the French market. The Spanish trade unionists were naturally furious. In 1986 the nationalist-minded French workers urged their employer to close the Renault plants in North America, a suggestion that angered the UAW.

In 1978 BL gave notice that its Liverpool plant would be shut down and 3,000 British workers made redundant. The British union leaders did not like this and countered with a concrete alternative that was put to the head office. Why not declare redundant the 2,700 workers at BL's subsidiary in Senesse and transfer the output of the closed Belgian factory to Liverpool?

"Equal pay for all employees of the same multi" is an attractive slogan, but few who proclaim it have considered how this ideal can be implemented in the real world. To be meaningful, international corporate wage parity implies that the length of the working week be harmonized globally. But this is only the first step. Wages per se account for only part of the emoluments: these consist of (current and deferred) pay plus fringe benefits. In the industrial world the latter constitutes at least one-third (and often more) of the renumeration package. Are fringe benefits to be equalized as well? Taxes on employment vary widely; is the demand for global wage parity to be formulated in terms of pre-tax or post-tax earnings? What of the disparate state subsidies for fringe benefits? In several countries occupational pensions are financed largely by the employers; in others mainly by the employees. In some economies, 50:50 contributions are the rule. Neither Perlmutter nor Levinson have so far told us how the global labor bargainers would deal with these and other conundrums.

Leaving aside the practical aspects of implementation, union leaders in several OECD economies have raised non-economic objections of a fundamental nature. Bert Lundin, the chief of Sweden's metal workers, explicitly rejected multinational collective contracts because the Swedish

Federation of Trade Unions (LO) was pledged to sustain national agreements covering all the country's manual workers. Global bargaining involving only the employees of given multis would clearly offend the credo to which the LO is attached. According to Lundin, the Swedish trade union movement has not sought to maximize the earnings of the top layers of industrial employees: its sights were set on a high level of egalitarianism. By uplifting the emoluments of employees in the subsidiaries of foreign MNCs, global bargaining "would reduce or stop our policy of raising the wages of lower-paid employees in Sweden" (174).

In November 1980 the Ford world council met in Valencia. Despite the displeasure of several delegates, representatives of the Japanese automobile workers union had been invited. The head of their delegation, Tetsuo Osone, was given a hard time. The calm that ordinarily prevailed at these talking shops was shattered by Bernard Bassingham, a shop steward who was a veteran of many Ford strikes in Britain. He depicted the situation in Japan in a light that made nonsense of international wage parity. Bassingham maintained that global wage negotiations would be largely irrelevant for Japanese automobile TNCs because only 13 percent of the workers in the motor industry were employed directly.

This minority is frequently portrayed as working in model conditions and having a job for life. . . . The Japanese policy is to buy in most of their components from free-booting, back-street enterprises . . . where long hours and low pay are the norm and where social security provisions, holidays and safety regulations are non-existent.

Bassingham probably exaggerated, but according to press reports his blistering intervention "did little to reinforce the spirit of international trade union solidarity which was the theme of this gathering of senior Ford union officials convened by the IMF."

The parity slogan, concerned with equal money wages for the international labor force of given multis, does not postulate equal productivity per work-hour. Responsible trade unions sometimes deliberately opt for relatively lower emoluments to compensate employers for relatively lower productivity per work-hour. In extreme cases, trade unions and management prefer to continue with outdated modes of production when the main consideration is to retain in employment individuals who would be surplus to requirement if the latest capital-intensive machinery was installed. The attempts by U.S. unions to ram wage parity down the throats of Canadian workers stirred up a public debate which highlighted some of the inimical side effects. David Blake, in the study already cited, has paraphrased the arguments against cross-border wage parity that were adduced by the Canadian government.

Equal wages coupled with a lower level of productivity would cause the corporations to expand their operations in the US at the expense of Canadian production. After all, if we equalise wages when we have a lower level of productivity, then the unit cost of production relative to that in the United States will be greater. Given this, what is the advantage for the corporations to expand production in Canada when it is actually cheaper to manufacture in the US? (143)

During the UAW parity negotiations in 1968, Massey-Ferguson, a Canadian multi with factories in both Canada and the United States, claimed that the transportation costs associated with shipping farm implements from Ontario plants to the United States made it uneconomic to pay equal wages. The company insisted that if, against its will, the UAW succeeded in establishing the parity principle, it would close down some of its Canadian operations and relocate closer to the market in the U.S. midwest. Blake quotes an anonymous official of the nationalist-minded Canadian Labor Congress.

It was felt quite strongly that President Reuther and the UAW sought wage parity as a means of protecting the jobs of American workers. Indeed, Walter Reuther quite often expounded this same theme. . . . The American union members were frequently told that it was necessary to gain parity in order to ensure that lower Canadian wages did not take jobs away from them.

If Canadians perceived that they might suffer from the parity ambitions of U.S. based unions, how much more intense is the vested interest of the workers, employed in LDCs by foreign multis, that there should be no global wage bargaining. LDC delegates have said so explicitly at meetings of the ITSs. David Lilienthal could not have been more wrong when he predicted that the workers in LDCs would bargain for the "same rates of pay and fringe benefits as American operators receive." The opposite is true. The (non-political) LDC unions actually tell foreign MNCs of their readiness to work at lower wages—even when their productivity equals that of the employees in the home country. They are also prepared to put up with health and safety provisions that are less stringent than those imposed in OECD economies. The union leaders from the LDCs, who are invited to conventions in Geneva, scorn offers of multinational labor action which, in effect, would raise the costs of employing their members.

For most of the postwar period the UK shipowners had a curious closed-shop arrangement with the National Union of Seamen (NUS). Its (predominantly white) members received, for identical work, substantially higher wages than the Asian (mainly Indian) seamen. P&O explained that if the Indian seamen were paid the NUS rates, many of the British cargo ships would be uneconomic and consequently many Indian

and British seamen would become redundant. The shipowners paid to
the NUS a yearly £15 penalty per Asian employee. The Indian government warmly supported this arrangement. It wanted no imported wage
inflation and stressed that the emoluments of their seamen must be kept
low lest the comprehensive Indian wage structure was upset. The appropriate ITS (the International Transport Workers Federation) disapproved of this dual wage agreement and advocated the blacking of British
ships to compel the shipowners to increase the wages of their Indian
employees. The employers deliberated seriously on their response; some
were ready to reach parity in stages. But in 1983 the ITS, the NUS, and
the British shipowners received an ugly jolt. The National Union of
Seamen of India intervened to express its anger about the parity proposals. It expressed the fear that its members would price themselves
out of jobs if they could be employed only at European rates.

Finally, I wish to mention the protectionist stance of unions which
blatantly contravenes the spirit of multinational labor action. The AFL-
CIO has spent many millions of dollars to persuade legislators in Washington to restrict the import of manufactured goods into the United
States. From the vantage point of the American unions this expenditure
is intended to enhance the material well-being of their members. It is
an investment in job security for residents of the United States but a
recipe for unemployment in the rest of the world. It is not improper for
U.S. unions to support financially protectionist legislation, but critics
regard it as despicable that these very unions should participate in ITSs
and propagate the gospel of international labor solidarity. Donald
MacDonald, president of the Canadian Labor Congress, has given vent
to his indignation that a portion of the dues, collected by U.S.-based
unions from their members in Canada, were disbursed on lobbying for
bills that, if enacted, would damage the interests of Canadian trade
unionists.

Since the mid–1960s it would have been incongruous for ITSs to ignore
Japan's trade unions. Increasingly, these are being enrolled as constit-
uent members. In consequence, representatives of Japanese workers
make frequent appearances at sessions of the world company councils.
Their presence has on several occasions provoked fellow delegates to
voice acrimonious attacks on the export tactics of Japanese corporations.
These prompted some ugly xenophobic reactions in the Western Press.
Some European and North American unions have after all been in the
forefront of national campaigns to limit the import of Japanese goods.
Not unnaturally, the overt and covert hostility of OECD-based trade
union leaders has devitalized the drive for international solidarity on
the part of Japanese unions. As a rule, Japanese delegates listen in silence
to the attacks on their country—but not always. One distinguished union
leader, who had specially come to Europe from Tokyo to attend a con-

gress on international labor solidarity, was so stung by the repeated demands of European speakers for embargoes on imports from Japan that he replied sharply: "If import controls were to be applied, they should be applied universally. How much real international union solidarity would there be if controls were applied to Japan only?"

15

NO MORE GUNBOATS

The public statements uttered by members of the American-based multinational community make it continuously more difficult to determine whether they are simply non American or un-American. The multinational has not only declared war on the jobs of American workers but on the traditional concept of Americanism.

AFL-CIO report to the U.S. Congress

Because of the unfriendly attitude of many host countries, it is not always easy for multis to make direct foreign investments. Sometimes, however, the hindrances emanating from the home countries are even more vexatious.

When a corporation imports goods that could have been procured at home, it courts disfavor for depriving workers of jobs and weakening the country's balance of payments. The identical economic consequences may be generated by establishing a manufacturing subsidiary abroad, but the menacing clamor then is pitched considerably higher. Corporations—particularly those which pride themselves on being "socially responsible"—hate being denounced for unpatriotic behavior. William Lever, the English founder of Unilever, was enrolled in the ranks of the

Liberal party and shrugged off the poisonous attacks of Conservative party politicians who accused him of creating unemployment by opening up factories in foreign lands. If today's CEO of Unilever were the butt of such widely disseminated abuse, would he be as nonchalant as the first holder of this office? In February 1990 Siemens, the electronic multi, was attacked for making direct investments in Australasia. Its critics said that, instead, the corporation should have used the capital to create jobs in East Germany.

Investing overseas may whip up wild rebukes from environmentalists, who glibly accuse multis of planning to ravage nature and harm the health of the downtrodden masses in the projected host countries. Impoverished Belize was delighted when several food multis announced that they would invest in the planting of orange trees, to be followed by the building of a processing plant. Yet Anglo-Saxon environmentalist groups agitated to halt these projects because of the allegedly adverse effects on subtropical forests. In 1989 Scott Paper pulled out of a $650 million eucalyptus project in Indonesia. This U.S. multi was frightened off by the U.S. environmentalist lobby that denounced it for endangering the tropical forest. The WCC may call upon God to chastise TNCs that are striving to build factories where low-wage natives will be exploited. The anti-racist campaigners have a list of countries in which it is deemed nefarious to build any kind of factory. As one British critic, David Warburton, put it: "Is it right that BP should invest £26 million of your money in South Africa to prop up their vile creed of apartheid while they reduce job opportunities at home?" Nowadays all this sanctimonious (and sometimes politically malevolent) propaganda is taken very seriously by corporations that are obsessed with their good name and fear that their products might be boycotted. Better then to let the poor in the LDCs suffer and avoid direct investments in public relations minefields!

THE TRADE UNION LOBBY

The AFL-CIO has not been satisfied with blackening the PR images of MNCs that have spread their tentacles beyond the home country. They have attempted to bring about legislation that would penalize financially U.S. corporations with subsidiaries abroad. Well-endowed campaigns by U.S. unions have been targeted at members of Congress to persuade them to enact laws that would punish U.S.-based multis. Among the many detailed proposals were demands for the imposition of a tax on the value of any patents, licenses, and technology that are exported; levies were to be laid on the royalties received by U.S.-based MNCs (166).

Earlier mention was made of ICI's predicament when fellow multis with German domicile strove to block its proposed building of a PVC plant in Germany. This foreign hurdle was overcome in 1979 but ICI also had to remove obstacles in its home country. For two years British unions had opposed this putative export of jobs from Britain to Germany. Some economic journals had even speculated that because of virulent attacks by the unions that represented the workers of its UK operations, ICI might desist from proceeding with the German investment. Protracted industrial disputes were already giving management severe headaches in 1977 and 1978. David Warburton, the chairman of a committee of 40 unions recognized to bargain on behalf of ICI employees, warned of the dire consequences if ICI built a plant in Wilhelmshaven.

There is a keen sense of betrayal. . . . I can only express my disgust at the way ICI has acted. . . . We are reaching the limit of joint discussions if ICI intend to go on like this. . . . There were reports that ICI intended to cut investment in Britain. . . . That was scandalous.

ICI's board was obviously convinced of the economic rationale underpinning this defamed project. It must also have suspected, right from the outset, that the unions would not cooperate; for this reason the UK chemical multi was coy about revealing details until the last moment. Hostile British press comments did not help. Perhaps surprisingly for the pre-Thatcher period, and uncharacteristic of the conduct of Western MNCs, ICI decided in this instance to disregard public opinion and brushed aside implied union threats in the home country.

Volkswagen's head office had for years realized the urgent need to manufacture in the United States and had been actively investigating suitable locations. Unlike ICI's board, the supervisory board of the German automobile MNC was not prepared to invest abroad unless the union bosses and the rank and file expressly blessed the venture. In 1974 the unions formally turned down the U.S. project and the vacillations of top management continued. Only in April 1976 was agreement reached (88). This belated approval from the unions cost the German multi dearly because during the years of wavering its market share in North America had declined.

During the 1980s, the major Japanese manufacturing corporations were turning themselves into TNCs, and consequently had to reckon with the hostility of their domestic unions. It was intended that Honda's projected subsidiary in the United States should also manufacture cars for export to the home country. This met with resistance from the Japanese labor force because of fears that it would "import unemployment." Only after some bickering did the leaders of Honda's company union reconcile themselves to management's promise that no jobs would be lost as a result of the U.S. investment. The plans for Nissan's subsidiary in Britain stayed on the drawingboard for a long time. It is said that the opposition to this project, announced in July 1983, by the Federation of Japan's Automobile Workers Union carried a great deal of weight. The chief union boss of Nissan, Ichiro Shioji, is credited with having held up the implementation of this manufacturing plant in Europe. Only after certain concessions were made to his union was he ready to state publicly that he had changed his mind and henceforth would support the management's proposals. According to Shioji, Nissan's board had had to accept that in future its foreign investment plans were to be scrutinized by the union. The budding Japanese TNCs may have learned the importance of consulting their unions at an early stage. In the past, all the barriers to Japanese corporations becoming international manufacturers were in the host countries; now some of them are clearly at home.

IN DAYS GONE BY

Multis of all nationalities used to be able to rely on the active assistance of helpful governments in their home country. The postulated right to invest overseas was often sustained by diplomatic pressure. The big powers intervened forcefully to protect investments owned by their nationals. If such interventions did not bear fruit, grovernments showed their displeasure by punishing the guilty host country.

Before World War II the burgeoning U.S. multis had cause to grumble that the European powers were hostile to U.S. investors in Europe and also tried to stop them advancing into India, the Dutch East Indies, and the Middle East. The victims complained loudly to Washington, and indeed "the State Department came to the assistance of American business by urging an 'open door' " (93). Such commercial contests between multis of different nationalities did not call for gunboats. A more arduous task was to put in place those host countries which from time to time sought to demonstrate their national virility by kicking out foreign investors or refusing to pay interest on loans that they had raised abroad. In those days financial institutions and MNCs could turn confidently to their government. The Royal Navy once sent a battleship as a gentle warning to the Guatemalan authorities when they had failed to service loans floated by London banks (139). Standard Oil of New Jersey played an important role in Peru for decades. In 1914 the Peruvians did not as yet dare to confiscate foreign-owned assets, but they aimed to penalize the U.S. oil multi by formulating sharp tax increases. In 1915 the U.S. ambassador in Lima, on direct instructions from Washington, told the Peruvians to think again—they did (96).

Today, Mexicans still celebrate the 18th of March as a national holiday, for on that day in 1938 the decree was signed expropriating all foreign oil holdings. The Western powers, but especially Washington, were incensed. They could not make Mexico change its mind. (Only at a much later stage was some kind of compensation paid under an arbitration award.) The foreign governments could not put the clock back and restore the property rights of the oil multis. But—and this is the basic difference between 1938 and 1988—they could make the Mexicans suffer. The country was placed on an international blacklist that kept it in an economic limbo until after the end of World War II. The stigma of expropriation and unsettled compensation meant that, with a handful of exceptions, no new foreign direct investments were made in any sector of the economy (164).

From the inception of its direct investments in Latin America, UFCO depended on real and metaphorical U.S. gunboats. Perhaps the last classical example—described by one critic as the "most sordid operation in American history" (165)—occurred during President Eisenhower's term of office. UFCO then employed, directly and indirectly, 40,000 people out of a total Guatemalan population of 3 million. The earthly paradise of this multi was devastated after a left-wing regime took over in 1945. By 1953 large tracts of land owned by UFCO had actually been expropriated. The company was offered $3 per acre. When the State Department delivered a formal complaint, the claim was for $75 per acre. Further expropriations and other irritations followed. UFCO then lobbied in Washington for help to overthrow the government of Jacobo Arbenez. Under the direction of the CIA and with the support of Eisenhower's administration, together with some UFCO money, Guatemala was 'liberated' in 1954 and the U.S. food multi's candidate, Castillo Armas, came to power. He returned the expropriated land, introduced a modest new income tax and subjugated the unions that had irked UFCO (99).

In 1962 Congress passed an amendment (named after Senator Hickenlooper) to the Foreign Assistance Act of 1961, which required the U.S. president to cut off assistance, after six months, to any government that had expropriated U.S. property without taking appropriate steps to pay compensation. The protagonists of the amendment hoped that it would prevent further expropriations and thus encourage multis to invest in LDCs (97). The fact that it was deemed necessary to enact such a provision indicated that U.S. TNCs which ran into trouble overseas could no longer expect automatic support from their government. Congress was therefore imposing a statutory duty on Washington to act. History, however, has shown that this did not bring back the good old days. President Kennedy, who had entered the White House in the year before the Hickenlooper amendment became law, did not disguise his hostility to a statute which betokened that Washington was obliged to assist U.S. TNCs.

Richard Olson is the author of a well-researched study of the application of the Hickenlooper amendment before it became dormant (101). In 1961 the extreme-left government of Ceylon, led by Sirima Bandaranaike, expropriated some (and later all) of the facilities of three oil multis: Esso, Caltex, and Shell. Initially, the U.S. chargé d'affaires and the British high commissioner made only mild representations in which they advised the host government that direct investments by foreign multis would be deterred by the prospect of expropriation. In a belligerent reply, the Ceylonese asserted that since gaining independence, Western multis had shown no interest in their country and consequently Ceylon had nothing to lose. Furthermore, the Soviet Union was willing to provide oil on advantageous terms. In 1962 the dispute hotted up and the U.S. ambassador cautioned that "aid from Washington might be stopped if American oil companies are not quickly compensated." In January 1963 there was a formal warning that the Hickenlooper amendment would be brought into play—as indeed it was. U.S. economic aid to Ceylon was curtailed drastically and Washington used its decisive influence to bring about parallel reductions in the disbursements of international agencies. Hickenlooper triumphed because the resultant economic distress largely accounted for the ousting of the Bandaranaike government at the 1965 elections. The new, more moderate, administration immediately compensated the oil multis and U.S. aid appropriations went up steadily.

According to Olson, the Ceylonese authorities had initially not believed that—in the changed climate of the 1960s—the U.S. government would put into practice the Hickenlooper amendment. *The Economist* was indignant about the United States precipitate action and "the uses made of foreign aid . . . to make an example of little Ceylon. . . . Washington could not care less for what happens in or to Ceylon." The British government maintained a low public profile. Some alleged that it was not upholding vigorously the compensation claims for the expropriated assets of Shell. By appeasing the Ceylonese, it was hoped to safeguard the assets of other British-based multis. In 1964 the Bandaranaike administration passed a law limiting the profit remittances of all foreign companies doing business in Ceylon. This general anti-multi legislation seems to have galvanized the British. Only then did London alter its stance and put formal pressure on Ceylon regarding the Shell assets.

UNFRIENDLY HOME GOVERNMENTS

As anti-multi populism was blossoming in the early 1960s, Western governments ceased to pretend that they were protecting their own TNCs. In the motherland of the mightiest international corporations, six presidents—Kennedy, Johnson, Nixon, Ford, Carter, and Reagan—proved that they no longer cared much if American multis were kicked around in foreign lands. Of course there were occasional mild protests but no gunboats were sent forth; no substantive punitive aid cuts were imposed; no boycotts were organized. The United States (and some other Western powers) did actually do all three for a number of foreign policy reasons, but not in order to restore the material fortunes of their TNCs. The host countries have understood the message only too well.

Perhaps it was not obvious in 1965 that the Ceylon affair signalled the end of an era in which multis could lean on the friendly shoulders of the government of the country in which they were domiciled. But in 1985 there was certainly no intellectual justification for the dissemination of the following caricature of the modern multis, which appeared in an English-language Communist guide.

To protect their own interests in the developing countries, the TNCs often seek support from the governments of the imperialist states. They make particularly frequent use of such methods as diplomatic pressure, threats that economic 'aid' will be discontinued, demonstrations of military might, in particular, the dispatch of naval forces to the shores of a given country, military diversions, economic and political boycotts, and the like (1).

Far from encouraging multis to invest overseas, certain countries have instituted specifically higher corporation taxes on profits earned abroad. When and where exchange controls function, governments have made good use of this administrative instrument to impede their companies from establishing foreign manufacturing subsidiaries. Inter alia, they have done so by charging hefty premiums on the official exchange rate when their TNCs were allotted foreign currency. A major proportion of the foreign-earned profits have had to be remitted home and there was no automatic entitlement to reinvest them abroad. Politicians have been known to prohibit altogether the export of capital to countries of which they disapproved. The influential vice president of the Bank of America, Walter Hoadley, thundered: "Our multinationals get no Brownie points from the State Department for getting a piece of the action for the U.S." (8). Instead, they must put up with anti-bribery laws, restrictions on trade with the COMECON, regulations forbidding them to comply with the Arab boycott, and so on. President Johnson implicitly subscribed to the legend that the U.S. TNCs were largely responsible for the BoP deficit of the United States. As a consequence, the 900 largest TNCs were brought under government surveillance. A special supervising agency was set up in Washington, whose officials ordered the international companies based in the U.S. to reduce drastically their projected capital outflow, return liquid assets from abroad, and make foreign subsidiaries remit an enhanced proportion of their profits.

Per capita, Sweden has more multis than any other country. Nevertheless, the Swedish authorities have had at times an ideological commitment not to encourage direct investments overseas. Sweden's politicians maintained that if the TNCs of their country intended to continue exploiting the oppressed masses of the LDCs, they should be made to comply with a number of 'social conditions': specific facilities were to be provided for native employees pertaining to health, housing, nutrition, libraries, and other leisure activities. Though such absurd injunctions were in fact promulgated, Robinson has found that most Swedish corporations just ignored them (9). Sweden is not alone in banning outright direct investments in blacklisted countries. Among others, Portugal and Chile have been on such a list and of course South Africa is an economy in which most Western governments do not want their multis to invest—at least not overtly.

Nowadays, governments assume no responsibility for the fate of their multis abroad. They say so with special vigor when implored to defend them because they are being harassed in host states. The opposite may occur. The authorities in the home countries have been known to bully their own TNCs by promulgating restrictions which prevent them from competing in the host countries on an equal basis with native businesses. In fact, their foreign subsidiaries may sometimes be asked to break the laws of the host country in order to comply with laws enacted in the home country. Washington once stopped the Canadian subsidiaries of three U.S. food multis from processing Canadian wheat that Ottawa had sold to Cuba. In 1982 the Le Havre plant of Dresser Industries was ordered by Washington not to go ahead with its plans to supply the contractors of a Soviet gas pipeline. This placed it at the center of a Franco-U.S. conflict, uniting all sections of French society against the U.S. multi, which was seen to place loyalty to its home government above the commercial interests of France. Another attempt by Washington to hold up the 'undesirable' sales by the French subsidiary of a US multi failed, largely because it was not wholly owned. Fruehauf's French subsidiary had undertaken to manufacture certain components that were to be incorporated by its customer, Berliet Automobiles, in 60 lorries destined for China. On the orders of the U.S. government, the head office of Fruehauf ordered its subsidiary not to proceed with this contract (11). Berliet threatened to sue for damages and the (French) minority shareholders persuaded the court to appoint a judicial administrator who had the authority to carry out this prohibited contract. As the very existence of the subsidiary was at stake—possibly 600 jobs could have been lost—French law empowered the court to intervene. It was held "that the interest of the subsidiary as a separate economic entity can be different and even superior to the concerns of the parent company" (12).

When Eisenhower became president, most of the major Latin American mining and oil concessions were owned by foreign, largely U.S.-based, multis. By the time Reagan left the White House, the overwhelming majority of these subsidiaries had been taken over. Why did the United States, the domicile of the majority of the world's largest TNCs, allow this to happen without retaliating? Kennedy, Johnson, Ford, and Carter prided themselves on being 'good guys.' With some exceptions, they rarely even went through the motions of threatening to punish guilty host governments that had blatantly stolen the property of U.S. corporations. As for actual punitive measures, the few that were applied were mild and did not last long. Nixon and Reagan did not choose to be known as presidents who were soft on the enemies of the United States, but they behaved in this context as if they too were seeking the approbation of the do-gooders at home and abroad. In a major speech President Nixon spelled out his attitude to rapacious Latin American governments. He told them that he would "not encourage U.S. private investment where it is not wanted or where local conditions face it with unwarranted risks." Fine words, but he had been expected to outline what the world's mightiest power would do when U.S. assets were expropriated unilaterally. The silence was deafening. Nixon only offered advice to foreign politicians who elected to behave in a manner inimical to existing investors: these countries must be ready for "a serious impairment of their ability to attract investment funds." Nobody was frightened.

Jessica Einhorn has clearly had access to internal sources of several administrations in Washington (97). Hers is a detailed examination of the disingenuous decision-making process in the Latin American Bureau of the State Department. No president has actually declared that the U.S. government would applaud all expropriations. But having declined to send gunboats, break off diplomatic relations, or fulfill their statutory obligations in accordance with the Hickenlooper amendment, U.S. administrations since the mid–1960s have been content merely to warn that "non-overt economic pressure" might be exerted. U.S. governments no longer have the will to wound and their postures—as valiant champions of beleaguered U.S. multis—are sometimes farcical and almost always futile. Why this changed attitude to multis in powerful countries of the OECD? The complex answer has been divided into eight parts.

1. Western public opinion does not tolerate neo-imperialism even if it means that some of its nationals are humiliated abroad. U.S. presidents of both parties do not wish to be seen as the handmaidens of the TNCs. In the last third of the twentieth century, the gringos sought to be loved in Latin America! Earlier in this chapter there was a reference to Eisenhower's old-fashioned intervention in favour of the UFCO multi. Yet soon after the fateful decision was made, the president was so stung by

hostile criticism at home and in Latin America that he looked benignly on the prosecution of UFCO by the Justice Department for violation of antitrust laws. UFCO became involved in protracted litigation with Washington that was to cost it dearly. Ironically, the company had to accept a consent decree that curtailed its business in Guatemala. Eisenhower was happy to have demonstrated, by default, that he was not the blind protector of *El Pulpo*.

President Kennedy did not want to appear merely unhelpful to U.S. multis. He wanted it known that at times he rejoiced in the tribulations of U.S. corporations abroad. (This attitude is not unique. Swedish and Dutch governments have openly sided with host countries against their own multis.) When Belaunde became president of Peru in 1963, he "concluded that without a doubt, Kennedy would not stand behind Esso in a confrontation between its Peruvian subsidiary and the government of Peru." The Peruvian capitalists could not at first understand why Kennedy was wavering in the defense of U.S. capital in Peru. Why did he not squash the attempts to expropriate Esso's La Brea y Parinas oil fields? They soon learned the truth. According to A. Pinelo, Robert Kennedy, brother of the president, made the right noises: "You Peruvians want to nationalize La Brea y Parinas. Well, do it. Nothing is going to happen" (96).

The testimony of Arthur Schlesinger, a politician and historian who was very close to the Kennedy family, must be taken very seriously. He has set out in detail how President John Kennedy and Attorney General Robert Kennedy implicitly encouraged the displacement of U.S. multis in the American hemisphere. When in April 1962 ITT properties were being expropriated in Brazil, "Congress was huffing and puffing." Geneen urged sanctions against Brazil but the president made it clear that he was "not defending the interests of big business" and, in any case, saw no future for foreign ownership in fields like telephones and other utilities. We owe a debt of gratitude to Schlesinger for revealing some of the Machiavellian cynicism of the Kennedy brothers. When Vice President Joao Goulart visited the White House, the president urged Brazil not to embarrass him by expropriating U.S. assets without compensation—because this would only annoy Congress. The president said that he wanted to see procedures adopted that would enable LDCs "to engage in 'frictionless' nationalization." Schlesinger rubs it in: "A striking change from previous American Presidents whose interest was in stopping nationalization per se." There were instances of crossed wires when threats to U.S. multis provoked official condemnations in Washington. The Kennedy brothers rebuked the responsible officials and politicians for being beastly to foreign rulers in the West Indies and Latin America who contrived to displace U.S. multis. In December 1962 Attorney General Robert Kennedy visited Brazil. To flaunt his anti-multi credentials to the whole of Latin America, Kennedy told his hosts that he himself "had struggled with some of the same [U.S.] companies with which the Brazilian Government was sometimes in conflict." He spoke in English but the message was translated into Portugese and Spanish (163).

2. It has been argued that TNCs are driven out of LDCs because the host governments have become "hypersensitive to anything that suggests colonialism." This is the sort of defense that U.S. liberals like George Ball put forward when U.S. multis had their assets confiscated. In fact, LDCs are more aggressive today because they have learned that expropriations and defaulting on loans are not the sort of things for which one gets punished heavily, if punished at all. L'appetit vient en mangeant.

John Saul and Elliot Miller, graduates of MIT, were the main actors in what became known as the Kenyan "ruby mine scandal." In the 1970s they staked out what promised to become the world's largest source of rubies. Saul and Miller naively thought that by taking in Kenyan partners, the 50:50 joint venture might protect their property rights.The authorities had other plans. They deported them, prohibiting their return to the country. The ownership of the mine was transferred to a public sector company in which the wife of President Kenyatta was a partner. The U.S. Department of State lodged formal protests against the mistreatment of the two U.S. entrepreneurs and the confiscation of U.S.-owned assets without compensation.

The Kenyan government, however, has not taken this protest seriously. Apparently it feels secure in the knowledge that no matter how outrageous the conduct of its officials and the flouting of the traditional rules of international law, the Kenyan government will not be brought to account. Third World countries like Kenya have taken the measure of the U.S. Department of State. They know that the greatest power in the world is unlikely to take any retaliatory action (189).

3. R. Vernon, one of the sophisticated critics of U.S. TNCs, has assured politicians in Washington that they need not feel guilty if they neglect to safeguard U.S.-based international corporations: there is "uncertainty as to whether [their] interests should be regarded as American" (147). After all, by the identity of their employees the foreign subsidiaries are less than 1 percent American; by source of funds, perhaps only 25 percent American; by the identity of the governments that receive their taxes, practically 100 percent foreign. Vernon condescingly concludes that the United States might still wish to foster the rights and interests of U.S. multis. However, he pours cold water on any policy of protecting effectively their assets overseas. Vernon explicitly questions the benefits that the United States derives from its multinational enterprises—so why send gunboats?

4. Host countries rarely proclaim the expropriation of all foreign assets, not even the confiscation of all the properties of the multis of one nationality. Usually they are knocked off one by one! Nixon certainly did not have the ambition of being evaluated by historians as a weakling. Nevertheless, when soon after taking office the Peruvian government of General Velasco confiscated Esso's oilfields in 1968–69, he acted almost as if he were imbued with the spirit of President Kennedy. Most of the facts are not in dispute though there is still some disagreement as to why Nixon acted as he did. J. Einhorn commences her book on this ironic note.

In April of 1969 the Nixon administration pleasantly surprised an interested public of Peru watchers in the U.S. by deferring the application of sanctions required by U.S. law in response to an expropriation that had occurred six months before. In August of that same year these sanctions were once again deferred—and then disappeared from public view (97).

President Nixon was made aware that any anti-Peru sanctions would strain relations with other Latin American countries and he did not wish to be seen sabotaging the Alliance for Progress. Velasco's "brilliant strategy" made use of a carrot, but mainly depended on wielding several blackmailing sticks. Peru's government gently pointed out that the expropriation of Esso's subsidiary was a unique case and that there was no intention of harming other U.S. interests. If, however, sanctions were applied, Peru would hit back by banning all profit remittances to the United States. Furthermore, much valuable property of U.S. TNCs would be confiscated. Finally, Nixon had to concede that if he applied the law, that is, the Hickenlooper amendment, it might have a domino effect all over Latin America and lead to additional expropriations in other LDCs (98). Nixon was advised to exercise expediency.

5. The seemingly perverse behavior of the Canadian government was not appreciated by its southern neighbor. However, other countries with TNCs of their own, and which concurrently also host the subsidiaries of foreign multis, saw the logic of Ottawa's position. The assets of Alcan's subsidiary in Guyana were nationalized because, as the host country claimed, the Canadian multi had refused to build a smelter. Alcan's head office requested its government to intervene actively. How naive! Though at first Guyana made no offer of any proper compensation, the sizable Canadian aid program to Guyana continued. When the World Bank proposed to make a loan to Guyana, the Canadian representative cast his vote for it. The U.S. government, however, wanted to uphold the principle that host governments should pay adequate, prompt, and effective compensation for nationalizations. Though Washington had no direct interest in the matter, it expressed its displeasure with Guyana

by abstaining from voting in favor of the loan (102). The Canadians behaved in this curious manner because they were intent on being seen to have clean hands should they consider it propitious to put the heat on the Canadian subsidiaries of U.S. multis. Canada sought to establish the right to proceed against U.S.-owned assets on its soil. If this happened, the Canadian politicians wanted to be morally entitled to demand a hands-off policy from Washington. Ottawa sacrificed the interests of a Canadian multi to neutralize possible future adverse reactions in the United States, which might be triggered off should the Canadian authorities find it expedient to harass U.S. TNCs.

6. It can prove instructive to peruse the annual reports of companies that have suffered financially through the expropriation of foreign subsidiaries. The reader will find the events recorded—accountancy rules and company law demand this. But rarely does one come across blistering criticism of the predatory governments that have unilaterally taken over the assets owned by foreign investors. This meekness is often linked to the illusion that if the company makes no noise, it might in time receive some morsels of compensation. Many ingenuous CEOs believe that if they were to scream loudly about the robbery in host country A, their subsidiaries in host countries B, C, and D would be endangered. Numerous multis, which are pounced upon in Latin America but cannot count on efficacious assistance from their own governments, prefer to withdraw quietly rather than put up a fight.

7. Some multis will do battle even if they have to step over the corpses of their confreres. The arms of U.S. presidents have been twisted by certain selfish TNCs that have urged Washington not to take punitive action against countries that have confiscated the assets of other multis. Several reports tell of the attitude of U.S. TNCs with subsidiaries in Peru that wanted Nixon to overlook the expropriation of Esso, saying that it "got what it deserved." British and U.S. banks have unashamedly provided loans to host governments which, following the nationalization of foreign properties, needed foreign currency to make some nominal payments.

8. R. Olson has conjectured that if the Ceylonese had not been so stiff-necked, they would not have been punished by the Americans (101). They ought to have used some diplomatic finesse, issued spurious counter-claims, and made some wild assertions about excessive profits by foreign oil multis. They would thus not have undermined the bureaucrats within the U.S. administration who were eager to sabotage the application of the Hickenlooper amendment by devising a token response to the expropriation. Had the Ceylonese been more devious, they could have avoided an aid cutoff.

In his description of the cynical behavior of LDCs that take over the assets of foreign multis, G. Philip writes (seemingly, with some appro-

bation) of the increasing sophistication shown by the expropriators. Formally, they are no longer thieves because they offer compensation of
some kind: they are flexible "as to the quantity, manner and timing of
such payments" (100). Governments that have instituted insurance
schemes for foreign direct investments, to cover their MNCs against
political risks, often find it difficult to ascertain how far "creeping expropriation"—for example, excessive taxation, the withdrawal of import
licenses, breaches of contract by public authorities—entitles the aggrieved corporations to compensation from the state agency that collected their premiums. Clear and explicit political expropriation has hit
TNCs in Cuba, Chile, Tanzania, and Uganda, but honest robbers are
now few and far between (103). One of Unilever's annual reports records
unemotionally that

in one or two countries it is being made very difficult for us to carry on business.
The extreme case is Burma, which now levies a tax of 99% on all profits over
£23,000. Our interest in Egypt is now limited to a fee for specialist assistance
and the use of trade-marks which we receive from the business of which we
formerly had a 50% share. This business was finally taken over by the state in
1963, compensation being payable in Egyptian state bonds. In Indonesia . . . there
have been attempts by trade unions to take over our factories and offices and
this has led to the business being put under the supervision of the Indonesian
Ministry of People's Industry, although we retain the ownership.

What about the Hickenlooper amendment when, in October 1969,
Bolivian authorities seized the local assets of Gulf Oil? The expropriators
provided a 'justification' that other LDCs governments have cited since.
Gulf Oil was told that not a single penny of compensation would be
handed over because the U.S. multi's past profits in Bolivia represented
'just compensation.' A year later Bolivia revised its position—or did it?
Gulf Oil had claimed that its seized assets represented investments made
over 14 years, of about $169 million. The Bolivian Minister of Mines and
Petroleum offered $79 million, but the true character of the 'compen-
sation' was clarified when the small print revealed that the money was
to be paid, interest-free, over a period exceeding 20 years.

Prime Minister Michael Manley seemed a contented man when, in an
orchestrated "display of friendship between Jamaica and the U.S.," the
California-based multi Kaiser signed away to his government 51 percent
of the local mining subsidiary. (Jamaica undertook to pay $25 million
over ten years with interest.) With mock humility Kaiser's CEO told the
specially invited journalists that the agreement was beneficial and fair;
it had helped to forge a new bond of understanding and trust. Nothing
was said on that occasion of what had really compelled Kaiser to agree.
Michael Manley had exerted effective pressure on the six U.S. multis
that had direct Jamaican investments in bauxite and aluminum. Jamaica,

the sovereign host country, had imposed unilaterally a tenfold increase in the bauxite export levy!

Nothing has been said so far about the attitude of the Japanese government. Does it also allow host countries to push around the MNCs of Asia's most powerful country? At first Tokyo thought that the new rules of the game did not apply to it and consequently considered retaliation against weak countries that behaved very naughtily to its nationals and companies. But Japan was soon forced to learn that LDCs regard it like any other homeland of MNCs. In November 1986 the new president of the Philippines visited Tokyo to beg for increased aid and also sought to attract more direct Japanese investments. Corazon Aquino was apparently given certain assurances. These were "adversely affected" when, shortly after her return, the head of Mitsui's subsidiary in Manila was kidnapped. Tokyo was angry with the Philippine government for not obtaining his speedy release. Japan did not send gunboats, but instead blacklisted Manila for tourism and slowed down its promised aid disbursements. Filipinos were outraged—not at their failure to find the kidnap victim but at the neo-imperialist measures directed against a poor LDC by the administration of an OECD giant. President Aquino lodged an official protest against the blacklisting. The Japanese were highly embarrassed and their embassy in Manila issued a statement implying that, irrespective of the fate of the Mitsui executive, Japan would after all provide the promised aid. The Mitsui executive was released after 136 days in captivity; he had been kept bound hand and foot. Before he was flown home, President Aquino chatted to the liberated Japanese businessman. She was able to tell the press that he had not been tortured. Japan marked the release by cancelling its standing warning to Japanese tourists not to visit the Philippines.

16

THE INHOSPITABLE HOST COUNTRIES

The global company overwhelming the small state has become a new ogre. ... If there is one thing more alarming to a small country than the presence of multinationals, it is their absence.

Anthony Sampson

Spain, Tanzania, the United States, Yugoslavia, and some one hundred other economies host subsidiaries of foreign multis. OECD and LDC state agencies encourge inward direct investment. Naturally, these stress the positive features of the host economy. The unpublished inhospitable features emanate from the native entrepreneurs (plus, sometimes, the established subsidiaries of foreign multis); the native unions; and the native political decision-makers who sway the investment climate (and formulate the regulations governing the scope of foreign-owned operations). In the very last section of this chapter it is suggested that nowadays the head offices of circumspect multis pay little heed to promises and current practices. Increasingly, they examine whether the host country is likely to honor its contractual undertakings. Wary TNCs strive to evaluate what radical changes might occur after the finishing touches have been put to their direct investments.

NATIVE ENTREPRENEURS

Many of the anti-multi vilifications imply that opposition to foreign MNCs is spearheaded by the left. This ideological depiction is not universally valid. In the LDCs particularly, the "nationalist right"—the "bourgeois pragmatists"—play a significant role in barring the entry of foreign corporations. The representatives of small businesses in South Korea have obstructed the establishment of certain foreign-owned factories that would have introduced innovative technology. In May 1988 Brazil's Constitutional Assembly came out with a set of anti-MNC restrictions that were meant to frighten off potential foreign investors and drive out existing ones. Brazil had been one of the few Latin American economies in which majority foreign participation in mining was still allowed. Now non-Brazilian TNCs were to be compelled to transfer their controlling ownership to native capitalists. Non-mining subsidiaries were being penalized in other ways. Though the left gave its support, the anti-multi measures were largely due to the influence of native Brazilian business leaders.

India furnishes a significant example of an LDC in which native non-left politicians and entrepreneurs were in the vanguard of a rabid anti-multi crusade. M. Kidron has recalled how, before independence, the Indian Merchants Chamber had propagated the repatriation of all British investments. When India became a sovereign country, the Birla and Tata families—the owners of India's largest manufacturing conglomerates—fanned the flames of economic xenophobia. The All-India Manufacturers' Organization attacked the socialist leaders of the Congress Party for not expelling the existing multis. (Many of the Indian left had actually sought to encourage the influx of direct investments.) When the native bourgeoisie portrayed this as a betrayal of the new nation–state, some of the left-wing politicians counter-attacked. The Birlas, Tatas, and their allies were warned that if the government was impelled to penalize foreign businesses, then this policy might be extended to smother the native capitalists. The Indian Minister of Finance spelled it out: "If we were to stop the remittance of dividends [by Indian subsidiaries to their foreign parents], then we might as well be driven to sequestrate the payment of dividends to Indian shareholders also" (41).

While Indira Gandhi was prime minister, the anti-multi campaign was at its height. One important exception was made and that was on ethnic grounds. Foreigners of Indian descent were given special privileges which put them in a more favorable position than either native Indians or non-Indian foreigners. Investments made in India by non-resident Indians—and foreign companies majority-controlled by them—were exempted from some of the restrictions that applied generally to the investments of TNCs headquartered outside India. When his mother was still India's ruler, Rajiv Gandhi applauded this ethnic discrimination: "They [the non-resident Indians] are our brothers and if they want to put their foreign exchange in this country, they are welcome." It was not the left but the native entrepreneurs who were displeased with this concession to 'foreign' capitalists. Things took a nasty turn when Swraj Paul, an Indian emigrant who had built up the London-based industrial conglomerate Caparo, announced that he was planning the takeover of several sizeable Indian companies. The governor of the National Bank warned that "while all reasonable facilities ought to be provided to attract funds from non-resident Indians, it is necessary to protect well managed companies against takeover bids from abroad." Paul's biographer recounts how an Indian industrialist, in charge of the targeted businesses, warned that Paul might be a front for multinational money and should consequently be resisted because "India has to protect itself from multinationals per se." He attacked non-resident Indians who were potential investors in India.

You have run away from the Indian conditions, the Indian wages and Indian high taxation. But we have stayed here. Therefore, we should be protected. . . . And I can tell you, you non-Indians of all hues and colours, you are all ruddy mercenaries (153).

In developed countries the language employed may differ from the colorful jargon in LDCs but the hostile sentiments of the native entrepreneurs are often not dissimilar. There is, however, a substantive difference: if a foreign MNC is determined to build a greenfield plant in the face of local opposition, this is frequently, but not always, possible. In all OECD countries certain segments of the economy are mandatorily closed to direct investments by foreign corporations.

Attitudes to hostile takeovers differ widely in the OECD. (The issue does not arise in LDCs because they harbor few suitable targets and, in any case, all direct foreign investments are controlled strictly.) Diehard Switzerland encourages its companies to formulate Articles of Association to make them bid-proof against corporate raiders in general and alien ones in particular. Swiss TNCs crave protection from encroachments by non-Swiss intruders, though their own global empires have been built through scores of bellicose takeovers. On the other end of the spectrum is the United States which, with very few exceptions, has so far allowed natives and foreigners to bid freely for the equity of American corporations. The United States does not spend taxpayers' money to encourage inward investment and yet has proved to be the most powerful magnet in the world to pull in foreign investors.

In between Switzerland and the United States there are varying degrees of intolerance toward hostile takeovers. In theory, France and

Germany tolerate them but in practice their gates are closed firmly. While Australia and Canada are somewhat more lax, they too treat with disdain the efforts of MNCs to expand by buying up existing native businesses on the open market. Japan and Sweden behave almost as sternly as Switzerland though there are instances in which foreigners were allowed to purchase small businesses. The large corporations, however, are shielded. Sweden's premier multi, the ballbearing manufacturer SKF, has always denounced xenophobic non-Swedish governments that have harassed its subsidiaries in many parts of the world. When Prime Minister Harold Wilson successfully halted SKF's attempt to acquire a British competitor through open-market share purchases, the Swedish TNC raged with anger. Howard Perlmutter was the corporation's mentor and regularly coached its executives on how to turn SKF into a truly geo-centric-oriented company. SKF's directors were of course internationalists, but they hated the thought that one day a powerful foreign TNC might bid for its equity. So they stipulated that non-Swedes could own only B shares which had one vote each; Swedes alone were permitted to own A shares of one thousand votes each.

Under both Labour and Conservative administrations, the United Kingdom has proved to be a relatively permissive society in relation to contested takeovers by foreign raiders. Nevertheless, besieged British companies with powerful allies have been able to exert sufficient pressure to persuade the UK authorities to frustrate hostile bids from abroad, ostensibly 'in the national interest.' To save face, UK politicians have sometimes extracted promises of good behavior from corporate bidders; these were ordinarily given with alacrity because both sides knew them to be worthless. During the 1960s the Labour government wielded a sophisticated, seemingly respectable, anti-multi weapon. A state merchant bank (the Industrial Reorganisation Corporation—IRC), with ample funds, could be instructed to counter-bid in the open market. Rather than ban outright the hostile takeover bids, it was considered expedient to have them defeated by 'market forces.' Alternatively, British target companies that were threatened by unwelcome bids from foreign TNCs could be rescued through the injection of IRC money. The head of this state bank, Charles Villiers, explained that his strategy was "to preserve our national assets where a British solution can be found."

NATIVE TRADE UNIONS

To the pleasant surprise of many TNCs, LDC unions—which are not manipulated for religious or ideological objectives—frequently welcome manufacturing operations by foreign multis. Almost invariably these are greenfield enterprises that do not adversely affect employment in existing union-organized factories. The newly created production facilities of MNCs are more likely to destroy the livelihood of small, non-unionized workshops. Rhetoric aside, LDC union leaders are not concerned primarily with the national level of employment. They strive to enlist the maximum number of members and recruiting efforts are most productive in large-scale enterprises. Many of the foreign MNCs actually seek out the native union leaders and offer help in organizing the labor force. The advent of employers, who voluntarily offer to pay higher wages than the native entrepreneurs, often gratifies the LDC unions. Enclaves of relatively high-paid workers, employed by the subsidiaries of foreign multis, prove helpful when the unions bargain with indigenous firms. (Hence private sector and public sector employers have cause to resist the invasion of their country by alien corporations.)

While (non-political) LDC unions have specific reasons to be friendly to foreign-based MNCs, unions in the developed economies may find themselves in a trying predicament. In hostile takeovers, unions (and unorganized employees) frequently team up with their bosses to repel the foreign multis. While the directors and senior executives of a targeted company may justifiably reflect that they personally would be displaced from their position of power, this consideration ought not to worry the majority of the employees. Nevertheless, xenophobia and apprehensions of the unknown grip many rank-and-file trade unionists. There are a number of cases on record in which even bids agreed to by the directors and shareholders could only be consummated after some special compensation had been paid to manual workers who, in any case, were guaranteed continued employment by the new owners.

OECD trade unions are also often in the forefront of the battle when foreign multis announce plans to build greenfield plants. Seemingly, these hold out the prospect of additional employment opportunities. National union leaders, however, are rightfully concerned that the *net* impact on their total membership will at best be neutral and may actually be negative. When the Japanese zip fastener MNC YKK came to Europe, it engaged hundreds of workers. However, many times that number lost their jobs because the superior production techniques of YKK's European subsidiaries brought about the demise of several indigenous zip fastener companies.

Most of the British union leaders allied themselves with the bosses of the European and U.S. automobile multis in agitating against Nissan's manufacturing project in the north of England. While Nissan was certain to take on thousands of unemployed in that region, the unions feared that Nissan's success would cause a big loss of jobs in the other UK car factories. The union leaders were also apprehensive that Nissan, while permitting its employees to join a union, would not compel them to do so. This was in contrast with the closed-shop contracts that prevailed in most of the existing plants in which the ensuing redundancies were likely to occur.

For many years the UAW, like many European unions, had been in favor of severe restrictions on the import of Japanese-made cars. To their horror the union leaders learned that Chrysler, Ford, and GM had taken minority equity stakes in Japanese automobile firms and were selling Japanese-made vehicles at home under U.S. logos. When the UAW had digested this 'betrayal' by U.S.-based multis, it took the lead in inviting Japanese car multis to establish themselves in the United States—local manufacturing was a lesser evil than imports! In 1984 the Federal Trade Commission approved a joint manufacturing project of GM and Toyota in Fremont. The UAW proved very flexible indeed. Perversely, as some would have it, it not only blessed the U.S. production of a Toyota model but agreed to wage rates that made the labor costs in Fremont 15 percent lower than those prevailing in the GM factories.

SOME OPERATIONAL HURDLES

The percentage of the equity that MNCs may own in their foreign subsidiaries or affiliates is often of decisive importance when evaluating a new project. The majority of LDCs nowadays insist that foreign multis may not have a controlling majority. Many host economies spell out explicitly the non-negotiable maximum stakes: 30, 40, or 49 percent. A few countries have officially flexible rules. Thus the Philippine government varies the percentages in accordance with the industrial branch that foreigners are encouraged to invest in. Malaysia too is prepared to deviate from its nominal 49 percent (maximum) rule: if the subsidiaries of foreign MNCs excel in exports, they are even allowed 100 percent ownership. The politicians of some LDCs, while they are on record as opposing 100 percent ownership by foreigners, have nevertheless let it be known that they are prepared to bargain. In addition to these LDCs, at one time or another, most developed countries have also been opposed to foreign companies owning the majority equity of their local subsidiaries. (The United States and Britain have been prominent and consistent exceptions.) Australia and Canada have for many years had statutory agencies that scrutinized applications by alien TNCs that wanted to set up 100 percent-owned manufacturing operations. The pragmatic French do not have a law on the statute book to prohibit foreign corporations from owning the whole equity of businesses functioning on French soil. But if the authorities in Paris have reason to dislike such an arrangement, they know how to thwart foreign multis with the ambition to have wholly-owned subsidiaries. In the 1980s all the Scandinavian countries, with the exception of Denmark, still attempted to safeguard the national purity of their industrial companies; foreign TNCs were generally not allowed to own a majority of the share capital of large, established indigenous enterprises.

The Brazilian government formally differentiates between 'Brazilian enterprises' (a euphemism for the subsidiaries of foreign multis) and 'Brazilian enterprises of domestic capital' (the appellation of truly Brazilian businesses). These official designations enable the authorities to discriminate when they disburse certain financial subventions that are meant for native-owned businesses only. This dualism is an LDC hallmark and TNCs must learn to live with it. Most OECD governments disdain such practices though at times indigenous entrepreneurs and unions urge them to imitate the LDCs. When ICI announced the building of a chemical plant in Germany, it aroused some resentment in the host country. Bonn would not prohibit this lawful investment. The opponents of the project then urged the authorities, as a second best, to deprive ICI of the incentives that were automatically available for direct investors in Germany. The British Plastics Federation objected to the plans of a Japanese multi, Showa Deoka, for the construction of a small factory in Wales. The UK manufacturers argued that if the Japanese firm could not be prevented from proceeding with its greenfield enterprise, then at least it should not receive the standard investment grants that by right were accorded to all British and non-British manufacturers.

Especially in the LDCs, a plethora of irksome rules awaits the TNCs when they are ready to manufacture. There are restrictions on the employment of expatriate experts and managers. In a host of countries foreign-owned firms are subject to special curbs when borrowing from local banks; sometimes they are charged more onerous terms than are demanded from their native competitors. Profits, or the payments for royalties and patents, cannot be remitted freely. Member-countries of Ancom (Andean Common Market) are pledged not to allow any payments of royalties to parent companies. There are cases in which profits can only be transferred if the parent agrees to take goods manufactured by its subsidiary. Host countries unashamedly decide at short notice to ban profit remittances altogether; Peru issued such a decree in 1986 which was to last for two years. In August 1989 Brazil announced the retention of all foreign companies' profit remittances in frozen accounts indefinitely. Numerous LDCs have played around with draconian—but pliant—price controls that are administered at the discretion of civil servants: foreign-owned corporations have often been victimized and some have 'voluntarily' liquidated their subsidiaries when they were punished in this way.

Almost all LDCs regulate imports and require licenses. Foreign-owned firms are frequently hampered because they are refused licenses to bring in machinery, components, and ingredients. They are bullied to purchase locally made inputs though these may not come up to the required quality standards. Japanese multis regard this as a major obstacle to investing in India, where such unreasonable demands plague the subsidiaries of many foreign companies.

Some TNCs establish subsidiaries abroad to exploit natural resources, while others seek to take advantage of low labor costs. Many multis, however, set up manufacturing operations in foreign countries in order to sell to local consumers. Foreign multis may be willing to put up with some of the discriminatory regulations that are applied to them but not to indigenous manufacturers, though these raise their unit production costs. What many TNCs find unacceptable, however, are situations in which the host country also applies the dualist approach to the sale of goods produced in local factories. There have been occasions when the output of the subsidiaries of foreign companies has been disparaged as being on par with imports. The procurement officers of the state sector and the patriotic public have been exhorted not to purchase such alien goods and to buy from native-owned producers instead. This occurs mainly in LDCs but there are also instances from the OECD, as the following story shows. In 1965 the British Labour government decided that whenever public money was expended on the procurement of a certain range of technological goods—for the state, nationalized corporations, universities, research laboratories, and so on—a "Buy British" policy must be enforced. Not only were imports to be vetoed but also the manufacturing output of UK companies owned by foreign multis. At first this policy was not admitted officially. Later the Wilson government conceded that a 25 percent rule was enforced unofficially by the civil servants who disbursed public funds. (Unless the subsidiary of the foreign-owned company was prepared to sell at prices that were at least 25 percent below those of their indigenous competitors, they were banned irrespective of any technical merits.) The British subsidiaries of Honeywell and IBM were penalized severely in order to prop the ailing British multi ICL. Though the affected foreign multis expressed their displeasure, they all accepted that they would have to live with the status of a second-class company—or pack up and go home.

If the CEOs of multis were quizzed on what they regarded as the most ominous drawback associated with a direct investment in a foreign economy—especially an LDC—many would reply: "Unpredictable costs and persecutions." They would not be referring to unforeseeable changes in macroeconomic conditions but to the uncertainties that are determined by the whims and fancies of the political decision-makers. Will they penalize MNCs to gain populist approbation? What financial favors will be demanded of individual multis? This is a subject that, by its very essence, is not detailed in books on the nature of MNCs. One light but piquant illustration is cited as a case in point for weightier matters. A correspondent of *The New York Times*, who had no inkling that this had any connection with the dreaded TNCs, noted that the new Indonesian restaurant Ramayana "was one of the most opulent and agreeable restaurants to open in Manhattan." The catering was superb and the Indonesian politicians were proud of their flagship in the United States. Only later was it disclosed that a number of French, Japanese, and U.S. multis—(including Mitsui, Mitsubishi, Arco, Armco Steel, Exxon, Schlumberger, Monsanto, and Mobil) that did, or hoped to do, business in Indonesia—had had their arms twisted by a government agency to 'persuade' them to buy shares in this million-dollar restaurant (88, 189).

CANDID AND DEVIOUS DESIGNS

There are intellectually honest opponents of multis who wish to close the door to foreign investors. As good nationalists, they fear that the independence of their countries might be impaired by modern, powerful, foreign corporations (59). Especially in LDCs, there are fears that when underdeveloped countries are dragged into the vortex of the world economy, their economic fortunes will be determined decisively by external events over which they have no control. Such is the view of the *dependencia* school. Its protagonists are first and foremost nationalists; not all of them are left-wingers. They do not stress the evil intent of MNCs and mostly have no truck with paranoiac anti-multi propaganda. Some of them concede implicitly that if multis were given free scope in their country, this would quickly induce a larger GDP and generally enhance living standards. While the *dependencia* visionaries do not deprecate material attainments, they are prepared to reach their goals at a slower pace. In the short term they prefer to be poor but honest. Such a political stance deserves respect provided the decision-makers in power declare openly that new ventures by foreign corporations are taboo. At one stage Burma said so; its rulers explained why on grounds of nationalism and socialism they had firmly shut the gate to all and sundry.

However, the vast majority of LDCs have not acted honorably. There is a big difference between giving a cold shoulder to new investment projects of foreigners and behaving antagonistically to MNCs that had invested before anti-multi laws were promulgated. Many host countries have disingenuously created circumstances that led to the enforced demise of the old subsidiaries of foreign-based MNCs. Rules stipulating that foreigners may not own more than a given minority stake in Nigerian companies were sufficiently publicized to frighten off new investors. But retroactive Nigerian indigenization was surely another matter. The compulsory sale of the equity of Unilever subsidiaries to natives was manipulated in such a manner that the parent of this European food MNC received 'compensation' which it rightly denounced as "most unfair by any international standard." India has also disdained the formal expropriation of the shares of foreigners in their Indian subsidiaries. They have merely shown vindictiveness by arbitrarily fixing selling prices far below their market value. In addition, the Indian politicians have prevented multis from selling to the highest native bidders and designated the buyers, who have often been public sector corporations.

The most cynical conduct is manifested when host governments lure multis to invest, promise them concessions, import licenses, lollipops, and so on—and on completion of the project, or soon thereafter, renege on their original undertakings. One European TNC, prominent in the building materials industry, was induced to build a factory in East Africa. After several years (and hefty investments, both in cash and capital goods) the factory was ready to be opened in full splendor by the president of the state, which had only recently become independent. A few days before the guests were scheduled to arrive from abroad, the government announced that 'in the national interest' this direct investment would be nationalized! Admittedly, it is a very crude example. The rapacious politicians of host countries are usually a little more considerate.

It must be stressed that the confiscation of the assets of foreign multis is usually a very popular policy. Not only 'progressive' church leaders and Marxist agitators play this xenophobic game; right-wing politicians and power-seeking generals have also learned that they can buy the adulation of their people by kicking out foreigners. But though anti-multi measures are clearly acclaimed at home, are they not self-defeating by discouraging foreigners from carrying out new investments? During most of the postwar period host countries have generally succeeded in escaping punishment for their Machiavellian conduct. If they defaulted on loans, other lenders were ready to step into the breach. The coerced divestitures by multis of their old investments have not always frightened off the foolish CEOs of new MNCs who naively think that their virgin investments will be immune from future expropriations.

In the late 1980s the pendulum swung against dishonest host countries. MNCs nowadays pay strict attention to the past performances of governments that proclaim their newly acquired love for multis. In the 1950s Burma closed its door to new investments and in the 1960s almost all existing foreign assets were taken over (with some compensation). Today Burma is again accepting applications from foreign MNCs but, somehow, few are listening. In January 1989 Nigeria became another self-proclaimed repentant host country. President Babangida renewed his commitment to an extensive privatization program. The infamous 40 percent ceiling on foreign equity holdings was abolished (except for financial and natural resource companies). Henceforth, foreign multis will again be allowed to own 100 percent of the equity of their Nigerian subsidiaries. India's protracted dastardly behavior to MNCs has not been forgotten though Rajiv Gandhi devoted much time and energy to woo foreign companies. India's ruler has expressed his surprise that the streams of MNC investments that are flowing into Communist China and other Asian economies are so very much more substantial than the "minuscule" brook reaching India. It is too simplistic to maintain, as he has done in public speeches, that if only the Indian government were more efficient and adopted superior administrative procedures, the capital and technological expertise of the world's multis would engulf India. Rajiv Gandhi ought to examine his mother's role vis-à-vis TNCs. Many international corporations still remember it vividly.

Malaysia launched a new economic policy in the 1970s which, inter alia, forbade foreign MNCs to retain majority ownership of their subsidiaries. In those days the country's top leaders were good at abusing multis. In the summer of 1985 economic pressures compelled Kuala Lumpur to change course. Its erstwhile enemies were wooed and business journals in the United States were asked to publicize that the old measures are now recognized to have been a serious error. Henceforth, so the message goes, the old investment barriers are being torn down and under the new guidelines TNCs will again be able to own majority stakes in their Malaysian operations. This euphoric news has also not been greeted abroad with any pronounced enthusiasm by the people who matter. The politicians of Kuala Lumpur are said to be disappointed. It appears that modern multis are not charitable. They seem unwilling to accept at face value the *mea culpa* announcements of host countries with a bad record. CEOs no longer trust foreign politicians just because they claim to be repentant sinners.

Increasingly, TNCs comprehend that agreements signed with a host country may have little validity when its government is replaced at the polls or overthrown by force. The successor administration can and does challenge the propriety of explicit, written undertakings given by its predecessor and may therefore refuse to honor them. Greece, now a member of the EC, illustrates why MNCs invest in that country at their peril. Between 1967 and 1974 a number of TNCs received the consent of the Athens authorities to proceed with certain negotiated investment projects. Soon after the military government was overthrown, the new administration introduced a law—passed unanimously in August 1975— that reneged on the signed investment deals of the deposed government. The new rulers commenced to 'renegotiate' contracts. The government sought to defend its conduct by asserting that the terms offered by the military junta had been too generous and that, in any case, parliament had given it legal backing to review the direct foreign investments of the past. This case demonstrates effectively that the Greek government, as the majority of host governments, refuses to be bound by the pledges of previous governments. It also explains why most direct investments are made today in those economies where MNCs believe that Greece's example is not likely to be followed.

17

MULTIS ARE HYPERSENSITIVE

> Large multinational companies, like large animals, tend to be very shy.
>
> Christopher Tugendhat

FOUR AFFLICTIONS

TNCs are unwieldy entities. Their managers are engaged in internecine battles. Yet according to myths that have gained wide currency, multis are able to exercise influential evil powers because of their international ramifications. Actually, it is their global reach that makes them vulnerable. News travels fast and, consequently, the reputation factor is discussed extensively at board meetings. The worldwide fortunes of a TNC may suffer from mishaps, supercilious behavior, misdeeds, and malicious allegations concerning one national subsidiary. An accusation—whether true or not—pertaining to a corrupt manager in Nicaragua can rebound on sales in Germany. A chemical explosion, racial labor practices, revelations relating to the former Nazi or Communist past of a director—such local affairs may prove commercially distressing for the whole of the international corporation.

In the 1960s a British government commission, investigating the duopoly of Unilever and Procter & Gamble, sought to ascertain whether their vast advertising expenditure constituted an anti-social component in the prices of their consumer products. The U.S. multi did not treat this as a matter that related only to its UK subsidiary. Top advisers were dispatched across the Atlantic to defend the merchandising techniques of Procter & Gamble because the head office feared that if an anti-advertising judgment was given in Britain, this would encourage vexatious adversaries in other national economies. The Swiss-based pharmaceutical multi Hoffmann-La Roche (HLR) was not as perceptive. It had convinced itself that each country could be coped with as a separate market in which pricing was determined by what the national traffic could bear. The corporation's CEO believed that if HLR's operations were enveloped in supersecrecy, events in one country need have no bearing on the multi's commercial and political standing in other parts of the world. Many of its products were unique. Their true production costs could not be ascertained by outsiders because of highly successful (and legal) maneuvers that ensured the transfer of most profits to the Swiss head office. It was the British government, via the National Health Service, that paid for almost all the HLR merchandise marketed in Britain. In response to routine enquiries, addressed to all British and foreign pharmaceutical suppliers, HLR—unlike its confreres—refused even to go through the motions of providing meaningful cost information. The company threatened, probably genuinely, that it was ready to abandon the UK market altogether, hoping that this would affect only a tiny portion of its global sales. Although the Swiss company refused to cooperate, the UK authorities initiated an official investigation into the HLR cost-price structure. The published factual findings spread like wildfire throughout the world. LDCs were too weak to use them as a stick to beat this multi. But HLR learned that its conduct in Britain had become a hot political potato in the United States. The German Cartel Office formally requested detailed information from London and proceedings were begun against the distributors of HLR pharmaceuticals. The secretive, mighty Swiss corporation had deluded itself into thinking that its behavior in Britain meant that it had stirred up a hornet's nest in only one national market. When, finally, HLR gave up the fight in Britain and settled out of court, the financial losses incurred there were but a minute part of the global damage that it had suffered as a result of the adverse publicity that had emanated from London. After replacing the old decision-makers, HLR was turned into a near-normal TNC and today employs press officers who are instructed to answer freely questions about the gospel of the company.

The second major curse afflicting the modern MNC is closely linked to the important role of public relations in our age. Corporations are compelled to contemplate their navels and defend their putative social responsibility. A company does not have a soul; nevertheless the PR agencies of Caterpillar, ICI, and Sony disseminate the glad tidings that their clients are magnanimous, progressive, and charitable. The British MNC Rowntree was the object of a global consumer boycott. This indignity was magnified when one of its largest shareholders—the Joseph Rowntree Charitable Trust, set up by the founders of the company—attacked it in public for manufacturing in South Africa. In the old days, the AGMs of large corporations were often attended by vocal critics who castigated the board for failing to maximize profits; many a director was abused because the dividend was not raised in accordance with the expectations of shareholders. Nowadays AGMs are often interrupted by outraged individuals who protest that the company is earning too much money or manufacturing in undesirable locations or employing the wrong type of worker. PR practitioners know that the perceived truth—even when based on falsehoods—can be very damaging. Hence multis are guided to behave in a manner that obviates criticism by individuals and institutions 'with a conscience.' CEOs are given cowardly but sound advice to anticipate events. They are counselled to abandon in time PR-sensitive situations.

Nestle, since then a wiser TNC, has experienced the trauma of a protracted worldwide consumer boycott of its numerous products. This was sparked off by its marketing of infant milk in the LDCs. Critics who felt strongly on the subject censured the company. The anti-Nestle propaganda was poisonously emotive: "Nestle Kills Babies" was the heading of one article, which was the subject of a libel suit by the food multi. Stupidly, the company had this issue vented in court. On the PR front, Nestle lost though it collected a few hundred francs in damages. The sale of dried milk as baby food in LDCs represents but a tiny segment of Nestle's total global turnover. Irrespective of the merits of the charge that food multis ought not to promote in poor countries the distribution of dried milk to uneducated mothers, Nestle—on grounds of expediency—should have cut its losses and withdrawn at an early stage. Of course, the motives of many of those who launched the onslaught on Nestle were suspect. But it was still a bad strategy by the Swiss TNC to finance lavishly on overt and covert propaganda to demonstrate that it was doing no harm. The ensuing publicity helped to nurture a damaging picture of this callous Swiss multi. Ultimately, Nestle (and some other food firms) offered money to child charities and agreed to abide by an International Code of Marketing Breast-Milk Substitutes that was drawn up by the World Health Organization. In 1984 the consumer boycott was suspended.

The following three excerpts bring to the fore the third feature of the sorry plight of corportions that are big, famous, and international: it is very hazardous for them to break the law. Shell has confessed that "large firms cannot afford to behave badly; that would damage their interests." Kidron, the Marxist detractor of multis, confirms this. He concedes that "the bulk of business in India evades taxation. . . . [F]oreign firms are generally thought to have a cleaner record than indigenous ones. . . . [T]heir greater size and the fact that they are exposed to a social, political-ly-inspired scrutiny make it unlikely that they would resort to the more blatant methods known." A prominent spokesman of Britain's Green lobby, the editor of the journal *Vole*, has put in a kind word for MNCs. Unlike many of his political colleagues, he has concluded that small companies behave more cruelly than big ones: "The multination-als, a favourite target, are not always angels . . . [but they] are more open to persuasion and the consciences of consumers than the many, very distant small-time entrepreneurs" (182).

Unlike national companies, multis can bribe only at great peril. It is also dangerous for them to buy and sell on the black market; only fool-hardy MNCs follow in the footsteps of those entrepreneurs who bravely break price and wage controls, smuggle, and cheat the taxman. While small companies are often not affected, the large corporation is always the first target of nationalizers. Frequently, multis cannot discharge their obligations only in accordance with legal requirements—they are expected to behave more charitably. Multis grit their teeth for they know that allegations of ungenerous behavior in one country may harm their reputation in other countries.

MNCs are not members of a fighting fraternity. Because of conflicting interests, they do not conspire together even when faced by a (seemingly) common enemy. (I hope this thesis has been argued convincingly in previous chapters.) It is therefore anomalous that the fourth afflication has to do with the frequent denunciations of all multis because of populist resentment against one of them. When HLR battled with the British National Health Service, the most bitter enemies of the Swiss-based multi were the other pharmaceutical MNCs (with UK involvement), including some which were headquartered in Switzerland. They had good reason to be angry with HLR, because in the public arena all pharmaceutical multis were deemed to be tarred with the same brush as HLR. There was a general demand to take strong measures against all multis supplying the National Health Service. The president of Pitney Bowes has stressed the superior corporate morality of his TNC and publicly distanced himself from corporations involved in "scandals we are reading about daily." In the United States, all sorts of TNCs were extremely annoyed with the conduct of ITT. Muckraking journalists, publicity-seeking politicians, and over-zealous government officials exploited the general anti-multi climate to probe the inner workings of moral and immoral multis. After the ITT disclosures some inquisitors stated publicly that all international firms must now expect to be treated with heightened suspicion.

WHY MULTIS ARE PUNISHED

Cross-border campaigns against individual MNCs are usually launched by protesters who disapprove of only a certain operation or one national location with which the company is associated. The real or purported crimes perpetrated by the multi may relate merely to a small proportion of its overall output or sales, but the campaigners aim to denigrate the company's multifarious activities in different countries. Sometimes the mere intention to devise an international boycott is enough to drive the head office into surrender, as the following examples show.

Though the ITSs of Chapter 14 have failed to organize cross-border strikes, they have on a few occasions registered successes by joining in the promotion of consumer boycotts. Rowntree's alleged anti-trade union behavior in South Africa brought in its wake a global boycott of KitKat, one of its popular chocolate brands. In 1980 an independent Coca-Cola bottler in Guatemala refused to recognize the local union. The IUF staged a global consumer ban on all Coca-Cola products. When this threatened to become effective, Coca-Cola's head office reacted. New owners were installed in Guatemala who negotiated a contract with the union. In 1984 another worldwide boycott campaign was in the offing when the owner of the Guatemalan Coca-Cola franchise had become bankrupt and was forced to close his factory, which was then occupied by the redundant workers. When the (U.S.) Chemical Workers Union led its members out on strike at American Cynamid's Lederle pharmaceutical factory in Pearl River, the Geneva headquarters of the ICF sent a cable to the head office of Cynamid. Levinson threatened that if the company did not change its manner of bargaining, a global boycott of Lederle products could be expected (120).

Multis are penalized for being (or planning to be) involved with countries, whose regimes are objectionable in the eyes of those who orchestrate the remonstrations. 'Involvement' is condemned if the corporation invests in, buys from, sells to, or trains the personnel of the accursed country. Textron was embarrassed by the global brouhaha caused by the news that it was tutoring helicopter pilots for Idi Amin's Uganda. Numerous MNCs have evoked enmity because they were marketing Chilean wines, Polish meat products, Brazilian leather shoes, Russian Vodka, or canned Israeli orange juice. The American multi Firestone was to have been boycotted if it proceeded with its plan to supply a synthetic rubber plant to Romania. (Firestone pulled out.) IBM was mauled in some media for agreeing to sell computers to the Soviet Union.

Several food TNCs have been castigated in the Western world for pro-
curing coffee from (colonial) Angola and (Amin's) Uganda. IBM, Control
Data, and Sperry Rand have been at the receiving end of bad publicity
(from the churches and other anti-multi forces) because of sales, or
intended sales, to Argentina, Brazil, Chile, and Uruguay. An article in
the trade journal *Computer Decisions* asked with righteous anger: "Would
you sell a computer to Hitler?" The subtitle would have it that "Latin
American dictatorships are using computers as tools of repression."

Processing food (bananas, beef, pineapples, fish, vegetables) obtained
from territories in which wages and working conditions are said to be
bad has given birth to several global consumer boycotts. Brooke Bond,
the British-based corporation, encountered much unpleasantness because of wide television coverage relating to its Asian tea estates.

Few TNCs have suffered as grievously as Gulf Oil. At one stage the
main accusation against it revolved around the oil concession in Cabinda,
on the West Coast of Africa, which had been granted by the Angolan
authorities. All over the world virtuous people were urged to have nothing to do with an MNC that "prolonged the agony of a people tortured
by Portugese colonialism" (48).

Charges that a TNC is guilty, by commission or tacit acquiescence, of
discrimination on religious, sexual, or racial grounds have laid the foundations for many global campaigns. RTZ and other multis operating in
Australia have been chastised for their oppression of the Aboriginal
people. A number of U.S.-based oil TNCs have been reproached for not
employing Jews in their head offices. Coca-Cola once faced a potential
international boycott due to the employment policy pursued by the
owners of a bottling plant in South Africa. It was not maintained that
blacks were being exploited for the benefit of the indigenous white
population. In the peculiar charge laid against the Coca-Cola bottler of
Port Elizabeth, it was alleged that the employer "paid higher wages to
coloured employees working part-time than to the black full-time workers" (157). HLR has been denounced as an anti-feminist corporation
because employment practices in its Spanish and U.S. subsidiaries are
said to have militated against women employees. Companies in Northern Ireland were alleged to be prejudiced against the recruitment of
Catholic workers. Twenty-four U.S.-based TNCs—including American
Brands, Ford, Du Pont, and GM—were warned in their home country
that dire consequences awaited them if they did not order their subsidiaries in Northern Ireland to subscribe to the MacBride Principles.
(MacBride was an erstwhile chief of staff of the IRA.) The Principles do
not deal with the abolition of discrimination. They are meant to put
pressure on the affected TNCs to introduce religious job quotas and
proclaim positive discrimination in favor of non-Protestants.

Social activists (as they like to be called) have been crusading against international companies for promoting in LDCs products that are luxuries, 'destructive of local cultural values', squander foreign currency, and so on. Quite a few MNCs have been condemned for exporting merchandise from LDCs that the campaigners considered should not have been exported. The food multi Del Monte was found guilty of harvesting pilchards in Namibian territorial waters and then canning them for exports, thus causing malnutrition in Namibia.

Industrial explosions, such as occurred in Union Carbide's Indian plant and in HLR's Italian factory, offer agitators an opportunity to denounce the safety provisions in *all* the facilities of the inculpated corporations.

Firms accused of polluting the environment in one national territory have their reputations blackened everywhere. RTZ's global image has been dented badly on this account.

Multis have become the targets of consumer boycotts because, inter alia, they supply materials for the armies of Western imperialism. Dow has featured in demonstrations in many countries on account of the napalm it manufactures in the United States.

Shell has been plagued by the global picketing of petrol and gasoline stations: the protestors reproved it for breaching oil sanctions against South Africa.

Some MNCs have suffered worldwide commercial opprobrium after deliberately opting to have no dealing with a given country, for example, firms that have disposed of their Israeli investments or refused to become involved with Israel. In 1964 Coca-Cola resolved that granting a franchise to a bottler in Israel would be incompatible with continued access to the Arab markets. It turned down pending applications, saying that the reasons for its rulings were, of course, commercial and not political. While many similar, and more far-reaching, decisions by other TNCs were not overturned as a result of pressure from concerned groups, Coca-Cola faced a vigorous onslaught that made it reverse its decision. The corporation did so because of the peculiar international ramifications of its activities. If it had had to chose between the more numerous Arab customers and the relatively few customers awaiting its entry into Israel, the choice would have been simple: it would have renounced the tiny Israeli market. But this (acceptable) anticipated loss of sales in Israel would have been dwarfed by the ensuing drop of sales within the United States. A large number of Jews stopped drinking Coca-Cola in 1966. This was coupled with the more serious threat that important wholesalers, distributors, restaurant chains, and hospitals would switch to other brands in order to express their disapproval of Coca-Cola's readiness to yield to the injunctions of the Damascus Boycott Office. In 1967 Coca-Cola conceded defeat in the home country and was immediately punished by the Arab League. In 1968 an Israeli bottling plant opened for business. Pepsi-Cola was delighted as it was allowed to take over the Arab facilities of its main competitor (156).

In the issues listed above the declared motives are often only the ostensible reasons for making particular TNCs the butt of planned hostility. Politically inspired activists are known to select items with wide humanitarian appeal which are therefore likely to cause maximum damage to corporate prestige. Sometimes their strategy is to cloak the true objective of the campaigners. When IBM was picketed for filing an application in Washington to sell a computer to a Soviet tourist agency, the organizers said that the TNC should desist because the computer might be used to keep track of political dissidents. The real intention of the campaigners was to weaken the Soviet regime but it was more palatable to hit IBM by enlisting public support for human rights. When the churches first persecuted Gulf Oil, they accused it of racism in Angola. This was soon proved to be sophistry. The protesters had to admit that they hated the Portuguese regime and wanted it overthrown: racialism had been a false charge, a pretext for attacking Gulf Oil which, indirectly, was paying taxes to Lisbon. The instigators of the boycott of U.S. companies with subsidiaries in Northern Ireland proclaimed that they wanted to do away with anti-Catholic job discrimination. This was only a minor consideration. The campaign was launched to embarrass the British government: the pressure on U.S. MNCs was to help bring about the unification of Northern and Southern Ireland.

Many of those who pull the strings of global campaigns dislike multis in general and disapprove in particular of their direct investments in LDCs. In 1974 Rev. Patrick O'Mahoney was commissioned by the Roman Catholic archbishop of Birmingham (England) to investigate the South African interests of fourteen UK multis (with special reference to Barclays Bank). This appeared to be an emotional—almost a spiritual—affair. A superficial observer could not have detected the general anti-multi principles of Father O'Mahoney. He recommended to the archbishop that the local church funds should be divested of shares in three depraved multis. But the Reverend Father also thought it right to examine the archdiocese's portfolio in accordance with broader criteria. He found that, for example, Burma Oil and RTZ had Australian connections. Was it proper for Catholics to invest in these TNCs? Did these companies provide handbasins for their Aboriginal employees? Did they have acceptable training facilities for the natives? What about minimum pay? The Reverend Father did not stop at that. He then considered whether shares might properly be held in corporations that had subsidiaries in India, Pakistan, and Brazil. Father O'Mahoney wanted to be assured that the fringe benefits paid to local workers in those countries were satisfactory and he also sought information on environmental damage that these TNCs might be causing. This produced of course an even longer list of corporations—the shares of which were to be taboo—than the original South African brief would have justified. The Reverend Father appealed in print to the government to withhold the services of the ECGD (Export Credits Guarantee Department) from multis which he deemed to be bad (159).

THEY HAVE REASON TO FEAR

If the populist legend on the might of MNCs had substance, corporations could shrug off with contempt international efforts to discredit them. Some macho CEOs have indeed boasted that a global consumer boycott could not hurt their company. There are few top executives who really believe this. The overwhelming majority of multis have cause to concern themselves with what their enemies say of them. They cannot afford to be indifferent.

At the height of the baby food campaign against Nestle, the Swiss TNC covertly supported the distribution of a partisan article that referred to "Marxists marching under the banner of Christ." Marxists and 'progressives' do indeed play a prominent role in the attacks on individual multis. However, it is simplistic indeed to propound that left-wingers always lead such crusades. IBM (and other multis with commercial links to the COMECON) have been slapped down by right-wingers for being 'soft on Communism.' The anti-Uganda action committees were not inspired by Marxism. The reputation of the UK-based multi Lonrho has remained blemished ever since Conservative Prime Minister Edward Heath denounced the corporation for displaying "the unacceptable face of capitalism." (The outburst was occasioned by the revelation that the emoluments of some of its directors were paid in the Cayman Islands, a notorious tax haven.) The politicians of the Gulf States, who finance the Damascus Boycott Office and penalize multis that have dealings with Israel, are not socialist revolutionaries. Firestone terminated negotiations for a contract in Romania because of pressure from the Young Americans for Freedom (103).

The Pope has so far confined himself to smiting MNCs as a group. Generalized attacks are not so dreaded as campaigns against named multis, which are initiated or supported by mullahs, priests, and rabbis— with or without clerical collars. Television stations in the developed countries screen pictures of nuns and monks who flaunt their habits and cassocks at rallies in LDCs against the subsidiaries of some wicked MNCs. Even a hard, secular-minded CEO becomes anxious when his company is branded as immoral by men and women who appear to speak in the name of God. A Church of England publication mentions cryptically that churches "may be in a position to exercise some leverage on managers and directors" (148). Many executives hate the thought that they are regarded as social pariahs. They do not want their children to be ashamed of them. Textbooks on the omnipotent, ruthless, fiendish multis do not tell us that these are managed by staff who crave love and respect from their neighbors.

TNCs are sensitive when their image is tarnished for not meeting the requirements of the social activists. They are also conscious of the various prosaic damages that global campaigns can inflict upon them. Violence has been used: the homes of executives have been bombed and corporate premises destroyed. TNCs are upset when, during recruiting drives on campuses, their adversaries seek to persuade students that 'decent people do not join company X and Y.' Gulf Oil, the "epitome of corruption," was picked out (in the United States) by the United Presbyterian Church and the United Church of Christ as a specially abominable company: "Boycott Gulf" advertisements, directed at black drivers, appeared in *Ebony* and other journals. Students seized for six days the Harvard university administrative building to protest Gulf's involvement with Portuguese imperialism; gasoline stations were picketed; its 1970 AGM was dominated by violent protesters who presented 'non-negotiable demands'; consumers were induced to tear up their Gulf credit card; a Gulf Boycott Coalition was formed in Dayton, Ohio, and the city was persuaded to cancel its contract with Gulf; Washington marches on African Liberation Day made Gulf a prominent target; and so on (48).

The strategists who prepare the battle plans have found that the head offices of TNCs are particularly worried about approaches to religious and political decision-makers who can influence decisively the procurement practices of public sector agencies, municipalities, churches, and trade unions. Anti-British groups in the United States exhorted U.S.-based TNCs either to liquidate their manufacturing subsidiaries in Northern Ireland or to subscribe to the MacBride Principles. When Ford paid no attention to these demands, the organizers wrote one million letters to Irish-Americans urging them to stop buying Ford cars. Senators and Representatives with many Irish constituents have presented bills to Congress that would halt imports into the United States of products made by Northern Ireland subsidiaries of multis that had not adopted the anti-discrimination propositions of the campaigners. Washington was lobbied to cancel defense contracts with British-owned firms that manufactured in Northern Ireland, and Boeing was urged not to buy supplies from UK corporations of which the organizers disapproved.

Several U.S. MNCs—among them Bell & Howell and Xerox—have confessed dolefully that selective contracting and outright purchasing boycotts by states, counties, and cities (aimed to hurt corporations with South African operations) were the major factor that impelled them to liquidate their subsidiaries in South Africa. The city of Gary, Indiana, passed a resolution instructing its officials to cease buying from Motorola, IBM, and others with South African ties. In Europe the biggest success of the anti-apartheid campaign was to make Barclays give up most of its involvements in South Africa. The bank had been plagued by the withdrawal of personal and institutional accounts; it feared that the trickle might turn into a flood.

In the latter part of the 1980s most of the major U.S.-based, and a large number of Europe-based, TNCs withdrew from South Africa. In many cases the decisive consideration was the corporation's standing on the world's bourses, which was deemed to be endangered. Many years before, ITT had experienced what the wrath of investors can do to a multi's share price. Denounced as "evil incarnate" because of unpalatable disclosures, and harassed by the governments of its home country and of several host countries, the price of ITT shares dropped from $60 to $20 in the 1972–74 period (88). It was the beginning of an era in which universities, publicity-sensitive banks, insurance companies, religious bodies, and, most importantly, pension funds tended to "withhold investments from companies they consider are engaged in anti-social activities" (103). After 1985 many U.S. states, spearheaded by California, threatened to implement divestment programs—totalling tens of billions of dollars—directed at corporations with business connections in South Africa. Governor Thomas Kean of New Jersey spoke to the gallery: "We will not countenance the brutality that is apartheid by nourishing it with our investments." Not surprisingly, many of the projected corporate victims hurried to mend their ways. Once the investment-boycott sword had been brandished to smite the 'friends' of apartheid, it was quickly put to good use to harass MNCs for other reasons. The politician Tom Hayden, who wanted to compel U.S. TNCs to subscribe to the MacBride Principles, proposed a law in California that would have forced the trustees of the pension funds, catering for the state's public employees and teachers, to dispose of shares and bonds of non-compliant U.S. corporations: "We can use our pension power to lobby for improved employment practices in Northern Ireland." In Europe institutional pressures have been more muted but, for example, the Commissioners of the Church of England demonstratively sold the Church's equity holdings in RTZ.

CEOs are conscious that the *overall* profit performance of their corporation is of primary interest to most shareholders even though a vocal minority at AGMs may give an impression to the contrary. How then can and should the head office react when one national subsidiary begets adverse international side effects? The response depends first and foremost on the visibility of its products and who buys them. If sales are made directly to personal consumers and/or the goods are purchased in large quantities by the procurement officials of politically sensitve institutions, the possibility of an effective global boycott cannot be ignored.

But if the TNC's output consists of industrial goods and private sector companies are the main purchasers, the multi is much less vulnerable. J. Boddewyn relates that the U.S. MNC Eaton advertised at one time: "We are probably the largest multinational company you have never heard of." Eaton's industrial goods were 'hidden' in the products of other companies as parts, supplies, machinery, and so on (160).

CEOs who are not as fortunate as the managers of Eaton will want to consider the expedient liquidation of the national subsidiary that is causing PR troubles for the other parts of the corporation. If the operation that is giving offense accounts for only a small portion of the multi's global output or if it is unprofitable, then this is an easy and relatively painless way out. But conditions may prevail when expediency dictates the severing of even profitable links with a certain country. In such a situation MNC A is not eager to act on its own lest competitors B and C are given the opportunity to flourish at its expense. For this reason the authorities of the home country may be approached with the suggestion that a mandatory order be issued to break commercial connections with the odious country. When a trade embargo is imposed, all competing MNCs (of a given nationality) suffer alike and shareholders can truthfully be told that the ensuing losses are due to a force majeure. The U.S.-based food multis, harassed for processing Ugandan coffee, were the agonized targets of Congressman Pease: "Are American coffee companies prepared to do business with a genocidist like Amin or Hitler if the price is right?" To resolve their dilemma, the international food corporations begged Washington to forbid by law the importation of Ugandan goods. At first the authorities turned down this request but in July 1978 the multis were jubilant because a trade embargo had finally been passed by Congress.

Several TNCs have sought to camouflage their national origin or disguise their ownership of sensitive operations. Unilever engaged Victor Cavendish-Bentinck as an international trouble-shooter. One of his tasks was to inquire into its existing affiliate in Israel. This was an enterprise that Unilever "did not wish to acknowledge openly for fear of being put on an Arab blacklist." The Anglo-Dutch food multi must have concluded that it was not worth taking the risk of retaining a direct investment in Israel; during the 1950s it was disposed of to natives (155). Why did U.S. Rubber, founded in 1892, change its name to Uniroyal? This rubber-cum-plastic multi suffered outside its home country, especially in Latin America, because of the U.S. predicament in Vietnam. Hostile acts against U.S. Rubber, which were motivated by a dislike of Washington's foreign policy, irked the board of the corporation. It was therefore resolved to change the 'nationalist' name to the universal designation, Uniroyal (149). The Board hoped that the world image of the corporation would then glitter in a 'progressive' light!

If an MNC is accused of behaving badly in a named country, it is often folly to try to disprove the charges. Having become a global target of hatred because of its operations in Angola, Gulf Oil's head office attempted to show that, in reality, it was an outstandingly benevolent employer. This U.S. oil TNC offered critical shareholders, church dignitaries, civil rights leaders, and journalists expense-paid visits to Angola. Gulf hired a black PR firm in the United States and made large grants to black organizations. Its executives pathetically publicized the fact that the company "had had the privilege of being involved in giving away money to black colleges and providing scholarships for black students." The policy did not work. At the end of the day Gulf learned that its expensive efforts to counter the accusation of racism did not impress the leaders of the campaign who called for the boycott of its products. The organizers presented three "non-negotiable demands": complete withdrawal from the Third World; breaking all commercial links with the Defense Department in Washington; the resignation of the board of directors, to be replaced by the elected representatives of the workers in the various communities where Gulf has direct investments (48).

The spokesmen of the campaigns against 'racist' Western-based TNCs with South African subsidiaries were not always candid. At first they demanded of corporations to cease applying apartheid in their own South African factories. Many multis were only too happy to comply. Ingenuously, a large number believed that this would be the end of the story. But it soon became obvious that the boycotts with which they had been threatened would still go ahead even though their hands were now apparently clean. From the beginning, the real but undisclosed aim had been to force TNCs to divest in South Africa irrespective of how they were treating their own native employees. When IBM finally had to throw in the towel, the senior executive of a British MNC, which was still retaining its South African subsidiary, said that the withdrawal of the world's most famous computer firm was particularly sad as the "company had done so much for its local black workers." This was surely true but proved irrelevant.

In 1987 the governing body of one of Britain's prestigious academic institutions, the London School of Economics and Political Science (LSE), asked its investment committee to divest the school's shareholdings in companies with a significant presence in South Africa. Some of the corporate victims had endowed LSE in the past. Despite this rebuff they thought it right to continue to help financially. One can only guess at the reason for these perverse decisions. No doubt they were arrived at in the hope that by striking a low profile the docile TNCs would escape further public chastisement from 'progressive' academics and avoid unpleasant publicity. Similar responses are reported from North America, though not all U.S.-based MNCs have behaved as spinelessly. Dow, for example, has hit back. When actress Jane Fonda was invited by the Central Michigan University to speak, and she denounced American multis in general and Dow in particular, this U.S. chemical MNC declared that it had cut its annual contribution to the university. After the trustees of the Michigan State University had demonstratively disposed of shares in companies doing business in South Africa, Dow did not flinch from announcing that it would not reduce operations there and enquired whether the university wished to continue to receive grants from the company. Dow, unlike most TNCs, recognized at an early stage that there is not much to be gained from offering the left cheek to those who have already slapped the corporation's right cheek.

GUIDELINES FOR EXEMPLARY BEHAVIOR

In 1949 the Paris-based International Chamber of Commerce (ICC) began drafting a convention relating to MNCs: "An International Code of Fair Treatment for Foreign Investment." This was addressed primarily to host countries which were asked to treat fairly the direct investments of foreign companies. In the 40 years since, a number of international organizations—among them various bodies of the UN, OECD, International Labour Office (ILO), International Confederation of Free Trade Unions, and the (revamped) ICC—have formulated radically different guidelines pertaining to MNCs. Overwhelmingly, these relate to the putative obligations of multis and hardly touch on the duty of host countries to behave as decent hosts. The new guidelines are intrinsically hostile to TNCs. The codes are the work of committees that have opted for compromises to accommodate the conflicting views of their members. Their intent was to make the guidelines acceptable to the governments of LDCs and OECD countries, to Communist and non-Communist nations. The most protracted negotiations were those that led to the publication of the draft of the *United Nations Code of Conduct on Transnational Corporations* (161). Work began in 1972 when the UN entreated a Group of Eminent Persons to devise the means of controlling TNCs. In 1974 a research center was established which in time became the secretariat of the Commission on Transnational Corporations (under the aegis of the UN's Economic and Social Council). Two-thirds of the Commission's 48 member-states were from LDCs. The highest priority was given to the formulation of a code, but when the authoritative draft was published in 1986, the UN conceded that as yet not all provisions had been agreed.

The following, arbitrarily selected, excerpts from three guidelines indicate the flavor of the verbose codes that teem with scores of trite and imprecise injunctions. Unenforceable by law and subject to diffuse interpretations, they constitute homilies that are (politely) ignored by TNCs and host countries. One wonders why numerous important people fought so many verbal battles to compose declarations that are largely meaningless and wholly ineffectual.

SOME OECD GUIDELINES

Enterprises, when granting licences for the use of technology, should do so on reasonable terms and conditions.

Enterprises should observe standards of employment . . . not less favourable than those observed by comparable employers in the host-country.

Enterprises should refrain from making use of . . . transfer pricing, which does not conform to an arm's length standard, for modifying in ways contrary to national laws the tax base on which [they] are assessed.

Enterprises should not render—and they not be solicited or expected to render—any bribe or other improper benefit, direct or indirect, to any public servant. . . .

Enterprises should favour close co-operation with the local community and business interests.

Every State has the right to prescribe the conditions under which multinational enterprises operate within its national jurisdiction. . . .

SOME PASSAGES FROM THE TRIPARTITE DECLARATION OF THE ILO

All the parties concerned by this Declaration should respect the sovereign right of States, obey the national laws. . . . [T]hey should also honour commitments which they freely entered into, in conformity with the national law and accepted international obligations.

Arbitrary dismissal procedures should be avoided.

Multinational enterprises should ensure that relevant training is provided . . . in the host-country . . . to meet the needs of the enterprise as well as the development policies of the country.

When multinational enterprises operate in developing countries, where comparable employers may not exist, they should provide the best possible wages, benefits and conditions of work. . . . Where they provide workers with basic amenities such as housing, medical care or food, these amenities should be of a good standard.

SOME POINTS FROM THE UN CODE OF CONDUCT ON TNCs

Contracts between Governments and transnational corporations should be negotiated and implemented in good faith.

Transnational corporations should/shall contribute to the managerial and technical training of nationals of the countries in which they operate. . . .

Transnational corporations shall avoid practices which adversely affect the international flow of technology. . . .

Transnational corporations shall/should . . . take steps to protect the environment.

Some individual multis have felt that they ought to be governed by very strict, self-imposed regulations; of course they take good care that the textual contents are publicized by their PR machine. The Swiss phar-maceutical MNC Ciba-Geigy has issued a pompous statement to its employees that tells them in some detail that their employer "is at the service of man and society." Mitsui has proclaimed a code of conduct especially geared to the company's activities outside Japan. Numerous U.S.-based corporations have drawn up documents to tell the world how much better they are than those other multis, which deserve to be abused for their greed and anti-social behavior. The "Code of Worldwide Business Conduct" of the Caterpillar Tractor company is perhaps the most famous of its kind. Caterpillar executives in Europe and its head office in Peoria, Illinois used to boast that Caterpillar differed from other TNCs in its attitude to operations in host countries. Caterpillar's lengthy guidelines have been cited frequently to exemplify responsible behavior by a global corporation. In view of what will be said in the next section, a few sentences from Caterpillar's famous code are reproduced below:

The law is a floor. Ethical business conduct should normally exist at a level well above the minimum required by the law. One of a company's most valuable assets is a reputation for integrity.

   With respect to pricing of goods . . . transferred within the Caterpillar orga-nization . . . such pricing is to be based on ethical business principles consistently applied throughout the enterprise. It is to reflect cost and a reasonable assess-ment of the value of the good . . . transferred. Prices are not to be influenced by superficial differences in taxation between countries.

   We desire to build functional, safe, attractive factories to the same high stan-dard worldwide, but with whatever modifications are appropriate to make them harmonious with national modes. . . . Facility operations should be planned with the long-term view in mind, in order to minimize impact of sudden change on the local work force and economy. . . . We intend to attempt to provide contin-uous employment and avoid capricious hiring practices. Employment stabili-zation is a major factor in corporate decisions (160).

GOOD CITIZENS

Geography Matters

   In the late 1970s multis commenced to publish social audits, which are meant to tell skeptics that respectable corporations do a lot of good. The message of Quaker Oats is contained in its *Social Progress Plan*. The output of other U.S. companies is named *Corporate Social Reporting*. Sev-eral European MNCs entitle their exercise the *Annual Social Report*. In Germany certain companies have joined together in a loose organization (*Arbeitskreis*) to discuss the practical aspects of the *Sozialbilanzen*, which they publish on a regular basis. In the past Dunlop and Unilever iden-tified the quantitative net social benefits, which they bestow upon countries harboring their subsidiaries, by means of cost-benefit analysis. (A senior executive of Dunlop once went on record to say that his company had created wealth in certain foreign territories which exceeded 15-fold what it had taken out in dividends and fees.) BOC expends a great deal of effort to produce a *Social Matrix*, which rates the company's performance in general and in such specific areas as pollution, treatment of women, mental health, civil rights, and so on.

The aspiration to appear as a good corporate citizen is widespread. Self-contradictory platitudes abound but they are not harmful. Perlmutter's acolytes, however, think that these barren PR recitations may cloak the duty imposed on card-carrying CEOs of genuine TNCs. The executives sans patrie are reminded that the world is their oyster and international corporations owe no loyalty to the home nation or host nations. Nevertheless, most multis seek to be known as socially responsible entities that care fervently for the well-being of the nations hosting their foreign operations. This of course is in accordance with the letter and spirit of the guidelines cited earlier. Some cautious MNCs, for example Motorola, stress that while they intend to respect the laws and customs of host countries, they "will not engage in any act . . . which may violate U.S. laws or its business ethics." Other MNCs, such as Armco Steel, do not hedge their "intent to be a good corporate citizen and to obey all laws." They state explicitly that if the laws of the home country clash with those of the country hosting their subsidiaries, they will "abide by the host-country's disposition of the conflict" (151).

Proclamations by TNCs about their responsibility to help promote progress in host countries earn them applause in the chambers of the UN and are quoted profusely by those who wish to present multis in a good light. Individual nation–states, however, are not impressed by generalities. The politicians and people of Portugal care not whether the multi BBB awards generous maternity benefits to its Albanian workers, builds a technologically advanced plant in Chile, and lavishly subsidizes the theater in Brazil. The self-centered Portuguese are concerned with how BBB is behaving, and is likely to behave in the future, in relation to its Portuguese subsidiary. When international companies profess that their social conscience makes them a good citizen in each country in which they operate, they are opening a Pandora's box. If the head office plans to increase global output by 5 percent, will this apply in equal measure to all national operations? An even more delicate question: if recession hits a 20-factory multi, will it cut employment in each plant by 10 percent or, instead, close down altogether the subsidiaries in countries X and Y?

In the 1970s Monsanto set up a European office for external affairs. Its director set out Monsanto's spirited approach in a presentation to business leaders, assembled in Brussels. The basic idea was to persuade opinion-makers that this multi was and would be a good corporate citizen in *every* European country in which it had manufacturing facilities. It was planned to publish annually a cost-benefit balance sheet for all major economies in the region. His speech outlined that Britain, where the company was heavily involved, had been chosen as the first national model. The listeners were given a detailed demonstration of Monsanto's positive contributions to that host country's GDP, balance of payments, employment, and technological advance. One member of the audience rose to express his dissent. He agreed that such a one-country social audit would help Monsanto score a PR victory in the current year. But, he asked rather naughtily, what would be the PR effect if, in subsequent years, Monsanto found it expedient to shut down some British plants? That is precisely what happened soon thereafter. The director of the European office for external affairs, who had been listened to with such awe, retired and returned to the United States and Monsanto stopped the exercises that were to have proved quantitatively that it was a good corporate citizen in individual European countries.

Caterpillar did not have only a private code. It repeatedly testified that it was also loyal to the various guidelines of the international bodies. Caterpillar was proud of its reputation as the most socially responsible multi of the United States. At the end of 1986 its head office in Peoria informed the British government that a $90 million expansion plan for its Scottish plant had been finalized. The purpose of the widely publicized message was to solicit subsidies that were indeed granted. More than £3 million had already been handed over when, only a few months later, an astounded British public read that Caterpillar was cancelling its heralded investment and closing down altogether the Scottish plant, laying off 1,200 workers. The cynicism of this brutal divestment was unprecedented during the seven years of the Thatcher administration. The prime minister was so taken aback that she personally wrote to Peoria to enquire whether her government could extend any assistance to make this multi change its mind. The answer was in the negative because the decision had nothing to do with any local industrial dispute or specific British factor. The corporation's board had been appraised that in the last quarter of 1986 a global loss was about to be registered. Hence the order was given to reduce the worldwide output immediately. The CEO had no intention of making cuts across the board, but had opted for the complete closure of two plants out of 32 manufacturing sites. The reason that this arbitrary treatment of the UK manufacturing facility aroused such consternation had of course to do with its celebrated "Code of Worldwide Business Conduct." This had specified that Caterpillar, unlike other MNCs, behaved humanely, as behooved a good corporate citizen in a host country. It so happened that by mid–1988 "substantial profits" were again earned. The axing of the Scottish plant in January 1987 was probably an over-hasty decision. But at the time, the directors of the parent company could justifiably defend it: unless drastic surgery is carried out at short notice, the viability of the whole company and the employment prospects of some 55,000 people are put at risk. It may therefore well have been a sound judgment to cut the worldwide output. As a multi, Caterpillar was in a position to pursue a flexible strategy that allowed for relatively fast adjustments. The means employed bore witness to the fact that being a good TNC in the global context did not mean being a good corporate citizen in every country of the world. Has Caterpillar's private code been withdrawn? If it has not, this document, which laid bare the social conscience of a caring TNC, is not likely to be cited in the future with the same religious fervor that was manifested before this episode.

The Dubious Independence of National Subsidiaries

The governments of host countries demand of foreign parents that the subsidiaries operating in their territories should meet effectively the requirements established by local policies and regulations. Though the equity is held by non-residents, it is the municipal law that is expected to prevail and the various guidelines affirm that this is how it ought to be. The UN has extended this principle. When the subsidiary of an international company has cause to complain of harassment by its host nation, it is deemed to be improper to enlist the support of the government of the home country in which the head office of the multi is located. To do so would offend the canons of social behavior to which modern, 'progressive' TNCs ought to subscribe: the global power of a TNC should not be summoned to help one constituent foreign operation that is victimized by native authorities. Article 3 of Mexico's Foreign Investment Law allows the confiscation of the Mexican property of any foreign company that invokes the protection of its own government against Mexico.

Whenever host governments want to squeeze some additional benefits out of operations that are controlled or owned by foreign multis, or refuse to implement contractual obligations that they have freely taken upon themselves, they stress the autonomous character of the subsidiaries. Interferences from head offices located abroad are decried. But when such subsidiaries lack the resources to comply with demands from (private and public) native claimants, the limited liability concept is disregarded. If a national subsidiary faces bankruptcy, then the board of the multi is supposed to rescue the creditors and pamper the redundant employees. TNCs are blackmailed easily. When the Belgian manufacturing subsidiary of the U.S.-based Raytheon company closed down because it had no work, local politicians took up the cudgels on behalf of the former employees and extracted gold from the head office of this foreign multi. Raytheon was made to hand over not just the officially prescribed severance pay but also additional substantive amounts. Did the recipients not deserve this supplementary compensation? Though employed by a company incorporated under Belgian law, had they not indirectly been toiling for a global corporation?

The ambiguous independence of national subsidiaries was spotlighted in 1978–80 during the Viggo affair in Sweden where the ILO and OECD guidelines played a decisive role. In 1973 London-based BOC bought a small Swedish company with 150 employees. Within five years Viggo, by then BOC's subsidiary, had a labor force of 600; during the acrimonious dispute it was not suggested that this number would be reduced. The Swedish unions had received formal notification, as Swedish law demanded, that some Viggo products might in future be manufactured in Britain and the United States because it was not economic to export them to these markets from Sweden. LO immediately opposed this, maintaining that "in the national interest" the Viggo subsidiary should be enlarged. Furthermore, the union bosses denied the right of Viggo managers to negotiate on this issue because they were not in charge of an independent company. LO requested to bargain on this matter with the head office of BOC in London. When this demand was turned down, the guidelines were cited to indicate that the British multi was in breach of these codes. The Swedish government assisted the LO and made representations on its behalf to the UK authorities, which in turn propounded that BOC had not contravened any applicable rules.

The Swedish Employers Confederation was very upset by the tactics of the Swedish unions. Its most powerful members, the Swedish-based TNCs, were frightened of the consequences that would ensue if the LO principle became an accepted practice: the autonomy of their foreign subsidiaries would be undermined and they might then be expected to bargain in Sweden with union representatives from all the many countries in which they had manufacturing facilities. The Confederation sent out a warning letter to the Swedish subsidiaries of foreign multis and to the CEOs of Swedish multis. Paying lip-service to the ILO and OECD guidelines, it was suggested that these should also be used in future as helpful indicators. But firms were admonished not to sign binding agreements regarding these guidelines because this would limit managerial prerogatives in the independent subsidiaries of Swedish and non-Swedish MNCs.

Swedish unions did not accept that Viggo was an autonomous company within the BOC empire and thus they insisted on negotiating with the head office in London. While the Viggo affair was at its height, LO unwittingly provided proof of how arbitrary are the challenges by host governments and unions to the independent status of the subsidiaries of foreign multis. In 1979 SKF closed down a French subsidiary and the aggrieved native employees refused to negotiate with the French management, saying that their rights would only be safeguarded if they could arrive at a settlement with the head office in Goeteborg. Not only did SKF's CEO refuse this demand but the Swedish unions too agreed that the French subsidiary was a wholly independent corporate body. One LO leader went on Swedish television to justify this stand on the ground that "we must look after our own unemployed" (174).

No one was more adamant than the Indian government in asserting that subsidiaries and affiliates of alien multis are subject to Indian laws and that undue meddling by foreign head offices would not be tolerated. One of the reasons that a settlement of the compensation claims for the victims of the 1984 Union Carbide Bhopal tragedy dragged on for many years was the attitude of the authorities in New Delhi. They maintained that the Indian subsidiary of Union Carbide—almost half of its equity was owned by the Indian government and indigenous shareholders—was not an independent legal body. Consequently, the claims were to be directed at the wealthy U.S.-based parent. The TNC in turn argued that the Bhopal plant had been built and managed by Indians; this subsidiary was said not to be receiving capital injections or managerial guidance from the United States so that the parent was just a shareholder in Union Carbide India.

Obey the Law of Host Countries?

The published guidelines of the UN, OECD, ILO, and ICC all stress that multis should not interfere in the political processes of host countries. There can be no question of MNCs actively supporting the overthrow of a government—this is universally condemned as improper. The Group of Eminent Persons conceded that multis should be allowed to express views concerning government policies if these affected directly their operations but they were warned to do so in a "circumspect way." The subsidiaries of multis controlled from abroad are expected to conduct themselves as "discreet foreigners" (154). The concept of TNCs as neutral, non-political corporate vehicles is one that most corporations are happy to embrace. UFCO belongs to history and it would make life easy for TNCs if they were allowed to follow these particular precepts of the guidelines. But in the real world they are not always given this opportunity. Their adversaries would like them to behave obsequiously to the rulers of 'progressive' regimes but to conduct themselves as bad citizens in countries that for one reason or another are pursuing policies of which some critics of TNCs disapprove. Irrespective of what the guidelines say, a multi is expected to fight actively against the government of a bad host nation or face a global boycott.

When ITT was crucified for its conduct in Latin America, some detractors unearthed that in the prewar years of Hitler's regime (1933–39) ITT's head office had appointed Nazis with good connections to the board of its German subsidiary in order to ingratiate itself with the rulers of the host country. In the 1970s the enemies of the U.S.-based TNC castigated it for this, allegedly depraved, conduct in the 1930s. ITT's defense is surely in consonance with the modern guidelines: its intention had been to demonstrate good citizenship and a readiness not to operate against German interests (139).

The campaign against U.S. multis with connections in Northern Ireland is clearly aimed at punishing them for not breaking UK regulations and for not supporting civil disobedience. These MNCs are being chastised precisely because they are conducting themselves as good citizens of the UK.

Thanks to a WCC pamphlet (19), some scolding rebukes for the Dutch multi Philips have become public knowledge. When Chile's Allende government was overthrown, the portrait of the new ruler, Pinochet, was hung in the boardroom of its Chilean subsidiary. This token of good citizenship (according to the guidelines, MNCs are not to take account of the political complexion of the government of the host nation) is denounced as an ominous sign that the only thing that matters with Philips is its own profit.

The same source tells of another crime perpetrated by Philips. A coup in Brazil brought to power a set of rulers whom the critics of this Dutch TNC did not like. Frits Philips, the chairman of the parent company, visited the Brazilian subsidiary and was photographed shaking hands with members of the new government.

Gulf Oil acted like a good citizen in Angola. A delegation of five U.S. church leaders, who were organizing a boycott of the corporation because they were opposed to Portugese imperialism, told the company: If you want our campaign to be halted, you must behave as a subversive corporate citizen in Angola—"you must openly support the forces of liberation financially and publicly" (48).

Central banks in all parts of the world instruct, order, or cajole banks within their jurisdiction to purchase government securities. When the South African affiliate of Barclays Bank complied with one such official request, it was condemned by anti-apartheid activists for propping up the hated regime. This was rather hard on Barclays, which had gone out of its way to be a bad corporate citizen whenever this was possible. By assisting one of its senior (black) employees to buy a house in a Johannesburg suburb that was reserved for whites, it had flouted a basic tenet of apartheid. Barclays also admitted that it was agitating for the scrapping of the segregation laws. In 1986 Shell too no longer pretended to obey the spirit of the guidelines, for it openly adopted a political stance hostile to the host government. Shell pledged itself to "do all within its powers to eradicate this unjust system," which Pretoria was administering. Years before its divestment decision was announced, GM had been encouraging non-whites to contravene the law of South Africa. At one stage—as a symbolic act of defiance—the subsidiary of the U.S.-based multi had offered legal assistance to its black employees who were prosecuted for swimming at whites-only beaches in Port Elizabeth. Demonstrating bad citizenship of a mild kind was not enough. To buy absolution Shell, Barclays, and GM would have had to give financial donations to the groups that were attempting to overthrow the South African government by violence. This they were apparently not prepared to do.

The OECD guidelines say that "enterprises must abstain from any improper involvement in local political activities." This trite generality poses several questions. Who is authorized to define what is 'improper'? Are all political interventions by multis always condemned by everybody as deplorable? The governments of India, Kenya, and Sri Lanka are accused in some quarters of oppressing Sikhs, Indians, and Tamils, respectively. Are TNCs with subsidiaries in these countries morally and politically obliged to support actively those groups that, by violent or non-violent means, strive to reverse the ethnic or religious policies of the host governments?

When white-skinned persons persecute non-whites, this is clearly racism. But, though many church leaders and 'progressive' politicians would disagree, these are not the only expressions of racial discrimination. Must TNCs adapt their 'social responsibility' when the regimes of the host countries exhibit unorthodox racist tendencies? Indonesia compelled all multis to reduce their equity in Indonesian-registered companies to below 50 percent. But, in a measure biased against the Chinese, the edict stated explicitly that the spun-off equity must go not just to indigenous Indonesians but only to non-Chinese Indonesians. President Moi of Kenya denounced South Africa's apartheid but when he affirmed his intention to place the controlling heights of his country's economy in the hands of African citizens, he was blatantly racist. Multis with Kenyan subsidiaries were expected to hand over 51 percent of the equity to indigenous Kenyans. This order was interpreted to exclude the Kenyan Asians and the Kenyan whites from the privileged group of "indigenous Kenyans". Malaysia's government pursued a racist line of action that forced foreign-owned companies to employ Bumiputras— "sons of the soil" who were regarded as the true indigenous Malays— and not those of Chinese or Indian origin. Between 1970 and 1986 Kuala Lumpur made foreign multis dispose of up to 70 percent of the equity of their Malaysian subsidiaries. They were, however, not free to sell to the Malaysian capitalists of their choice. The transfer of the divested equity was to be executed in such a manner that priority was given mandatorily to Bumiputras rather than to those Malays who belonged to the Chinese and Indian communities.

Only one conclusion seems to evolve with certainty from this discussion. There are no objective standards that regulate the conduct of a company in order to qualify it as a good corporate citizen. In their relationship with the authorities of host nations, TNCs must play it by ear, which is precisely what most of them do. It is also why the guidelines do not deserve serious attention.

PART III

LIVING WITH THE FUTURE

18

THE TIDE IS RECEDING

MNCs have never been in greater danger. . . . Make plans for disinvestment.

BINCO's warning, March 1984

The preceding chapters were composed with the aim of dispelling the myth that stresses the evil influence of the TNCs' collective might and attributes supranational domineering strength to the individual corporations. The legend pertaining to the influence of the multinational corporation is beginning to lose its sting. Even during the days when the four founding fathers were formulating their theories on the nature of the TNC, multis were not the omnipotent vehicles that vainglorious company presidents, trendy clerics, and Marxist agitators made them out to be. Today this is becoming blatantly obvious. With hindsight we know now how fragile were the Seven Sisters, which were generally believed to be mighty companies; their assets were expropriated at the whim of seemingly insignificant autocratic rulers. Older readers will recall when the vilified ITT was portrayed as a prototypical specimen of the accursed multis and was the victim of a worldwide hate campaign. Anthony Sampson published a hostile biography, tendentiously entitled

The Sovereign State (133). He said of ITT: "I had the powerful impression that here was a company that was accountable to no nation, anywhere." Its dictatorial chief, Harold Geneen, was probably flattered. Even then an unemotional analysis would have revealed what was clearly discernible after Geneen left the corporation's driving seat: ITT was politically impotent, subject to being kicked around by LDCs, OECD governments, and the administration of its own home country. Beneath the gloss, this "corporate centipede"—a hotchpotch of multifarious companies, active in a hundred countries—was basically a pitiable, weak creature. Rand Araskog, the CEO who was later to dismantle the ungainly outfit—this epitome of multinational and multiproduct diversification—had a task that was compared to "turning the Queen Mary around in the middle of the floes" (167). In a short time he rid the TNC of 95 businesses worth $4 billion and then commenced the divestiture of the core business that had endowed it with its corporate name. ITT transferred most of its global telecommunication equipment assets to a new company, majority-controlled by a French nationalized organization. Wall Street loved the axe-man who was destroying Geneen's empire. The refurbished multi desecrated Geneen's memory by inserting apposite advertisements in the financial press.

As we've said all along, at ITT it's a different world today. . . . We promised that ITT was going to reshape itself. . . . And we've done so. We've already divested ourselves of dozens of companies. . . . No doubt about it. We're a very different company today.

I predict that, increasingly, the veil of the multi legend will be pierced to reveal the intrinsic nonsense on which it rested. In the next century the legend will have faded away altogether. It would be agreeable to believe that this will have come about solely because of the rising perceptiveness of our fellow citizens. Maybe—but the legend is in any case doomed to wither with the gradual decline of the present OECD multis during the next two decades. Internationally oriented enterprises will grow in number and flourish, but few of the old-fashioned TNCs will have survived by the year 2010—unless they have radically transformed themselves.

My glimpse into the future makes a number of assumptions.

1. The citizens of the OECD countries will become progressively more prosperous and, consequently, the price of goods will not be the main determinant in consumer choice. Concomitantly, low-cost processes will not necessarily have an edge over more costly modes of production.

2. The gates of the OECD countries will be locked firmly to stem the influx of work-seeking individuals from the poorer parts of the world.

3. While I envisage a spurt in nationalist sentiments, I do not forecast a substantive rise in protectionism, which would seriously impede international merchandise trade. (If I am wrong and protectionism becomes a weighty instrument of policy, then my predicted decline of the conventional multis will take place at a somewhat slower pace.) I surmise that, on balance, the OECD countries will not attempt to curtail the import of most goods from the LDCs. My main reason for thinking so is set out below, where I argue that in future the OECD will have less reason than at present to fear the 'cheap labor' incorporated in the exports marketed by the poorer countries.

Chapter 19 deals with the metamorphosis of those conventional multis that seek to survive as a fundamentally different kind of international corporation. It will be more difficult to make the multi legend sound plausible when the size of the new type of TNC is much reduced and mammoth corporations are primarily cross-border purveyors of services rather than manufacturers in foreign locations. Thirty years after BINCO was founded, its chiefs announced a principled ideological retreat. They admitted dolefully to their corporate members that the "MNC of tomorrow" will be a radically changed creature which will no longer find it necessary to own "the means of production." They might well have added that neither will most of the future MNCs be the direct employers of the workers who produce goods for them in foreign lands.

Chapter 20 recalls that the protagonists of the TNC have linked the blossoming of multis with the emasculation of the nation–state and the advent of world government. In my prognosis the nation–state will strengthen and tighten its grip on the international corporation. The decline of the multi legend will be speeded up by the enormous drop in the number and weight of U.S.-based corporations within the totality of TNCs.

THE MAINSPRINGS ARE RUSTING

This current chapter is devoted to a reexamination of the bread-and-butter causes that brought about the birth of the majority of multis. A few blips on the horizon favor the continued expansion of conventional TNCs. However, most of the features that are conjectured to dominate our lives in the next two decades will curtail the scope of OECD-based multis. The raison d'être of numerous existing multis will gradually abate. In 2010 there will be no application for the rationale that led to their international expansion in the years up to, say, 1975. From this generalization Japanese corporations must as yet be excluded, because for some time to come, they will still have reason to spread their tentacles as the old OECD TNCs used to do. There are also bright prospects for the parturition of new MNCs in LDCs. Though many of these will indeed shoot forth and thus swell the number of TNCs in the world, they are unlikely to shield the multi legend from sinking into oblivion. TNCs with head offices in Bangladesh and Nigeria will not be abused in the same vituperative fashion that the WCC and other anti-multi zealots now reserve for TNCs from the OECD.

The harsh disciplines demanded from executives sans patrie were appropriate for the internal life force of the multi prototype designed by Perlmutter. But nowadays a growing number of executives do not agree to be moved from one national location to another, from one corporate function to another. More attention is being paid to the needs of the children and, above all, wives now have a greater say. Many are working and do not wish to give up careers to help their husbands step up the promotion ladder. Multis are being weakened also in another respect. The geocentric concept is increasingly treated as unrealistic. Corporations are loosening the reins that tie subsidiaries to the center. Some multis, such as NCR, go out of their way to proclaim the new stance: more freedom is being granted to affiliates and subsidiaries. The Woolworth-BAT-RTZ model is gaining admirers. Many of the manufacturing TNCs, which are setting up an autonomous structure for the constituent parts of their global operations, are digging their own grave. Unwittingly, they are conveying the message that there is no economic justification for a corporate framework with diverse product groups and manufacturing facilities in different national locations. Such 'modernized' multis invite corporate raiders to break them up.

The emaciated shadows of the most important causes that led to the rise of TNCs and nurtured the multi legend are discussed under four headings: cheap labor; the risks of direct investments; old-fashioned backward integration; and the masking of the national origin of TNC subsidiaries. Several minor causes that drove companies to expand overseas are now also on the wane. One of these is tariff jumping. Import duties are generally unimportant today and it is difficult to believe that a large national company would nowadays want to transform itself into an international company primarily in order to escape from the tariff burden. The proportion of the retail price of imported merchandise, accounted for by import duties, is dwindling. One recalls with nostalgia Wicander, a company manufacturing bottle-cork, which was Sweden's earliest multi. The first of its factories abroad was built in Finland. That national location was chosen because Finland was close to the large market of Russia, where its goods enjoyed far-reaching tax privileges. Then rumors became current that a tariff barrier would be erected between Finland and Russia. For this reason and this reason only, Wicander built a manufacturing plant in Russia which served it well when import duties were indeed enacted in 1888 (175).

The "balloon-sized world of post-World War II has been shrunk to the size of a grape by the modern technology of transportation and communication" (34). This hyperbole by Orville Freeman was intended to herald the news that world government is nigh. In my view there is no connection between the intensity of nationalism and the time it takes to fly by Concorde from Lisbon to Los Angeles. While the quotation emphasized the enhanced speed of modern travel, in our context it matters more to highlight transportation costs in the evolution of TNCs. This factor was once a midwife, helping to give birth to numerous foreign manufacturing subsidiaries but is now of little significance. Unit transportation costs have tumbled and dispatching goods overseas has become a fast routine, considerably more dependable than in the early years of this century. In some industrial branches sending freight to foreign destinations by air has had a remarkable impact. Not only is this often cheaper than conveying it by rail and/or shipping, but it also obviates the need to store inventories in local depots; foreign customers are supplied directly from the home country. Vendors of capital goods are able to make available at short notice spare parts and technicians for servicing equipment in operational use. The expected further drop in unit transportation costs will pull multis into diametrically opposed directions. Companies will find it commercially more feasible to manufacture overseas, shipping back some of the output to the home country. However, lower freight charges will provide an additional impetus to liquidate manufacturing subsidiaries abroad and supply foreign markets with exports from the home base. On balance, the second aspect will prove to be more influential.

Whatever may have been the case in the past, large international corporations will face increased dangers when they strive to collect corporate rewards from tax avoidance schemes and flagrant tax evasions. For their own sake and to protect the PR image of their corporation, top executives sans patrie are already fighting shy of exploiting opportunities their predecessors would have grasped in years gone by. Several national revenue authorities have organized special bodies to examine cross-border, intracorporate dealings. This has reportedly closed some real and imagined transfer pricing loopholes. Head offices are finding it less worthwhile to set up dummy companies in foreign lands. Revenue officials in countries in which TNCs source their inputs and market their finished goods have become more disposed to make 'true' tax assessments. They ignore the actual invoices and instead postulate arbitrary prices. These decisions are of course challenged, but multis do not enjoy such altercations. The CEO of the modern TNC has also become aware that there is little to be gained from 'ornamental' and 'screwdriver' subsidiaries because most nations now understand that these are cunning corporate devices that bestow few benefits on the host country. In the immediate postwar years the concept of value-added was an academic abstraction. Today, in OECD and LDC economies, manufacturing subsidiaries are scrutinized for their value-added. Unless this is an acceptable proportion of their output, host countries will not treat the operations as genuine direct investments.

To implement contrived transfer pricing, it is helpful to enlist as accomplices willing, though passive, host countries. The Republic of Ireland, well known as a country that is not very concerned with value-added, once urged the multis of the world to partake of its facilities. The Irish did not discriminate: they welcomed companies from Communist and anti-Communist countries, from LDCs and from the OECD. Hundreds of MNCs located assembly plants and repackaging companies in hospitable Ireland. When it was on offer, they were happy to take advantage of the long-term 100 percent tax holiday. But other nations, in particular members of the EC, resented this assistance to TNCs that excelled in cross-border price machinations. Ireland was forced to rescind the 100 percent tax abatement. More pressure is likely to be exerted on Ireland and the other havens that harbor 'enterprising' international companies.

Multis have to adapt themselves to the idiosyncracies of the national economies in which they choose to have subsidiaries. Hitherto, it was understood that—PR considerations apart—the limited liability concept prevailed; that is, country A's sovereignty was brought to bear only on those operations of multis that relate directly to country A. Things are changing. There are signs that a multi investing in A must expect to be subjected to interventions by the government of A relating to its global reach. TNCs with large undertakings in Germany have had to acknowledge that the municipal law of *Mitbestimmung* [codetermination] covers also their local subsidiaries: worker-directors are elected to the *Aufsichtsrat* [supervisory board] and certain statutory disclosures must be made. But there is clamor—warmly supported by the supreme bodies of the EC—that this principle should be extended so that companies with subsidiaries outside their home country will have to make disclosures on their worldwide activities. Furthermore, host country A will claim authority to make the foreign parent responsible for the liabilities of its incorporated subsidiary in A. The Bhopal and Viggo affairs, noted in chapter 17, tell perceptive, imaginative CEOs how the wind is likely to blow in the next century. The implementation of 'unitary' taxation in the United States is still facing formidable obstacles. If, however, the opposition of the multis is overcome and the technique is adopted widely within the U.S., other countries are bound to emulate it. In the future, head offices intending to set up a subsidiary in A will have to consider that this may entail an involvement in matters that are not connected with the actual operations in A. Under those circumstances corporations, which shrink from writing open checks, will curtail their direct investments abroad.

The majority of OECD economies—most noticeably the English-speaking countries—abandoned in the 1980s some long-established state support measures for investments. In many of the years following the end of World War II the twins, investing and saving, were pampered; they were fitted out with expensive garbs and given costly toys to play with. Consumption was deemed to be a bad thing. Not by chance was the period during which investing and saving were glorified also one in which full employment dominated the labor market. While investing per se was spurred by OECD governments, incidental side effects benefited corporations which laid the foundations for manufacturing operations abroad. They could collect subsidies relating to installed capital goods. Some Western governments even apportioned funds from their foreign aid budgets to such infrastructure as would induce privately-owned multis to open subsidiaries in LDCs. The UK authorities gave the French multi Club Méditerranée a tax holiday in a British dependency in the Caribbean and built a special airport to lure the company into investing in a tourist facility. Weightier examples are found in several developing economies in which Western-based multis had been encouraged to establish production facilities; with the help of the aid budgets of their home countries they purchased the requisite machinery. It is outside the orbit of this book to detail how in the 1980s opportunities to receive subventions for capital expenditure were wiped out or at least emasculated. Britain used to be the most extreme country in its promotion of the investment mania: for several years 100 percent first-year depreciation of virtually all machinery and equipment could be written off against current tax liability. Those days are over. Western states no longer accord priority to the subsidizing of investments. Instead, they prefer to subsidize people; that is, employers are given financial subventions commensurate with the number of people they employ. If indeed this is a long-term trend, coupled with the abatement of certain fiscal advantages that used to accrue to multis on overseas profits arising in overseas subsidiaries, TNCs will have to learn to play a new ball game. In future, OECD taxpayers will subsidize more generously production in the home country and give relatively more aid to exporters.

"CHEAP LABOR" IS IMMATERIAL

The most frequently cited 'evidence' for the evil-mindedness of OECD-based multis is their choice of LDCs in which to exploit the low-paid, obsequious, unorganized, non-white (and largely female) native workers. It is a stark exaggeration to say, as anti-multi zealots do, that this is the predominant reason why foreign-owned manufacturing subsidiaries were established. To the limited extent that this factor furnishes a valid historical explanation for the birth of TNCs, it also illuminates why numerous multis are liquidating, or contemplating to liquidate, some of their foreign manufacturing operations.

A German TNC once justified its decision to build a plant in Singapore on the ground that its home country was groaning under full employment. In future, OECD economies will not suffer from such labor shortages as to induce corporations to set up shop abroad.

In the 1960s and 1970s Western European employers had difficulties in recruiting indigenous youngsters to take up highly remunerative but monotonous jobs in assembly plants. Volvo demonstrated in Goeteborg that the level of the wage offered was not significant. Young Swedes preferred to take up other, less well-paid, employment or subsist on the benefits of the welfare state rather than manufacture cars. Volvo and other European car firms solved the problem by importing *Gastarbeiter*. There were forecasters in those days who concluded that certain repetitious factory work would tend to be transferred to LDCs and that this would stimulate the overseas expansion of OECD-based multis. The automation of assembly work in the rich economies has countered this, once seemingly logical, trend and the growing use of robots and computers will progressively eliminate many of the tiresome and tedious features of factory production.

Some of the long-term forecasts, published in the 1970s, suggested that international companies will increasingly locate their labor-intensive plants in countries in which management is not challenged by a rebellious workforce. Several LDCs wooed OECD-based multis by explicitly drawing attention to their low-wage rates and also to the imposed industrial peace that prevailed and would prevail in the future. There are already enough indications to be able to assert that this is not how the world will be in the twenty-first century. Some countries, such as Taiwan, which had banned strikes, have now legalized them. Local manufacturers have already had a foretaste of what the future will be like. South Korea has been engulfed by (non-political) strikes, the dimensions of which were unimaginable only a decade ago. As industrial workers are flexing their muscles in the Asian LDCs, the character of their unions is also undergoing a radical change. While previously many LDC unions were approved and supported by the government, the new type of unions are independent of both employers and the state. It was a former senior executive of strike-prone BL who helped to lay the foundations of South Korea's largest car plant. When it was opened, commentators would have it that this was a signpost that pointed to the production of cars in a peaceful industrial environment; ultimately these cars would flood the markets of the OECD. In June 1988 Hyundai car workers returned to work with a 30 percent pay raise after a turbulent 25-day work stoppage.

Lester Thurow believes that the following will affect the expansion policies of U.S. TNCs.

Multinationals need low wages . . . to establish facilities that can compete with those in the U.S. In Europe low wages are already gone. And they are rapidly disappearing in [some] parts of Asia, e.g. Korea, Taiwan, Hong Kong, Singapore (178).

Many others besides Thurow consider that the cheap-labor attractions of LDCs are about to disappear because of the narrowing of the wage differentials between the poorer and richer parts of the world. This will undoubtedly occur in some developing economies but is not a generalization which will be universally valid. In the year 2010 there will still exist a very wide gap between the labor costs of the OECD and, say, the People's Republic of China or Bangladesh. There is a more profound reason why, nevertheless, the magnetism of cheap labor is not likely to stimulate many OECD corporations to build plants overseas.

K. Ohmae has calculated some of the expensive side effects arising from manufacturing abroad, such as the expenditure on insurance, transport, and other items that would not have been incurred if the production had taken place in the United States (177). The drawbacks arising from production in foreign lands have clearly been offset in the past by the savings that arose from employing low-cost labor. This was especially true where labor costs were a substantial factor and amounted to more than 40 percent of the ex-factory price. We are in the midst of an era that is experiencing a radical drop in the proportion of labor costs out of total costs. There are already many technologically advanced production processes (chemicals, electronics) in which direct labor costs are down to below 10 percent; many more hover between 10 percent and 20 percent. The number of TNCs with direct labor costs below 20 percent is set to grow dramatically in the next two decades. On balance, they would be at a disadvantage if they manufactured in countries whose main attraction is low labor costs. Those with direct labor costs of 20–40 percent will have no, or only a minimal, incentive to manufacture abroad because of the mirage of cheap labor.

THE UNATTRACTIVENESS OF DIRECT FOREIGN INVESTMENTS

The learning curve of OECD-based TNCs is a long, crooked line. Many have already concluded that they no longer wish to bear the onerous burden of being involved in the politics of LDCs. Consequently, they are running down their existing foreign direct investments. Even more corporations disdain making new greenfield investments abroad. (Japanese TNCs are still sui generis.) This general tendency is pervasive but does not as yet apply to direct investments in the United States, Britain, and a few other OECD economies. But even in these favored locations, the proportion of the total volume of direct investments represented by the building of greenfield manufacturing plants is now much smaller than in the past. The overwhelming majority of the recent mammoth direct investments in the United States and Britain by foreign (non-Japanese) TNCs are acquisitions of existing enterprises.

Skepticism abounds, particularly in relation to those LDCs where numerous TNCs have been wounded severely in the past. India and Venezuela, for example, now claim to be reformed host countries; they intend to behave well to foreign investors. It is making little impression. Perhaps for decades to come, the conduct of most LDCs after World War II will be remembered by Western corporate decision-makers. Have the LDC leopards changed their spots? The present-day CEOs of multis do not believe they have. The expropriations, broken promises, punitive taxes, mandatory orders to use local (inferior) inputs, kidnapping of executives, prohibitions to remit profits and royalties—these and other harassments of corporations, which had originally been invited to invest, have made OECD-based companies unwilling to rely on solemn undertakings by most potential host countries. The terrible tragedy in Bhopal has taught many Western TNCs once again to beware of operating subsidiaries in certain foreign lands, particularly in countries like India where xenophobia is stirred up when factory accidents occur and where corporations—if they are foreign-owned and said to be wealthy—are found guilty before even a trial has taken place. Had the accident occurred in the home country, the matter would have been adjudged on the merits of the case. Anyone who has witnessed the officially inspired and orchestrated anti-U.S. multi hate campaign taken up by Union Carbide's detractors throughout the world can be left in no doubt that it is the involvement of a *foreign-owned* corporation that seemed to matter most. No court has yet determined whether the 1984 incident was due to Union Carbide's neglect, local sabotage, or other factors. For global PR reasons the Union Carbide parent agreed in 1989 to an Indian Supreme Court ruling that the U.S. multi should make a compensation payment of $470 million. This will be cited as a precedent in the years to come. India has given notice to the TNCs of the world that it is the parent company that is deemed to be liable for any putative misdeeds and mishaps of its foreign subsidiaries. OECD-based multis will note another dismal fact. Having defeated Rajiv Ghandi at the polls, the new administration—unilaterally—reopened the case for damages and set aside its predecessor's compensation claim as "totally inadequate."

The rights of multis in LDCs are precarious indeed. This was illustrated superbly when eight directors of the board of the UK-based TNC Lonrho sought to dismiss the CEO Roland Rowland. The lawyer who appeared for the endangered executive at the High Court had a peculiar brief. Affidavits by the governments of Ghana, Zambia, Kenya, and the Sudan were submitted. These would have it that if Rowland were dismissed, Lonrho's operations would cease in their countries. There were also references to a letter from a diplomat of Zaire that gave "an unmistakable warning which the defendants would disregard at their risk." This was capped by the ludicrous spectacle of the governor of Zambia's Central Bank threatening to nationalize immediately Lonrho's assets in his country should Rowland cease to be the CEO of the global corporation. If direct investments in African LDCs can be menaced because of such whims on the part of capricious rulers, what security is there for Western shareholders who foolishly hold equity stakes in multis with direct investments in Africa? Some pertinent testimony appears in the published history of Metal Box, a UK multi that learned to its shareholders' regret what it meant to 'own' manufacturing subsidiaries in the new Africa.

The subsidiaries of an international company are at the mercy of the governments of countries where they operate, not in any sense their masters. Moreover, once capital has been committed and factories have been built, it is almost impossible to get out without heavy losses, no matter how difficult life may become (135).

Though most of the disillusionment with foreign investments stems from developing economies, some disheartening experiences were gained in developed countries. They all add up to make plausible the prediction that the enthusiasm for the international expansion of national companies will be dampened in the years to come.

Raytheon, an American electronics firm, had a Sicilian subsidiary with a history of losses and labour unrest. Eventually they decided to close it. . . . The Mayor of Palermo promptly occupied the plant, so Raytheon then declared its Italian subsidiary bankrupt. . . . But Raytheon cannot even sell the plant to make good some of its losses because IRI [a state agency] has managed to scare off all potential bidders while waiting for Raytheon to come down to a price it is willing to pay (180).

The British automobile multi BL had a lot of financial troubles at home and was consequently pressed to liquidate its direct investments abroad. After announcing the closing of its Belgian assembly operation, BL was blackmailed into paying huge amounts—for which there was no legal foundation—in order to preserve its sales image in Belgium. The British multi's experience has been not dissimilar to that of other TNCs, particularly U.S. ones, which have suffered in silence though they have stored up their resentment. TNCs have learned from these episodes to think also of the possible costs of divestment. A business journal, appearing in Geneva, summed it up.

Before companies accept investment-aid packages from Belgium's regional governments—or, for that matter, from any other authority—they should be aware of a possible pitfall. They could be letting themselves in for official arm-twisting, should they make cutbacks in staff or manufacturing capacity. . . . BL was bluntly presented with . . . paying out extralegal compensation. . . . The message for companies is clear. When contemplating investment in Belgium, do not simply take into account the [subsidised] capital costs of entry. Factor in a realistic projection of the [inflated] costs of exit too and remember that regional governments are able to force 'generous' settlements on companies that have accepted their help in the past (179).

When multis are wooed to set up a greenfield plant in Timbuktu, they rarely think of what would happen if they had to disinvest. Investors in India have had to learn the bitter lesson that they cannot dispose of their equity holdings to the Indian buyer who is willing to pay the highest price. Foreign multi vendors need a permit from the government. The Controller of Capital Issues frequently sets the price below the market rate and may also 'suggest' the buyer. France is not an LDC, but curious things have happened there too. In the fall of 1988 Gillette's global rationalization program called for the closure of its plant at Annecy. The French government formally intervened, condemning the proposal as "unacceptable." The minister of industry warned the company that it was taking a big risk if it went ahead with the closure. Without detailing in public what this meant, an official spokesman commented ominously that the U.S. multi had understood the message of the "serious warning."

It is somewhat difficult to provoke moral indignation at, say, a Dutch TNC investing in a high-cost country like Germany. This is why the WCC literature is full of allusions to the depravity of Western multis that exploit the poor in developing economies. The multi legend is based on the implicit assumption that most direct foreign investments are in LDCs. Facts do not destroy myths disseminated by zealots even when, as in this context, easily ascertainable data challenge the message of this fairy tale. The investments of MNCs in LDCs fall into three categories: (1) extraction industries of which more will be said in the next section; (2) the production of goods meant to be sold entirely (or mainly) in the host country (when protectionist barriers effectively exclude imports, the level of wages is not very significant); and (3) manufacturing for the purpose of exporting all or most of the output to other national markets, including the multi's home country. It is this third category that is mainly responsible for arousing the wrath of 'progressives' in the developed countries. Though hundreds of such subsidiaries have been established, they have always constituted a minority of total foreign investments by OECD-based TNCs. (Once again we are excluding Japanese firms from this analysis.)

Although the multi legend would have it that Western TNCs beg for the privilege of investing in LDCs, the opposite is true. As a form of charitable aid for the Third World, a number of rich countries (the United States, Britain, Germany, Japan, and so on) have provided state-backed insurance to safeguard reluctant corporate investors against the risks that are associated with investments in LDCs. (The World Bank also joined in.) The taxpayers of the rich countries provided carrots to induce multis to exploit the developing countries. These incentives have proved a spectacular failure; only few companies have been prepared to start foolhardy ventures despite the promise that they would be bailed out if things went wrong. The UN, which has played its role in frightening off multis from having subsidiaries in LDCs, has had to report that TNCs have reduced their flows of direct investments to LDCs in the 1980s. TNCs have "made greater use of non-equity arrangements . . . which allow firms to maintain an economic presence without the risks associated with direct investments" (186).

In 1986 the Japanese government expressed its displeasure that, in the previous eight years, Japanese TNCs had decreased progressively the proportion of their total direct foreign investments that went to Asian LDCs and increased instead their investments in North America and Europe. In Germany the parallel proportional decline assumed such distressing dimensions that the Minister of Economic Cooperation publicly expressed his concern at the conduct of German TNCs. He opined that German investors appeared to have lost confidence in the economic stability of the developing world. Already in 1980 the German trade union IG Metall had cited statistics that attested to the unwillingness of German multis to establish manufacturing subsidiaries in the LDCs. It was used as a stick to beat the employers. The latter were reproached for threatening disingenuously to transfer production to LDCs because 'wages are too high in Germany.' IG Metall could demonstrate with ease that, overwhelmingly, the direct foreign investments of German multis took place in economies in which high wages had to be paid: "Despite low hourly wage rates, LDCs have proved to be territories which are not attractive."

In the 1985–89 period 85–90 percent of all direct foreign investments by European TNCs were located outside the LDCs. (Those that were carried out in LDCs were made almost exclusively in the richer countries of the LDC classification.) The absolute and relative decline of new manufacturing investments in the Third World, which are owned or controlled by foreign multis, is pronounced.

WHY BACKWARD INTEGRATION?

Before World War I backward vertical integration, that is, investments to procure raw materials for use in the factories of the home country, was the main motor in the development of TNCs. In the days of atomic power and jet airplanes, it is facile to look askance at the motivations that propelled the managers of the early multis. "Unilever's interests in Africa [are] . . . a legacy of the active imagination of William Lever. [He was] haunted by the fear that raw material shortages might limit his enterprise" (104). Firms were then genuinely concerned with security of supply and the ability to obtain inputs at steady prices. More importantly, corporations could then not just buy at will copper, oil, bananas, and so on. Pioneering multis—among them the Rockefellers and Guggenheims—had to invest in geological searches for the required raw materials, build mines, lay pipelines, and construct the infrastructure (roads and ports) so that the discovered natural resources could be shipped to foreign lands.

For a variety of reasons foreign-owned subsidiaries in agriculture and the extraction industries have largely disappeared. It has proved rewarding to stir up economic nationalism in the Third World relating to natural resource development. No doubt there is great satisfaction among the illiterate poor when rabble-rousers promise them a better life after the shoe factory of an alien corporation is confiscated or burned down. But it has proved a still more persuasive formula to propound that the country's national destiny would be served best if ownership and control of natural resources was taken away from aliens and 'restored' to natives. The appeal was and is overwhelming.

Unilever, like so many of the modern TNCs, has had to learn that even the undisputed legal ownership and control of natural resources does not guarantee the secure procurement of reasonably priced inputs. Sovereign governments—of the OECD and in the LDCs—have mastered the art of rendering ineffective 'ownership.' Some of the brazen-faced administrations laugh at multis that insist on operating in accordance with signed franchises and authorized exploration concessions. As TNCs have no gunboats, who is to stop governments, which meticulously avoid confiscating foreign-owned property, from imposing exorbitant export taxes? What can multis do when they are prohibited from exporting the output of their subsidiaries?

The English Queen Elizabeth I, who proscribed the export of raw wool in order to assist the domestic woollen manufacturers, has been imitated widely ever since but particularly in the period following World War II. Host governments want indigenous raw materials to be incorporated in locally manufactured goods; exports of the latter are to be encouraged while those of the former are to be penalized or stopped altogether. Among a host of countries that have taken measures to implement such a strategy are Pakistan, Peru, Bolivia, Sri Lanka, and Brazil. But rich countries too have followed unashamedly in the footsteps of Elizabeth I. France once imposed an ad valorem tax on timber exports after successful pressure was exerted by indigenous pulp producers. MITI has chided Washington for behaving in a manner that is not consonant with its avowed belief in free trade. Tokyo had been eager to buy logs from North America but "both Canada and the U.S. want to export manufactured goods; they won't sell logs" (81). Export restrictions are applied frequently by LDCs, such as Brazil and India, as an anti-inflationary weapon. The mighty United States too has not hesitated to make us of its Export Administration Act to behave in a similar fashion. In 1973 a sensational ban on the export of soya beans was promulgated. Preparations were in hand to ban also the export of logs, which the Japanese were trying to buy up en masse. The threat sufficed and Tokyo promised to practice 'voluntary' buying restraint.

Unlike assembly plants for television sets in Asian LDCs, backward vertical integration necessitates capital-intensive investments with lengthy pay-out periods. Considering the political risks of expropriation and the inability of TNCs to rely on low-priced, secure supplies, why bother to have such subsidiaries? In the days of William Lever there were no international commodity exchanges with buffer stocks. Today Western manufacturers are able to buy natural resources without being involved in their production. With the help of financial hedging, manufacturers are in a position to safeguard themselves against sharp price fluctuations. If the facilities available at the end of the twentieth century had existed at the end of the nineteenth century, William Lever would never have carved "great plantations out of the jungle." In the 1980s his successors are busy acquiring manufacturing companies in the United States and would not dream of setting up new raw materials subsidiaries in LDCs.

Technological advances are lessening the dependence of the OECD economies on LDC raw materials. (Polymers and plastics have already hit hard the producers of wool and of some basic metals.) There are two unrelated causes. First, natural resources are being substituted for increasingly by artificial products manufactured in industrial countries. Second, the input of traditional raw materials, as a proportion of the final price of (capital and consumer) goods, is declining sharply and expected to fall further.

Notwithstanding the events of the postwar years, there are still a few

OECD-based multis that are ready to be enticed by the prospects of investing in LDCs' natural resources. In 1986 Ecuador liberalized its mining laws and went out of its way to induce foreign TNCs to make bids for exploration and exploitation contracts of its mineral wealth. Ecuador succeeded in signing up several Western corporations. Throughout the post–1945 period the Japanese have attempted to buy 'national security,' that is, to offset their lack of raw materials, by making direct investments in foreign metal-extraction plants. These, however, are exceptions to the general rule that TNCs now subscribe to overwhelmingly: with the end of colonial rule, OECD-based manufacturing companies that are the owners of (foreign) plantations, mines, and oil fields rarely have an edge over companies that satisfy their requirements through purchases on the commodity markets.

DISGUISING THE NATIONAL ORIGIN

The early multis (but also some of more recent vintage) were very conscious of the actual or attributed xenophobia of the potential buyers of their products. (This was said not to have been a problem in Canada where Mira Wilkins discovered only one large business, Imperial Oil, that tried to take on a Canadian appearance and disguise its U.S. parentage.) Many TNCs were convinced that by giving up exports and instead establishing manufacturing operations in host countries, they had solved this problem. A large number of corporations were quickly disabused of this illusion, and consequently endeavored to disguise the true (foreign) ownership of their subsidiaries. Global businesses frequently operated under separate local names wherever the market warranted it. Until a volte face in the 1980s, GM as such did not exist in Europe: it was Vauxhall in Britain, Opel in Germany, and so on. Swedish multis were advised that "even if it costs a little national pride, we should refrain from raising the national colours over 'Swedish' factories abroad" (173). The United States has contributed to the English language the expression "to pass," denoting the attempts by individuals to cloak their ethnic origin. Similarly, large corporations have deliberately adopted appellations and brand names that do not enlighten the non-curious purchaser as to the national identity of the home country. The Japanese Konishiroku company, selling a wide range of goods, felt it more expedient to be known as KONICA. It is said that American Metal Climax changed to AMAX to dissociate itself from "American" in its original designation (38). British Leyland hoped that its new name, BL, would be a more suitable title for a corporation aiming to sell in the markets of the world. The architect of one of the most outstanding merchandising successes in the postwar years has revealed why SONY—which does not evoke a Japanese affiliation—was chosen as the name of his international company.

We did not purposely try to hide our national identity . . . but we certainly did not want to emphasise it and run the risk of being rejected. . . . But I must confess that in the early days we printed the line 'Made in Japan' as small as possible, once too small for U.S. Customs, which made us make it bigger on one product (115).

If it was difficult or impossible to disguise the fact that the ownership of a subsidiary was in the hands of a foreign-based company, efforts were made to persuade the local customers that—despite this handicap—it was not really foreign. For this reason many TNCs considered it helpful if the leading executives of their operations abroad, who were not necessarily the top decision-makers, were natives. If they were aliens, they were ordered to conduct themselves in a manner that would endear them to the indigenous population. The plant manager of YKK's subsidiary in England was asked why, when there were so many Japanese-made cars on British roads, he was driving a Ford car. He is quoted as having replied: "It is against the YKK policy to use a Japanese car when you are on an overseas assignment" (172). IBM, in PR material distributed in Britain, has compared itself with the prestigious UK retail chain Marks & Spencer. Pointing to the co-founder, Michael Marks, who was born in a Polish village, IBM-UK claimed that though it too had foreign parentage, it now was an integral part of Britain's economy. IBM-UK asked to be considered as an essentially native manufacturer: "How British do you have to be to contribute to Britain?"

The customers of the overseas subsidiaries of some lucky TNCs were not aware that they were buying goods from a foreign-owned company. Singer is an outstanding example. The buyers of its products believed that they were acquiring goods from native manufacturers. The German, French, and British public thought that Singer is a German, French, and British name, respectively. The U.S. customers were of course enlightened that the sewing machines are produced by a U.S. multi. Various surveys have shown that the majority of the European customers of Ford, Nestle, Philips, and Shell were wrongly informed as to the companies' national parentage. McDonald's-Japan has 600 outlets and is the largest foreign venture of this U.S.-based fast-food business. According to the CEO of the Japanese affiliate, Japanese visitors to the United States are often shocked to discover the U.S. origin of McDonald's.

Many of the world's large corporations now consider that the fear of xenophobia, which propelled a large number of multis to set up manufacturing subsidiaries abroad, is no longer as solid a factor as it once was. In the OECD countries the public—as distinct from political deci-

sion-makers and union leaders, concerned to maximize employment—
faces both ways. Nationalist sentiments are still very strong and I predict
they will gather even more strength in the years to come. At the same
time there is a greater proclivity to spend holidays abroad and there are
fewer compunctions about purchasing foreign-made goods. Several
TNCs have noted that cloaking their national identity can work to their
disadvantage. Some customers, who had hitherto bought certain goods
believing them to have been produced by an indigenous firm, are delighted to be informed that it is in fact the subsidiary of a reputable
global corporation. For more than half a century GM has cloaked carefully its scores of European subsidiaries from being blemished by association with a Detroit-based MNC. The U.S. automobile giant was
surprised at the findings of a survey that it commissioned in the mid–
1980s. The majority of the European respondents were indeed not aware
that certain European manufacturing companies, of which they knew,
were members of the GM group. But when told that this was so, the
news was received very positively. As a result GM has changed its stance
and initiated corporate image advertising that explicitly stresses the U.S.
affiliation of Vauxhall and other European subsidiaries. New TNCs no
longer even bother to camouflage the foreign ownership of their subsidiaries by appointing natives to leading posts. One of Italy's food
multis, Ferrero, does not feel guilty and actually boasts about it: "All
top jobs in our corporation, at home and abroad, are filled with Italians."
In 1989 ICI's chairman announced in New Delhi that, as a demonstrative
gesture to emphasize that his company is a true TNC, he is changing
the name of the local subsidiary from Indian Explosives Limited to ICI
India. Until 1988 Philips had been operating in Britain by retaining the
British names of companies that it had taken over decades previously.
An advertising campaign was aimed at telling the public that things are
now different.

Why would Britain's No. 1 electronic component company change its name?
We were Mullard. Now we're Philips Components. The fact is, Mullard has
been an integral part of Philips for over 60 years and the new name simply
emphasises the worldwide resources . . . from which our customers will continue
to benefit.

Another European TNC quickly followed suit. Paris-based Rhone-Poulenc spent money to give this message, so indicative of the changed
atmosphere now prevailing at the head offices of many TNCs.

You've been dealing with us for 60 years. Perhaps we should introduce ourselves. In 1927 Rhone-Poulenc, one of the world's largest chemical companies,
bought May & Baker, one of the leading names in the field in Britain. But the
name May & Baker remained. . . . From May 31st we'll be introducing the name

of Rhone-Poulenc. What difference will it make . . . to you? Well, you may just find it reassuring to be reminded that when you deal with us, you're dealing with a company that employs over 83,000 people in 140 countries worldwide.

If the public—knowing the true nationality of the owners and controllers—is happy to buy the locally made products of a foreign multi, would it not be even happier to buy them when they are manufactured in the home country of that corporation? In the LDCs the answer is assuredly in the affirmative. The governments of the developing countries, which allow TNCs to manufacture locally for the domestic market, insist that many local inputs must be used. Even though the brand name of the foreign corporation remains, the LDC-produced goods are of inferior quality, or are deemed to be so. For this reason the question of masking the OECD origin of goods does not arise in LDCs. The opposite is the case. An imported article has considerable scarcity-value as compared with products made by indigenous entrepreneurs or even with output produced locally under licence from a respectable foreign multi.

The merchandise marks acts of some countries provide merely that imported articles should be stamped with the words "Foreign Made" (or words to that effect). At the end of the nineteenth century Britain annoyed its competitors, especially Germany, when it legislated that the country of origin must be shown. Some German manufacturers had sought to market shoddy goods in the British Isles, pretending that they were locally made. All sorts of tricks were employed so that the British customer could not notice the "Made in Germany" label. After Germany had acquired repute as a producer of high-quality goods, German companies went out of their way to affix prominent marks, attesting to the products' German origin. History has repeated itself. Until the early 1970s many Japanese exporters attempted to frustrate the statutory requirement to label imports in a manner that indicates clearly the country of origin. The Japanese used proper and improper subterfuges at a time when Japanese goods, admittedly cheap, were deemed to be of low quality. All this changed radically once the Japanese were perceived to be manufacturing high-quality, technologically advanced, and reliable products. Sony and others then went into reverse. The size of the label "Made in Japan" became bigger and bigger. In 1987 an accolade was bestowed in Britain upon Japanese industry. A famous British electrical goods chain was fined for the offense of having passed off as Japanese products television sets, refrigerators, recorders, and freezers that had in fact been manufactured in Britain, Italy, Singapore, and Yugoslavia. This large retail organization had very cleverly devised the brand name of Matsui and a logo resembling the rising sun. To mask its deceptive strategy the merchandise was advertised under the slogan: "Japanese technology made perfect."

Whatever other reasons there may be in future to establish manufacturing subsidiaries abroad, the xenophobia argument will not sound very convincing. An important caveat must be entered here. The above refers to the private sector only. Different rules apply to the procurement practices of the public sector, where political considerations weigh heavily. The foreign parent of a manufacturing subsidiary in country X receives the red carpet treatment while foreign companies that seek to export to X are rebuffed. But this generalization has ceased to be valid universally. In previous chapters some—as yet rare—instances were mentioned when OECD and LDC host governments no longer treated the manufacturing subsidiaries of foreign multis on par with indigenously-owned enterprises. If official edicts would have it that certain public sector contracts are to be awarded only to domestic producers, but the *local manufacturing operations of foreign multis do not qualify*, some TNCs must revise their global strategy. Why should they maintain subsidiaries that were set up primarily in order to be able to supply the public sector in fair competition with indigenous firms? Another reason for liquidating existing subsidiaries overseas?

19

THE MULTIS OF THE TWENTY-FIRST CENTURY

> An industry is a customer-satisfying process, not a goods-producing process.
>
> Theodore Levitt

Will all the disseminators of the multi conspiracy hear and digest the message? Several friends and foes of multis have been whispering it for years but now it is shouted from the rooftops: the familiar TNCs are in the midst of a far-reaching metamorphosis. They are shedding several of their old functions and it will soon be difficult to berate their subsidiaries in foreign lands as alien capitalists and alien employers. The R&D that is generated (mainly) in the home country will continue to be spread around the world, but not via production subsidiaries. *The Economist*, reporting on a New York-based hotel group that aimed to cash in on a global brand image, praised its CEO for "having realised that the trick with hotels is not to own them, but to operate them." The Brandt Report sought to enlighten its anti-multi constituency: "A foreign company need not always bring capital with it, for it can borrow in local markets. It is mainly technology, management or marketing that it provides." Perhaps the most fascinating testimony is that of Gyorgy Adam, the head of the economic research section of the Hungarian Academy of Science. Aware of the current trends, he told the UN that there is a growing school of economists in the developed countries who advocate the replacement of the traditional forms of direct foreign investment by contractual obligations, with ownership left wholly or in controlling part in national hands. According to Adam, the whole structure of multinational corporations is schemed to be transformed into something resembling that of personal service firms. Speaking as a "citizen of a socialist country," he warned that these proposals would ensure the continued presence of TNCs in the developing countries under new rules. This "recent tool of expansion . . . threatens the LDCs with transformation from 'banana-republics' into 'pyjama-republics' or 'branch-plant economies' " (27).

NOT BY MANUFACTURING ALONE...

Elsewhere I have elaborated on why the conventional GDP is neither a meaningful, comprehensive index of human welfare nor an accurate enumeration of all wealth-creating activities (69). The volume of the abstract, true national cake cannot be quantified, but one can assert with certitude that it has been growing and will continue to grow at a much faster rate than the conventional GDP. It follows that the output of MNCs, registered of course only in the conventional national accounts, is diminishing as a proportion of the all-embracing national cakes of the world's richer economies.

The old-type multi is also declining in significance because of the steep diminution of manufacturing as a segment of the national product. The service sector is burgeoning! The trend is too pronounced for the facts to be challenged but, wrapped in nostalgia, many bemoan this 'erosion of the industrial base.' It is alleged that national security and economic independence are being undermined. Harold Wilson's Labour governments in the 1960s still pursued policies that supported 'productive' manufacturing at the expense of the less worthy servicing activities. In order to contrive the transfer of resources from the service sector to manufacturing, payroll taxes were imposed on the former, the proceeds of which were paid out as subsidies to the latter. Michael Stewart was in the cabinet office at the time and is therefore a primary source. He has since ridiculed the motivations of his former colleagues. According to his evidence, the left welcomed these fiscal measures "on the puritanical ground that they were penalising the service sector which was candyfloss and bad, and favouring the manufacturing sector, which was real and good" (171). This antediluvian approach was also extended to exporting. Labour politicians laughed out of court the suggestion that foreign currency earned from invisible exports were as valuable as those earned by the exports of merchandise. Hence state subsidies were lavished only on visible exports. Such old-fashioned economic philosophy was applied to the bestowal of the Queen's Awards for Export Achievements. The matter was raised in the House of Commons. The columns of *Hansard* have immortalized the nonsense of the Labour government's insistence that it would not propose, for Her Majesty's approval, any company that had helped the balance of payments through invisible exports: the awards were to be a recognition for the success of "industrial units" only.

Against this background it is perhaps easier to comprehend why the four founding fathers were so resolute that only manufacturing corporations could be proper TNCs and why, at first, BINCO was reluctant to admit to its association international companies from the service sector. If one were to retain the orthodox definition and count in the next century only the output of the old-style multis, their weight within the OECD economies would be remarkably light. It therefore makes sense to abandon this—now—unrealistic definition, say good-bye to the pioneering theoreticians of the TNC, and a fortiori cease to worship manufacturing as a symbol of corporate virility. Multinational companies, providing services globally, will soon be more numerous than those corporations that manufacture worldwide. Under the new liberal rules the multi fraternity will thus have many more members. Concurrently, many of the manufacturing TNCs will so structure themselves that their profit-earning activities outside the home country will be more concerned with intangibles than the physical production of goods. They will straddle the manufacturing and servicing sectors. GDP statisticians may have a hard time when allocating their respective output-values to the appropriate compartments of the national accounts.

What of the impact on the multi legend? The representative of the COMINTERN who was quoted earlier implied that we are not really witnessing a substantive metamorphosis, as TNCs will continue to exploit LDCs. It is a dubious argument. But even if true, in future the old anti-multi slogans will sound less enticing. The foreign subsidiaries of service TNCs and of the new-type manufacturing TNCs (which no longer manufacture directly abroad though they have a presence outside the home country) are likely to be less conspicuous. They will be deemed less obnoxious than the corporations that once boasted of owning banana plantations and steel works. TNCs with representative offices in foreign countries that offer design, financial, tourist, catering, medical, and educational services, are not likely to bring grist to the mill of the rabble-rousers who espouse today the cause of the multi conspiracies.

Service multis are relatively labor-intensive. But however influential their foreign involvements, these will not be matched by the direct employment of large numbers in locations outside the home country. Why maintain a large staff of architects in the Middle East when some of them could be working in San Francisco on the preparation of plans for facsimile transmission to a contractor building a refinery in Kuwait?

On parallel lines, a diminishing proportion of the global labor force of the new-type manufacturing TNCs will be working abroad. The operational mode of Coca-Cola and Pepsico will be emulated widely. The majority of their production facilities in some 150 countries are managed, owned, and financed indigenously. The parent companies own and operate a few plants which manufacture the syrup concentrates that are sold worldwide to the independent franchised bottling companies. The head offices of the two food multis exercise quality and management controls over all the bottling-cum-distribution facilities. The parent companies are responsible for global advertising and auxiliary services. They intervene actively when franchises do not perform well. Acting as brokers, they then buy and sell the equity of their associated bottlers.

THE PLUSES AND THE MINUSES

The old-type TNC usually backed direct investments abroad with some of its own financial resources. The new-type TNC strives strenuously to avoid tying up capital in ventures abroad. As already noted, it also seeks to extricate itself from manufacturing outside the home country. Despite these curbs the international corporation of the twenty-first century will nevertheless prove attractive to potential host nations on two counts. First, it can offer them the commercial exploitation of its established reputation and/or globally promoted brand name(s). Second, it has for sale innovative ideas and expertise that are incorporated in equipment, individuals (who are available for hire), and patents/designs/know-how.

Management Contracts

These furnish some service multis with their bread and butter. (However, for the majority of manufacturing TNCs, they are and will remain mere adjuncts to their core activities.) The foreign enterprises draw upon the managerial, production, or marketing expertise transmitted through specialized teams of executives and technicians. LDC governments are the main—but not the only—users of management contracts for agricultural and mineral projects, railways, hospitals, hotels, airports, and so on when the know-how of international companies is valuable. Flat-rate fees are usually negotiated but sometimes the arrangements provide for payments linked to the size of turnover or profits. Somewhat perversely, Western TNCs are being requested by host nations that effectively confiscated their manufacturing subsidiaries to manage the nationalized factories—preferably with the expatriate staff that had been made redundant. The mammoth oil companies, forcibly removed from their concessions by host nations, were left with experienced staff on their payroll who cried out for the kind of work for which they had been trained. Concurrently, few of the countries that expropriated the subsidiaries of oil multis have enough trained and experienced personnel to carry out all aspects of a geological, petroleum, and development program. This is where management contracts come in handy. They entail the hiring of external groups of experts who happen to be supervised by the head offices of the oil TNCs. No proprietary rights are granted. The LDC authorities do not anticipate domestic political complications. For some oil companies this is now an important, albeit unorthodox, source of income.

Licensing

Licensing is often the only way to enter a market from which the TNC is excluded because exports and/or the establishment of a manufacturing subsidiary are not feasible. To prevent encroachments upon other markets, it is vital for the licensor to impose conditions on the sale of the output outside the borders of the licensee's country. Multinational companies, selling the fruits of their R&D in this manner, are frequently not concerned with how the licensee produces and do not specify the type of equipment to be employed. Some offer licenses of patented and unpatented processes as part of a more comprehensive agreement that includes technical assistance in setting up manufacturing operations and bringing them on-stream.

Licensing may sometimes be employed as a political subterfuge. Under pressure, several of the world's automobile multis have closed down their wholly-owned car assembly plants in South Africa. A few have licensed South African-owned companies to assemble their models.

Franchising

Franchising affords an independent native entrepreneur the opportunity to sell his output under the name of a famous corporation. His customers are ready to pay a premium because of the superior quality of the goods and services which the franchisor's name conveys. The international mold of the multi consigning franchises is an additional attraction. In contrast to licensing, the head office of the franchising company imposes strict uniformity on the operations of the franchisees. The contracts that allow the franchisees to make use of the multi's name can (and often are) terminated at short notice, particularly if quality falls below the required standard. Many TNCs favor comprehensive franchising; that is, the franchisees must buy certain inputs and equipment from the franchisor (as in the case of the two Cola firms). The head office of the international corporation is responsible for global advertising and sometimes for cross-border services such as international booking systems for car rental firms (Avis) and hotels (Hilton). Members of the public who deal with franchises frequently believe them to be subsidiaries of global companies.

Collaborative Manufacturing

This arrangement epitomizes the evolution of international corporations with few or no manufacturing subsidiaries abroad. Using their own brand names, the new-type multis market goods produced by others. TNCs that opt for collaborative manufacturing make long-term arrangements with independent companies that undertake to manufacture under their guidance. These foreign collaborators may be told what inputs to use. The designs are likely to come from the multi's head office. Many of the old-fashioned TNCs have already swallowed their pride and are experimenting with this method for peripheral production. Some of the new global OECD-based companies are using this operational technique exclusively. Caterpillar has signed several collaborative manufacturing deals of this kind. For many years Philips was selling refrigerators of the Italian Ignis company in European markets under the Philips name. If customers were to learn that goods bearing the brand name of a renowned multi were not actually manufactured in a factory operated by that multi, many would feel cheated. The multis respond to this reproach by asserting that they are supervising scrupulously the quality of the articles made for them by other producers. No doubt this is true but it is still not a completely satisfactory answer. In any case collaborative—sometimes also called contract—manufacturing is here to stay and will expand greatly in the near future.

The advantages of the operational modes that serve the evolving new-type multis can be summarized as fewer financial worries, no industrial relations headaches, and more flexibility. These must be contrasted with the drawbacks of direct investments, especially of joint ventures. Some of these have engendered expensive and PR-damaging squabbles with minority shareholders in overseas subsidiaries. Host goverments determine—often arbitrarily—the percentage of the equity that the foreign parent might own. In the home country, accusations surrounding the 'flight of capital' are publicized; where exchange controls prevail, the requisite foreign currency is not always allotted. Home countries have been known to demand that all profits earned abroad are remitted to the parent while host nations frequently restrict the transfer of profits to alien multis. (In the 1960s 45 percent of the global net profits of the UK-based MNC Lonrho were "unremittable," frozen by the dictates of

African host countries.) Financial worries of this kind are nonexistent when the parent conducts its foreign transactions in a manner that avoids monetary involvements abroad. There are also fewer requirements to raise money (or lower dividends) in order to invest in bricks, turbines, and the holding of inventories. Such capital spending is financed by native licensees, franchisees, and collaborative manufacturers—not by the multis. The treasurers of the future TNCs are freed from the fear that their overseas investments might be confiscated, expropriated, or nationalized with some pitiful, delayed compensation. Contracts providing for licensing and franchising fees or lump sums are treated as invisible exports, and the parent company can insure these either with state export insurance agencies or with private carriers. The balance sheets of the new-type multis are less encumbered by debt (bonds or bank borrowings) than those of the traditional international corporations. In takeover situations today, a company saddled with a high debt-to-assets ratio and a low return on capital is in a precarious position. The anxious CEO producing a defense document tells stockholders that they should not accept the predator's offer because 'in the course of time—over years to come—the past investments will pay off. In the long run it will be proved to have been a wise decision to borrow funds to invest in countries X and Y even though it has meant a temporary cut in dividends.' Alas, most stockholders are lacking in gratitude. The CEO of the new-type TNC will not have to worry.

The parturition of TNCs was accompanied by public outrage at national companies which, by becoming international companies, were creating unemployment at home and "exporting jobs." Unions in the home country have organized strikes when learning of plans by the parent company to open a manufacturing subsidiary abroad. In foreign lands the host governments expect alien multis to behave more benevolently than native employers. At home, to show solidarity, demonstrators may break the windows of the parent company's office and voice their indignation at the multi's exploitation of foreign workers (particularly of women and children) and the damage to the environment caused by its manufacturing subsidiaries. Sometimes the WCC screams. On other occasions consumer boycotts are threatened. All those headaches will belong to the past when TNCs cease to be the alien owners of factories and farms and are no longer direct employers.

The TNCs of the future will not be chained for an indeterminately long period to given national locations. Unlike corporations that have invested in fixed assets in foreign subsidiaries, the new-type multis are able to switch production from one country to another at short notice. The subsidiaries of the old-type TNCs cannot break the law or pay bribes with the same ease as native businesses. The collaborative manufacturers, producing goods for associated multis, have fewer inhibitions and enjoy more flexibility. For this reason the multis' resultant profits from marketing the output of native-owned factories are sometimes more substantial than the net earnings that would have been gained by producing the same goods in manufacturing subsidiaries under all sorts of restrictions. PR-conscious TNCs will be delighted that some of the new arrangements help to remove blemishes from their global image. But this does not always work. Coca-Cola's head office in Atlanta was upset by the worldwide reports about its Guatemalan operations. For the sake of its brand name in 149 other countries, the CEO found it expedient to intervene—though the alleged culprits were franchisees and not managers of a subsidiary. While some adversaries of the new-type multis could be nasty, the material damage that they are able to cause *to the multi's shareholders* is not very great. When demonstrating against U.S. involvement in the Vietnam war, it was rewarding to discover a Coca-Cola plant in order to set it ablaze. If the demonstrators could not find one, they chose what in those days was the next best symbol of U.S. imperialism—a Hilton hotel. Of course, the head offices of these two U.S. TNCs did not like to hear of the burning down of their franchised facilities. But, not being in the same boat as the old-fashioned oil multis, ITT and UFCO, they could afford to regard these political misfortunes with some equanimity. The directors comforted themselves that their corporations did not own the bottling plants and hotel fixtures and could not be held to ransom in relation to the redundant employees on the payroll of the franchisees.

What of the disadvantages of the new modi operandi? They necessitate tighter quality controls than are necessary in a multi's own manufacturing subsidiaries. Trademark protection and the enforcement of licensing contracts present many complications, especially in LDCs. TNCs frequently opt to have only loose contractual ties with collaborative manufacturers. Having trained them, some of the enterprising native firms may seek to cut loose and branch out for themselves, perhaps by exporting directly to OECD markets or by selling their newly acquired production expertise to another TNC. There is always the danger that the licensee will eventually emerge as a major competitor, swamping the original licensor of the brand or technology.

Triple-pronged attacks have been launched on the efficacy of licensing/franchising arrangements. They highlight obstruction from the host nations, opposition in the home country, and failures to maximize the profits from R&D. Some LDCs—India and Mexico are prominent examples—are reluctant to register licensing agreements between TNCs and native entrepreneurs. If permission is granted, the time span of the agreement is often short: five years is the rule in India and an extension is difficult to obtain. Annual royalties are extremely low by OECD standards and ceilings of 1–3 percent of the ex-factory value of the output are not unusual. Native licensees have been known to cheat their own authorities by paying (illicitly) lump-sum disclosure fees to foreign licensors in order to induce them to sign the government-determined contracts. Sometimes a sense of humor is helpful. A well-informed source would have it that Pakistani administrators are often not helpful in giving official consent to royalty payments for licenses. However, they are happy to approve contracts that stipulate the remittance of technical fees!

Unions in the home countries of the OECD have consistently described foreign direct investments as "runaway plants." Since the early 1970s the sweep of this offensive has been widened. The AFL-CIO has propagated the view that the transfer of technology is as detrimental to the job security of their members as the establishment of manufacturing subsidiaries abroad.

The licensing transfer of any U.S. patent outside the U.S. would contribute to unemployment in the U.S. . . . . America is witnessing the export of its future technological base. . . . McDonnell Douglas has licensed Mitsubishi of Japan to build the famous Phantom fighter. . . . [T]he company has made a contract with the Japanese to furnish the blueprints, the technology and, where necessary, technicians. . . . The result is a heavy loss of employment among highly trained U.S. aircraft technicians, the loss of paychecks to St. Louis (54).

A strike threat to frustrate licensing is reported from Birmingham (England). The UK multi Lucas found that the Russians were not prepared to buy from it certain advanced electronical engine controls. The workers' leaders alleged that—as an alternative—Lucas had offered a licensing agreement so that the controls could be produced in the Soviet Union. The shop stewards demanded that this deal be stopped because it destroyed jobs in Britain.

Several critics have argued that TNCs receive only inadequate returns on the licensing of technological inventions. They say that it is more profitable for TNCs to utilize the fruits of their R&D by manufacturing the endproducts in their own factories at home and abroad. One such detailed charge was made public by J. Goldman (senior vice president in charge of R&D at Xerox's parent) His accusation centered on the British glass multi Pilkington, which in the 1960s had licensed its revolutionary floating-glass process to manufacturers in the United States, Japan, France, and many other OECD, LDC, and COMECON countries. Goldman suggested that from the standpoint of the TNC's shareholders, the process could have been exploited much more effectively.

The Pilkington process is, in fact, one of the great innovations of the century that has had profound economic and technical impact on the entire glass industry. But nevertheless significant economic gains accrued to others abroad.

. . . It's a magnificent concept, very original and technologically viable. . . . But who's making the real money out of the process? The Pilkington people . . . have done it by licensing. True, it's an income-producing formula but not nearly as effective in terms of economic growth as if they themselves had been able to dominate the entire thing, which they could have done (169, 183).

Weighing up the pluses and the minuses—to ascertain whether multis will gain more than they lose from abandoning the ownership and direct control of foreign manufacturing subsidiaries—is not an ideological exercise. Both specific internal and general external circumstances are decisive. When the spokesman for the Lucas workers told the press that in their view it would be better to manufacture the company's technologically advanced instruments in the home country rather than issue licenses to foreign producers, they were stating a platitudinous but irrelevant truism. The issue revolved around the absolute refusal of the Russians to buy certain instruments. Lucas had to face reality: unable to export to the Soviet Union, should it accept the limited revenue available through licensing or forego this as a matter of principle? In the 1950s the British leisure multi Rank acquired the worldwide rights to Xerox's technology outside the United States. With hindsight this could be condemned as a wrong decision. It netted vast profits to Rank and ipso facto Xerox's stockholders endured vast "notional" losses. No doubt Goldman would argue that U.S.-based Xerox ought to have built its own manufacturing subsidiaries abroad rather than let a foreign company produce Xerox products under license. But was this a feasible alternative? The inventor of the world's first electrostatic copying device, Chester Carlson, was unable to interest backers though he approached many large companies, including IBM. It was a medium-sized family company (Haloid of Rochester) that took the risk and, gambling $75 million between 1947 and 1960 on the development of the invention, made it ready for production. This investment in an uncertain venture was twice the amount that Haloid was earning from its regular activities. Thus when a foreign TNC came along and offered to manufacture abroad, the proposed licensing arrangement was welcomed warmly. At that time the Haloid funds barely sufficed to produce for the domestic market.

Pilkington is today a TNC with a stock exchange quotation and thousands of (non-family) stockholders. It is able to expand overseas both through licensing and its own manufacturing subsidiaries. This freedom of choice was not on hand when, in the 1960s, its R&D department came up with a revolutionary floating-glass process. Goldman was almost certainly unaware that Pilkington was then a family business with scores of passive, but discontented, stockholders. The CEO, Harry Pilkington, had bullied them into accepting over many years low dividends so that the heavy costs of researching the technology of the new process could be financed. Having finally proved to them that their patient (or not so patient) waiting had paid off, they clamored for immediate rewards. Harry Pilkington personally would no doubt have liked to build manufacturing plants all over the globe. As head of a family firm he was pushed into choosing the alternative, that is, licensing the invention abroad.

The metamorphosis of TNCs that we are currently witnessing has little to do with the intellectual merits of the listed pluses and minuses. It is the world that is changing and forcing the old-type multis to rethink global strategy—or be wiped out. The bitter experiences suffered by so many of them at the hands of hostile host nations are one side of the coin. On the other side are the heightened difficulties in most parts of the world to obtain permission for new manufacturing operations that can be controlled meaningfully by the multi's head office. Observing one's navel and talking of the good old days are not constructive deeds. Alternatives must be chosen so that TNCs can continue to have some kind of presence abroad. As the following cases show, some firms are grasping the nettle.

SOME NEW-TYPE MULTIS

Two Global Shoe Corporations

Tennis champion John McEnroe and Olympic gold medallist Sebastian Coe have helped to promote the athletic footwear of what used to be the private Oregon-based company Nike. When its goods were first marketed in 1972, annual revenue totalled less than $2 million; they jumped to almost $500 million in 1981, the year Nike became a public corporation. It had by then succeeded in becoming a globally renowned firm that specialized in relatively high-priced shoes for competitive and recreational uses. Yet only 10 percent of its output was produced in U.S. factories. Ninety percent was manufactured on a contract basis by some 20 collaborative manufacturers in South Korea, Taiwan, Britain, Japan, the Philippines, Hong Kong, Malaysia, and Thailand. Nike's board of directors announced that negotiations were pending concerning the contract production of shoes in the People's Republic of China. Despite this prodigious turnover, Nike had on its payroll only 2,700 employees. Members of the staff who controlled the production of the foreign-made footwear played a pivotal role. They prepared detailed specifications and supervised the control inspections of each collaborating producer. Vast sums were spent by the company on the Sports Research Laboratory which, it claimed, was the most comprehensive facility of its kind in North America. One hundred employees worked there on R&D projects that involved high-speed photographic analyses of the body in motion, the study of athletes on treadmills, the testing of new materials, and allied activities. There is not a word in the Nike annual reports on the confiscation of any of its corporate assets in an LDC!

In some ways the achievements and cross-border ramifications of the Wortmann company (Internationale Schuhproduktionen) are the more remarkable because of the small number of its direct employees—about 170 at the Detmold headquarters and in the field. Horst Wortmann founded his shoe business in 1967. He cherished independence and disdained bank loans and equity subscriptions by outsiders. This stance meant that he could not produce in factories of his own at home or abroad. Making a virtue of necessity, he operated solely with foreign collabortive manufacturers. Though the home market was and is Germany, he was determined that not a single pair of shoes would be produced locally, so great was his fear of the mandatory redundancy payments and the power of the unions. Within 20 years his turnover had risen to exceed DM 300 million. Marketing remains centralized at the head office. Most of the shoes are delivered to German warehouses; one-third of the volume is exported.

Horst Wortmann is adamant that he is not a buyer who goes to low-cost countries to acquire foreign-made shoes off the shelf. His company closely controls the execution of production by collaborative manufacturers in some 40 countries, among them Greece, Italy, Spain, Yugoslavia, Taiwan, and Hong Kong. The Wortmann company jealously guards the quality of the footwear, marketed under the trademark "Tamaris." Every year its designers prepare a fashion collection in Germany. Wortmann technicians work closely with the foreign producers who are obliged to follow prescribed guidelines. These include instructions on designated inputs, some of which are sourced in Germany (181).

Löwenbräu

This company's directors told their stockholders with pride that more than two-thirds of all the beer sold worldwide under its trademark is brewed outside the home country. Undoubtedly, the company became entitled in 1984 to call itself a Bavarian-based TNC, a connotation that—until recently—would have offended the then diehard owners and managers. The metamorphosis commenced in 1977, due to circumstances that left management with little choice: it was forced to restructure its operations. During the whole postwar period Löwenbräu had brewed primarily for the German market. Its presence abroad had been effected through very rewarding exports, overwhelmingly to the United States. The crisis came to a boiling point after profits on domestic sales had evaporated and the once lucrative export sales were carried out at considerable loss because of the rise in the external value of the DM vis-à-vis the U.S. dollar. The company had no inclination—and probably not the financial clout—to make acquisitions abroad or invest in foreign greenfield projects. This induced it to halt exports to the United States and sign a licensing contract with Miller Brewing Company, part of the Philip Morris group. Miller was followed by licensees in Greece, Sweden, Panama, Hong Kong, Japan, and Canada. In Britain a two-pronged strategy is pursued: while the Munich-based company has licensed there the brewing of its beer sold in barrels, bottled beer is exported from Germany. Seven years after the parochially oriented Bavarian company had become a fully fledged global corporation, profits from foreign licenses far exceeded the income gained from domestic sales and direct exports (168).

Cadbury Schweppes

This firm used to be an orthodox, established MNC with roots in the nineteenth century when the Quaker family Cadbury manufactured chocolates and cocoa drinks in a company town, Bournville. The sales of these products were promoted as a moral alternative to the consumption of beer by the laboring classes. Cadbury's first international links as an influential buyer of cocoa were with the West Coast of Africa but these play no significant role in the life of the corporation today. Most of its turnover relates to confectionery (with the Cadbury brand name), tonic water, and some other soft drinks (marketed mainly under the Schweppes brand name). The output is distributed in some one hundred countries. While some production licenses and franchises have been granted, most of the endproducts are made in company-owned plants in the home country and in a variety of foreign manufacturing subsidiaries and affiliates of which the parent owns a minority, majority, or all of the equity. There are export sales from Britain and also from some of its overseas operations. Some 33,000 people were on the payroll in 1986 when global sales topped £2 billion.

In the mid–1980s the board took the strategic decision to expand global sales of Schweppes in a financially painless manner. Instead of recruiting capital to enhance production capacity, it was resolved to franchise the brand name abroad; this was done in several countries, including some in the COMECON.

But the U.S. confectionery market was sui generis and this food MNC tackled it both by making acquisitions and by establishing new manufacturing facilities. It became the owner of three U.S. plants (two in Pennsylvania and one in Connecticut) and had an 8 percent market share. There were plans to invest further in North America and the corporation was indeed in a position to finance them either through a rights issue or by raising funds externally. But in the summer of 1988 a non-British corporation dropped strong hints about launching a hostile bid for Cadbury Schweppes. When a powerful angel of death breathes down your neck, you tear up existing plans, give up old habits, and cast away hallowed traditions. Cadbury Schweppes sold to Hershey, the largest chocolate company in the United States, all of its U.S. physical assets in the confectionery field. Hershey agreed to make annual royalty payments in a 40-year period, during which it was entitled to produce Cadbury products under license.

The managing director of the British MNC's confectionery division proclaimed that "the strength we had was the great brand names. I had to find a way of exploiting those. It was then that I looked at our soft drinks interests and realised franchising had to be the way" (170). There is no cause to challenge this reasoning, but surely there was another aspect too. The licensing contract with Hershey was bound to make the 1989 P&L and balance sheet of Cadbury Schweppes look very much healthier than if the company had proceeded to finance the planned manufacturing expansion in North America under its own steam. This new-type MNC is still not immune from being taken over in the future by some unwelcome bidder, but the Hershey arrangement has at least made it easier to repel predatory raids. That consideration will have been duly noted by the vigilant board of directors of the beleaguered corporation.

20

NOT BIGGER BUT SMALLER

One of the great paradoxes of business today is that, superficially, the world is becoming more and more a single market, while in reality, national differences are becoming accentuated.

John Harvey-Jones

LEVITT VERSUS KOTLER

Two eminent professors of marketing, Philip Kotler of Northwestern University and Theodore Levitt of Harvard Business School, have each enunciated diametrically opposed theses on the future of internationally-oriented corporations. Sneering at academic oracles is a century-old game, played by self-styled pragmatic businessmen. But times have changed and today's CEOs are following with great interest the Kotler-Levitt controversy. Of the two, Levitt has gained very much more publicity, due partly to his flamboyant style. In addition, the revolutionary hypothesis that he is marketing so avidly sounds more exciting than the conservative views of his intellectual adversary. Levitt's astounding proposition is reminiscent of the sensation caused a quarter of a century ago by another professor, Howard Perlmutter, who also grabbed the headlines when he forecast the triumphant accession of the geocentric MNC.

Kotler favors the internationalization of large companies. However, he does not believe that this can and should be implemented by the full standardization of a company's products destined for worldwide distribution. According to Kotler, the successful entry of many internationally-oriented corporations into different national markets owed much to imaginative planners at the head offices. They paid attention to varying regional and national preferences and adapted production so as to please the specific tastes of differing consumer groups (152). Such a strategy, Kotler opines, ought to be pursued also in the future. In recent times some celebrated advertising giants have pleaded with corporate clients to embark upon global promotion campaigns. These are to be directed at all potential consumers; more or less identical logos, pictures, slogans, packaging, and brand names are to be employed. Kotler rejects this advocacy on the ground that in most cases such campaigns would prove inefficacious.

Levitt spurns the nomenclature of "multinational" to depict the modern-type global corporation, the coming of which he has been inspired to proclaim. He highlights the convergent tendency of our age "for everything to become more like everything else." Levitt prays that it will prove plausible to homogenize universally the tastes and wants of real human beings.

The future belongs to the globally, not multinationally, oriented corporation. . . . More and more, people everywhere are growing more alike . . . whether we are talking of jeans . . . or milling machines. This means that the world explodes into a gigantic market in place of what used to be thought of as small segments or uniquely national markets. . . . The global corporation operates with resolute constancy . . . as if the entire world were a single, largely identical entity; it does and sells the same things in the same single way everywhere (146).

Levitt's philosophy has been translated into language that yuppies can relate to. He has publicly castigated the U.S. MNC Hoover for commissioning European market research to ascertain the disparate consumer preferences for its washing machines in Sweden, Britain, Italy, Germany, and France. Some housewives preferred top-loading, and others, front-loading machines. The desired capacity of the machines varied, by national origin, between four and six kilos. Italians were apparently enamored with enamel drums, while the Swedes wanted stainless steel. There were other national factors that determined the choice of the consumers' ideal washing machine. Levitt thundered at this nonsense. If Hoover intended to customize to these preferences, the unit costs of its washing machines would be higher than if only one global type were manufactured. He denounced the old-fashioned Hoover executives for bothering to ask people what they wanted in the way of special features. Levitt said that "thoughtlessness and dumbness" had induced them to think of making "products tailored attentively to each nation." He would have it that one global model should be launched aggressively, consumers being told that it was good for them—and, above all, that it was cheaper.

So far Kotler has been scoring heavily against Levitt. Most academics side with him. All agree that some products have already been marketed globally in identical shape and form. Coca-Cola and Sony's Walkman are cited as examples. But these are not harbingers of the Levitt future in which almost all companies will perish if they do not follow his precepts. Is it supercilious or pompous to assert, as Levitt did, that "nothing is exempt, and nothing can stop it"? Though they flock to his lectures, most executives sans patrie are courting Levitt's damnation. David Stout, Unilever's chief economist, has ridiculed global selling as "globaloney." Nestle agrees. Ford's dream to build a "world car" in the 1970s was an innovative idea at the time. Students in universities throughout the world are nowadays asked to write essays on why the dream never came true. Heinz's tomato soups, Rowntree's KitKats, Cadbury's chocolate bars are all marketed worldwide under the same brand name. Yet there are important diversities. Heinz goes to much trouble to ascertain regional tastes and varies accordingly the ingredients. Cadbury Schweppes introduced in 1984 an "international formula" and "international wrappers" for their chocolate bars, which are produced in many parts of the world. Yet the company can only assert, for example, of the output of its Indian affiliate, that "with regard to quality . . . the chocolate in Bombay is now made to a similar process to that in the UK" (184). Cadbury Schweppes does not elaborate on what "similar" means. However, it indicates that the "difference in the fat content of the chocolate . . . is lower in India to enable the product to stand up better to the high temperatures that are prevalent there." Jean Guerin, the chairman of Rowntree's European region, has pointed to the diverse (national) product sizes in his area. Traditionally, national markets demand varying product sizes because standard retail prices are geared to product weights. This means that five-fingered KitKats have had to be produced for French consumers and three-fingered ones for Italy (158). If these appear to be trifling instances, there is strong anti-Levitt testimony also from several Japanese manufacturers who originally had been attracted by the global message from Harvard. Levitt had claimed in support of his thesis that

the global commonality of what's preferred leads inescapably to the global standardisation of products, of manufacturing. . . . That, and little else, explains much of the surging success of such a variety of Japanese companies (146).

Several rising Japanese TNCs have chosen to deny that they are following in Levitt's footsteps. Canon has come out against complete world standardization. Matsushita emphasized (with seeming pride) that its products, sold worldwide, differ considerably in design and other attributes. Nissan, in 1986, referred to the discredited doctrine of producing one "world car." The most outspoken critic of Levitt is the Sharp company, which conceded that in the past it had indeed considered making global products but now its policy was to manufacture several variants.

In one respect Levitt is blazing a new trail, one in which he stands apart from the four founding fathers, the original theoreticians of the multi. The touchstone of a corporation's international dedication used to be its production facilities outside the home country. Levitt is scornful of this criterion, saying that however gigantic or geographically dispersed are such efforts, by themselves they do not typify a global corporation. This, he maintains, is achieved by "operating customer-getting presence of meaningful scale in a variety of national markets." Levitt's doctrine—emphasizing the preeminence of *selling* identical products under one brand name in different national markets—is compatible with the new-type manufacturing multi, described in chapter 19. If marketing furnishes the supreme test, Levitt's futuristic global corporation may well arrange to have its products made by collaborative manufacturers while the head office supervises R&D, quality control, and the promotion of the branded goods.

ECONOMIES OF SCALE

In the last resort, forecasts of mammoth TNCs dominating the world in the next century are based upon the prophets' faith in the beneficial effects flowing from ever-increasing economies of scale. They do not only predict that large companies will become larger, but also that the size of single production units is set to rise. Employing the economies-of-scale argument, these prophets refer primarily to production and generally play down other features of corporate life (R&D, financial clout, managerial acumen). Donald Kendall, Pepsico's CEO, spoke succinctly for many of his confreres in the multi club: "My company has Pepsi-Cola plants all around the world. From our standpoint, I would love to have one big, efficient, automated plant in the United States making Pepsi-Cola concentrate and shipping it all over the world" (54). Levitt prognosticates that corporations geared to his recipe of global marketing will generate "enormous economies of scale. . . . [W]hen they translate these into equivalently reduced world prices, they devastate competitors." Perlmutter had said that too at the beginning of his forecasting career. He told of the discussions he had had with political and business leaders:

There was surprising agreement that we are moving towards a world of very large multinational firms and very small entrepreneurial firms, of the 'one man show' variety. The fate of the middle-sized firm seems dubious (26).

Famous TNCs, the CEOs of which were Perlmutter's disciples, have put up manufacturing facilities in different parts of the world. Ideally, each of the factories was specialized to turn out only one product, the output being supplied to all the company's customers in the world (or a given region). In some cases the specialization embraced not end-products but vital components and ingredients that served as manufacturing inputs in several plants. To serve its consumers in continental Europe, Rowntree concentrated all production of KitKat in a Hamburg factory, while chocolate marketed under the brand names of Quality Street and Lion Bar were produced in Dijon and Paris, respectively. Suchard closed several of its manufacturing units (some of which it had inherited with acquisitions) in order to produce in a smaller number of (specialist) factories goods that were to be marketed throughout the whole of Europe. Thus its plant in Berne was reserved for Tobler products; the Callebaut (Belgium) factory concentrated on "industrial chocolate"; Strassbourg (mainly) on Suchard confectionery; Loerrach (Germany) on chocolate with the Milka brand name; and Vienna on hazelnut wafers marketed under the Milka Nussini label. By the mid-1980s Sweden's Electrolux had become—in part through acquisitions—one of the world's largest kitchen appliance makers. To attain maximum economies of scale it opted for a policy of centralizing the manufacturing of various appliances in single factories. In the subsequent structural reorganization, Italy was destined to supply Electrolux front-loading washing machines throughout Europe while a new factory was commissioned in Luton (England) to make microwave ovens for the whole region.

The economies-of-scale consideration does not always generate the targeted cost savings. Even when it does, the financial advantages must be set against the potential dangers that are lurking in the wings. Natural disasters, industrial disputes, wars, and revolutions assailing one national economy can upset the global or regional applecart of a TNC that depends on supplies from the affected location. If something terrible were to happen in Austria and, in consequence, the Suchard TNC would be unable to provide its European buying public with the delicious Milka Nussini chocolate-covered wafers, this would no doubt be seen at the corporation's head office as a human and commercial calamity. But this would not interfere with the marketing of other products from the var-

ious Suchard factories. However, when TNCs—for the sake of economies of scale—concentrate in one manufacturing facility the production
of components needed in several factories, they are in greater peril than
corporations such as Suchard. Ford and GM have learned to their cost
how risky is such a strategy. Within a few days of GM's plant in Bochum
(Germany) being hit by a strike, 7,000 workers at the GM Antwerp plant
had to be laid off because the Belgian operation depended on the supply
of several components from Bochum. Ford's factory in Cologne has also
had to endure industrial stoppages that led within a very short time to
Ford's employees in other countries—at the Genk and Saar factories—
being sent home. When a UK national Ford strike shut the engine plant
in Cardiff, this triggered off ten days later a close-down of Ford's Belgian
factory.

The glory of economies of scale is also impaired for a variety of other
reasons. These have led some MNCs to assert—as, for example, Sony
and Toyota did—that they are deliberately foregoing the benefits of
concentrating world production in one location in order to reap com-
pensating advantages in other respects. The confession by Pepsico's
CEO, regarding his wish to manufacture cost-effectively in one plant
the global requirements for Pepsi-Cola concentrate, was not cited in full
earlier. Donald Kendall, having paid homage to the economies of scale
that could be achieved, then went on to outline his corporation's reluctant strategy: "Unfortunately, we can't do that. You have to put up
concentrate plants in some countries, or you're not going to be in their
markets" (54). According to the Swedish MNC Ericsson, the global demand for its goods would ideally be produced in one plant. It has in
fact 30 manufacturing plants. Non-tariff barriers (and not the level of
customs duties) account for this. The corporation is fully conscious that
political factors decisively affect the purchasing decisions for its products. The Rowntree system of consolidating production in a few European factories was intended as a cost-saving exercise. Jean Guerin,
responsible for these economies of scale, has hinted obliquely at the
intracorporate discontent that this policy could engender (158). He has
pointed out that if the managers of Rowntree's Italian subsidiary made
a special effort to promote the sale of KitKat—which is made for the
whole continent of Europe in one plant in Hamburg—most of the 'financial credit' would accrue to the German subsidiary and not to the
Italian one. Guerin, who ought to know, says that this distorts the true
"national effort" made by the Italian employees in the furtherance of
Rowntree's global profits.

When the growth of mammoth TNCs is predicated on the ground of
increasing economies of scale in manufacturing, one can assuredly reject
the prognosis. The scaling-up of plants was once regarded as a proven
method of lowering unit production costs. Now there is much disen-

chantment. Too many instances of dashed expectations have come to light in which the gains were very modest and some have thrown up negative results. Perlmutter and Levitt notwithstanding, the output of small and medium-sized production facilities will account in the future for an ever-rising proportion of national output in the OECD countries.

Advances in technology have given birth to new scaled-down industrial equipment that effectively decreases the optimum run-sizes of batch production and lowers the level of the plateau at which optimum economies of scale are achieved. In old plants unit costs were expected to drop unremittingly until, say, one million cars of a certain type had been produced; today there are no gains from economies of scale beyond, say, 250,000 cars. Working with antiquated printing machinery, newspaper proprietors had declining unit costs of production commensurate with the increase in the number of copies printed each night. The optimum used to be 2 to 3 million copies. Present day equipment promises no, or only very small, gains beyond a print run of 500,000 copies. In the chemical industry very satisfactory economies of scale were actualized when 500,000 tons of chemical X could be manufactured uninterruptedly; modern technology has lowered this optimum to 100,000 tons. Until the 1970s, power stations got bigger and bigger in order to heighten thermal efficiencies and generate power more cheaply. Now, smaller-sized (non-nuclear) plants are the vogue. They are said to score because they are quicker to build, have relatively lower servicing costs (for the equipment is more reliable), and, thanks to new fuel-efficient technologies, their generation costs of electricity are below those of the very large power stations.

Robots and semi-automated machinery have stirred up structural changes on another front. The economies-of-scale argument used to be adduced to stress the economic merit of concentrating in one factory the manufacture of one standardized product. Switching from one product-type to another meant halting the existing assembly line and reconstituting it. Today robots can be constantly reprogrammed and machines centrally linked to computers that control their production runs. This makes for much greater flexibility. In lay language, the modern factory is capable of manufacturing economically several types of a given product group, each with short run-sizes.

Small firms have also benefited from this development, which has given many of them an opportunity to operate successfully in competition with their big brothers. Capital goods manufacturers now offer a wide choice of scaled-down equipment suitable for short-run, small-batch production. Thus many firms with low-volume production requirements are able to meet the once insurmountable challenge presented by the high-volume runs of very large factories. It is becoming feasible to cater to the tastes of consumers who disdain standardized products. In future, products offered to minority consumer groups will still be more expensive than standardized products, but the price differential is set to narrow.

To the impoverished citizens of Bangladesh, the prices that they have to pay for their essential purchases are of supreme significance. But will the future prices of nonessentials in the OECD economies also play a momentous role? Levitt answers in the affirmative. In fact his forecast, relating to the rising power of global corporations in the next century, leans on the explicit assumption that the expansion of already large corporations will be facilitated by additional economies of scale from ever-longer production runs. All this is predicted to come about because of the putative price-sensitivity of consumers who are ready to forego the satisfaction of acquiring the products of their choice when cheap standardized products are available. Levitt's doctrine may be outrageous, but he deserves to be quoted at length because his supercilious prognostication is spelled out unambiguously.

When . . . lower costs are offered to the international multitudes, markets are expanded doubly, as previous holdouts for local preferences in product features, design, and functionality sacrifice these to the superior attractions of price alone. . . . In this way the new technological juggernaut taps into an ancient motivation to make one's money go as far as possible. . . . The global corporation knows: if you can get the price low enough, the increasingly homogenized world will increasingly take your world-standardized offering, even if it isn't exactly what your old mother said was suitable, what immemorial custom decreed as right, or what market-research fabulists asserted was preferred. . . . The lower the price the greater the likelihood that the world will accept standardized modernity in all its major sectors and segments rather than insist on higher-priced customization to inherited preferences and ancient practices. . . . People will prefer in overwhelming numbers lower-priced, more or less standardized quality products over higher-priced customized products. . . . It is not unreasonable to suppose that the microprocessor . . . will change what's so powerfully built into our immemorial genes (146).

This is not a perception of the future that I share. My fellow citizens in the OECD are about to get even richer (materially) than they already are. They will become highly indifferent to the cost-price level of most consumer goods. People will shun increasingly standardized, low-priced goods and seek out novelties. They will want to be different from their neighbors and indeed will be able to afford the luxury of not keeping up with the Joneses. To Levitt they are "multitudes"; to me they are individuals who will be able to indulge themselves by gratifying their individualistic tastes. This privilege was denied to previous, materially poorer, generations and is still likely to be denied to many in the LDCs during the coming years. If Levitt's views on standardization are not

validated, what then of his prediction on the mushrooming growth of
the global corporation?

POLITICAL DECISION-MAKING

The world is indeed getting smaller. A nuclear disaster in the Soviet
Union adversely affects Welsh sheep farmers. Long-range missiles in
Cuba present a direct threat to the military security of the United States.
British power stations cause 'dirty rain' to descend upon the Swedish
countryside. Cross-border collaboration between the flight controllers
of different nations helps to ensure safety in the air. Pictures of the
bloody overthrow of the Burmese government are seen on the actual
day by television viewers in all parts of the world. Important as these
developments are, do they presage the speedy coming of a world government with effective powers? Dreamers apart, few observers believe
that we shall be ruled by a world government in the year 2010. Many,
however, think that we are about to witness the formation of larger
nation–states through the amalgamation of smaller-sized countries.
There are prominent Europeans who advocate the formation of a United
States of Europe in the near future. They want Brussels to become the
capital of a new superpower. While some matters (for example, the
police, museums) would be left to the national provinces, the central
authorities of the United States of Europe are to determine the things
that matter. The provinces will no longer have an independent currency
of their own and their parliaments will not be allowed to legislate on
foreign affairs, pornography, employment, taxation, company mergers,
social welfare, and so on. Though I do not share it, there is a widely
held view that this is an unstoppable process that will come to fruition
before 2010.

Large nation–states are a breeding ground for extraparliamentary actions by disgruntled and frustrated citizens. The more educated they
are, the more conscious will be the residents of huge countries that they
have little influence on the way they are governed. Despite universal
franchise, general elections or referenda in states with a population of
1 billion (or 500 or 250 million) are not very meaningful. The links between the governors and the governed are tenuous and geographically
remote. The projected parliament (with significant legislative powers)
of the United States of Europe is to be elected directly by voters from
places as far apart as Dublin, Palermo, Copenhagen, and (perhaps) An-
kara. There will undoubtedly be politicians who would hail this as a
victory for democracy. In practice it would be a formal, barren exercise.
The distant legislators would merely accelerate the alienation of the
public from the government of an unwieldy state.

Catching a glimpse of the future, I see humanity marching in the opposite direction. I predict that political decision-making will increasingly be devolved downward to smaller national bodies with sovereign powers. Very populous countries may break up into smaller sovereign nation–states. The EC, should its organization survive, will be very much less powerful than its protagonists wish it to be; perhaps the United States of Europe may even be stillborn. The intense national rivalries among the participating Communist states have already seriously strained the unity of COMECON; its complete disintegration is only a matter of time. Some federally governed countries will continue to exist, albeit with the authority of their central government weakened because weighty powers will have been handed on to constituent provinces or states.

In the next century the smaller nation–states, with their enhanced social cohesion, will compare favorably in many respects with the populous 'powerful' countries that are being weakened by internal dissensions. All this is highly relevant to the future of OECD-based TNCs. Some of the choice morsels reported below are indicative illustrations that point to the devolution of political decision-making that is ahead of us.

After 40 years of incessant bickering, Belgium took a further big step toward genuine federalism in the summer of 1988 when its two-chamber parliament devolved substantial powers to its three regions (Flanders, Wallonia, and Brussels).

For decades many Kremlinologists have predicted the collapse of the Soviet regime. This, some said, would come about following defeat at the hands of an invading foreign power. Others opined that the masses of the Soviet Union would revolt because of the failure of the ruling Communist party to raise living standards. It now appears that the most concrete threat to the hegemony of Moscow's rulers emanates from discontent among the constituent republics. Georgians, Latvians, Armenians, and Ukrainians are among those groups that feel oppressed, not so much by the Communist character of the central government as by the putative tyranny that subjugates national and ethnic minorities. Some of the leaders of the rebellious republics have affirmed their loyalty to the tenets of Karl Marx: they demand to be allowed to put into practice their own versions of national Marxism. The matter was raised at the nineteenth Communist party conference when spokesmen from republics, facing an upsurge in nationalist sentiment, urged Gorbachev to change the constitution to provide for more autonomy, and thus avert the complete break-up of the Soviet Union. By now it is probably too late and the 1990s will witness the birth of several new nation-states, former republics of the USSR.

Foreign companies selling to the Commonwealth of Australia (the central government) have found themselves under pressure to make counterpurchases equal to about 30 percent of their sales. Adam Smith and the Geneva-based controllers of GATT (General Agreement on Tariffs and Trade) surely disapprove, but it is a fact of life. The foreign vendors to Australia's public sector may discharge their countertrade obligations by buying goods anywhere in the Commonwealth. The authorities of the Australian states also impose certain countertrade conditions on foreign suppliers or contractors who want to do business with them; these, however, can only be met by making purchases from companies resident within their territorial jurisdiction. The states also implement a parallel ('parochial') policy pertaining to direct investments by foreign multis. They are not concerned with Australian ownership of companies; they want the ownership to be vested in companies resident in their states. Reckitt & Colman, a British food TNC, aimed to divest itself of an Australian wine subsidiary. In stepped the state government of South Australia. It offered financial backing to a local group so that it could buy-out Reckitt & Colman. The Labor administration of South Australia was eager that corporate assets located in its state should not be 'lost' either to foreign-based multis or to capitalists in other Australian states.

Though mild, the impact of Scottish nationalism on economic life in Britain has surprised several foreign TNCs that planned to serve—without any nationalistic complications—the whole of the country (and, hopefully, the whole of the EC) from one manufacturing location. This factor has also been encountered during amalgamations involving UK-based corporations on both sides of the Scotland-England border. When BP—the mammoth London-based oil multi—bid for Britoil, a company with headquarters north of the border, there were loud screams that once again an English company, swallowing up Scottish assets, would be moving the decision-making apparatus out of the region. Guinness, making a hostile bid for the Scottish whisky firm Distillers, stirred up nationalistic feelings that did not augur well for the success of its offer. The outrage was great. Guinness found it necessary to undertake that if its bid succeeded, Distillers would remain an autonomous unit within the enlarged corporation with its own head office in Scotland and a Scotsman would be appointed as CEO.

Will India fall apart? There are certainly enough centrifugal forces that make this a strong possibility. In the meantime the central government authorities are encouraging each state to develop autonomously, though this may not always be in the overall interest of India. This can present difficulties for those TNCs that have ventured into this lion's den. General Tire would have liked to operate, or supply technology on a fee basis, for one large manufacturing facility supplying the whole of the Indian market.

When the Indian government decided to de-centralise the tire industry and to de-emphasise the dominant foreign ownership in this field, it was proposed that individual Indian states should have their own tire factories. Under normal circumstances, such relatively small factories would not be viable and, in truth, local investors in India found it hard to find international tire companies willing to supply know-how on an individual basis. General Tire, on the basis of a technical service contract, undertook to establish a Centre which will serve not only as a local consultancy but will channel all of General Tire's technology to these infant tire factories (27).

In the Soviet Union, ethnic and national minorities complain of being oppressed by the dominant Russian nation. In Yugoslavia the various regions are fighting it out among themselves: their common enemy is the central government in Belgrade. The leaders of the warring regions, who have helped to bring about a great deal of decentralization, are faithful veteran members of the central committee of the Yugoslav Communist party. The autonomy now enjoyed by the regions is so substantial that some observers doubt whether the country can still be regarded as a unitary state. The far-reaching and political reforms carried out by the leaders of the Slovenian Communist party are at variance with the practices prevailing in the other regions; they are also not esteemed by the federal authorities in Belgrade. Foreign corporations, having signed contracts with the government of the country, find that the regional authorities do not necessarily honor these. In theory, the centralists in Belgrade are working according to an overall plan. In practice, however, regional administrations are prepared to sabotage the national strategy in order to enhance the economic fortunes of their areas. This is highlighted by Yugoslavia's perennial foreign exchange shortages. The regional bosses strive to obtain foreign currency to finance imports for enterprises in their bailiwick. Over the years many foreign companies have not been able to fulfill the countertrade requirements imposed on them by the central government. A corporation delivering foreign equipment for a factory in region A, is supposed to be paid with goods sourced in Yugoslavia, which it may take out of the country. But what if the authorities of regions B and C will not let it buy goods from sources under their control? They justify their refusal by saying that they hope to export themselves these very goods to earn foreign currency for their own regions. In any case, what benefits do regions B and C derive from a factory located in region A? It has been said that the name "Yugoslavia" has already lost its meaning.

Levitt sneers that the "multinational corporation's accommodating mode to visible national differences is medieval." Maybe—but whether you call them global or multinational, all internationally-oriented corporations will have to accommodate themselves to the combined consequences that flow from greater devolved political decision-making and the introduction of scaled-down capital goods that optimize economies of scale with shorter production runs. The economic rationale of multis will be affected by traffic in both directions. Let us hypothesize that a large, populous country—say, India—has been split up into several independent nation–states. It would follow that certain TNCs may not wish to retain existing (or establish new) manufacturing subsidiaries that are located in one of these new states. This would be the case if their production operation is only viable with untrammelled access to a very much bigger market.

The other side of the coin beckons TNCs to open up in states whose market-size would previously have deterred them. The CEO of a U.S. chemical corporation has postulated that new vistas are being opened up. Instead of making one mammoth investment abroad once every ten years, his TNC will in future build several smaller, more flexibly-scaled factories at more frequent intervals. Because of the changed dimensions of economies of scale, the new-type multi will have opportunities to license its R&D to many more foreign-based companies.

Import restrictions and/or high customs duties, together with exhortations to buy locally made goods, have often been inimical to the material welfare of small nations. (True nationalists are of course prepared to pay this price.) As a result of modern technology, which enables smaller-sized manufacturing operations to compete successfully with large-sized factories, the protection of domestic industries does not depress living standards as severely as in the past. This is not written to commend protectionism to small and medium-sized economies. However, multis would do well to be on guard because some political decision-makers will surely succumb to the temptation.

THE DECLINE OF U.S. MULTIS

When in 1909 International Harvester contemplated building a factory in Czarist Russia, the authorities were told that it planned to employ Russian workers, use Russian lumber, "and in every way possible conduct the enterprise as a Russian company." The minister of finance was pleased but pointed out that what was really important to him was that the capital and management of the subsidiary should remain in U.S. hands—that is, not pass to Western Europeans. In those days the embryonic European MNCs were deemed a menace to Russian sovereignty, while U.S. corporations constituted no such threat. When, 50 years later, the multi legend was born, it was the U.S. parentage of the then prominent TNCs that kindled the fires of hatred for the multinational corporation per se. This evil corporate vehicle was actualy defined in many quarters as an "international company with its head office in America." The denunciations of the wicked multis might not have become so pervasive had it not been for the nationality of the most numerous and mighty TNCs. During its infancy the legend was constantly nurtured by anti-Americanism. The proportional decline of U.S.-based TNCs is now evident even to many of those who once disseminated the legend. The increasingly non-American composition of the multi fraternity will hasten the expiry of the legend.

Between 1955 and 1975 it appeared plausible to prognosticate on the domination of the Western world's non-U.S. manufacturing output by U.S. subsidiaries, though many of the quantitative estimates were wide off the mark (65). In some of the technologically advanced segments of European industry it was indeed accurate to say that U.S.-based "rogue elephants" called the shots. The ideologist of economic anti-Americanism was Jean-Jacques Servan-Schreiber. He was an ambitious, left-of-center, journalist-cum-politician who gained world fame as the author of *Le Défi Américain*. Published in 1967, it predicted that in the 1980s the third industrial power (after the United States and the Soviet Union) would be "American industry in Europe" (193). The invaders were portrayed as "rolling from Naples to Amsterdam with the ease of Israeli tanks in Sinai." Servan-Schreiber rallied his fellow citizens to organize resistance. He called for specific anti-U.S. actions by the governments of Europe and also proposed the formation of trans-European corporations that could repel the giant U.S. TNCs. The book is no longer on the reading lists of most business schools as it once was: its contents are seen by hindsight to be ludicrous. At a later stage, sooner than some of his admirers, Servan-Schreiber was to recognize that the anti-multi legend, written in language of anti-Americanism, was out of date. Only those who can recall his former international fame as a scourge of U.S. TNCs will appreciate the irony of what has happened to him since. In 1982 he founded and became the president of Le Centre Mondial in Paris, which was to promote computer and information technologies. In 1985 he told President Mitterrand that he was resigning because the French government favored the procurement of French equipment for France's schools instead of buying the computers of a U.S. corporation, which he thought were to be preferred. In 1984 he became a director of the huge Pittsburgh-based TNC Allegheny International! In 1988 he set out to frighten the U.S. public with his newly discovered bugbear. He pointed to the "intensification of the Japanese penetration. The hold of the Japanese has become all but impregnable. Their . . . networks are spread all over the United States. The Japanese economy employs today so many Americans—American voters—that the issue has become delicate indeed" (190).

Until the 1980s LDCs differentiated between the iniquitous multis in general, and the specially vile and dangerous multis of the United States (and to a minor extent of Britain). Italy's state-owned oil TNC ENI was able to obtain several concessions in Africa after Enrico Mattei, its dynamic CEO, waved the Italian flag, telling the native politicians that their countries ought not to be dependent on U.S.-Anglo-Dutch TNCs. The neutrality of Switzerland and Sweden was regarded by their multis as a commercially vital asset. A U.S. observer has suggested that the French and German flags lacked the imperialist connotations of the U.S. and UK emblems and, consequently, French and German TNCs were in a position to perform well in the Third World and the COMECON. Howard Perlmutter favored the location of the head offices of TNCs in countries with a "low political profile." He comforted the British TNCs that the attractions of the UK location would "rise as its military power sinks" (70).

Readers of the business press cannot help noticing the current growth of TNCs from the less powerful member-states of the OECD (Ireland, Spain, Canada, Australia, New Zealand). Even more substantial is the upsurge of Asian multis, which are now expanding through acquisitions and greenfield projects in the Third World and the English-speaking countries. (To cite but one illustration: in August 1989 a nascent Thai TNC paid $270 million for Seafoods, a subsidiary of the U.S. multi Pillsbury). The erstwhile insuperable might of U.S. TNCs is being challenged by the Japanese multis which, at the time, had been ignored by Servan-Schreiber. They have been depicted as "timid transnationals." Timid or not, by the end of this century, output of their foreign manufacturing subsidiaries might well surpass those of U.S.-based multis. Firestone Tire & Rubber is an old MNC and features in some of the early attacks on U.S. economic imperialism. In March 1988 it was swallowed up by a $2.6 billion cash offer from Bridgestone, Japan's largest tire corporation. Japanese TNCs are now emulating the U.S. multis by making hostile acquisitions; in 1987 Dai Nippon Ink paid $540 million to acquire Reichhold Chemicals in this manner. While the WCC is still treating kindly MNCs with head offices in LDCs, it has finally caught up with reality and is devoting space in its publications to castigate Japanese multis. Eleven Japanese companies that had manufacturing facilities in Korea are rebuked for closing their factories and leaving Korea, "owing workers . . . earned wages, bonuses and retirement benefits" (47).

At the commencement of the 1960s, two-thirds of the direct foreign investments of all countries were owned or controlled by U.S.-head-quartered MNCs. Twenty-five years later the proportion had dropped to below one-third and has registered a further decline in every subsequent year. This realignment has occurred because a number of U.S. TNCs have divested themselves of foreign subsidiaries and because U.S. multis in toto are executing fewer new direct investments (including those financed by retained earnings) than the established, and host of infant, non-U.S. TNCs. The recorded value of foreign direct investment holdings in the United States first exceeded U.S. direct investments abroad at some point in the second half of the 1980s. These (official) sensational data were in part misleading because they refer to book values. Judged by the relevant stock market indices, the balance is probably still slightly in favor of the United States at the beginning of 1990 (191). But this numerate superiority is shrinking fast and if the present trend continues, within a few years foreign multis will have more assets in the United States than U.S. multis will own abroad.

Two consequences follow, the first of which is very relevant to the sociopolitical theme of this book. In the 1960s one could forgive the man in the street if he thought that all multinational corporations were in fact U.S.-based TNCs. This perception is now fading fast and with it, the populist anti-multi sentiments.

The relative decline of the power of U.S. TNCs has engendered within the United States xenophobic agitation that in previous decades had been rampant outside the United States (and not only in LDCs). Until recently Washington was wary of taking steps to halt the multi invasion lest this harm the expansion plans of U.S.-based multis. But now there is less fear of retaliation. Headlines in *Fortune* tell of investors from abroad who are "gobbling up . . . giant U.S. companies." The Democratic presidential candidate whipped up patriotic feelings in the fall of 1988 by attacking foreign investments in the United States. (In previous years politicians had also appealed to patriotism but then they did so by castigating U.S. companies for investing abroad.) Public opinion polls support congressional leaders who are proposing that special taxes should be imposed on foreign investors in the United States. But the most significant plank in the program of the U.S. anti-multi protagonists is their plea that the United States ought to follow the precepts of other host countries. If they have their way, foreign-based TNCs are to be required in future to obtain explicit approval from Washington for the purchase of U.S. assets.

CODA

But for the sentimental reason that their grandfather is the author, I cannot envisage any inducement for my grandchildren to read this text in the year 2010. Taking wings into the future, I shall be assuming that they will be residing in an OECD country, one of the many that has put up firm barriers to impede the entry of the numerous potential immigrants from the poorer parts of the world. In that rich society there will be few material shortages. People will strive for the privilege to work, not primarily to earn money, but in order to have something to do. Issues such as euthanasia, expeditions to the moon, and test tube procreation will arouse political passions—and not devaluations and investment grants. There are not likely to be many job opportunities for economists. Maximizing output and optimizing economies of scale will not be exciting exercises when labor saving technological advances will make it even more difficult to devise the means by which (unwanted) leisure time can be endured without suffering excessive boredom. Offices and factories will be smaller-sized than now. Companies will be smaller. Nation–states will be smaller in area and population. Should a few self-styled TNCs survive, they will have little in common with the multis depicted by the four founding fathers.

I hope that my grandchildren (and perhaps some of their friends) will find interest in what I have written of the historical foundations of the multinational corporation. Should they peruse the whole of this book, they will note with some incredulity the strange birth of the multi legend. The baby was fed, cuddled, and later raised to manhood by anti-American zealots, idealistic believers in a world government, disciples of Karl Marx, and a variety of religious and secular do-gooders. Will the coming generations comprehend how sane scientists joined with starry-eyed business executives to proclaim the social and moral mission of the TNC? They will already have discerned some of the abuse hurled at these international companies. But will they understand with hindsight why international religious conferences voiced, devoutly and routinely, strong opposition to the evil multis? (At the multinational 1988 Lambeth conference of the bishops of the Anglican Communion, it seemed at first as if the ritual condemnation of TNCs might be omitted. There was a happy ending in that a resolution was finally passed that mentioned, inter alia, the exploiting multis.)

It is too early for me to know whether my grandchildren will be avid students of history. If this proves to be so, then they will of course have learned that in the dark past of humanity there have been many legends, embedded in superstitions and irrationalities, that remained influential for protracted periods. But what of the enlightened twentieth century? How is it that so many respectable and erudite opinion-makers and political leaders nurtured this legend for several decades? Why did the multi legend survive so long? I have no convincing answer.

BIBLIOGRAPHY OF
CITED SOURCES

1. A. Buznev, *Transnational Corporations and Militarism*. Moscow: Progress Publishers, 1985.

2. Eldridge Haynes, *Collective Action by Multinational Corporations*. New York: BINCO, January 1972.

3. U.S. Congress, *A Foreign Economic Policy*. Congressional Documents IV, Washington, 1970.

4. E. Nukhovich, *International Monopolies and Developing Countries*. Moscow: Progress Publishers, 1980.

5. World Council of Churches, *Churches and the Transnational Corporations*. Geneva: WCC, 1983.

6. H. Wilson, *Individual Choice in Democracy*. London: Labour Party, 1973.

7. B. Connell, "Anthony Wedgwood Benn," (London), *The Times* July 18, 1977.

8. R. Barnet, *The Lean Years*. London: Sphere, 1981.

9. R. Robinson, *National Control of Foreign Business Entry*. New York: Praeger, 1976.

10. H. Sklar (ed.), *Trilateralism*. Montreal: Black Rose Books, 1980.

11. M. O'Neal, *Multinationale Unternehmen unter Staatsaufsicht*. Heidelberg: Institut für Politische Wissenschaft, 1979.

12. Organization for Economic Cooperation and Development, *Responsibility of Parent Companies for their Subsidiaries*. Paris: OECD, 1980.

13. S. Nilus, *Protocols of the Meetings of the Learned Elders of Zion*. London: Britons, 1936.

14. S. Knight, *The Brotherhood*. London: Panther, 1985.

15. D. Lipson, *Freemasonry*. Princeton: Princeton University Press, 1977.

16. L. Ratner, *Antimasonry*. Englewood: Prentice Hall, 1969.

17. D. Schwarz, *Die Freimaurerei*. Berlin: Eher, 1938.

18. W. Vaugh, *The Antimasonic Party*. Lexington: University Press of Kentucky, 1983.

19. World Council of Churches, *Churches' Report on Transnational Corporations*. Geneva: WCC, 1984.

20. L. Turner, *Invisible Empires*. London: Hamish Hamilton, 1970.

21. M. Anshen and G. Bach (eds.), *Management and Corporations 1985*. New York: McGraw-Hill, 1960.

22. S. Hymer, *The Multinational Corporation*. London: Cambridge University Press, 1979.

23. *Hansard*, House of Lords. London: HMSO, April 16, 1975.

24. *Hansard*, House of Lords. London: HMSO, June 16, 1974.

25. "The Firms Who follow No Flag," *Industrial News*. London: TUC, March 12, 1970.

26. H. Perlmutter, *Adjusting Corporate Policy to a Changing World*. New York: BINCO, 1986.

27. United Nations, *Summary of the Hearings Before the Group of Eminent Persons to Study the Impact of Multinational Corporations*. New York: UN, 1974.

28. M. Stevens, *The Big Eight*. London: Macmillan, 1981.

29. Church of England, *The Churches and the Multinationals*. London: General Synod of the Church of England, 1978.

30. F. von Krossigk, "Marx, Universalism, and Contemporary World Business," *International Studies Quarterly*, Stoneham, December 1972.

31. H. Radice (ed.), *International Firms and Modern Imperialism*. London: Penguin, 1975.

32. O. Reinhold (ed.), *Der Imperialismus der BRD*. Frankfurt: Marxistische Blaetter, 1972.

33. R. Hilferding, *Finance Capital*. London: Routledge, 1981.

34. O. Freeman, *The Multinational Corporation*. New York: BINCO, 1973.

35. M. Steuer et al., *The Impact of Foreign Direct Investment on the United Kingdom*. London: HMSO, 1973.

36. H. Perlmutter, "The Tortuous Evolution of the Multinational Corporation," *Columbia Journal of World Business*, New York, January 1969.

37. U.S. Congress, *Hearings on the Trade Reform Act*. Congressional Documents III, Washington, 1973.

38. R. J. Barnet and R. E. Müller, *Global Reach*. London: Cape, 1975.

39. U.S. Congress, *Hearings on the Trade Reform Act*. Congressional Documents V, Washington, 1973.

40. United Nations, *The Impact of Multinational Corporations on Development*. New York: UN, 1974.

41. M. Kidron, *Foreign Investments in India*. Oxford: Oxford University Press, 1965.

42. Methodist Church, *Just Trading*. London: Methodist Church, 1979.

43. C. Payer, *The Debt Trap*. London: Penguin, 1974.

44. B. Edwards, *Multinational Companies and the Trade Unions*. Nottingham: Spokesman Books, 1977.

45. W. Brandt (chairman), *North-South*. London: Pan, 1980.

46. International Labour Organization, *Multinational Enterprises and Social Policy*. Geneva: ILO, 1973.

47. World Council of Churches, *The Impact of Transnational Corporations on the Quality of Work*. Geneva: WCC, 1981.

48. C. Powers (ed.), *People/Profits*. New York: Council on Religion and International Affairs, 1972.

49. U.S. Congress, *Technology Trade*. Congressional Documents (hearings), Washington, 1980.

50. U.S. Congress, *World Trade and Investment Issues*. Congressional Documents (hearings), Washington, 1971.

51. U.S. Congress, *Hearings on the Trade Reform Act*. Congressional Documents IV, Washington, 1973.

52. C. Wilson, *The History of Unilever*, vols. 1–2. London: Cassell, 1954.

53. Labour Party, *News Release*. London: Labour Party, April 18, 1973.

54. U.S. Congress, *Hearings on Multinational Corporations*. Congressional Documents, Washington, 1973.

55. A. Kamin (ed.), *Western European Labor and the American Corporation*. Washington: Bureau of National Affairs, 1970.

56. J. Winpenny, *Brazil*. London: Grant & Cutler, 1971.

57. B. Ward, *Progress for a Small Planet*. London: Penguin, 1979.

58. A. Chetley, *The Politics of Baby Foods*. London: Pinter, 1986.

59. C. Kindleberger, *Multinational Excursions*. Cambridge, MIT Press, 1984.

60. BINCO, *The United Nations and the Business World*. New York: BINCO, 1967.

61. F. Vogl, "Mr. Ralph Nader Set to Take on Multinationals." *The Times* (London), February 4, 1980.

62. E. Woodroofe, "Multinationals Shape a Global Economy," *The Guardian* (London), May 11, 1972.

63. J. Lindsay, "Directing International Operations," *Commerce International*, London, February 1971.

64. P. Brookes, "Unions with World-Wide Ambitions," *Daily Telegraph* (London), October 22, 1970.

65. A. Said and L. Simmons (eds.), *The New Sovereigns*. Englewood: Prentice-Hall, 1975.

66. R. Desatnik and M. Bennett, *Human Resource Management in the Multinational Company*. Farnborough: Gower, 1977.

67. *Yearbook of International Organisations*. Brussels: Union of International Associations, 1969.

68. *An Examination of the Multinational Corporation*, New York: Corporate Information Center, 1973.

69. A. Rubner, *Three Sacred Cows of Economics*. London: MacGibbon & Kee, 1970.

70. *The Multinational Company* (summary of lectures and discussion). London: Business and Industrial Training, November 1970.

71. BINCO, *Where in the World Are We Going?* New York: BINCO, 1974.

72. E. Weiss et al., *Der Fall General Motors.* Vienna: Forum Alternativ, 1980.

73. A. Akinsanya, *The Expropriation of Multi-National Property in the Third World.* New York: Praeger, 1980.

74. J. M. Stopford, J. Dunning, and K. O. Haberich, *The World Directory of Multinational Enterprises.* London: Macmillan, 1980.

75. R. Stauffer, *Nation-Building in a Global Economy.* Beverly Hills: Sage, 1973.

76. L. Fox, *Multinationals Take over Australia.* Sydney: APCOL, 1981.

77. G. Temple, *Als wär's der liebe Gott: Die Weltmacht der Konzerne.* Gütersloh: Bertelsmann, 1971.

78. J. de Santa Ana, *Transnational Corporations from the Point of View of the Churches.* Geneva: WCC, 1981.

79. United Nations, *Multinational Corporations in World Development.* New York: UN, 1973.

80. "*The Multinationals and the Swedish Labour Market*". *Svenska Dagbladet,* Stockholm, 1973.

81. A Rubner, *The Export Cult.* Aldershot: Gower, 1987.

82. *Minutes of Meeting,* Parliamentary Group for World Government. London, July 7, 1969.

83. T. Aitken, *The Multinational Man.* London: Allen and Unwin, 1973.

84. Y. Aharoni and C. Baden, *Business in the International Environment.* London: Macmillan, 1977.

85. W. Laqueur, *The Age of Terrorism.* London: Weidenfeld and Nicolson, 1987.

86. Owens-Illinois, *Background Material.* Toledo, August 1986.

87. C. Cheape, *Family Firm to Modern Multinational.* Cambridge: Harvard University Press, 1985.

88. T. Gladwin and I. Walter, *Multinationals Under Fire.* New York: Wiley, 1980.

89. IBM, *Letter to the Author.* Paris, November 4, 1986.

90. C. Levinson, *International Trade Unionism.* London: Allen and Unwin, 1972.

91. Elliott Haynes, *Alert Roundtable on the International Labor Movement.* New York: BINCO, March 1970.

92. M. Wilkins, *The Emergence of Multinational Enterprise.* Cambridge: Harvard University Press, 1970.

93. M. Wilkins, *The Maturing of Multinational Enterprise.* Cambridge: Harvard University Press, 1974.

94. "Chemical Industry Section Conference," *ICF Bulletin.* Geneva, June 1969.

95. J. Behrman, *National Interests and the Multinational Enterprise.* Englewood: Prentice-Hall, 1970.

96. A. Pinelo, *The Multinational Corporation as a Force in Latin American Politics.* New York: Praeger, 1973.

97. J. Einhorn, *Expropriation Politics.* Lexington: Lexington Books, 1974.

98. R. Olson, "Economic Coercion in International Disputes," *The Journal of Developing Areas,* Macomb, April 1975.

99. S. Schlesinger and S. Kinzer, *Bitter Fruit.* London: Sinclair Browne, 1982.

100. G. Philip, "The Political Economy of Expropriation," *Millenium*, London, Winter 1977.

101. R. Olson, "Expropriation and International Economic Coercion." *The Journal of Developing Areas*, Macomb, January 1977.

102. K. Sauvant and F. Lavipour (eds.), *Controlling Multinational Enterprises*. London: Wilton House, 1976.

103. B. Lloyd, *Political Risk Management*. London: Keith Shipton, 1976.

104. C. Wilson, *Unilever 1945–1965*. London: Cassell, 1968.

105. A. Sloan, *My Years with General Motors*. London: Sidgwick and Jackson, 1986.

106. N. Faith, *The Infiltrators*. London: Hamish Hamilton, 1971.

107. W. Reader, *Imperial Chemical Industries*, vol. 2. Oxford: Oxford University Press, 1975.

108. P. Harrison, *Inside the Third World*. London: Penguin, 1984.

109. A. Mockler, *The New Mercenaries*. London: Sidgwick & Jackson, 1985.

110. R. Eels, *Global Corporations*. New York: Free Press, 1972.

111. C. Gerstacker, *The Structure of the Corporation*. Midland: Dow Chemical Company, 1972.

112. G. Ball, "Cosmocorp: the Importance of Being Stateless." *Columbia Journal of World Business*, New York, November 1967.

113. J. Boddington (ed.), *Speeches by Tony Benn*. Nottingham: Spokesman Books, 1974.

114. H. Mertz, *Peace and Affluence through the Multinational Corporations*. Bryn Mawr: Dorrance, 1984.

115. A. Morita, *Made in Japan*. London: Collins, 1987

116. "Close Watch on Eminent Persons," *Financial Times* (London), June 1, 1978.

117. J. Kunen, *The Strawberry Statement: Notes of a College Revolutionary*. New York: Avon, 1970.

118. Eldridge Haynes, *The Mission of Business International*. New York: BINCO, 1969.

119. H. Northrup and R. Rowan, "Multinational Collective Bargaining Activity," part I. *Columbia Journal of World Business*, New York, Spring 1974.

120. H. Northrup and R. Rowan, "Multinational Collective Bargaining Activity," part II. *Columbia Journal of World Business*, New York, Summer 1974.

121. J. Dunning, *International Production and the Multinational Enterprise*. London, Allen and Unwin, 1981.

122. R. Helfgott, "American Unions and Multinational Companies," *Columbia Journal of World Business*, New York, Summer 1983.

123. A. Altman, *L. M. Ericsson*. Stockholm: Ericsson, 1977.

124. U.S. Congress, *Hearings before the Joint Economic Committee*. Congressional Documents, Washington, 1970.

125. J. O'Hagan (ed.), *The Economy of Ireland*. Dublin: Irish Management Institute, 1975.

126. S. Vogel, "Akai Comes to the Champs Elysees." *Euro-Asia Business Review*, Chichester, May 1985.

127. J. McDonald, "New Organisational Concept of the World Enterprise." *Management International*, Wiesbaden, 1961.

128. "Why Sony Has Yet to Find a Solution to the Complexity of World Markets," *Financial Times* (London), December 4, 1987.

129. R. Sobel, *IBM*. London: Sidgwick and Jackson, 1984.

130. A. Hammer, *Hammer*. London: Simon and Schuster, 1987.

131. GEC, *Letter to the Author*. London, September 15, 1987.

132. C. Bergsten, T. Horst, and T. Moran, *American Multinationals and American Interests*. Washington: Brookings Institution, 1978.

133. A. Sampson, *The Sovereign State*. London: Hodder and Stoughton, 1973.

134. D. Channon and M. Jalland, *Multinational Strategic Planning*. London: Macmillan, 1979.

135. W. Reader, *Metal Box*. London: Heinemann, 1976.

136. B. Goldwater, *With No Apologies*. New York: Morrow, 1975.

137. Pepsico, *Background Material*. Purchase, September 1986.

138. C. Tugendhat, *The Multinationals*. London: Penguin, 1973.

139. R. Sobel, *ITT*. London: Sidgwick and Jackson, 1982.

140. B. Saporito, "Black & Decker's Gamble on Globalization," *Fortune*, New York, May 14, 1984.

141. T. Barka, *The Glassmakers*. London: Weidenfeld and Nicolson, 1977.

142. L. Grunberg, *Failed Multinational Ventures*. Toronto: Lexington Books, 1981.

143. D. Blake, *A Case Study of 1967 UAW-Chrysler Agreement*. Geneva: International Institute for Labour Studies, May 1969.

144. S. Fay, "Car Firms Face Euro-Union Ban," *Sunday Times* (London), December 7, 1969.

145. C. McMillan, *Multinationals from the Second World*. London: Macmillan, 1987.

146. T. Levitt, *The Marketing Imagination*. New York: Free Press, 1986.

147. R. Vernon, "The Multinational Enterprise." *Foreign Affairs*, New York, July 1971.

148. Church of England, *Transnational Corporations*. London: Church of England, 1983.

149. A. Room, *Dictionary of Trade Name Origins*. London: Routledge, 1982.

150. Crown Cork Company, *Letter to the Author*. (London), March 30, 1988.

151. J. Kline, *International Codes and Multinational Business*. Westport: Quorum Books, 1985.

152. P. Kotler, *Marketing Management*. Englewood: Prentice-Hall, 1972.

153. C. Karadia, *The Swraj Paul Affair*. London: Slatecourt, 1984.

154. United Nations, *Material Relevant to the Formulation of a Code of Conduct*. New York: UN Center on Transnational Corporations, 1977.

155. P. Howarth, *Intelligence Chief Extraordinary*. London: Bodley Head, 1986.

156. S. Sethi, *Advanced Cases in Multinational Business Operations*. Pacific Palisades: Goodyear, 1972.

157. "Global Newswatch," *Multinational Monitor 2*, Washington, 1982.

158. L. Wood, "The Tricky Task of Tickling Taste-Buds," *Financial Times* (London), December 21, 1987.

159. P. O'Mahoney, *Multinationals and Human Rights*. Essex: Mayhew-McCrimmon, 1980.

160. J. Boddewyn, *Corporate External Affairs*. Geneva: BISA, 1975.

161. United Nations, *The United Nations Code of Conduct on Transnational Corporations*. New York: UN, 1986.

162. *The UK Electronic Components Industry—the Future?* London: Mullard, 1978.

163. Arthur Schlesinger, *Robert Kennedy and His Times*. London: André Deutsch, 1978.

164. J. Rovira, T. Berry, and R. Diaz, *Investment Strategies in Mexico*. New York: BINCO, 1979.

165. P. Brendon, *IKE*. London: Secker and Warburg, 1987.

166. AFL-CIO, *The Critical Need for New International Trade and Investment Legislation*. Atlanta: AFL-CIO Executive Council, 1971.

167. "Will Araskog's Radical Surgery Work?" *Business Week*, New York, July 14, 1986.

168. H. Bössenecker, "Nur der Name bringt Gewinn." *Die Zeit*, Hamburg, May 4, 1984.

169. K. Owen, "Industrial Research would Strengthen British Innovation," *The Times* (London), April 18, 1969.

170. N. Goodway, "Cadbury's Hershey Deal." *Observer* (London), July 24, 1988.

171. M. Stewart, *The Jekyll and Hyde Years*. London: Dent, 1977.

172. S. Davis (ed.), *Managing and Organising Multinational Corporations*. Oxford: Pergamon, 1979.

173. S. Ramel, *The Cross-National Society*. Stockholm: Swedish Marketing Association, October 1970.

174. N. Parsons, *Letters to Author*. Stockholm, February 2, 1980.

175. P. Hertner and G. Jones (eds.), *Multinationals: Theory and History*. Brookfield: Gower, 1986.

176. A. Rubner, *The Price of a Free Lunch*. London: Wildwood House, 1979.

177. K. Ohmae, *Triad Power*. New York: Free Press, 1985.

178. L. Thurow, *The Zero-Sum Society*. New York: Basic Books, 1980.

179. "How the Walloon Government Forced BL to be Generous." *Business Europe*, Geneva, March 13, 1981.

180. L. Turner, *Politics and the Multinational Company*. London: Fabian Society, 1969.

181. Horst Wortmann, *Background Material*. Detmold, September 1986.

182. R. North, *The Real Cost*. London: Chatto & Windus, 1986.

183. J. Goldman, *Technology and Multinationalism*. London: Science Policy Foundation, October 1973.

184. Cadbury Schweppes, *Letter to Author*. London, September 18, 1986.

185. Allegheny International, *1985 Annual Report*. Pittsburgh, 1986.

186. United Nations, *Transnational Corporations in World Development*. New York: UN Centre on Transnational Corporations, 1988.

187. G. Allen and L. Abraham, *None Dare Call it Conspiracy*. Seattle: Double A Publications, 1983.

188. J. Harvey-Jones, *Making it Happen*. London: Collins, 1988.

189. N. Jacoby, P. Nehemkis, and R. Eels, *Bribery and Extortion in World Business*. New York: Macmillan, 1977.

190. Jean-Jacques Servan-Schreiber, *The Chosen and the Choice*. London, Futura, 1988.

191. Morgan Guaranty, "Foreign Direct Investment in the United States." *World Financial Markets*, New York, June 1989.

192. R. Enrico, *The Other Guy Blinked*. New York: Bantam, 1986.

193. Jean-Jacques Servan-Schreiber, *Le Défi Américain*, Paris: Denoël, 1967.

194. Tony Benn, *Office Without Power*. London: Arrow, 1988.

Grateful acknowledgement is made to the publishers and authors of the material listed above. The sources of some of the factual data—the scores of company practices described in the book—could not always be acknowledged individually. The following publications especially have provided much useful, and often authoritative, information.

Busimag

Business Latin America

Business Week

Catholic Herald

Daily Telegraph

Der Spiegel

Die Dritte Welt

Far Eastern Economic Review

Financial Times

Fortune

Handelsblatt

Harvard Business Review

International Management

Journal of Business Ethics

Journal of International Business Studies

Le Monde

Multinational Business

Neue Züricher Zeitung

New York Times

Svenska Dagbladet

The Developing Economies (Tokyo)

The Economist

The Irish Times

The Sunday Times

The Sydney Morning Herald

The Times (London)

The Times of India

Third World Quarterly

Wall Street Journal

Wirtschaftswoche

INDEX

accountancy partnerships, 14
accounting practices, 140–46, 148–49.
  See also transfer pricing
Adam, Gyorgy, 245
advertising, 14, 200. *See also* public
  relations
African subsidiaries, 235. *See also spe-
  cific corporations, countries*
agricultural subsidiaries, 238
Alcan, 182
American Federation of Labor–Con-
  gress of Industrial Organizations
  (AFL-CIO), 23–25, 57, 156, 161,
  172, 253
American Selling Price, 150
Angola, 204, 211, 220
anti-Semitism, 5–7, 128
anti-trust laws, 92, 125
Arab league, 205
Argentina, 64–68, 163
arms manufacture, 30, 88
Australia, xii, 50, 86, 124, 268–69

Austria, 35, 105
auto manufacturers: supplier links,
  109–10; unions and, xii, 73, 156–61,
  165–66, 173–74, 192. *See also specific
  companies*
automation, 232, 265

Ball, George, 43–44, 94, 96
bankruptcy, 217
banks, 220
Barclays Bank, 209, 220
Barlow Rand, 134
Belgium, 236, 264
Benn, Tony, xv, 39, 49, 89–90
Black & Decker, 150–51
Bolivia, 184
borrowing, 142
boycotts, 128, 144, 202, 205, 207, 208,
  211
Brazil, 36, 48, 180–81, 188
bribes, 125, 128, 202
Britain: BINCO and, 83; Ford and,

119; hostile takeovers, 190; investment promotion, 231; Japanese MNCs and, 117; percent equity ownership and, 49–50, 51–53; Scottish nationalism and, 269; tariffs in, 105; taxes and, 93–94. *See also* British MNCs; British subsidiaries

British Leyland (BL), 154–55, 232, 240

British MNCs, 132–33; Africa and, 235; foreign MNCs and, 125–27; unions and, 154–56, 173. *See also specific corporations*

British Oxygen, 218–19

British subsidiaries: "buy British" policy, 194; inter-MNC contacts, 92; percent equity ownership of, 49–53; subsidiary nationalism and, 149; unions and, xii, 158–61

Burma, 184, 196

business culture, 29

Business International Corporation (BINCO), xvi, 79; CIA and, 85–86; corporations belonging to, 81; employment research, 121; Freeman and, 84–85; Haynes and, 80–84; international mobility and, 56; island headquarters idea, 97–98; Levinson and, 69–70, 76–77; *Mission* of, 83–84; South Africa and, 79; UN and, 96

Cadbury Schweppes, 257–58, 261

Canada, 178, 182–83; BINCO and, 82; gay bankers and, 36; unions and, 153–54, 158, 165; wage parity and, 167–68

Carter, Jimmy, xv

Caterpillar Tractor Company, 214, 216–17, 250

Central Intelligence Agency (CIA), 85–86

Ceylon, 176, 183

chemical MNCs, 111–12, 150

Chile, 48, 129–30, 220

Chrysler, xii, 39–40, 49, 156, 158–59

churches, xv, 15, 23, 28–29, 208; environmentalism and, 112; South Africa and, 206

Coca-Cola, 28, 47, 125, 203, 205, 252

codetermination, 230

coffee companies, 210

COMECON, 15, 88, 162

computers, 204, 206, 232, 265, 272

consolidated accounts, 141

conspiracy theories, 4–10

consumer preferences, 28–29, 110–11, 260–62

Council of the Americas, 92

credit, 142

Crown Cork & Seal, 51–52

Damascus Boycott Office, 128, 205, 207

Danish MNCs, 133–34

dependencia school, 28, 195

direct foreign investment, 124–28, 233–38, 273–74

discrimination, 29, 63, 204

diversification, 135–38

divestiture, 74, 209, 211, 226

dividend policy, 51–52

Dunlop, 58

Du Pont, 75

economies of scale, 110, 262–67

Egypt, 184

employment, 21; BINCO research, 121; global estimate, 37; in home country, 21, 24; in host country, 26–27; labor laws, 63; technology transfer and, 253–55; tokenism and, 41–42

Enrico, Roger, 59

environmentalism, 29, 111–12, 172, 205

Esso, 64–66, 180, 182

ethnocentric firms, 42

Europe, United States of, 267

exchange rate, 108, 142–43

executives. *See* managers, multinational

exports: criticism of, 27–28; indige-

nous raw materials and, 239; service sector and, 246–48
Exxon, 26, 65

Faith, Nicholas, 103–4
families of international managers, 55–56
Farley, Laurence, 150–51
Fiat, 67–68
finance capitalism, 16, 101
financial resources, 102
food MNCs, 178, 210, 257–58. *See also specific corporations*
Ford, 119, 127–28, 149, 156, 159–61
Ford, Henry, 6, 116
Ford, Henry II, 147
foreign aid, 175–76
France: disinvestment in, 236; French MNCs, 166; Japanese MNCs and, 117; nationalism in, 149, 178; subsidiaries and, 125, 149
franchising, 249–50, 257
free trade, 102, 122–24, 150. *See also* protectionism
Freeman, Orville, 20, 80, 84–85, 97, 121
Freemasons, 7–9
fringe benefits, 62, 166

Gandhi, Indira, 188
Gandhi, Rajiv, 79, 189, 197, 234
Great Britain. *See* Britain
Geneen, Harold, 129–30, 147
General Foods, 125–26
General Motors, 34–35, 103, 124, 240, 242; managerial infighting, 139; overseas division, 132, 133; South Africa and, 221; unions and, 156–58, 165–66; Venezuela and, 48
General Tire, 48
geocentric corporation, 43–44, 55, 70, 228
German MNCs, 103–4, 125–27, 172–73, 237
German subsidiaries, 148, 160–61, 173, 264; codetermination and, 230; Japan and, 116–17; unions and, 160–61, 165–66

Gerstacker, Carl, 96–97
global economy, MNC domination and, 30–37
Gott, Ken, 86
grandmother arrangement, 133–34
Greece, 197–98
greenfield enterprise, 189, 234
gross national product (GNP), 33–36
Grundig, 105
Guatemala, 175, 203, 252
Gulf Oil, 184, 204, 206, 220, 211
gunboat diplomacy, 174
Guyana, 182
Gyllenhammar, Pehr, 92

Hammer, Armand, 128–29
Haynes, Eldridge, xii, 44, 80–90, 95, 97–98
Hickenlooper amendment, 175–76
Hilferding, Rudolf, 16
Hitachi, 126–27
Hitler, Adolf, 8
Hoffman-La Roche, 200
home country: change of, 95–96; criticism in, 24–25; employment in, 21, 24; loyalty to, 40; pressure from, 176–84; support for MNCs, 171–85. *See also specific corporations, countries*
homosexuals, 36
Honda, 173
Hoover, 52–53, 260
host country: attractions of, 106–8; dishonest practices of, 195–96; government changes and, 197–98; guidelines for treatment of inhospitability of, 188–98; investors, 212–14; labor market in, 26–27; MNC attractions for, 248; MNC disunity and, 128–30; national tastes, 110–11; native businesses, 188–90; native trade unions and, 190–92; political impact in, 25–26, 219–22; repentance of, 196–97, 234; risk assessment, 119–20; undesirable countries, 117–18. *See also* subsidiaries; *specific countries*
hostile takeovers, 189–90

Hungarian MNCs, 106
Hymer, Stephen, xii, 40, 89

IG Metal, 160, 165
illicit activities, 128, 138–40, 202
Imperial Chemical Industries (ICI), 59, 125, 137, 172–73, 242
India, 197, 242; collapse of, 269–70; native businesses in, 188–89; percent equity ownership and, 46, 47; tax avoidance and, 114, 116; Union Carbide and, 205, 219, 234; unions and, 168–69
Indonesia, 184, 195
Institut pour l'Étude des Methodes de Direction de l'Enterprise (IMEDE), 60
International Business Machines (IBM), 47, 118–19, 132, 133; German subsidiaries, 148; India and, 47; South Africa, 211; Soviet Union and, 206
international division, 132–35
International Harvester, 111, 271
internationalism: cross-border mobility and, 228; executives and, 55–68, 146–51; Perlmutter and, 40–42; product standardization and, 262
international management development (IMD), 58–64
International Metalworkers Federation (IMF), 73, 75
International Telephone & Telegraph (ITT), xiii, 129–30, 136, 202, 209, 220, 225–26
International Trade Secretariats (ITS), 71–72, 75, 154, 162, 164, 169. *See also* unions
Ireland, Republic of, 114, 230
Island headquarters, 96–98
Israel, 205, 207, 210
Italy, 155, 272–73

Jamaica, 184–85
Japanese MNCs, 19–20, 109–10, 273; Asian investment by, 237; Britain and, 106, 126–27; free trade and,

123–24; Germany and, 117; international executives and, 62–63; Philippines and, 185; product standardization and, 262; South Africa and, 118; unions, 129, 166–67, 169–70, 173–74; unitary taxes and, 94; U.S. labor laws and, 63; wholly-owned subsidiaries and, 50–51, 103
Jews, 5–7, 205
Johnson, Lyndon, xi–xii
joint ventures, 48, 103, 181

Kendall, Donald, 262, 264
Kennedy, John, 84, 180
Kennedy, Robert, 180
Kenya, 181, 221
kidnapping, 64–68, 185
Knights of Labor, 154
Kotler, Philip, 259–62

labor force, 26–27; cheap labor, 106–8, 231–33; import of, 112–232; labor laws, 63. *See also* employment; unions
language, 41, 60–61, 117, 189
Latin America, 92, 174–75, 178–82. *See also specific countries*
less developed countries (LDCs): cheap labor and, 231–33; inhospitability of, 188–98; perils of investment in, 234–38; reform in, 234; unions in, 232. *See also* host country; *specific countries*
Lever, William, 104, 110–11, 171–72
Levinson, Charles, xii, 44, 69–77, 157
Levitt, Theodore, 259–62, 266
Libya, 129
licensing agreements, 249, 252–55
Lilienthal, David, 11, 55–56, 154
local-contents rules, 110, 127, 194
Löwenbräu, 256–57

MacBride Principles, 204, 208, 209
McDonald's, 241
Maisonrouge, Jacques, 44, 58, 148

Malaysia, 197, 221
management contracts, 248–49
managers, multinational, 55–68; accounting practices and, 140–46, 148–49; compensation of, 61–64; disunity of, 147; foreign languages and, 60–61; kidnapping of, 64–68; mobility of, 228; nationalism and, 146–51; third-country nationals, 148; unethical behavior, 138–40
manufacturing: collaborative, 250–55; decline in, 246; economies of scale and, 262–67; global standardization, 260–62; indigenous raw materials and, 239; "made in" labels, 243; national tastes and, 110–11; supplier links, 109–10
Marks & Spencer, 50
Marxism, 15–17, 268
Meany, George, 23
Mertz, H., 94–95
Metal Box, 132–33, 235
Mexico, 106, 107, 174–75, 217
multinational corporations (MNCs): blacklisted countries and, 203–204; collaboration of, 91–94; collective influence of, 30–37; decline of, 226, 271–74; definition of, 13–15; discriminatory regulations and, 193–95; disguising origin of, 240–44; disunity of, 121–29, 128–30, 202; domestic vs. international division, 132–35; enemies of, 207–12; exaggerated power of, 9–10; formation of, 101–20; 228; future development of, 245–75; as geocentric, 43–44; guidelines for treatment of, 212–14; heterogeneity of, 35–36; illicit behavior, 138–40, 202; island headquarters for, 96–98; modernization of, 228–31; negative attributes, 22–30; negative publicity issues and, 203–9; new strategies of, 246–51; Perlmutter categorization, 42–43; political activities of, 219–22; positive attributes, 20–22; social standards and, 221–22; statelessness and, 94–98; synonymous appella-

tions, 11–13; trivial motivations, 114–17; union of, 79–80, 94–95; vulnerability, 131–51. *See also* home country; host country; subsidiaries; *specific corporations, countries*
mobility, cross-border, 40–41, 55–60
monopolies, 109
Monsanto, 73, 215–16
Mussolini, Benito, 8
Myrdal, Hans-Goeran, 70

Nader, Ralph, 41, 111
Namibia, 205
National Cash Register Company, 57
national interests, 40–41, 57
nationalism, 20, 25, 195; BINCO and, 88–89; European subsidiaries and, 149–51, 178; executives and, 146–51; lower-rank employees, 146; Scottish, 269; Soviet Union and, 268; unions and, 165–67; nationalization, 174–76, 179–80; British MNCs and, 132–33; France and, 14–15; management contracts and, 248–49; Mexican law, 217; oil companies and, xiv, 174–76, 182, 184; repentance of, 196–97; U.S. investment vs., 120
National Union of Seamen (NUS), 168–69
native businesses, 188–90
natural resources, 104–5, 238–40
Nazis, 8, 220
Nestle, 74, 201, 207
Netherlands, 75–76, 132
newspapers, 60, 66, 80
Nigeria, 195–97
Nike, 255–56
Nilus, Sergey, 5–7
Nissan, 127–28, 173–74, 191
Nixon, Richard, 179, 182
non-tariff barriers, 105, 123–24
Northern Ireland, 102, 204, 206, 208

oil companies, 128–29; boycotts of, 208; finance capitalism and, 16; na-

tionalization of, xiv, 174–76, 182, 184. *See also specific companies*
Organization of Petroleum-Exporting Countries (OPEC), 16
ornamental subsidiaries, 118
ownership: disguise of, 210, 240–44; of natural resources, 238; percent equity, 39–40, 45–53, 190, 192

pacifism, 88
Pakistan, 93
Peccei, Aurelio, 89
Pepsico, 59, 139–40, 262, 264
Perlmutter, Howard, xii, 20, 39–44, 55, 70, 88, 190, 262–63
Peru, 174, 180
pharmaceutical MNCs, 200, 202
Philips of Eindhoven, 50, 58, 75, 126–27, 132, 220, 242, 250
Philippines, 185
Pilkington, 253–55
pollution, 29, 111, 205
polycentric firm, 42–43
price, standardization and, 266. *See also* Transfer pricing
Procter & Gamble, 200
product divisions, 135–38
production: foreign share of, 34; value-added, 33–34; vs. wages, 167–68
profit and loss, 102; accounting practices and, 140–46; factors affecting, 131; MNC definitions and, 14; transfer pricing and, 23–24
proprietary secrets, 47
protectionism, 105–6, 122–24, 156, 169, 227
public relations, 113, 117–19, 194, 199–201; anti-MNC groups and, 207–12; damage control, 209–12; illicit activities and, 202; negative publicity issues, 203–209; social propaganda, 214–17; public sector, foreign goods and, 108–9

racism, 29, 41–42, 63, 172, 204, 211, 221
raw materials, 104–5, 238–40

regional organizations, 133
Renault, 166
research and development, 29–30, 111, 118, 143, 147–48, 253, 255
Reuther, Victor, 157
Reuther, Walter, 156
Rhodesia, 144
risk assessment, 119–20
Rockefeller, David, 4
Roman Catholic church, 23, 206, 207
Rowland, Roland, 235
Rowntree, 263
royalties, 143, 252
runaway corporations, 24, 253
Russia, 271. *See also* Soviet Union

Saint Gobain, 14–15, 72, 75
Sampson, Anthony, 225–26
Saudi Arabia, 81
Scargill, Arthur, 161–62
Schlesinger, Arthur, 180
Scottish nationalism, 269
screwdriver subsidiaries, 113–14, 229
Servan-Schreiber, Jean-Jacques, 272
service sector, 14, 246–48
sexism, 29
Shell, 176, 220–21
shoe corporations, 255–56
Singer, 241
Sklar, Holly, 4, 10
small businesses, 188–90
Smith, Adam, 123
social audits, 214–17
socialism, 15–17
Sony, 119, 124, 240–41
Sophus Behrendsen, 133–34
South Africa, 79, 117–18, 134, 204, 206, 208–9, 211, 220–21
South Korea, 188, 232
sovereignty issues, 25, 46, 195
Soviet Union, 15–17, 206, 268
Spain, 166
standardization, 260–62, 265–66
steel industry, 155–56
stock market, 209

strikes, 26–27, 74, 107, 155–64, 203, 264

subsidiaries: cooperative action, 93; disguised ownership of, 210, 240–44; disunity of, 147; domestic division vs., 132–35; independence of, 35–36, 217–19; interdependence of, 264; local authority of, 43–44; ornamental, 118; percent equity ownership, 39–40, 45–53, 192; product divisions, 135–38; relative performance of, 144; token plants, 143–44. *See also* host countries; *specific corporations*

subsidies, 113, 231

supplier links, 109–10, 143, 193–94

Sweden, 109; equity ownership and, 190; MNCs from, 120, 123, 144, 148, 177–78; trade unions and, 166–67; U.S. and, 120; Viggo affair, 218–19

Swiss MNCs, 92, 112–14, 189, 200

tariff-jumping, 105, 228

tariffs, selective, 111

taxes: avoidance of, 23–24, 41, 62, 229; MNC evolution and, 113–14; unitary taxation, 93–94, 230

technology transfer, 253–55

terrorists, 64–68

Thatcher, Margaret, 124

third country nationals, 61, 148

tobacco companies, 74

tokenism, 41–42

token plants, 143–44

toxic products, 111–12

Toynbee, Arnold, 97

training, 59–61

transfer pricing, 23–24, 45–56, 113–14, 142, 229–30

transnational corporations. *See* multinational corporations

transport costs, 108

Trilateral Commission, 4–6

Uganda, 210

unemployment. *See* employment

Unilever, 104, 110–11, 163, 195, 200, 210, 238

Union Carbide, 205, 219, 234

unions, 24–25, 172–74; associations of, 71–72; auto manufacturers and, xii, 73, 156–61, 165–66, 173–74, 192; boycotts and, 203; Canada and, 153–54; COMECON and, 162; cynical solidarity of, 154–56; indigenous, 190–92, 232; international wage parity and, 166; Japanese MNCs and, 126; Levinson, 69–77; licensing agreements and, 253; nationalism and, 165–67; no-strike promises, 107; protectionism and, 156, 169; steel industry and, 155–56; strikebreaking, 26–27; subsidiary independence and, 218; true solidarity of, 161–63

Uniroyal, 210

unitary taxation, 93–94, 230

United Automobile Workers (UAW), 156–61; 165, 168, 191

United Fruit Company (UFCO), xiv, 104–5, 175, 179–80

United Nations, 15, 96, 212

United Rubber Workers, 76

United Shoe Machinery, 136

United States, foreign subsidiaries in, 63, 120, 150. *See also specific corporations*

U.S. MNCs: competition between, 125; decline of, 271–74; government support for, xi–xii, 174–85; Latin America and, 174–75, 178–82; percent equity ownership and, 51–52. *See also specific corporations*

value-added production, 33–34, 118, 229–30

Vauxhall, 240, 242

Venezuela, 48, 64–66, 129, 234

Vernon, B., 181

Vertical integration, 104–5, 238–40

Viggo, 218–19

Volkswagen, 173

Volvo, 73, 232

wages: cheap labor, 106–8, 231–33; cross-border problems and, 154; inflation of, 27, 204; international parity, 166; irrelevance of, 231–33, 237; productivity vs., 167–68
wholly-owned subsidiaries, 39–40, 45–53, 103, 192
Wilson, Harold, 190

Woodcock, Leonard, 157–58
World Council of Churches (WCC), xv, 23, 29
world government, 6, 20, 80, 85, 89, 229, 267

York, John, 59
Yugoslavia, 270

ABOUT THE AUTHOR

ALEX RUBNER is a business economist who received his Ph.D. from the London University. He has lectured widely at business schools, universities, and management seminars. He is a frequent contributor to the in-house forums of international companies.

During forty years of writing on socio-political-economic subjects, Rubner has published hundreds of often controversial articles in both academic and general journals. Among his eleven published books are *The Ensnared Shareholder, The Economics of Gambling,* and *The Export Cult.*

This current work draws on his experiences as a counselor to multinational corporations, which he advises on cross-border issues stemming from foreign investments.